D1443810

CIVICS

GOVERNMENT
AND
CITIZENSHIP

CIVICS

GOVERNMENT AND CITIZENSHIP

Jack R. Fraenkel

Frank T. Kane

Alvin Wolf

PRENTICE HALL

Needham, Massachusetts • Englewood Cliffs, New Jersey

About the Authors

JACK R. FRAENKEL is Professor of Interdisciplinary Studies in Education and Director of the Research and Development Center in the School of Education at San Francisco State University. Dr. Fraenkel has also taught social studies at the junior high and high school levels. He was Associate Director of the internationally recognized Taba Curriculum Development Project at San Francisco State University. He frequently serves as a consultant on the development of thinking and values clarification in students.

FRANK T. KANE is former Chairperson of the Social Studies Department of Jefferson Union High School, Daly City, California. He has since served as a curriculum consultant and as a coordinator for many high school Model UN programs in the San Francisco Bay Area.

ALVIN WOLF is Professor of Education at California State University, San Bernardino. A former high school teacher, he is the author of *American Consumers, Foreign Policy, and Lobbies and Lobbyists.*

Reviewers/Consultants

Mariela Arango
Social Studies Teacher
W.R. Thomas Middle School
Dade County, Florida

Marylou Barnhorn Bay
Social Studies Teacher/
  Education Specialist
Queen of Peace School
Archdiocese of Cincinnati
Hamilton, Ohio

Miriam Glessner
Supervisor of Social Studies
Columbus Public Schools
Columbus, Ohio

Francis X. Hardy
Social Studies Department Chairman
Peabody Veterans Memorial High School
Peabody, Massachusetts

Farley M. Hill
Social Studies Teacher
Palchaven High School
Memphis City Schools
Memphis, Tennessee

Mary Frances Lavin
Social Science Chair
Lanphier High School
Springfield Public Schools
Springfield, Illinois

Donald W. Prince
Social Studies Teacher
Central Middle School
Broken Arrow, Oklahoma

Charles A. Ptolemy, Jr.
Social Studies Department Head
Stadium High School
Tacoma, Washington

Staff Credit

Executive Editor: Darrell J. Kozlowski
Project Editor: Kathryn A. Kline
Editorial Services: Susan Judge, Elizabeth Grube, Julie Mines, Bruce Morgan, Kathleen Krokar, Peter Guthrie, Donald B. Armin, Peter Pappas
Production Product Line Specialist: Pauline P. Wright
Production/Copy Editors: Deborah Sargent, Shyamol Bhattacherya
Product Marketing Director: Jeffrey M. Ikler
Product Marketing Manager: David R. Zarowin

Design Director: L. Christopher Valente
Design Manager: Stuart Wallace
Design: George McLean, Linda Dana Willis, Marie McAdam, Michael Burggren, Eve Melnechuk
Cover Design: John Martucci, Stuart Wallace
Cover Photo: American Flag: Martucci Studio, Michael Sielcken; Statue of Liberty: SuperStock
Buyer: Roger Powers
Photo Research: Laurel Anderson

© Copyright 1990, by Prentice-Hall, Inc.

All rights reserved. No part of the material protected by this copyright notice may be reproduced or utilized in any form, or by any means, electronic or mechanical, including photocopying and recording, or by any informational storage and retrieval system, without written permission from Prentice Hall.

Printed in the United States of America.

ISBN 013-135070-6

1 2 3 4 5 6 7 8 9   95 94 93 92 91 90

A Simon & Schuster Company

Contents

Focus On Decision Making

Case Studies

Citizenship

Government and Law

Sharpening Your Skills

Citizenship Skills

Critical Thinking Skills

Study Skills

People Helping People

Maps, Graphs, Charts, Diagrams

The Meaning of American Citizenship

In the summer of 1986, 50 college students on bicycles left San Francisco, California, in high spirits. They billed themselves as the "Ride for Life," a grass-roots group pledged to raise money —through individual and corporate sponsors—to help feed the hungry in this country and abroad. Every mile they pedaled earned more money for the cause. By trail's end in Boston, Massachusetts, nearly $200,000 had been raised.

Citizenship means many things, but part of what it means is generosity, a willingness to give freely to others for the common good. To be good citizens, it is also important that we understand how our government works and what our rights and responsibilities are. That's what civics is all about—studying the nature of government and the rights and duties of American citizens.

"We the people" of the United States can take pride in being citizens of a country built on the ideals of freedom, equality, and democracy.
▼

What do you think of when you hear the word "politics"? The President making decisions in Washington, D.C.? Members of Congress passing new laws? Candidates giving speeches? All these groups have something to do with politics, but ordinary citizens are part of the political process, too. Whether it's by voting, working in a campaign, or expressing your views to newspaper editors or public officials, you and other citizens can make your voices heard.

The 535 men and women we elect to Congress represent the interests of nearly 250 million Americans.
▼

▲
Young people can become involved in the political process long before they cast their first vote.

Political conventions are ▶
occasions for rousing
displays of patriotism
and party loyalty.

Political leaders like Jesse Jackson
have inspired Americans to believe
that each individual can make a
difference in government.
▼

No single public official has more
responsibility than the President.
Here, President George Bush talks
with Vice President Dan Quayle.
▼

Have you ever stopped to think about the influence of laws in your daily life? The milk on your breakfast table has to pass a legal inspection. The look of your neighborhood is set partly by local zoning laws. The education you are getting at school is shaped by the legal requirements of your state. And every time you stop at a red light or pay a sales tax, you are observing laws. Of course, participating in the legal system can mean much more. Active, involved citizens serve on juries, take problems to the courts when necessary, and work for the passage of fair laws.

The motto engraved above the entrance to the Supreme Court Building, "Equal justice under law," sums up the philosophy behind our legal system.
▼

Judges are ▶
expected to apply
the law fairly and to
safeguard the rights
of all citizens.

▲
Traffic laws exist to
ensure the safety
of drivers on our
nation's roads and
highways.

Federal laws require ▶
the inspection of
fruits and vegetables.

You may not read the financial pages of the newspaper or follow the ups and downs of the stock market. The world of banking and business may seem remote to you. All the same, you and other citizens take part in that world every day. Working, spending, paying taxes, saving—these are all activities that keep our economy running smoothly. Thus, understanding basic economic ideas and making wise economic decisions is an important part of citizenship.

The American economy depends on the production of a wide variety of goods—from hats to airplanes.

The men and women ▶
who make up the
work force are the
backbone of our
economic system.

The American
consumer keeps the
pulse of the
economy beating.
▼

Saving money provides an
essential resource for the
growth of the economy.
▼

Alexis de Tocqueville, a Frenchman who visited the United States in the 1830s, wrote that "Americans of all ages, all conditions, and all descriptions constantly form associations . . . of a thousand different kinds." That hasn't changed much in the last 160 years. Family groups, school groups, churches, sports teams, work groups—these are what bind our social system together. Today, more than half of all adult citizens give something back to the community by volunteering for a cause. For many Americans, service to others is the true measure of citizenship.

As these volunteers struggle to save a stranded whale, they are helping to protect America's wildlife.

Nurturing the next ▶
generation is one of
the most important
investments we can
make in the future.

Concern for the health of
others leads some
Americans to volunteer in
hospitals or to work for the
Red Cross.

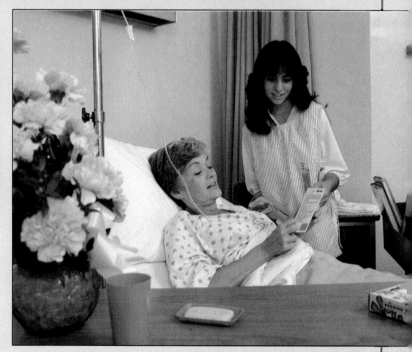

Government and Citizenship

Previewing the Unit

In the summer of 1787, fifty-five leaders from the newly formed United States met in Philadelphia. They were lawyers, merchants, and planters; war heroes and politicians; men as young as 26 and as old as 81. Day after day they argued about how to create a workable plan of government for their young nation. They had straw and mud spread on the cobblestone street outside so they would not be disturbed by the sounds of passing carriages. They sacrificed comfort for privacy, keeping the doors and windows of their meeting room shut tight despite the broiling heat. Finally, after nearly four months of work, the leaders unveiled their blueprint for government—the Constitution of the United States.

Those who wrote this document created a masterpiece that continues to guide our lives and laws. In this unit, you will learn about the Constitution's beginnings and about the nature of American government and citizenship.

Chapters in This Unit

1 Introduction to Government
2 Founding a New Nation
3 The Constitution of the United States
4 The Rights and Duties of American Citizens

◀ Now more than 200 years old, the original Constitution is sealed under glass in a display in the National Archives Building in Washington, D.C.

1

Introduction to Government

This float honoring the United States Constitution was part of a patriotic parade in Washington, D.C.

Sections in This Chapter

Previewing the Chapter

If you ride a school bus in the morning, governments on the national, state, and local levels have touched your life through a variety of safety regulations. Decisions made at the different levels of government are intended to protect our rights and to guide our actions. This chapter defines what government is and describes the various levels of government in the United States.

■ **Before you read,** look up these key terms in the Glossary at the back of this book: *dictatorship, democracy, law, tax, boycott, rebellion.*

■ **As you read,** look for answers to these questions:
1. What are four key ideas on which a democracy is based?
2. What are three main functions of our governments?
3. What were some major reasons for the American rebellion against Great Britain?

1 What Is Government?

What do the following kinds of people have in common: police officers, teachers in the public schools, park rangers, judges, county clerks, and the President of the United States? They all are a part of either a town, city, state, county, or national government. A **government** is made up of all the people who decide how a community, such as a city, state, or nation, is to be run.

There are many levels of government in the United States. There are town governments, city governments, county governments, state governments, and our national government. Millions of people work for government in cities like Boston and Seattle, in states like Texas and Iowa, and in Washington, D.C., our nation's capital.

Governments in the United States

SKILL BUILDER   Which level of government is the most powerful?

THREE LEVELS OF GOVERNMENT IN THE UNITED STATES

THE U.S. CONSTITUTION
sets up a government in which power is shared
by a national government and state governments.

▽

THE NATIONAL GOVERNMENT
has power over the entire nation. The laws of the U.S. Congress
apply to all 50 states—as do the decisions of the President and the federal courts.

▽

THE STATE GOVERNMENTS
have the power to manage affairs within their borders.
State laws may not violate or contradict federal laws.

▽

THE LOCAL GOVERNMENTS
—cities, towns, counties, and other forms—have the power to manage
their own affairs, provided they do not violate any national or state laws.

All of us are affected by government. Indeed, government enters into a large part of our daily life. On your way to school, you are expected to obey certain traffic rules. You may pay a sales tax on many of the things you buy. Your parents pay a property tax on their home if they own it. Those who are caught and convicted of breaking the law must pay a fine or go to jail.

We cannot legally go hunting, drive a car, fly an airplane, or build a house without government permission. We need a license or a permit to do each of these things. When we are born, the certificate of our birth is issued by the government. So is the certificate of our death when we die. Government plays a big part in all of our lives.

Dictatorships

One way to describe government is by saying whether it is a dictatorship or a democracy. In a **dictatorship**, all the power of the government is held by one person or a small group of persons. The authority of this person or group is absolute (total). The people usually do not challenge it, because if they do, they may be imprisoned or put to death. Some countries that have dictator-

SKILL BUILDER

Which type of government is based on control by the people?

HOW DICTATORSHIPS DIFFER FROM DEMOCRACIES

	DICTATORSHIPS	DEMOCRACIES
GOVERNMENT POWER	All power is held by one individual or by a small group.	The people are the final source of power.
PEOPLE	The people have little or no control over their own lives. They cannot disagree with the government.	The people have control over what they do with their lives. They are free to question and even protest government decisions.
POLITICAL PROCESS	Elections are controlled by the government. The people have no opportunity to change the government if they do not like what it does.	Elections are held regularly. The people may decide not to reelect those in government of whom they do not approve.
INDIVIDUAL CITIZEN	Individuals have value only in terms of what they can do for the government.	Individuals have value simply for themselves.

ships today are the Soviet Union, the People's Republic of China, and Cuba.

Dictatorships today also tend to be totalitarian in nature. A **totalitarian** government is one which holds control over every part of the people's lives. The government's power covers everything the people do. Schools, churches, businesses, labor unions—all are controlled by the government. Usually there is some form of secret police to make sure that the people do not do anything of which the government disapproves.

Democracies

Democracies are quite different from dictatorships. In a **democracy** the final authority rests with the people. The word comes from the Greek words *demos*, meaning "the people," and *kratos*, meaning "rule." Thus, the Greek word *demokratia* means "the people rule." Those who govern do so by permission of the people. Government is run, in other words, with the people's consent. The United States of America is an example of a democracy.

Democracies may be either direct or indirect. A **direct democracy** is one in which the people themselves, usually in a group meeting, make decisions about what the government will do. Direct democracies do not work very well in large communities. It is almost impossible to get all of the people together in one place. Not many direct democracies exist today, although in some small towns in New England, **town meetings** are held. In these meetings, members of the community meet to discuss issues affecting

Working on a school newspaper provides a valuable lesson in democracy.

the town. Then they vote to decide what they think the town should do. A **majority vote** (at least one more than half) of the people determines what the town government's action(s) will be.

An **indirect democracy** is one in which a few people are elected to represent everyone else in the community. For this reason, indirect democracies are also called **representative democracies**. These representatives are held responsible by the people for the day-to-day operation of the government. If the people are unhappy with the performance of their representatives, they may vote them out of office during the next election.

Key Ideas on Which Democracies Are Based

All democracies are based on certain key ideas. These ideas include a respect for individual worth, equality, majority rule, and freedom.

Respect for Individual Worth. In a democracy, individuals are of the utmost importance. Every human being, no matter what his or her race, position, or economic condition may be, is considered to be a person of worth. All people, no matter who they are or what they do, should be given respect simply because they are human beings. This belief—that every individual has worth—is perhaps the most basic of all democratic ideals. Every other idea on which democracy is based grows out of this belief.

Equality. Individuals in a democracy are not only considered as being of worth. They are also considered to be of *equal* worth. This does not mean that all individuals are thought to be equal in ability or talent. This is plainly not the case. What is meant here is that people should be given equal opportunity. **Equal opportunity** means that people should have the same chance to show what they can do with their natural talents and abilities. They should not be prevented from doing so because they are of a certain color, sex, ethnic background, age, or religion.

People also should be treated equally before the law. This means that all people should be given the same rights and treatment in a court of law, no matter what their position is or how much influence they have.

Majority rule. A third basic idea of democracy is that of **majority rule.** This means that if a disagreement arises between different groups within a community, the group that obtains a majority vote gets its way. Related to this idea is the idea of minority rights. The rights of the minority—the outnumbered side in a disagreement—must be protected. Otherwise, the majority group could destroy the minority group by forcing harsh policies and practices on it.

The United States **Constitution** is the basic law of our land. It protects the rights of minorities in many ways. For example, the government may not take away the right of any person to worship as he or she pleases. No person may be denied the right to vote because he or she is of a certain race or color, or because he or she is poor. No state may deny any person within the state equal protection of the state's laws. The President of the United States has the power to prevent laws from being passed that would be harmful to minorities. The U.S. Supreme Court, the highest court in the land, can **nullify** (cancel) any laws that take away the basic rights that are listed in the Constitution.

Freedom.   Democracies cannot survive without freedom. What is freedom? It is the right of individuals to do as they wish, provided they do not stop others from having the same right. The idea of freedom has limits, however. It does not mean that people are free to do anything they please. No one is completely free. If people could do anything they wanted, they could take away the freedom of others. A famous justice of the Supreme Court, Oliver Wendell Holmes, put it this way: "The right to swing my fist ends where the other man's nose begins."

In a democracy, therefore, we are free to do as we wish only if we do not take away someone else's freedom. To protect the freedom of every individual, the government puts limits on what we are free to do. If we are caught telling lies about someone in print, for example, we can be sued in court. We can also be tried if we physically attack another person, steal someone else's possessions, or damage his or her property. All of these actions are forbidden by law. In each case, they would deny another person his or her freedom.

PEOPLE HELPING PEOPLE

From Boardroom to Hospice

Not everyone would willingly walk away from $500,000 a year and a successful career, to help people die with dignity. But Joseph Kordick is not your average business executive.

Born to a poor Czechoslovakian family in a Chicago ghetto, Kordick joined the Ford Motor Company in 1954 and quickly rose through the ranks. Within 20 years he headed Ford's parts and service division. Kordick won a reputation for "managing with love" and led the company to record profits.

In 1988, Kordick decided to trade corporate life for something even more rewarding. The former executive now spends up to 80 hours a week volunteering in a hospice program near his home in Stuart, Florida. (A hospice is a homelike place that cares for people with terminal illnesses.) Kordick runs errands, comforts patients, even handles their yardwork. "I've always had a deep desire to serve society," he explains.

Defining Key Terms

1. Define: government, dictatorship, totalitarian, democracy, direct democracy, town meeting, majority vote, indirect democracy, representative democracy, equal opportunity, majority rule, Constitution, nullify.

Recalling the Facts

2. What are the three levels of government that exist in the United States?
3. What are some of the differences between a dictatorship and a democracy?
4. Give an example of direct democracy in the United States today.

Reviewing the Main Idea

5. Answer "As you read . . ." question 1 on page 2: What are four key ideas on which a democracy is based?

Critical Thinking

6. **Recognizing Cause and Effect.** How do ideas about government affect people's daily lives?

2 Why Do We Need Government?

Although most of us do not think about it, life as we know it would be impossible without government. The governments of our nation determine to a large extent what life in our towns and cities will be like. They make and enforce laws. They help to settle disputes. They provide us with many services that otherwise we would not have.

Making and Enforcing Laws

The governments of our cities, states, and nation decide what our laws will be. They also decide how they will be enforced. A **law** is a written rule that says how people who live in our nation are expected to behave. Laws spell out certain things we may and may not do if we wish to live in the United States. They provide guide-

Americans are required by law to go to school. These students are registering their bicycles at the beginning of the school year.

lines about how we are to act in our daily lives as we deal with other people. For example, we are required by law to go to school and to pay taxes. We are forbidden by law to steal another person's possessions. We must obey the laws that set state highway speed limits. By law we are guaranteed a fair trial in any of the courts of the land.

Laws also tell governments what they can and cannot do. The Constitution of the United States says what our government can do. It also forbids the government to do many things. The government is allowed by law to collect taxes, to borrow money, and to establish post offices. On the other hand, the government is forbidden to take away our freedom of speech or religion.

Disputes and disagreements develop in any community. A **dispute** is an argument or a quarrel. Whenever there are laws, people are likely to disagree or argue over what the laws mean and to whom they apply. Two neighbors, for example, may disagree over where the boundaries of their properties meet. An apartment dweller may refuse to pay an increase in rent because he or she feels it is too high. The members of a religious group may refuse to send their children to high school because they feel the children do not need more than an eighth-grade education.

How are such disputes settled? Where government does not exist, as has happened at various times in the past, people have turned to force to settle a disagreement. The person or group that is the strongest—that has the most physical strength or military might—is the one that wins. It does not matter who is right. The weak, without strength or strong friends, have no chance.

Where there is a government, courts are set up to provide a fairer way to settle disputes. Arguments on both sides are presented. Evidence is given to support the position of each side.

Settling Disputes

Government provides such services as firefighting, day-care, and city planning.

Then a judge or jury (a group of people selected to decide on the dispute) makes a decision based on the evidence.

Providing Services

Government also provides us with many services we otherwise would not have. A **service** is work performed for other people. The work of police and fire departments is a good example of the many services that government provides. Such services, however, are not free. We pay for them in the form of taxes and fees. A **tax** is a sum of money that a person is required to pay to the government each year. A **fee** is a payment made by an individual to obtain a permit or service that the government provides. Taxes and fees are used to pay government expenses, including salaries.

SECTION 2 *Review*

Defining Key Terms
1. Define: law, dispute, service, tax, fee.

Recalling the Facts
2. Name some of the services that government provides.
3. What law defines and limits what the government of the United States may do?

Reviewing the Main Idea
4. Answer "As you read . . ." question 2 on page 2: What are three main functions of our governments?

Critical Thinking
5. **Predicting Consequences.** How would your life be different if there were no government?

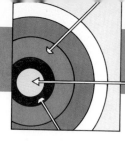

Sharpening Your Skills

Study Skills

Researching Information

Imagine that your teacher has just assigned you a research report. A wave of panic rushes through you. Where do you start to gather information? Then it comes to you: Aha! The library!

A library contains many different sources of information. *Primary sources* are firsthand or eyewitness accounts of an event, scene, or period in history. Primary sources include autobiographies, letters, diaries, and newspapers or newsreels of actual events. *Secondary sources* are probably the materials you are most familiar with. Secondary sources are written not by eyewitnesses or participants, but by researchers who have studied all the information available to them. Textbooks, biographies, and encyclopedias are all secondary sources.

An *encyclopedia* is a book or set of books containing general information on a variety of topics. You can find more detailed facts and up-to-date statistics in an *almanac*. An *atlas* contains maps and may provide other tables and charts. If you need specific books, you can check the card catalogue, which lists books by author, title, and subject. The *call numbers,* in the top left corner of each card, will help you find the books on the shelves.

Most books have a *table of contents* and an *index* to help you locate specific information. The table of contents appears at the beginning of the book. It lists the major parts of the book and gives their page numbers. The index appears at the back of a book. An index is more specific than a table of contents. It provides page numbers for a detailed list of topics arranged in alphabetical order. The information you need may be listed under several index entries. For example, in this book you will find "democracies" as an entry in its own right and as a subentry under "government(s)."

If you want to find recent magazine or journal articles, the place to start is the *Readers' Guide to Periodical Literature.* This source indexes articles by subject and author, using abbreviations that are explained at the beginning of each volume. If you looked up "education," for example, you might find an entry like this:

Democratic education in action.
G. H. Wood. *The Education Digest*
53: 10-13 Mr '88

The title of the article and the author's name are listed first. The name of the magazine follows, written in italics. The volume number is shown next, and, after the colon, the page numbers are given. At the end of the listing, you see the date the magazine was issued (the month's abbreviation and the year). With this information, a reference librarian can locate the magazine for you. All you have to do then is start reading!

Practicing Skills

1. Which would be more useful if you were looking for information on dictatorships: the table of contents or the index? Why?
2. How would you locate a current magazine article about taxes?
3. **Drawing Conclusions.** Which do you think is more likely to be accurate—a primary or a secondary source? Explain.

3 The Beginnings of the Government of the United States

During the 1600s, many people came to America from Europe to set up colonies. A **colony** is a group of people living in one land who are ruled by the government of another land. The people who live in a colony are called **colonists.** Some of the earliest colonies in North America were established by people from France, Spain, Holland, and England.

The English Colonies

The first English Colony was established in North America in 1607. By the early part of the 1700s, there were 13 English colonies. They were scattered from one end of the eastern coast of North America to the other. Each of these 13 colonies had its own government. Nevertheless, the colonists still thought of themselves as a part of England. They felt bound by the laws and the rule of the English government.

The English Tax the Colonies

By the middle of the 1700s, England had become the strongest power on the North American continent. It had defeated France in a major war in 1763. By doing so, it gained control of all land in North America east of the Mississippi River.

The war had cost England a great deal of money. To get back some of this money, the English government decided to tax its North American colonies. The colonists answered by boycotting English goods. A **boycott** is a refusal to buy goods from someone. The colonists also protested to England that they were being taxed against their will, since they had no representatives from the colonies in the English government.

The English government did **repeal** (do away with) most of the taxes. It still argued, however, that it had the right to tax the colonists whenever it wished to do so. Furthermore, angered by the colonial boycott, England began to pass laws that took away some of the rights of the colonists under English law. These laws, for example, stated that if a colonist was accused of not paying taxes, he or she could not have a trial by jury. English soldiers also were given the right to search people's homes to see if they could find any smuggled goods. In Boston, the colonists had to let English soldiers live in their homes whether they wanted them there or not. If English soldiers were charged with breaking any laws, they were not to be tried in colonial courts. They were to be sent to England for trial.

These laws made many colonists very angry. Fighting broke out between colonists and English soldiers. A general meeting of all the colonies was called, to which 12 of the 13 colonies sent **delegates** (representatives). Most of the delegates, however, still felt loyal to England. They did not want to separate from England. They were fighting, they insisted, "in defense of the freedom that is our birthright." If the English government would only give them the rights which they should have as loyal English subjects, they would lay down their arms and cease their resistance.

The English government did not share the colonial view, however. The king of England thought the colonists were disloyal subjects. He declared the colonies to be in a state of rebellion. A **rebellion** is an armed uprising against the government of a nation. The king sent more soldiers to North America. He expected to crush the colonial army quickly. Several battles took place, with both sides winning some victories.

This painting shows a tax collector being tarred and feathered.

The Declaration of Independence

By early 1776, more and more colonists were beginning to favor independence. **Independence** means freedom from the control of others. A second meeting of all the colonies was called. At this meeting, every colony was advised to set up a state government independent of England. Then in June, 1776, Thomas Jefferson of Virginia was asked to prepare a statement of independence. This entire document is shown on pages 504–505. Let us consider some of the more important phrases contained in the Declaration of Independence.

"We hold these truths to be self-evident, that all men are created equal, that they are endowed by their Creator with certain unalienable Rights, that among these are Life, Liberty, and the pursuit of Happiness." Jefferson put it clearly right at the start. The colonists believed that there were certain truths, or basic facts, about human beings that all governments should recognize. What are these truths? The first truth is that "all men [all people] are created equal." The second truth is that government cannot take away certain rights given to people by God. These include "Life, Liberty, and the pursuit of Happiness."

Governments are set up by human beings, Jefferson wrote, "to secure these rights." Government, in other words, is the means by which people make sure that every person has these rights. Government gets its power through the people's consent or agreement. The people agree to be governed.

What if government should seek to take away the people's rights? Then the people have both a right and a duty to change or do away with government. As Jefferson wrote, the people have a right "to abolish" a government that interferes with or destroys the people's rights.

Jefferson's words showed how many of the colonists felt. They felt they had good reasons for seeking independence. The English government had, in their eyes, taken away many of their basic rights.

The War for Independence

Not all of the colonists favored independence, however. Many remained loyal to England. The American Revolution was carried on by less than half of the colonists. Nevertheless, to the surprise of most of the world, the colonies, under the leadership of George Washington, won the war. After several losses, a major victory for the colonists at Saratoga in New York persuaded France to send money and advisers to help the United States. This was the beginning of the end for the English. Finally, in 1783, England surrendered. The War for Independence was over, and Americans were faced with the challenge of founding a new government for their new nation.

This engraving by John McRae is entitled "Raising the Liberty Pole."

SECTION 3 *Review*

Defining Key Terms

1. Define: colony, colonists, boycott, repeal, delegate, rebellion, independence.

Recalling the Facts

2. Why was the Declaration of Independence written?
3. What are some of the basic ideas contained in the Declaration of Independence?

Reviewing the Main Idea

4. Answer "As you read . . ." question 3 on page 2: What were some major reasons for the American rebellion against Great Britain?

Critical Thinking

5. **Identifying Central Issues.** What does the Declaration of Independence say is the purpose of government?

Government and Law

How Do Representatives Represent?

Representative Nancy Johnson of Connecticut talks to some young people from her district.

The scene is the Capitol in Washington, D.C. For the past three hours, members of Congress have been going over testimony and debating. They have before them a bill to create a national youth service program. It would work this way: volunteers who joined the program would spend a year doing community service in exchange for a monthly paycheck and money for college.

With just 15 minutes to vote, supporters and opponents of the bill are twisting the arms of their undecided colleagues. The digital timer is ticking down. Three minutes, two minutes, one minute. The presiding speaker lifts his gavel and bangs it down. "No more voting," he bellows.

How do elected officials cast their votes? Some see their role as that of a *trustee.* They believe that the people who elected them *trust* their judgment. Thus they rely on their own wisdom, values, and personal experience to make decisions.

Delegates, on the other hand, believe that they must follow the wishes of the people they represent. Unlike trustees, they try not to let their personal views on an issue influence their decisions. Instead, they respond to the demands of voters, expressed through phone and letter-writing campaigns, public opinion polls, and face-to-face meetings with their representatives.

Partisans are guided by a sense of loyalty to their political party. For their party to remain effective, they think its members should show a united front. Thus, they vote in line with the positions taken by party leaders.

Many elected officials try to combine all three of the roles just described. Representatives of this type might be called *politicos.* They consider their own views of what is best for their community or state, the wishes of the people they represent, and the position taken by their political party. Not surprisingly, it is often a tough balancing act!

Questions to think about:

1. If you were an elected official, which of the four roles described above would you choose for yourself? Explain your choice.
2. Studies have shown that partisanship (loyalty to one's political party) has a greater influence on representatives' votes than any other factor. Why do you think this is true?

CHAPTER SUMMARY

Section 1   A government consists of all the persons who supervise the operation of a town, city, state, or nation. Two of the most important types of government in the world today are dictatorships and democracies. In a dictatorship, all power is held by one person or a small group of persons while the rest of the people have little or no power. In a democracy, power is held by the people, who elect officials to make decisions and run the government. Although democracies can be direct or indirect, most democracies today are indirect. All democracies are based on certain key ideas including respect for individual worth, equality, majority rule, and freedom.

Section 2   Life as we know it today would be impossible without government. The government passes and enforces laws to set guidelines for our actions. It also sets up courts to help us settle disputes. The government also provides many important services that affect our health and safety, including food inspection and police and fire protection.

Section 3   In the 1600s, England established several colonies in North America. England ruled and taxed these colonies. Many colonists believed that England had passed unfair laws that denied the colonists' their rights. The colonies rebelled, and in 1776 Thomas Jefferson wrote the Declaration of Independence to announce the colonies' independence from England. Although less than half the colonists supported independence, they managed to defeat the English army by 1783.

Reviewing Key Terms

Match the following terms with the definitions below. Write your answers on a separate sheet of paper.

dictatorship   tax
democracy   boycott
law   rebellion

1. money paid to the government

2. an armed uprising against a government

3. a refusal to buy goods from someone or some group

4. a government in which final power is held by the people

5. a form of government in which all power is held either by one person or by a small group of persons

6. a written rule stating how people in our nation are expected to behave

Understanding Main Ideas

1. Identify five ways that government affects our lives.

2. What is the basic difference between a dictatorship and a democracy?

3. How is a direct democracy different from a representative democracy?

4. What is the principle of equal opportunity?

5. What are some ways in which minority rights are protected in the United States?

6. How do laws protect people against the government?

7. How do governments help to settle disputes?

8. Name three laws passed by the English government that denied the colonists their rights under English law.

9. Describe two of Thomas Jefferson's basic ideas about government as explained in the Declaration of Independence.

Critical Thinking

1. **Predicting Consequences.** Some people say that without government only those who are physically strong would survive. Some things, such as art or music, probably would not exist. Do you agree? Explain.

2. **Testing Conclusions.** An absolutely essential task for any government is to maintain order. Does this mean, then, that the freedom of some citizens has to be restricted? Some people say this is necessary if we are to have freedom at all. They say the basic difference between a democracy and a dictatorship is the way in which each restricts the freedom of the people. What do you think?

3. **Demonstrating Reasoned Judgment.** Is too much power a bad thing? Does everyone need to have some limits placed on how much power he or she holds at any given time? Why or why not?

Practicing Skills

1. **Researching Information.** Suppose you are writing a report on the Bill of Rights. Check the table of contents of this textbook and list the chapter and page numbers having information on the Bill of Rights. Then check the index to find any other pages with information on this topic and list them.

2. **Using an Index.** As you learned in this chapter, most of the money for running our government comes from taxes. Check the index of this textbook for the heading "Taxes," and list all the pages that have information about taxes.

Focusing on Citizenship

1. **Understanding Decision Making.** John Adams was a leading American patriot. At one time, however, he supported the English position. Use books in your school library to find out why he changed his views.

2. **Writing a Report.** Using an encyclopedia or other library books, research and write a brief report about Abigail Adams. Tell about the role she played during the American Revolution and the early years of our nation. Include her views on women's rights and racial discrimination.

3. **Predicting Consequences.** Make a list of at least 20 services we would lack if there were no town, city, state, or national government to provide them.

CHAPTER 2

Founding a New Nation

This painting shows George Washington, who chaired the Constitutional Convention and became our first President.

Previewing the Chapter

Imagine that you are an American leader during the Revolutionary War. You hope that when the war is over, the American colonies will no longer be subject to the laws of Great Britain. The question remains, however, what kinds of laws *should* there be in the new nation? This chapter describes the creation of the United States Constitution, the basic law that defines our government to the present day.

■ **Before you read,** look up these key terms in the Glossary at the back of this book: *ratify, amend, debtor, compromise, Federalist.*

■ **As you read,** look for answers to these questions:
   1. Why did the 13 original states not want a strong central government?
   2. Why are the years 1781–1787 considered a critical period in American history?
   3. What was the purpose of the Constitutional Convention?

1 The First Attempts to Form a Government

The Articles of Confederation

Even before the American Revolution ended, the colonists realized they needed a stronger central government to deal with their problems. They saw that if they were to defeat England, they would have to work together.

The general meetings of the colonists (known as the First and Second Continental Congresses), hastily called to discuss the situation with England, were not intended to be a permanent government. In November, 1777, therefore, a plan for a more permanent arrangement was suggested by the Second Continental Congress. This plan, known as the **Articles of Confederation**, took more than three years to be approved. Maryland, the last state to **ratify** (approve) the Articles, did not do so until February, 1781. The Congress then set March 1, 1781, as the date the Articles were to go into effect.

The Articles provided for a Congress in which each state was to be represented by no fewer than two nor more than seven delegates. Each state was to have one vote, no matter what its size. Delegates to the Congress were chosen by the state legislatures and paid by them. There was no national executive or judicial branch.

Under the Articles, Congress was given power to make war and peace. It could enter into treaties and alliances with other countries. It could coin and borrow money. It could send and receive ambassadors. It could build and equip a navy. It could establish a postal system. It could appoint senior officers of the United States Army. Soldiers for the army, however, had to be requested from the states.

The Articles did *not* set up a national government. Instead, they created a "firm league of friendship and cooperation." Although the states had jointly declared their independence from England, they still viewed themselves as free and independent of one another. People had stronger loyalties to their home states than to the new United States. They did not want to give up any of their newly won rights and freedoms. They had fought a war to free themselves from a strong central government. Not surprisingly, they had no wish to submit themselves to another such government, even though it would be American and not English. A strong central government, they feared, might take away all they had won in the War for Independence. As a result, Americans were reluctant to give Congress too much power over the states.

Members of the Second Continental Congress drew up the Articles of Confederation.

Weaknesses of the Articles of Confederation

Because of the way the new states felt, certain powers were denied Congress under the Articles. Two were very important. First, Congress had no power to tax. English taxes had helped to cause the American Revolution. To obtain money, all Congress could do was to borrow from another nation or ask for money from the states. Most of the nations of Europe, however, did not want to lend money to the new nation. They feared they would never be paid back. Congress's only hope was that the state governments would collect taxes and turn this money over to the central government.

Congress also had no power to **regulate** (control) trade among the states. It could not pass laws of any kind that would encourage trade throughout the United States.

Congress simply could not do very much. It could not protect the nation from invasion because it had no army. It had no way to settle trade or other disputes between the states because it had no courts. It could not enforce any of the laws it passed because there was no executive branch. It could not pay any of its debts because there was no national money worth anything. (The paper money which Congress had issued during the Revolutionary War was worth only about 1/1000 of its face value.) Even those powers that Congress did have could be used only if delegates from nine of the 13 states agreed. Congress under the Articles, then, was weak.

The state legislatures, not the voters, ratified the Articles. The people as a whole did not vote on them. The states promised to follow the Articles and the decisions of Congress, but there was no way to be sure that they would. Furthermore, all of the states had to agree before any changes could be made in the Articles.

Defining Key Terms

1. Define: Articles of Confederation, ratify, regulate.

Recalling the Facts

2. What were some of the powers given to the Congress under the Articles of Confederation?

3. What powers were denied the Congress under the Articles?

Reviewing the Main Idea

4. Answer "As you read . . ." question 1 on page 19: Why did the 13 original states not want a strong central government?

Critical Thinking

5. Demonstrating Reasoned Judgment. Could a government survive without at least some power to collect taxes? Explain your reasoning.

2 The Critical Period

By the time the Articles of Confederation went into effect in March, 1781, the new nation already had many problems. The central government was unable to provide the strong leadership the country needed. In fact, the years from 1781 through 1787 have become known as a "critical period" in American history.

Events Leading to the Constitutional Convention

The states disagreed among themselves about almost everything. Each printed its own money, which varied widely in value. They taxed each other's goods. They sometimes would not trade with other states. Many had their own armies and navies. Often they refused to obey the laws that Congress passed.

The central government had very little power to act. Favorable foreign trade treaties could not be **negotiated** (worked out) because most European nations believed the states could not live up to the treaties. Few people would lend money to the central government because they doubted it could pay them back. The states themselves began to **default** on (not pay) their debts to the central government.

Things soon went from bad to worse. Prices rose higher and higher. More and more people defaulted on their debts. People

The Fugio cent was minted in 1787. The 13 links on the back of the coin, above right, represent the 13 colonies united as one nation.

who had a lot to lose, such as property owners, merchants, and **creditors** (people who loaned out money), became convinced that something had to be done. The government under the Articles of Confederation was simply too weak to solve the nation's problems.

It was not long, therefore, before more and more property owners and creditors felt that some changes had to be made. But they did not think it would be enough just to **amend** (change) the Articles. They wanted a stronger central government with power to enforce any laws it passed. They wanted to give Congress the power to tax and to regulate trade. They wanted a strong national government to control unrest at home, to provide military protection, and to obtain favorable trade treaties with other nations.

Many people, however, still feared the idea of having a strong central government. They did not think things were too bad. They thought things certainly were not bad enough to change the basic plan of the government. Nevertheless, problems—of boundaries, trade, taxes, and many more—continued. Such problems were common to most, if not all, of the states.

In the fall of 1786, the Virginia legislature invited the states to send delegates to a meeting at Annapolis, Maryland. The stated purpose of the meeting was to discuss the idea of setting up trade regulations that would be the same in all states. What many hoped would really happen, however, was that the delegates would discuss ways to amend the Articles of Confederation. However, only five states sent delegates. Hopes sank. Alexander Hamilton, who was later to become the first Secretary of the Treasury, called for another meeting in Philadelphia in May of 1787. Congress still did not want to act. A few states appointed delegates. Most, however, did not.

Incident in Massachusetts

In some of the states, **debtors** (people who owed money), mostly small farmers, gained control of the state legislatures. Almost immediately, they printed an oversupply of paper money. Having an oversupply meant the money was almost worthless. In Rhode Island, the debtor-controlled state legislature passed a law requiring creditors to accept the worthless money.

In Massachusetts, creditors gained control of the legislature. To pay off its Revolutionary War debts, the legislature placed heavy taxes on anyone who owned property. The small farmers of the state, most of whom were already heavily in debt, could not pay these taxes. As a result, the state courts began to **foreclose** on (take away) the farmers' property. Many farmers faced possible imprisonment.

Shays' Rebellion

In 1786, Daniel Shays, a captain in the Revolutionary Army, led a group of about 1,000 armed farmers and other debtors to complain about what the Massachusetts courts were doing. The state militia (soldiers) easily defeated them. Shays' Rebellion, as the uprising came to be called, frightened many people and increased interest in the Philadelphia convention. Seven states immediately appointed delegates to the meeting. Congress then asked all of the states to appoint delegates for the "sole and express purpose of revising the Articles of Confederation." Every state except Rhode Island sent delegates.

SECTION 2 *Review*

Defining Key Terms

1. Define: negotiate, default, creditor, amend, debtor, foreclose.

Recalling the Facts

2. Why did Alexander Hamilton call for a convention of delegates in Philadelphia?
3. Why was Shays' Rebellion significant?

Reviewing the Main Idea

4. Answer "As you read . . ." question 2 on page 19: Why are the years 1781–1787 considered a critical period in American history?

Critical Thinking

5. **Expressing Problems Clearly.** What problems would occur today if the value of money varied from state to state?

3 The Constitutional Convention

The development of a truly independent nation was closer to reality. The first step had been to break away from England. The second step had been to create new state governments to replace the English-controlled colonial governments. The meeting in Philadelphia in 1787, which we now call the Constitutional Convention, was the third step.

Many important men attended the Philadelphia convention. Most were successful merchants, planters, bankers, lawyers, or politicians. Few workers or small farmers attended. George Washington was elected to preside over the meetings.

The delegates agreed on many things. Almost all favored a republican form of government. A **republican form of government** is one in which the people elect representatives to govern them. These representatives are then responsible to the people.

All delegates wanted a written constitution. All were in favor of a balanced government. They wanted to set up a national government in which no particular interest group could control what went on. Most delegates, however, wanted to protect property and business. Most of the delegates thought that landowners were the best protectors of liberty. All agreed that the right to vote should be limited to property owners. They differed, however, over the kind and the amount of property that a person had to own in order to vote.

All of the delegates had been instructed to suggest amendments to the Articles of Confederation. Yet within five days of the start of the convention, almost all of the delegates voted to establish a "national government . . . consisting of a supreme legislative, executive, and judiciary." This was a key decision. It basically changed the nature of the central government. No longer would it be merely a union of states, but rather a national government, with power over all the states.

There was little disagreement with the idea of giving the new Congress all the powers of the old, plus certain other powers it might need to govern the new nation. A strong executive, which did not exist under the Articles, was accepted as necessary to provide direction for the central government. An independent court system was also accepted without much argument. In addition, it was agreed that the legislature would consist of two houses.

There were some serious differences and disagreements among the delegates. The large states differed with the small

Writing a Constitution

Governments of the United States: 1781 and 1789

How the Weaknesses of the Articles of Confederation Were Corrected by the Constitution

Articles of Confederation	Constitution of the United States
States have most of the power. The national government has little.	States have some power, but most power is given to the national government.
No executive officer to carry out the laws of Congress.	A President heads the executive branch of the government.
No national courts. Only state courts exist.	Both national and state courts exist.
Congress is responsible to the states.	Congress is responsible to the people.
Nine out of 13 states have to approve a law before it can go into effect.	Laws may be passed by a majority vote of both houses of Congress.
Congress has no power to tax.	Congress given the power to tax.
Congress can not regulate trade among the states.	Congress given the power to regulate interstate and foreign trade.
Each state coins its own money. There is no national currency.	Only the national government has the power to coin money.

states over representation in Congress. The states in the North disagreed with those in the South over the counting of slaves to determine taxation and representation. The northern and southern states also differed over the regulation and taxation of foreign **commerce** (trade). These differences were resolved by three famous compromises. A **compromise** is an agreement between two parties in which each gives up some of his or her original demands to gain others.

As you might expect, the large states hoped to control the new government. The small states were anxious to keep this from happening. The large states wanted representation in both houses of the new Congress to be based on population or on the amount of money a state gave to support the central government. This would give the states with the most people, such as Virginia, Massachusetts, and Pennsylvania, a majority in Congress.

The small states insisted that the states had to be represented equally in Congress, at least in the upper house. Neither side would give in. Finally, a committee was elected to work out a compromise.

The Connecticut delegates played a leading role in the work of this committee. Therefore, the plan they worked out was called the *Connecticut Compromise.* This compromise called for an upper house in which each state would have an equal vote. There would be a lower house in which representation would be based on population. Also, all **appropriation** bills (bills approving the

The Connecticut Compromise

Oliver Ellsworth helped to work out the Connecticut Compromise.

spending (or money) would start in the lower house. The larger states agreed to the compromise only when the small states said they would not join the Union if the compromise was not accepted.

The Three-Fifths Compromise

As soon as the question of representation was settled, another question came up. Should slaves be counted in determining the size of a state's population? The southern states wanted slaves to be counted. The northern states said that slaves should not be counted. It was finally agreed that a slave should count as three-fifths of a person in determining a state's population. The Thirteenth Amendment to the Constitution, passed in 1865, which freed the slaves, made this compromise outdated.

The Commerce and Slave Trade Compromise

The northern states wanted to make sure that the national government had the power to control commerce. The southern states were afraid that a northern-controlled Congress would place a heavy tax on the South's flourishing trade in agricultural products with England. Again, a compromise was reached. Congress was given the power to regulate interstate and foreign trade. **Interstate** trade means trade between two or more states. Congress was forbidden to tax exports or to favor one location over another. The southern delegates also pushed through a requirement that all treaties had to be ratified by a two-thirds majority in the Senate. Furthermore, the slave trade (buying and selling of black people as slaves), which existed then, could not be prohibited for another 20 years.

George Washington presided over the Constitutional Convention.

The delegates differed on the method of electing the President. Twice, they approved election by Congress, but opponents argued that this would mean legislative control of the executive. The opponents finally won out. The Electoral College was chosen as the method of presidential election. Under the Electoral College, electors would choose the President and Vice President. **Electors** are men and women voted for by the people.

Finally, on September 17, 1787, the delegates stopped debating. Their work was finished. They came together to sign the document on which they had worked for nearly four months. Benjamin Franklin, at 81 the oldest of the delegates, summed up their feelings when he wrote:

> I agree to this Constitution, with all its faults, if they are such; . . . I doubt whether any other Convention we can obtain may be able to make a better Constitution . . . for when you assemble a number of men to have the advantage of their joint wisdom, you inevitably assemble . . . all their prejudices, their passions, their errors of opinion, their local interests, and their selfish views. From such an assembly, can a perfect production be expected?

Other Compromises

The Articles of Confederation could be adopted only with the approval of *all* states. The **Framers** (writers) of the Constitution had seen how difficult it was to meet such a requirement. Article 7 of the Constitution, therefore, stated that the Constitution would go into effect when two-thirds (nine) states ratified it.

On September 28, 1787, they sent the Constitution out to the states to review. Both supporters and opponents of the Constitution appeared quickly. The supporters became known as **Federalists**. The opponents were called **Anti-Federalists**. The Federalists were led by many of the delegates who had attended the Philadelphia Convention. Their main argument for approving the new Constitution centered around the failure of the Articles of Confederation. They argued that the Articles were much too weak. Unless a strong national government was created, the nation could not survive.

The Anti-Federalists were opposed to almost every phrase in the Constitution. But their main objections were that it gave too much power to the national government at the expense of the states. Also, it lacked a Bill of Rights. The Constitution did not guarantee certain basic liberties, such as freedom of speech and of religion, to the people. The Federalists finally gave in on this point. They agreed to add a Bill of Rights when and if the new Constitution was approved.

Ratification

Constitution Trivia

How many of the following questions can you answer correctly?

1. Who wrote most of the Constitution?
  a. Thomas Jefferson
  b. James Madison
  c. Gouverneur Morris
  d. George Washington

2. How many words are in the document?
  a. 3,219
  b. 4,440
  c. 7,605
  d. 8,050

3. How often does the word *democracy* appear?
  a. not once
  b. 7 times
  c. 11 times
  d. 21 times

4. A clerk named Jacob Shallus had the job of copying the Constitution neatly onto parchment. He spent 40 hours on the task. How much did he earn?
  a. nothing
  b. $30
  c. $80
  d. $100

5. How many countries have written charters that are modeled either directly or indirectly on our Constitution?
  a. 12
  b. about 70
  c. about 125
  d. more than 160

Answers: 1. c 2. b 3. a 4. b 5. d

By June, 1788, nine of the states had ratified the Constitution, and the new government was officially in effect. In May, 1790, the last two states approved the Constitution.

SECTION 3 *Review*

Defining Key Terms

1. Define: republican form of government, commerce, compromise, appropriation, interstate, Framers, Federalists, Anti-Federalists.

Recalling the Facts

2. What were some of the disagreements among the delegates at the Philadelphia Convention?

3. What were some of the delegates' compromises?

Reviewing the Main Idea

4. Answer "As you read . . ." question 3 on page 19: Why was the Constitutional Convention important?

Critical Thinking

5. Identifying Central Issues. Why did the Anti-Federalists want a Bill of Rights added to the Constitution?

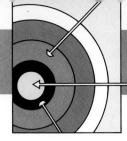
Critical Thinking Skills

Identifying Central Issues

A wealth of information is available to us from many sources, including textbooks, magazines, newspapers, radio, television, films, and other people. One way to begin to make sense of this information is to identify *central issues*—the main ideas or most important points in the material.

In addition to helping you sort out and make sense of information, identifying central issues is a way to check your comprehension (understanding). A group of specific facts will only be meaningful to you if you are able to grasp the central issues. If you can state the central issue in a speech or a newspaper editorial, for example, you are probably "getting the message." The same is true when you are studying the information in your textbook. If you can pick out the central issue in each paragraph, then you have probably understood what you have read.

Identifying central issues can also help you organize information. Central issues are like magnets that hold related bits of information together. When you identify central issues and then look for related information, such as details or examples, you are more likely to remember and make use of the information.

How can you identify central issues? Sometimes a writer or speaker will tell you directly what the central issue is. In other cases, you will have to figure it out yourself. You can successfully spot central issues if you look for (1) the major purpose of the information, (2) the points that are empha-sized, and (3) the ideas that are so impor-tant that the rest of the information would not make sense without them.

See how well you can identify the central issue as you read the paragraph below. Read the paragraph carefully and then apply the three steps listed in the preceding paragraph.

> When the Revolutionary War ended in 1781, the new nation's economic and political problems came into sharp focus. The weaknesses of the Articles of Confederation soon surfaced. With a central government unable to act, the states bickered among themselves and grew increasingly jealous and suspicious of one another. They sent little money to the new central government, and they failed to support it in other ways as well. Several of them made agreements with foreign governments, even though that was forbidden by the Articles. Most even organized their own military forces.

Practicing Skills

Refer to the paragraph above to answer the following questions on a separate sheet of paper.
1. What is the central issue of the paragraph?
2. Would you say that the central issue is clear and easy to identify? Explain your answer.
3. **Testing Conclusions.** Think of the central issue that you named in question 1 as a conclusion. What facts in the paragraph support this conclusion?

Citizenship

The Daughters of the American Revolution

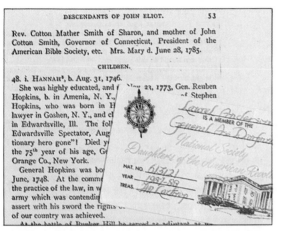

At the DAR's library in Washington, D.C., DAR members and the public can research their family histories.

"Antonelli." "Bernstein." "Chang." "Diaz." If you thumb through the telephone book, you can get a good idea of our country's rich ethnic mix. Most Americans have their family roots in another country. Their parents or grandparents or great-grandparents came to the United States sometime during the 1800s or 1900s.

For a small number of American women, though, the family tree can be traced straight back to the colonists who fought for American independence in the late 1700s. These women are proud members of a patriotic society called the Daughters of the American Revolution (DAR). Founded in 1890, the DAR now boasts more than 200,000 members.

"America's Fan Club," as it is sometimes called, aims to preserve American history and to promote patriotism, citizenship, and education. Since 1920, the DAR has helped immigrants to become United States citizens with its *Manual for Citizenship.* This booklet summarizes American history, explains our form of government, and outlines the rules for becoming a citizen.

Each year the DAR gives time and money to local anti-pollution and conservation efforts—planting thousands of trees and shrubs on public property and feeding birds and other wild animals. The Daughters have also helped to restore several of America's oldest structures, such as the Connecticut birthplace of Revolutionary War artist John Trumbull.

The DAR also reaches out to young people. The organization sponsors a Good Citizens scholarship for high school students. It funds scholarships for American Indians and students of American history. And it runs schools for needy children in Alabama, North Carolina, South Carolina, and Kentucky. As the DAR says, "What can be more important than to offer an education to disadvantaged young people?"

Questions to think about

1. In what ways does one's ethnic background play a role in American life?
2. How might you think of yourself and your country differently if you were a member of an organization such as the DAR?

CHAPTER SUMMARY

Section 1   During the American Revolution, the colonists decided they needed some form of central government to deal with their problems. The first plan for this government was called the Articles of Confederation. The Articles were weak, however, because they did not give Congress enough authority to raise money, to control trade, to protect the nation, or to settle disputes.

Section 2   The problems facing the nation became so bad between 1781 and 1787 that these years are known as the "critical period" of American history. The states could not agree on anything. Money became almost worthless. The states could not protect ships at sea or negotiate treaties with foreign countries. Both creditors and debtors began to rebel and call for change.

Section 3   As a result, American leaders held a convention and decided to write a new plan for government, the Constitution of the United States. The Constitution established a strong national government made up of three branches: legislative, executive, and judicial. Convention delegates settled disagreements by three famous compromises. One compromise decided how states would be represented in Congress. The second decided how slaves were to be counted in determining a state's population. The third allowed Congress to tax interstate commerce.

Reviewing Key Terms

On a separate sheet of paper, use the following terms to complete the sentences below.

debtor   ratify
amend   compromise
Federalist

1. To approve a constitution is to __?__ it.

2. To change a constitution is to __?__ it.

3. A person who owes money is a __?__ .

4. An agreement in which both parties give in a little is called a __?__ .

5. Someone who supported the Constitution was called a __?__ .

Understanding Main Ideas

1. What were the Articles of Confederation?

2. Name three powers and three weaknesses of the central government under the Articles of Confederation.

3. Why are the years 1781–1787 called the "critical period"?

4. What was Shays' Rebellion?

5. Identify five ways in which the Constitution corrected the weaknesses of the Articles of Confederation.

6. What did the northern and southern states disagree about during the Constitutional Convention? The large and small states?

7. What was the Connecticut Compromise?

8. Describe two other important compromises at the Constitutional Convention.

Critical Thinking

1. **Demonstrating Reasoned Judgment.** Consider how the new national government changed in the ten years after the Declaration of Independence. Do you think change in society can be brought about by only a few people? Why or why not?

2. **Drawing Conclusions.** The new Constitution was based on several important compromises. Do you think compromise is necessary in a democratic form of government? Why or why not?

3. **Recognizing Bias.** The delegates to the Constitutional Convention were all wealthy and successful landowners, merchants, and professional men. There were no small farmers, workers, nonwhites, or women. Does the Constitution reflect only the interests of these men? Explain your answer.

Practicing Skills

1. **Identifying Central Issues.** Scan your local newspaper for a brief article about the federal government. Cut out the article and attach it to a sheet of paper. Then, identify and state the central issue of the article. Share your article and central issue statement with the class. If others do not understand your statement, revise it so the most important points of the article are clearly stated.

2. **Summarizing.** In your own words, summarize the main weaknesses of the Articles of Confederation.

3. **Writing a Letter.** Imagine you are a delegate to the Constitutional Convention. Write a letter to the other delegates in which you try to convince them to vote for or against the new Constitution. Read your letter aloud to the class.

Focusing on Citizenship

1. **Writing a Report.** Using library resources, write a short report on the role played by each of the following at the Constitutional Convention: George Washington, James Madison, Alexander Hamilton, Benjamin Franklin, Gouverneur Morris.

2. **Staging a Mock Constitutional Convention.** Divide the class into groups of delegates from the 13 original states. Each group should find out whether it represents a large or small state, a southern or northern state. Then, have the delegates debate the major issues of the new Constitution: These issues would include how many legislative votes to give each state, whether to count slaves in the voting population, and how to regulate trade.

3. **Doing Field Research.** Contact your representative to the city council or state legislature. Invite the representative to visit your class to discuss the importance of compromise in lawmaking today.

CHAPTER 3

The Constitution of the United States

The United States Constitution has provided a remarkably stable foundation for our government for more than 200 years.

Previewing the Chapter

When the Framers met more than 200 years ago, the challenge they faced was not just to establish a government that would work *then*. The challenge was to produce a plan of government that could adapt–change if necessary–and thus serve people *far into the future*. The timeless ideals and beliefs held by the first leaders of our nation are stated in the opening paragraph of the Constitution. This chapter outlines the Constitution and shows how it promotes and protects the rights of citizens and limits the powers of government.

- ■ **Before you read,** look up these key terms in the Glossary at the back of this book: *Preamble*, *impeach*, *enumerated powers*, *elastic clause*, *amendment*, *extradition*.

- ■ **As you read,** look for answers to these questions:
  1. What were the two goals that guided the work of the writers of the Constitution?
  2. What are the three branches of the national government and the function of each?
  3. What are the basic principles on which the American system of government is based?
  4. In what ways do the national and state governments work together?

1 The Preamble

As you recall, the 55 delegates who met at the Philadelphia convention in 1787 did not originally set out to write the Constitution. Their aim at first was simply to revise the Articles of Confederation. Yet they soon saw that only a new plan of government would do.

The Framers had two goals in mind. First, they wanted to create a strong central government. Under the Articles, they had what George Washington described as "a half-starved limping government that appears to be always moving upon crutches and tottering at every step." The Framers' second goal was to set up a government that treated people fairly and was not cruel.

The writers of the Constitution developed a system of government to achieve these two goals. The Constitution describes the basic features of our system of government in a preamble and in seven other parts called articles. The **Preamble** is a statement of purpose. It explains why the government of the United States was created. The Preamble states: "We the People of the United States, in order to form a more perfect Union, establish Justice, insure domestic Tranquility, provide for the common defence, promote the general Welfare, and secure the Blessings of Liberty to ourselves and our Posterity, do ordain and establish this Constitution for the United States of America." What do these words mean? Continue reading to find out.

"We the People of the United States . . ."

When the Constitution was written, "people" referred only to free male property owners. Persons who did not own property could not vote; neither could women or slaves. They had no say in approving the final document. The term "United States" referred only to the original 13 colonies on the eastern seaboard.

". . . in order to form a more perfect Union . . ."

The Constitution helped to create a single nation of many states. It created a strong national government with powers to tax and to regulate trade between the states. It stated that only the national government could coin money or declare war. It created a strong executive branch to govern the entire nation. It established a national court system. It gave Congress the power to build roads in order to move mail and to connect various parts of the country. It stated that the Constitution would be the supreme law of the land.

". . . establish Justice . . ."

The Constitution provides for a system of **federal** (national) courts. The courts establish justice by settling disputes between

PEOPLE HELPING PEOPLE

The Warmth of Arizona

Ruth Haywood, is a retiree who chose to settle in Arizona for its famous sunny climate and soothing heat. But she has been bringing a special warmth of her own to the desert town of Casa Grande, halfway between Tucson and Phoenix.

In 1979, upset at the hunger in her community, Haywood began handing out sandwiches to her neighbors from the backseat of her car. Next she organized holiday meals. This was just a start. Haywood soon realized that many of the people she was serving needed help year round. She began an "Adopt-a-Family" program that delivers donated food, furniture, clothing, and toys to those most desperate for these things.

"We publish a list of what's needed," says the town's newspaper editor, "and the people of our community really respond."

individuals, between individuals and the national government, or between the states. The courts also establish justice by hearing cases against people accused of breaking laws. The courts try to make sure that accused people are not punished unless law enforcement officials are able to prove charges against them.

". . . insure domestic Tranquility . . ."

Domestic means at home. Tranquility means peace. Domestic tranquility means peace within the United States. The Constitution permits Congress to call out the state National Guard (soldiers) if necessary to keep law and order. Although local and state police usually enforce the laws, the National Guard is used in serious emergencies, such as riots or floods.

". . . provide for the common defence . . ."

The Constitution says that Congress "may raise and support Armies," and "provide and maintain a Navy" to protect the United States. Today, the United States has one of the strongest armed forces in the world, including not only an Army and Navy, but also an Air Force, Marine Corps, and Coast Guard.

". . . promote the general Welfare . . ."

The Constitution gives Congress the power to collect taxes to provide for the general welfare of all citizens. The **general welfare** refers to the needs of all the people of the United States. Congress has provided money to the states to help the unemployed. It has aided cities in rebuilding old neighborhoods. It has sent food and other assistance to the states when floods and earthquakes have occurred. It has given money to school districts to help them improve their education programs.

"... and secure the Blessings of Liberty to ourselves and our Posterity ..."

Liberty means that we are free to do as we please, as long as we obey the law and do not take away the rights of others. We have the right to select our leaders and to remove them from office if we do not like what they do. The states have the power to hold elections and to decide how these elections will be conducted. Several amendments have been added to the Constitution over the years to guarantee all adult citizens of our country the right to vote. These amendments are explained in the next chapter. The Bill of Rights, the first ten amendments to the Constitution, lists many of the freedoms which the people of the United States have.

Posterity means the people of the future. The rights guaranteed to us today under the Constitution are also to be guaranteed to all those who come after us.

In summary, then, the writers of the Constitution created a united nation made up of independent states, and a government which does as the people want. The purpose of this government is to protect and serve all of us and our descendants.

SECTION *1* *Review*

Defining Key Terms
1. Define: Preamble, federal, general welfare, liberty, posterity.

Recalling the Facts
2. Why was the Preamble of the Constitution written?
3. What are some ways the Constitution helps establish justice?

Reviewing the Main Idea
4. Answer "As you read ..." question 1 on page 35: What were the two goals that guided the work of the writers of the Constitution?

Critical Thinking
5. **Determining Relevance.** Which one of the purposes stated in the Preamble would you say is the most important? Why?

2 The Three Branches of the National Government

The Constitution divided the national government into a legislative branch (the Congress), an executive branch (the Presidency), and a judicial branch (the courts). It thus created a government based on the principle of **separation of powers**. Each branch is separate from, yet equal to, the other branches. The writers of the Constitution believed that separating the powers of the central government would prevent one person or a group of people from having too much power. The first three articles of the Constitution describe the powers of each branch. They also describe how officials are selected in each branch, how long they hold their positions, and how they may be removed.

The **legislative branch** consists of a Congress with two houses, the Senate and the House of Representatives. The legislative branch makes the laws.

Article 1 tells the qualifications and method of electing members of the House and Senate. It gives the power of *impeachment* to the House, but states that the Senate shall try an impeachment case. To **impeach** a public official means to bring a charge of wrongdoing against that official. The only punishment that can be given is to remove the wrongdoer from office. The Article also states that all tax bills must start in the House. It allows the President to sign or veto a bill. It gives Congress the power to overturn a President's veto by a two-thirds vote of both houses.

Article 1: Legislative Branch

SEPARATION OF POWERS

THE CONGRESS MAKES THE LAWS	THE PRESIDENT ENFORCES THE LAWS	THE COURTS MAKE DECISIONS ABOUT QUESTIONS OF LAW
↑	↑	↑
THE LEGISLATIVE BRANCH	THE EXECUTIVE BRANCH	THE JUDICIAL BRANCH

SKILL BUILDER

What is the main function of the executive branch of government?

Article 1, Section 8 gives Congress the power to tax, to provide for the "general welfare," to borrow and coin money, to regulate commerce, and to give aliens citizenship. An **alien** is a person from another country who lives in the United States. Section 8 also empowers (allows) Congress to punish counterfeiters, to establish a post office, to create courts, and to declare war.

Sections 4 and 5 state that Congress must meet at least once every year. Congress is to be the judge of the qualifications of its members. Each house may punish its members for improper behavior and even expel them (say they are no longer members). Section 9 provides certain basic protections for citizens against acts of Congress, such as passing a bill of attainder or an *ex post facto* law. (These protections are described in Chapter 9.)

Article 2: Executive Branch

Article 2 provides for an **executive branch**, the President. The President carries out the laws. Article 2 states the qualifications for office, term, and method of election. The writers of the Constitution did not provide for election of the President by the people. Instead, as was mentioned in Chapter 2, they established the Electoral College. Each state has as many electors as it has Representatives and Senators in Congress. All of the electoral votes of a state normally go to the presidential candidate who gets the largest number of popular votes in that state. (The Electoral College is discussed further in Chapter 18.)

Article 2 also provides for a Vice President to take over the powers and duties of the President if the President should die, be removed from office, or be unable to serve. It describes the President's powers and duties and the reasons for which either the President or the Vice President may be removed from office before completing his or her elected term.

Article 2 also specifies that the President, upon taking office, shall take the following oath: "I do solemnly swear [affirm] that I will faithfully execute the office of President of the United States, and will, to the best of my ability, preserve, protect, and defend the Constitution of the United States." The Presidential oath of office confirms the fact that the Constitution is the highest law of our land.

Article 3: Judicial Branch

Article 3 provides for a federal court system consisting of one Supreme Court and any other lower courts that Congress may create. The federal courts are the **judicial branch** of our national government.

Article 3 describes the powers of the federal courts. It also tells what kinds of cases are to be heard in the federal courts. (The operations of the federal court system will be described in more detail in Chapter 9.)

Chief Justice William Rehnquist administers the oath of office to President George Bush on January 20, 1989.

Separating the powers of the national government into three branches provides for a system of **checks and balances.** Each branch checks or limits the power of the other branches. For example, the President may check the Congress by **vetoing** (refusing to sign) bills that Congress passes. Congress may check the President by a two-thirds vote to override his veto. The President may negotiate a treaty with another country, but the Senate may refuse to approve it. A two-thirds Senate vote is required to ratify treaties. Congress may provide money for various federal projects, but the President may refuse to spend this money. The President may not spend money without the approval of Congress.

The President names federal judges to the Supreme Court, but the Senate has the power to reject the President's appointments. The Senate can also reject the President's appointment of an ambassador to another country, or the head of an executive department. Laws passed by Congress can be reviewed by the federal courts. The courts may declare a law unconstitutional. The President also names judges to the lower federal courts, but again the Senate has the power to reject his choices. As you can see in the chart on page 42, each of the three branches checks the activities of the other two.

Checks and Balances

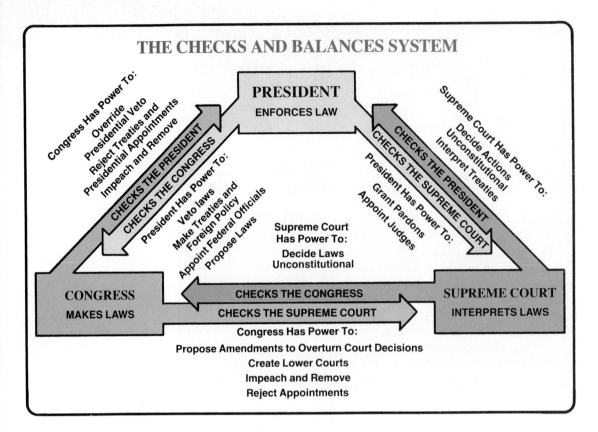

THE CHECKS AND BALANCES SYSTEM

PRESIDENT
ENFORCES LAW

Congress Has Power To:
Override
Presidential Veto
Reject Treaties and
Presidential Appointments
Impeach and Remove

Supreme Court Has Power To:
Decide Actions
Unconstitutional
Interpret Treaties

CHECKS THE PRESIDENT

CHECKS THE CONGRESS

CHECKS THE SUPREME COURT

CHECKS THE PRESIDENT

President Has Power To:
Veto laws
Make Treaties and
Foreign Policy
Appoint Federal Officials
Propose Laws

President Has Power To:
Grant Pardons
Appoint Judges

Supreme Court
Has Power To:

Decide Laws
Unconstitutional

CONGRESS
MAKES LAWS

CHECKS THE CONGRESS

CHECKS THE SUPREME COURT

SUPREME COURT
INTERPRETS LAWS

Congress Has Power To:

Propose Amendments to Overturn Court Decisions

Create Lower Courts

Impeach and Remove

Reject Appointments

▲ **SKILL BUILDER**

In what way does the Supreme Court check Congress's power?

SECTION 2 *Review*

Defining Key Terms

1. Define: separation of powers, legislative branch, impeach, alien, executive branch, judicial branch, checks and balances, veto.

Recalling the Facts

2. What are some powers given to each of the three branches of our government by the Constitution?

Reviewing the Main Idea

3. Answer "As you read . . ." question 2 on page 35: What are the three main branches of the national government and the function of each?

Critical Thinking

4. Predicting Consequences. Without a system of checks and balances, what might occur?

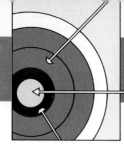

Sharpening Your Skills

Citizenship Skills

Analyzing the News

Every day, every hour, thousands of newsworthy events are happening all over the world. To stay informed about current events, most people depend on newspapers and television. Developing your skills as a critical reader, viewer, and listener can help you to analyze the news and thus to understand it better.

Newspapers offer more stories and more detailed information than television can provide. Most newspaper articles follow a standard format, or plan. The *headline* —the title of an article—captures the main idea of the story. The largest headlines and the most important stories appear on the front page.

Just below the headline are the byline and the dateline. The *byline* tells who wrote the article—either an individual or a news service. The two largest news services are the United Press International (UPI) and the Associated Press (AP). The *dateline* includes the place where the story was filed and sometimes the date. The first sentence, which summarizes the main idea of the story, is called the *lead.* A good lead tells who did what, where, when, and how. The why of the story and other details follow in the *body,* or remainder, of the story.

Television news programs offer more up-to-the minute reporting than newspapers, but they usually cover stories in less depth. The structure of an evening news program is much like that of a newspaper. Major stories, like front-page articles, are broadcast first, along with on-the-scene reports. Lighter feature stories, sports, and weather reports usually come after the headline news.

Understanding the following points can help you to be a more critical consumer of the news.

- **News stories should state the facts without expressing opinions.** If opinions are expressed by a newspaper, they appear in *editorials.* News editorials on television are announced as *commentary* or as *station editorials.*
- **Time and space limit the news.** No newspaper or television news show can possibly cover everything. Thus, consulting more than one news source will keep you better informed.
- **News is business.** Newspapers want to sell as many copies as possible, and television stations want to boost their ratings. Editors select many news stories on the basis of how entertaining they will be to readers and viewers. For example, a dramatic rescue at sea might get more coverage than a dry political speech.

Practicing Skills

1. If you want a full description of a new government budget proposal, would you turn to a newspaper or a television news report? Why?
2. **Making Comparisons.** Watch an evening news program on television, taking special note of the lead story. Then read about the same story in the next day's newspaper. Compare the quantity and quality of the accounts.

3 Basic Principles of Our Government

As you studied in Chapter 1, our Constitution is based on certain principles of government. A **principle** is a basic rule or code of conduct. The principles on which our system of government is based include separation of powers, checks and balances, federalism, limited government, popular sovereignty, and flexibility. Separation of powers and checks and balances were described in Section 2. We shall discuss each of the other principles in this section.

Federalism

The government of the United States is based on the idea of **federalism**. It is a federal system. Such a system has two main features.

First, the powers and activities of government are divided between the national government and the states. The national government makes and enforces laws that affect the whole nation. It makes laws, for example, to control communication among the states. Thus, the Federal Communications Commission licenses television and radio stations in the various states and decides how they may operate. The state governments, on the other hand, take care of matters that affect only the people within their borders. Utah has a law that forbids gambling, while Nevada permits it.

Second, the federal government can overrule the state governments. If a federal law and a state law conflict, it is the federal law that the people are to obey. The state law is set aside. Furthermore, federal courts can overrule a state court if they disagree with the state court's interpretation of a law. State courts, however, may not overrule federal courts.

The powers of the federal government are listed in the Constitution. These listed powers are often referred to as the **enumerated (listed) powers**.

The powers of the states are not listed in the body of the Constitution itself. They are found in the Tenth Amendment. The Tenth Amendment says the states have all those powers not given to the national government or forbidden to them by the Constitution. The powers of the states are called **reserved powers**.

A few powers, called **concurrent powers**, are held by both the national and state governments. Both governments have the power to tax. The national government uses these powers in matters that involve the nation as a whole. The states use these powers to govern affairs within their borders. The chart on page 46

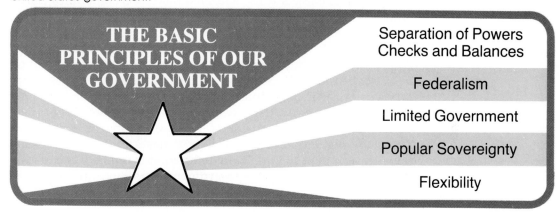

THE BASIC
PRINCIPLES OF OUR
GOVERNMENT

Separation of Powers
Checks and Balances

Federalism

Limited Government

Popular Sovereignty

Flexibility

gives some examples of these enumerated, reserved, and concurrent powers.

Limited Government

Our government cannot do everything it wants. The powers of each branch of government are limited, or restricted, in many ways by the Constitution. First of all, the national government may use only those powers the Constitution provides. Second, Article 1, Section 9 of the Constitution denies certain powers to the national government. It may not, for example, place a tax on goods **exported** (sent) to other nations, or spend money except as permitted by law.

The Constitution also limits the powers of the states. Article 1, Section 10 denies certain powers to the states. The powers denied the states include all those denied the national government. In addition, the states may not sign a treaty with a foreign country, coin money, or collect taxes on imported goods. Article 6 forbids the states to make any laws that go against federal laws, the Constitution, or a treaty made with another country.

Popular Sovereignty

The principle of popular sovereignty means that the people of the United States are the source of government power. The government needs the consent of the people before it can act.

Flexibility

The Constitution is a flexible document because of two provisions—the elastic clause and the amendment process.
The Elastic Clause.   Article 1, Section 8 gives Congress power to make all laws that are necessary and proper for carrying out the powers listed in the Constitution. This is sometimes called the **elastic clause.** This clause allows the national government to adapt its powers to the needs of the times. Because of the elastic clause, the need for frequent constitutional amendments has

been reduced. The idea that Congress can do all things necessary and proper to carry out its delegated powers is sometimes called **implied powers**.

Federal regulations that involve railroads illustrate the idea of implied powers. The writers of the Constitution could not have known that some day there would be a need for the government to regulate the railroads. No railroads existed when the Constitution was written. But the Constitution gives Congress the power to regulate commerce (trade) between the states. A railroad that travels between states is considered to be engaging in commerce. Thus, the regulation of railroads becomes a matter for the national government to handle. In doing so, it is implied, because of the elastic clause, that the government can determine the fares the railroads may charge, or require that they maintain certain safety standards.

The Amendment Process. The writers of the Constitution realized that some changes probably would be necessary in the future. Hence they provided in Article 5 that the Constitution could be amended. An **amendment** is a change in an original document. There are four ways by which this can be done, as shown in the figure on page 47.

SKILL BUILDER

Which set of powers is given to the federal government? To state governments? To both?

The Federal System

Enumerated Powers

- Regulate foreign and interstate commerce
- Make treaties
- Establish naturalization laws
- Coin money
- Establish post offices
- Issue copyrights and patents
- Declare war
- Provide and maintain armed services
- Fix standards of weights and measures
- Admit new states
- Establish a court system

Concurrent Powers

- Make and enforce laws
- Maintain courts
- Collect taxes
- Borrow money
- Charter banks
- Protect health and welfare of the people
- Call out the militia

Reserved Powers

- Provide for education
- Establish local governments
- Conduct elections
- Protect public safety and morals
- Build highways
- Raise a state militia
- Issue licenses
- Incorporate businesses
- Regulate intrastate commerce

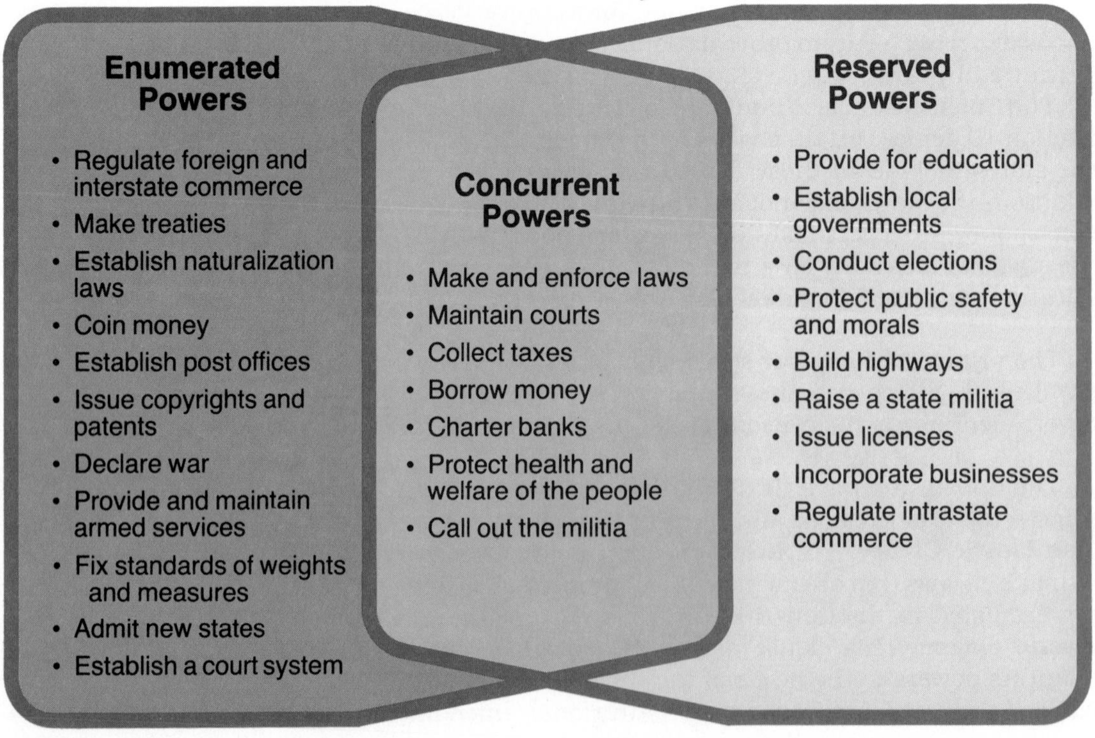

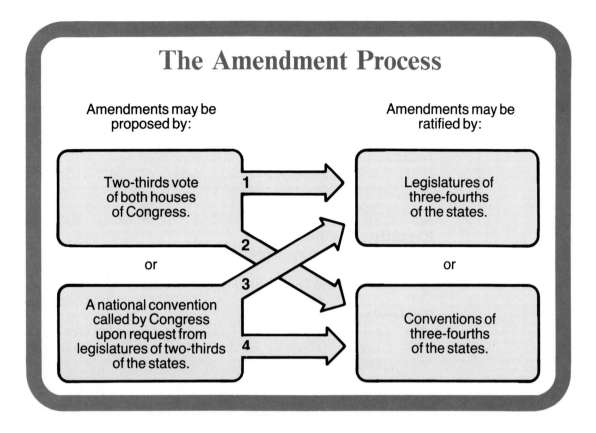

The Amendment Process

Amendments may be proposed by:

Two-thirds vote of both houses of Congress.

or

A national convention called by Congress upon request from legislatures of two-thirds of the states.

Amendments may be ratified by:

Legislatures of three-fourths of the states.

or

Conventions of three-fourths of the states.

1 2 3 4

Any proposed amendment always says what method of ratification is to be used. One way is for two-thirds of both houses of Congress to propose an amendment. The proposal is then sent to the state legislatures. It becomes law when three-fourths of the legislatures ratify it. Usually a proposed amendment must be ratified in seven years.

A second way also starts with having two-thirds of both houses of Congress propose an amendment. But then it is sent to the states where specially called conventions (meetings) consider ratification. Three-fourths of the states again must ratify it before the amendment can become law. This way has been used only once, to ratify the Twenty-first Amendment.

The third and fourth ways involve having a special national convention propose an amendment. This convention is called by Congress when two-thirds of the state legislatures ask for it. The proposal is then sent to the states for consideration by either their legislatures or by a special convention. In either case, three-fourths of the states again need to ratify the amendment for it to become law. Neither of these methods has ever been used.

These six principles are the basic framework on which our system of government rests. The powers given to the national gov-

SKILL BUILDER

Would an amendment ratified by 25 states become part of the Constitution? Explain.

ernment enable it to govern us. The limits placed on the national government provide ways to keep it from misusing its powers.

SECTION 3 *Review*

Defining Key Terms
1. Define: principle, federalism, enumerated powers, reserved powers, concurrent powers, export, elastic clause, implied powers amendment.

Recalling the Facts
2. What are two main features of a federal system of government?
3. How can the Constitution be amended?

Reviewing the Main Idea
4. Answer "As you read . . ." question 3 on page 35: What are the basic principles on which the American system of government is based?

Critical Thinking
5. **Making Comparisons.** How would the Constitution be different without the elastic clause?

4 Relationships Between the National and State Governments

The Constitution provides for relationships between the national government and the states. The Constitution requires the national government to guarantee every state a republican, or representative, form of government.

Article 4: State Relations

New States. Article 4 gives Congress the power to admit new states to the Union. It may not however, form new states out of those that already exist, unless the legislatures of the states involved give their approval. Congress has set up rules for bringing new states into the Union. A proposed state must have a minimum number of people, as decided by Congress. After a proposed

When approximately 980,000 acres of Yellowstone National Park burned in 1988, members of the U.S. Armed Forces and the Wyoming National Guard helped to put out the fire.

state meets this requirement, the Congress examines its constitution to see whether it is in agreement with the U.S. Constitution. The most recent states admitted to the United States were Alaska and Hawaii. Both of these states were admitted in 1959.

Protection of the States.   The states participate in defending the country. Congress may call the National Guard into national service at any time. When this happens, the President replaces the governors of the states as the acting commander in chief of these soldiers.

The national government also protects each state from invasion. It sends soldiers into a state when the governor asks for help during emergencies such as civil disorders or riots. On many occasions, Presidents have sent soldiers and equipment into a state that has suffered natural disasters such as hurricanes.

Full Faith and Credit.   Article 4 also provides for relations between the states. The Constitution provides that "full faith and credit shall be given in each state to the public acts, records, and judicial proceedings of every other state." The **full faith and credit clause** ensures that rights established under wills, contracts, deeds, and other property rights will be honored in all states. For example, marriages, drivers' licenses, and arrest warrants are honored in every state. This clause protects the legal rights of citizens as they move about the various states. It also prevents citizens from evading legal responsibilities.

A state, however, may require a new resident to apply for a driver's license within a certain period of time. Most states also require that doctors, lawyers, teachers, and other professional people apply for a license to work in their state when moving there from another state. Suppose you are a doctor who has moved from North Carolina to Texas. You may have to take whatever courses and training Texas requires in order to get a license to practice your profession in that state.

Returning Criminals. States also cooperate in pursuing wanted criminals. If a person commits a crime in Indiana and flees to Kentucky, the Indiana police may pursue and arrest that person in Kentucky. If a criminal escapes from jail in Kansas and flees to Missouri, the governor of Kansas may request the state of Missouri to return the criminal. This practice, called **extradition**, prevents a criminal from escaping justice by leaving the state.

Articles 5, 6, and 7

Article 5 describes how Congress and the states can amend the Constitution. Article 6 states that the Constitution is the highest law in the land. It requires that all government officials take an oath to support it. Article 7 states that the Constitution was to be in effect after nine states ratified it.

Although there are many ways in which the national and state governments are tied together, there are many other ways in which the states operate independently. These will be described later in Unit Three.

SECTION 4 *Review*

Defining Key Terms
1. Define: full faith and credit clause, extradition.

Recalling the Facts
2. What are some ways by which the Constitution provides for cooperation among the states?
3. How can a territory become a state?

Reviewing the Main Idea
4. Answer "As you read . . ." question 4 on page 35: In what ways do the national and state governments work together?

Critical Thinking
5. **Predicting Consequences.** Discuss some problems that would arise if contracts made in one state were not valid in another state.

Citizenship

Helping the Hungry

One day in 1983, Carolyn North, a California writer, saw a man looking through a garbage can for crusts of bread. As she watched, she realized there were people in her community who went hungry—and she realized she could help them. North began by bringing loaves of bread to an emergency food distribution center. Today she runs a group called the Daily Bread Project. Each month her group collects about 25 tons of extra food from local bakeries and restaurants. The food is distributed to local residents who would otherwise go hungry.

Like the man North saw, hundreds of thousands of Americans don't get enough to eat. Among the hungry are people who are out of work, the homeless, and people who are sick or disabled. These people are, for one reason or another, unable to feed themselves. Who should feed them?

The federal government shoulders some of the responsibility. It distributes food stamps to the needy, for example, and helps pay for school lunch programs. Such aid is one way the government tries to "promote the general Welfare," as called for in the Constitution. But the government alone cannot solve the problem of hunger—nor should it, say many. Some Americans feel that people must help themselves. Others think that private citizens should reach out to those less fortunate than themselves. That's why people like Carolyn North have stepped in to help. They volunteer their efforts and focus on a local rather than national level. They form groups, like the Daily Bread Project, that aim to distribute food directly to those in need.

Bags of food for the needy cover the floor of a church in Chicago.

Among the many groups that help the hungry are the three described below. Each one was started by concerned citizens working on a volunteer basis. Each group is an example of what ordinary citizens can do to reduce the problem of hunger across the country.

- **Kentucky Harvest** was begun in 1987 by citizens in Louisville, Kentucky. The group's founders were concerned about the amount of edible, nutritious food thrown away by local restaurants and hotels. In its first two years of operation, Kentucky Harvest collected nearly 1.5 million pounds of food from these sources.

The Constitution of the United States **51**

Relying entirely on volunteers, Kentucky Harvest does not accept funds from the state or federal government or from individuals. It does, however, vigorously campaign for donations of food from restaurants, hotels, caterers, and bakeries—even from private parties. This food is then used to feed hungry people in the Louisville area and, in fact, throughout Kentucky and Southern Indiana. U.S.A. Harvest, an outgrowth of Kentucky Harvest, has now been established to set up chapters to feed the hungry in other regions throughout the country.

- **The Perishable Foods Program** in Chicago, Illinois, also helps people in need. The program delivers empty containers to local restaurants, hotels, and caterers. The businesses then fill the containers with extra food that has never been served to customers. Restaurants, for example, contribute cuts of meat and poultry that don't quite meet their desired weight standard.

With these donations, the Perishable Foods Program was able to provide 28,000 meals a month in 1989—amounting to 336,000 meals a year. The cafeteria in the Chicago Sears Building alone donates 300 to 400 pounds of food a week. Other donations sometimes come from unusual sources, including food photographers and vending machine companies.

- Ruth Brinker, an energetic San Franciscan, worked for years as director of Meals on Wheels, a program that delivers meals to the elderly. Then a friend of hers died of AIDS. Although her friend had people nearby to help him, he often had to go without meals as he became too weak to cook for himself. This experience helped Brinker recognize a need to provide food for the growing number of people with AIDS who could no longer prepare their own meals and had nowhere to turn for help. **Project Open Hand** was founded in 1985 when Brinker began serving daily meals to seven people who were infected with the AIDS virus.

Since that time, Project Open Hand has grown quickly. It now serves two home-cooked meals a day to more than 1,000 people with AIDS in the San Francisco area. Like the other programs discussed here, Project Open Hand provides nutritious, well-balanced meals and something perhaps as important—comfort and kindness toward people in need.

Questions to think about

1. What programs for feeding the hungry are there in your community? How are these programs funded?
2. If you were starting a program to feed the hungry in your community, where would you get food? How would you staff your program?

CHAPTER SUMMARY

Section 1   The United States Constitution is the basic law of our land. Written over 200 years ago, it describes the framework of our government. It also lists the rights and privileges of individual American citizens. The first part of the Constitution is the Preamble. The Preamble is a brief introduction explaining the purpose of our government.

Section 2   The Constitution divides the national government into three main branches. The legislative branch (Congress) makes the laws. The executive branch (the Presidency) enforces the laws. The judicial branch (the courts) interprets the laws and settles disputes. Separating the powers of the national government into three branches provides for a system of checks and balances.

Section 3   Our Constitution is based on certain principles. These include separation of powers, federalism, limited government, popular sovereignty, and flexibility. These principles ensure that power is divided among the branches of government and between the national and state governments. Also, the people are the basic source of government power, and laws can be changed to handle new situations.

Section 4   The Constitution divides power between the national and state governments. The national government is superior to the state governments. Certain powers, however, are denied the national government and reserved for the states. The United States Constitution is the supreme law of the land.

Reviewing Key Terms

Match the following terms with the definitions below. Write your answers on a separate sheet of paper.

Preamble	elastic clause
impeach	amendment
enumerated powers	extradition

1. the statement of purpose that is the first part of the Constitution

2. the return of an escaped prisoner from one state to the state from which the excape was made

3. to bring charges of wrongdoing against a government official with the aim of removing the official from office

4. part of the Constitution that gives Congress certain implied powers

5. powers of the federal government listed in the Constitution

6. a change in the Constitution

Understanding Main Ideas

1. According to the Preamble to the Constitution, what are five purposes for establishing the new government?

2. What is the function of the legislative branch? Name five powers given to the legislative branch.

3. What is the function of the executive branch? The judicial branch?

4. What are some of the ways by which each branch of government can check the powers of the other two?

5. What are the two main features of a federal system of government?

6. List three powers given only to the national government, three powers reserved for the states, and three powers given to both state and federal governments.

7. What are implied powers?

8. Describe three ways to amend the Constitution.

9. What are three ways that the states must cooperate with the national government and with one another?

Critical Thinking

1. **Demonstrating Reasoned Judgment.** Should removing elected officials from office if they behave wrongly be left to the people rather than to Congress? Explain your answer.

2. **Predicting Consequences.** Would it be possible for a democratic government to govern effectively without a constitution? Why or why not?

3. **Recognizing Cause and Effect.** How does the separation of powers in the Constitution help to maintain freedom in the United States today?

Practicing Skills

1. **Analyzing the News.** Find a recent newspaper article about an issue involving the national government or the Constitution. Write a summary that tells what the issue is and why it is important.

2. **Researching an Amendment.** The *Readers' Guide to Periodical Literature* is an index of magazine articles. Use the *Readers' Guide* to find three articles on an amendment that has been proposed in the past five years. Look under the topics ''Amendments,'' ''United States Government,'' and ''United States Constitution.'' Read the articles and give a report on the proposed amendment, including the purpose of the amendment.

Focusing on Citizenship

1. **Improving Student Government.** Study the constitution of your student government. In what ways does it provide for separation of powers? Does it provide for amendments? If so, write a proposed amendment that would bring about a needed change. If you do not have a constitution, make plans to write one.

2. **Debating an Issue.** As a class, propose an amendment to the United States Constitution. Research an issue and select two teams, one to support the amendment and the other to oppose it. Have the two teams debate the amendment. Then let other class members vote to decide whether the amendment should pass or fail.

In this ceremony, immigrants are taking the final step to become American citizens.

The Rights and Duties of American Citizens

Previewing the Chapter

You may have heard people say, "It's a free country. I can do whatever I want." The truth, of course, is that they can't. No one can do anything that takes away another person's rights, because the rights of every citizen are protected equally under the Constitution. This chapter describes the basic rights and freedoms guaranteed to all United States citizens.

■ **Before you read,** look up these key terms in the Glossary at the back of this book: *bail, search warrant, double jeopardy, poll tax, discrimination, petition.*

■ **As you read,** look for answers to these questions:
   1. What is the purpose of the Bill of Rights?
   2. What are some of the rights guaranteed by the last 16 amendments to the Constitution?
   3. What are some of the responsibilities that go along with American citizens' rights?

1 The Bill of Rights

What do you think of when you hear the word *rights*? Do you think of your right to drive a car, to take a job of your own choosing, or perhaps your right to get married? These are examples of rights that many people might mention. But you have many other rights. Some go back for more than 200 years in our nation's history. Others are more recent. Many of your rights are stated in the **Bill of Rights** (the first ten amendments to the Constitution) and in later amendments. In this chapter, you will learn what your rights and responsibilities are. See pages 518–520 for the text of the Bill of Rights.

As mentioned in Chapter 2, many citizens wanted a national Bill of Rights. They feared that the national government might take their rights away. A number of states agreed to ratify the Constitution only if a Bill of Rights was added to it. Therefore, the first ten amendments were added to the Constitution in 1791, about two years after the new national government began operations.

The Need for a Bill of Rights

The need many people felt for a Bill of Rights grew out of the experiences of the colonists under English rule. The experience of John Peter Zenger is an example. In 1732, Zenger, a printer in New York, was arrested. He was accused of printing stories which claimed that the governor was dishonest. He was charged with writing lies and trying to turn the people against the governor. Zenger was kept in jail for nine months before being brought to trial. He was not given bail. **Bail** is money an accused person gives a court. The money is forfeited (lost) if the accused does not show up for his or her trial.

Zenger's first lawyers dropped the case when the governor threatened to take away their law license if they defended Zenger. The governor was afraid, however, to threaten Zenger's second lawyer, for he was a well-known and respected man. The lawyer admitted at the trial that Zenger was trying to stir up feelings against the governor. He added that Zenger had a good reason, however. Zenger's articles were true! Zenger should have the right to print the truth, the lawyer continued, even if it hurt the governor. The people have the right to know what the governor is doing, he argued. The jury accepted the lawyer's arguments and found Zenger not guilty. The governor's efforts to silence the press failed.

The people of the new United States did not want to suffer any more experiences like that of Zenger. They wanted to be sure the new government would protect their rights and freedoms. After all, the Preamble to the Constitution mentioned establishing jus-

Some Freedoms of the Bill of Rights

FREEDOM OF RELIGION   FREEDOM OF THE PRESS   FREEDOM OF SPEECH   FREEDOM OF ASSEMBLY

SKILL BUILDER

Which freedom in the Bill of Rights allows a newspaper to print an article criticizing the government?

tice and securing liberty as reasons for making a new government. They added the Bill of Rights to make sure certain rights and freedoms would be protected. What does the Bill of Rights protect?

The First Amendment. This amendment guarantees freedom of religion. Congress cannot pass a law that would make one religion the official religion of this country. Also, the government cannot forbid us to follow the religion of our choice. We have the right to worship (or not to worship) as we wish. In other words, the church and government must be separate. This idea is known as the **separation of church and state**.

The First Amendment also guarantees freedom of speech and the press. This freedom includes the right to criticize the government and the right to express opinions that are not popular. However, there are limits to both of these freedoms. The right to free expression carries the responsibility not to harm others. For example, a person does not have the right to go into a crowded theater and yell "fire" when there is no fire. A news reporter does not have the right to print lies about another person. If this should happen, the law allows the injured person to sue the reporter for **libel** (printing false statements). A heavy fine may be the result of court action.

The First Amendment also protects our right to take part in political activities. Citizens may send messages to government officials. They may hold public meetings to speak for or against a government policy. In most cases, however, city or town governments require groups to get a permit if they are going to use the streets for a march or parade.

The Second Amendment. This amendment was added to the Constitution in order to give the states the right to keep a militia. A **militia** is a home guard. It is made up of people who volunteer to serve their state. When the Constitution was written, the states and the national government needed the militia for defense.

The Third Amendment. This amendment prevents the government from requiring us to provide food or shelter to soldiers without our consent during peacetime. In wartime, Congress could require us to do this. Up to the present time, however, the government has never done this.

The Fourth Amendment. The Fourth Amendment is sometimes called the "privacy" amendment. It forbids the search of our homes or the seizure of our property without a search warrant. A **search warrant** is a written order signed by a judge, allowing officials to search a home or to seize property. A warrant must give the reason for the search, the name(s) of the officer(s) who can use the warrant, and the exact location of the search or seizure.

The Fifth Amendment. This amendment explains the rights of a person accused of a crime. A citizen of the United States cannot be brought to trial for a serious crime unless a grand jury (a special kind of jury) decides that there is enough evidence to hold that person for trial. If a trial does take place, the accused person does not have to give evidence which could be used against her or him. Furthermore, a person found not guilty of certain charges may not be placed in **double jeopardy**. That is, he or she may not be tried again on the same charges. The Fifth Amendment also says that all accused persons must receive equal treatment under the law.

Finally, the Fifth Amendment explains the idea of **eminent domain**. This is the right of the government to take over private property for public use, such as for a post office. However, the government must pay the owner of the property a fair price for the loss.

The Sixth Amendment. This amendment deals with criminal proceedings. It protects the following rights of persons accused of crimes: (1) the right to a speedy and public trial, (2) the right to be tried by an impartial (fair) jury, (3) the right to be informed of the charges against them, (4) the right to face witnesses and to question them, (5) the right to have witnesses for their own defense, and (6) the right to a lawyer.

The Seventh Amendment. This amendment states that a jury may be used in a civil (noncriminal) case, when asked for by either of the parties concerned. However, the amount of money involved in the case must be over $20. Otherwise, a civil case would be heard by a judge, without a jury, in a small claims court.

The Eighth Amendment. This amendment says that bail or fines should not be too high. The amendment also says that punishments given by courts should not be cruel or unusual.

The Ninth Amendment. This amendment states that we have rights that are not stated in the Constitution. Laws passed by Congress or a state legislature, for example, give people the right to join labor unions, to strike, or to attend private schools.

The Sixth Amendment guarantees a person accused of a crime the right to a lawyer. Here we see a client with his lawyer.

The Tenth Amendment. This amendment gives the states all powers that are not directly given to the national government in the Constitution nor forbidden to the states. Through the powers granted by this amendment, for example, the states run public school systems, take control of all elections, and pass laws that deal with marriage and divorce.

The amendments in the Bill of Rights were written to protect us from the national government. Today, the Bill of Rights puts limits on the power of *both* the national and the state governments in order to protect our rights.

SECTION 1 *Review*

Defining Key Terms
1. Define: Bill of Rights, bail, separation of church and state, libel, militia, search warrant, double jeopardy, eminent domain.

Recalling the Facts
2. What basic rights were involved in the Zenger case?
3. What basic rights are guaranteed in the Bill of Rights?

Reviewing the Main Idea
4. Answer "As you read . . ." question 1 on page 55: What is the purpose of the Bill of Rights?

Critical Thinking
5. **Drawing Conclusions.** Which of the original amendments in the Bill of Rights do you feel is the most important? Explain.

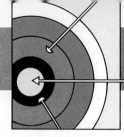

Critical Thinking Skills

Making Decisions

Decisions, decisions! Hardly a day goes by that you don't have to make choices —choices that can affect you deeply in one way or another. The signers of the Constitution, whom you read about earlier, had decisions to make about the nation's future. The choices you face in your own life can shape your own future. Should you take an art class or a computer class? Should you try out for the basketball team or find an after-school job?

Decision making is something you'll do all your life. Some decisions will be economic, such as whether to buy a car. Other decisions will be political, such as which candidate to support for President. No matter what kind of a decision you face, following the checklist below can help you make the best choice.

1. Clarify the problem.
2. Create a list of possible solutions.
3. Compare the pros (positives) and cons (negatives) of each solution.
4. Consider your values and goals.
5. Choose a course of action.

Clarify the problem. First, look closely at the decision you must make. What exactly *is* the problem? Is it important enough to justify using the checklist? Some problems have obvious solutions right from the start. Others, such as deciding whether to go to college, require greater thought. Sometimes a problem seems more complicated than it actually is. If you separate out all its parts, it may become more manageable. Get to the root of the problem. Talk to other people. An outsider can sometimes see a problem more clearly.

Create a list of possible solutions. Once the problem is clear, it will be easier to see ways that it can be solved. Start a list of possible solutions. Then gather any information you may need. You may do research or interview people. As you inform yourself about the options, you may add other possible solutions to your list.

Compare the pros and cons. After your list is complete, think about the positive and negative consequences of each possible solution. It might help to list these on a piece of paper, putting benefits on one side and drawbacks on the other. That way you can compare all of the pros and cons.

Consider your values and goals. The choice that is right for others may not be best for you. You have your own values (the things you strongly believe) and goals (the things you would like to accomplish). Paying attention to your values and goals can help you make the best decisions.

Choose a course of action. After you have worked through the steps above, you should be ready to make a decision. Put together a plan of action and set realistic deadlines for carrying it out. Be sure to follow up later by evaluating your decision.

Practicing Skills

1. After a theft at your school, school authorities randomly search lockers, including your own. You think that your rights have been violated. Make a list of possible actions you could take.
2. **Demonstrating Reasoned Judgment.** Now compare the pros and cons of each action. Taking into account your goals and values, what course of action would you take? Explain your reasons.

2 The Bill of Rights Expanded

The Bill of Rights does not contain all of the rights that we are guaranteed by law. Attempts have been made to increase the people's rights throughout the history of our country. The Constitution has been amended 16 times since the Bill of Rights was added. Eight of the 16 other amendments involve rights.

Equal Treatment

Several million black people in the United States were slaves for 69 years after the Constitution was approved. In a case that challenged slavery in 1857, the Supreme Court ruled that the Constitution did not view black people as citizens. The Chief Justice of the Supreme Court stated that blacks were not included in the phrase "people" in either the Declaration of Independence or the Constitution. At that time, although the practice was unjust, black people's right to citizenship was not recognized.

Slaves had to wait until the Thirteenth and Fourteenth Amendments were passed to have some of their rights recognized. The Thirteenth Amendment ended slavery. The Fourteenth Amendment made black people citizens. It states that:

- All people born or naturalized in the United States and subject to its laws are citizens. (A **naturalized citizen** is one who was not born a citizen but became one later.)
- No state may take away a citizen's Constitutional rights.
- The states must treat all citizens equally.

The Fourteenth Amendment is important because it guarantees full Constitutional rights to all of us, no matter what our race, color, national background, or religious belief.

The Right to Vote

In the early years of our nation, the states did not permit women to vote. In many states, only white males over 21 who owned property valued at a given amount could vote. For years less than half the adult population was eligible to vote.

Today, all born or naturalized citizens 18 or over may vote. Aliens may not vote, nor may inmates of mental institutions or any persons who have been legally found to be mentally incompetent. In nearly all states, persons convicted of serious crimes may not vote. Two qualifications for voting in all states are that a person must be a citizen of the United States and must live in that state. The states are allowed to decide voting qualifications with certain restrictions. For example, voting qualifications may not

The Fourteenth Amendment guarantees full Constitutional rights to all. James Meredith, the first black student to attend the University of Mississippi, is shown at left in this photo with his lawyer, Constance Motley.

conflict with the Constitution or other laws that protect the right to vote. The right to vote has been given to all citizens of the United States through the passage of the following six amendments.

The Fifteenth Amendment (added in 1870). No person may have the right to vote taken away because of race, color, or having been a slave. This amendment removed many voting restrictions (limits) against blacks. Some states, however, found ways to limit black people's voting rights. In 1965, Congress passed the Voting Rights Act to make sure that no qualified citizen would be denied the right to vote.

The Seventeenth Amendment (added in 1913). Senators are to be elected by the people. The Constitution originally stated that Senators were to be chosen by their state legislatures, rather than by the vote of the people. As a result, powerful groups in a state often picked candidates whom they wanted elected, and the legislature then chose them. The amendment guarantees that the interests of all the people will be better represented.

The Nineteenth Amendment (added in 1920). No citizen may be prevented from voting because of sex. This amendment brought to a happy ending a long campaign to secure the right to vote for women.

The Twenty-third Amendment (added in 1961).   The people of Washington, D.C. may vote for President. Before this amendment passed, they could not vote for President. The city was given the number of electoral votes it would have if it were a small state. Currently it has three electoral votes.

The Twenty-fourth Amendment (added in 1964).   No person may be denied the right to vote because he or she cannot pay

An eighteen-year-old woman exercising her right to vote.

taxes. Previously, some states had used a poll tax to prevent black people from voting. A **poll tax** is a sum of money a person must pay in order to vote. Since many blacks were poor and could not pay this tax, they could not vote before the Twenty-fourth Amendment was passed.

The Twenty-sixth Amendment (added in 1971).   No citizen 18 years of age or older may be denied the right to vote because of age. Previously, the voting age in most states had been 21.

Unratified Amendments.   A total of seven amendments have been approved by Congress but have failed to be ratified by the states. If ratification does not occur within a specific time period, the amendment "dies." One example is the Equal Rights Amendment (ERA) of 1972, which died in 1982. It proposed: "Equality of rights shall not be denied or abridged by the United States or by any state on account of sex." Supporters of the original ERA are working toward another ratification attempt.

In 1978, Congress sent to the states a proposed amendment to give the people of Washington, D.C., the same voting representation they would have if the city were a state. Currently the people of that city have no representation in Congress. The proposal must be ratified by the states before it can become an amendment to the Constitution.

Rooting for Nature

Nearly 20 years ago at summer camp, in an effort to improve the environment, Andy Lipkis planted a few trees. "It was backbreaking work," he says now, "but for me it was a life-altering experience." Lipkis, 34, is not exaggerating one bit. He has become a sort of modern-day Johnny Appleseed. As head of Tree-People, the worldwide organization he founded in 1974, he has planted more than 170 million trees.

The fragile state of the world's environment worries Lipkis. He speaks about the "greenhouse effect"—a warming of the atmosphere caused by the buildup of carbon dioxide gas. TreePeople promotes tree planting as the easiest solution to the warming trend. A single tree can absorb as much as 48 pounds of carbon dioxide in a year.

Lipkis works hard to convince people that his plan has merit. He recruits volunteers from grade schools and senior citizens' homes. He asks public and private agencies to do what they can to help. He talks nurseries into giving him unsold seedlings they would otherwise toss into the trash. Thanks in large part to Lipkis's efforts, a citizens' campaign is now underway to plant 100 million trees across the United States.

SECTION 2 *Review*

Defining Key Terms
1. Define: naturalized citizen, poll tax.

Recalling the Facts
2. How many amendments have been added to the original Constitution?

3. What do the Fourteenth and the Nineteenth Amendments say regarding the rights of citizens?

Reviewing the Main Idea
4. Answer "As you read . . ." question 2 on page 55: What are some of the rights guaranteed by the last 16 amendments to the Constitution?

Critical Thinking
5. Identifying Central Issues. What is the importance of the Twenty-sixth Amendment?

3 Rights Include Responsibilities

The Bill of Rights lies at the heart of an idea called the American's Creed. The American's Creed is a basic belief that all people are to be given equal opportunity to show what they can do. Thomas Jefferson had this in mind when he said in the Declaration of Independence that "all men are created equal." This means that all people, men and women, have equal rights "to life, liberty, and the pursuit of happiness." These rights cannot be taken away from us by our government.

All rights include responsibilities, however. Each of us has a responsibility, or a duty, to respect and protect the rights of others, to take part in political activities, and to work for improvement of life in our communities.

Respect the Rights of Others

The United States is a **pluralistic** society. This means that people from many different national, racial, and religious backgrounds live in our country. Our ancestors came from both Western and Eastern Europe—from England, France, Spain, Germany, Holland, and Sweden, and from Poland, Czechoslovakia, and Russia. They came from every part of Africa and from Lebanon, Syria, and other Middle Eastern countries. They came from countries in Asia including China, Japan, and Vietnam. Some came thousands of years ago, and were here when the first Europeans arrived in the late 15th and early 16th centuries.

A majority (more than half) of all Americans are white Protestants. Their ancestors came from Northern Europe. Many other citizens, however, belong to **minority groups**. They are set apart from the majority by their race or religion or national background. Because a minority, by definition, has fewer people than the majority, they usually have less voice in making decisions.

Members of minority groups have often been victims of prejudice and discrimination in our society. **Prejudice** is an unfair opinion formed without really looking at the facts. **Discrimination** is an unfair attitude toward or treatment of a particular person or group. Throughout our history, some members of minority groups have been treated unfairly. Catholics and Jews have been discriminated against. Irish Americans, black Americans, Native Americans, Mexican Americans, and Japanese and Chinese Americans have also faced discrimination. In addition, women, although they are not a minority, have been victims of prejudice and discrimination.

Prejudice and discrimination are serious problems in any society, but particularly so in ours. This is because they go against basic American beliefs. They result in many of our people being treated unfairly. Prejudice and discrimination continue even though all our governments—local, state, and national—have laws that forbid them. The spirit of the Bill of Rights, of other amendments, and of the Declaration of Independence calls on each of us to respect the rights and property of others. Nothing less will do.

Protect People's Rights

All of us must be on guard to protect our Constitutional rights if we wish to keep them. Here are three suggestions for doing this:

First, know what your rights are. You can learn about these rights by taking courses in history, government, and current affairs. Get booklets about government and Constitutional guarantees by writing to the Government Printing Office in Washington, D.C. The American Civil Liberties Union (ACLU) will also give you information. The ACLU is a nonprofit organization that helps to protect our rights.

Rights and Responsibilities of Citizenship

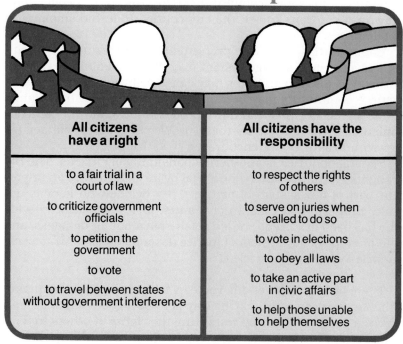

All citizens have a right	All citizens have the responsibility
to a fair trial in a court of law	to respect the rights of others
to criticize government officials	to serve on juries when called to do so
to petition the government	to vote in elections
to vote	to obey all laws
to travel between states without government interference	to take an active part in civic affairs
	to help those unable to help themselves

SKILL BUILDER

Through what types of activities could a citizen fulfill the responsibility to help others?

Second, do not allow any government agency or private organization to take away any of your rights. You can get the help of the ACLU and the Legal Aid Society if you feel your rights, or anyone else's, are being violated. The ACLU will defend people in court if one or more of their Constitutional rights appear to have been taken away.

Third, watch the news and read newspapers for cases involving people's rights. Express your support of Constitutional rights in public meetings, letters to government officials, and letters to newspapers.

You have a right and a responsibility to participate in the activities of your government. How well government serves us depends upon how well we let those in government know what we want. Voting is an important responsibility of citizenship. The quality of the leaders we choose determines the quality of government we get. Our leaders need help and guidance from us. We have the responsibility to attend meetings of our city council and school board, as well as public meetings on special issues with which the government must deal.

Participate in Political Activities

We can write letters to government officials and to newspapers. We can participate in petition campaigns. A **petition** is a document voters sign that asks the government to do or to stop doing something. In some communities, for example, people have drawn up petitions to ask the city council to forbid smoking in public places.

Communities often face problems that call for action by citizens. A neglected sewage system may cause flooding in a neighborhood. A town incinerator may cause pollution of the environment. A community may need more parks, schools, street lights, traffic signals, or police and fire protection. Community officials sometimes will not act on these problems, or they will act too slowly, unless they are encouraged by citizens.

Serving on juries is another responsibility of citizens. The Bill of Rights guarantees everyone a trial by jury. Juries are an important part of our system of justice. They decide who is or is not guilty in a criminal case. In civil suits, juries sometimes decide who has been hurt, who should receive payment for damages, and who must pay. Our system of justice depends on all of us to serve on juries when we are called.

Participate in Community Life

There are various actions you can take to improve the quality of life in your community. One way is to be a good neighbor. You can be a good neighbor by respecting the rights of others to have clean and quiet neighborhoods. You can be a good citizen by obeying traffic laws and other laws that protect the health and safety of your community.

You can also help to improve life in your community by volunteering to provide services. You might help as an aide in a hospital, nursing home, school, or recreation center. You could help senior citizens to repair and paint their homes or help parents who cannot afford to hire a babysitter. You could work with the handicapped or tutor other students. You could join or start groups to clean up parks, beaches, hiking and picnic areas, and highways. You could participate in walk-a-thons, bike-a-thons, and read-a-thons to raise money for charities. You might coach teams of elementary school children in baseball, soccer, or other sports.

Rights and Responsibilities of Students

The courts have recently made a number of decisions concerning the rights of students. The Supreme Court has ruled that students have specific Constitutional rights. Federal and state courts have applied this ruling in several cases involving the First, Fourth, Fifth, and Sixth Amendments. The courts have stated that students may publish school newspapers and give speeches on school grounds. Students faced with being expelled from school have the right to have the reasons explained to them and their parents. Expelled students have the right to appeal to the board of

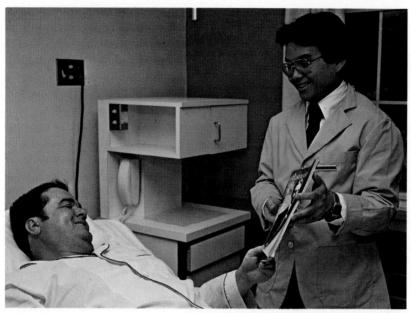

Rights and responsibilities go hand in hand. Here is a teenager helping to care for a person in a hospital.

education. If they are dissatisfied with the board's decision, they can appeal to a court of law. The power of school officials to search students or their possessions (including their school lockers) has been limited.

Rights, however, go hand in hand with responsibilities. For example, students are expected to obey reasonable rules. Articles which contain obscene language or which suggest breaking the law may not be printed in student newspapers. School officials have the right to censor (remove parts of) such articles. Speeches designed to get people to destroy property may not be given on school grounds. School officials have the right to decide where and when meetings on school grounds may be held. They also have the right to forbid students to bring weapons or other dangerous objects to school. If they have good reason to believe they may find evidence that a law has been broken, they have the right to search students or their lockers.

Rights, then, are never without some limits. They are not to be taken lightly. They are a vital part of our democratic background. But they do not entitle us to take away someone else's rights. We have a responsibility to respect and protect the rights of others as well as our own.

These young people are participating in a bike-a-thon to help raise money for the March of Dimes.

SECTION 3 *Review*

Defining Key Terms
1. Define: pluralistic, minority group, prejudice, discrimination, petition.

Recalling the Facts
2. What are three ways we can help protect our rights?
3. What are some of the rights and responsibilities of students in the United States?

Reviewing the Main Idea
4. Answer "As you read . . ." question 3 on page 55: What are some of the responsibilities that go along with American citizens' rights?

Critical Thinking
5. **Identifying Alternatives.** What are some ways we can help improve relations among the various ethnic and religious peoples within our country (or town)?

Government and Law

Religious Freedom and the Schools

"Almighty God, we acknowledge our dependence on Thee, and we beg Thy blessings upon us, our parents, our teachers, and our country." This may seem like a simple prayer. In New York, however, when students began to recite it each day in school, controversy arose. Parents filed suit, and the case, *Engel* v. *Vitale*, went all the way to the United States Supreme Court. In 1962, the Court made a landmark decision: prayer in public schools is a violation of the First Amendment to the Constitution.

The First Amendment states that Congress shall "make no law respecting an establishment of religion, or prohibiting the free exercise thereof." In other words, the government cannot force us to worship, nor can it prevent us from choosing our beliefs. Americans are fortunate to enjoy freedom of religion, but drawing a line between church and state is not always easy. Here's how the United States Supreme Court interpreted the law in a few other important cases.

In *Cochran* v. *Louisiana* (1930) and in *Board of Education* v. *Allen* (1968), the Supreme Court ruled that states may provide non-religious textbooks to children in parochial (church-related) schools. In 1947, in *Everson* v. *Board of Education*, the Court upheld a New Jersey state law providing public funds for busing students to parochial schools. The Court decided that such laws benefited children but did not promote religion.

The matter of prayers in school remains controversial. About half the states now

Prayer is part of the normal daily routine in our nation's parochial schools.

have laws permitting a "moment of silence" at the beginning of the school day. Former President Ronald Reagan proposed amending the Constitution to permit voluntary school prayer, and pro-prayer legislation has been introduced many times in Congress. No doubt the issue will be debated for years to come.

Questions to think about:

1. Some people suggest that a "moment of silence" in school, like a prayer, violates the First Amendment. What do you think?
2. Daily sessions of Congress begin with a prayer. The Supreme Court has approved this practice on the grounds that lawmakers, unlike schoolchildren, will not accept religious teachings uncritically. Do you agree with the Court's decision? Why or why not?

CHAPTER SUMMARY

Section 1   After the Constitution was written, some people were unhappy with it. Although a strong national government had been created, many citizens feared it might be too strong. In 1791, a Bill of Rights was added to the Constitution to protect the people's rights. The Bill of Rights consists of ten amendments to the Constitution that guarantee certain rights and freedoms to the people of the United States. The national government is forbidden to take away these rights and freedoms. These rights include freedom to practice any religion, freedom to express opinions, protection from unwarranted search and seizure of property, and protection in criminal proceedings.

Section 2   The Bill of Rights does not list all the rights that we are guaranteed by law. The Constitution has been amended 16 times since the Bill of Rights was added. Eight of the 16 amendments list additional rights that we have. The Fourteenth Amendment extends the protections in the Bill of Rights to all citizens in all states. Several other amendments extend voting rights to all citizens 18 years old or over.

Section 3   Rights include responsibilities. Each of us has a responsibility to respect and protect the rights of others, to take part in political and other civic activities, and to work to improve life in our communities.

Reviewing Key Terms

On a separate sheet of paper, use the following terms to complete the sentences below.

bail
search warrant
double jeopardy

poll tax
discrimination
petition

1. The Fifth Amendment protects citizens from being placed in ___?___ .

2. An act of ___?___ is unfair treatment of a particular group of people.

3. A ___?___ is an order issued by a judge allowing property to be searched.

4. The payment of money that sets an accused person free until the time of trial is called ___?___ .

5. A ___?___ is a request to the government to take a certain course of action.

6. A sum of money that a person must pay in order to vote is a ___?___ .

Understanding Main Ideas

1. Who was John Peter Zenger? Why is he important?

2. What is the Bill of Rights?

3. What are four freedoms guaranteed by the First Amendment?

4. What is meant by the "separation of church and state"?

5. What limitations are placed on our use of the rights guaranteed in the First Amendment?

6. How does the Bill of Rights limit the power of government?

Critical Thinking

1. Expressing Problems Clearly. How might freedom of speech, press, and assembly for all groups result in conflict?

2. Recognizing Cause and Effect. How does the separation of church and state help to protect religious freedom in the United States?

3. Drawing Conclusions. The Seventh Amendment allows a jury to be used in a civil case if either of the parties involved asks for one. Why might someone prefer to have a jury? Why might someone prefer not to have one?

4. Predicting Consequences. What might happen to our Constitutional rights if we did not have the Fourteenth Amendment? Give at least four examples.

Practicing Skills

1. Making Decisions. Suppose the government passed a law requiring all people with green eyes to live in particular areas, go to separate schools, and work in low-paying jobs. If you had green eyes, would you obey this law? If you did not have green eyes, how

would you respond to it? Explain your decision-making process.

2. Organizing Information. Review the case of John Peter Zenger on page 56. On a sheet of paper, make a two-column chart. In the left column, list the things that happened to Zenger that violate a person's rights under the Constitution. In the right column, list the amendment that now protects that specific right.

3. Researching Information. Use your school or local library to find out what happened to the Equal Rights Amendment that was proposed by Congress in 1972. How many states ratified it? Which national leaders were in favor of it? Which were against it? What were their reasons?

Focusing on Citizenship

1. Improving School Government. Obtain and discuss the list of student rights in your school or school district. If necessary, propose changes. If no list has been developed, form a committee to make one.

2. Determining Relevance. Ask a police officer how the Fourth, Fifth, and Sixth Amendments affect the work of the police. Share what you have learned in a class discussion.

3. Doing a Survey. Conduct a survey by asking five students and five adults this question: "Suppose a person is convicted of a serious crime, but the evidence used at the trial was not obtained through a search warrant, as required by the Fourth Amendment. Should the convicted person be sent to prison or set free?" Work with several other students to make the survey and put all the findings together.

What Are the Limits of Free Speech?

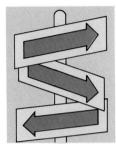

"The mayor is a champagne-sipping bum. . . . The 15th ward of this city is run by corrupt politicians. . . . The President is a bum. . . . You people should rise up and fight for your rights by going arm and arm to the Hotel Syracuse to the meeting of the Young Progesssives of America."

The Issue in Question

A young student named Irv Feiner used these words to address a crowd in Syracuse, New York, in 1949. Did Feiner have the right to say these things?

The First Amendment. The issue of what Americans have the right to say in public has been debated since the founding of our country more than 200 years ago. The First Amendment to the United States Constitution states, "Congress shall make no law . . . abridging the freedom of speech, or of the press, or the right of people to peaceably assemble, and to petition the government for a redress of grievances."

But does the First Amendment guarantee you the right to shout fire in a crowded theater? Or to say insulting things about the President, as Irv Feiner did? How far does a person's right of free speech extend? At what point do the speaker's rights interfere with the rights of others? The United States Supreme Court has made numerous rulings concerning the limits of free speech. In each of these rulings, the Court

has had to weigh individual rights against the public good.

Background on the Case

As the opening quotation suggests, Irv Feiner was a harsh critic of the American political and social system. On the evening of March 8, 1949, Irv Feiner stood on a large wooden box and used a portable loud speaker to address a crowd that had gathered around him on a city sidewalk. He urged people to attend a political meeting to be held that night, and his speech included strong statements against the President, the city's mayor, and other politicians.

The crowd of people listening to Feiner blocked the sidewalk and spilled out into the street. Two police officers who responded to a telephone complaint observed the scene from the other side of the road. They reported that Feiner stirred up the crowd and spoke in a "loud, high-pitched voice."

The crowd appeared to include both supporters and critics of Feiner's speech, and the police feared that a fight might break out between the two groups. One man shouted at the police, "If you don't [get him down], I'll go over and get him off there myself." The police approached Feiner and asked him to stop his speech and break up the crowd. Feiner went on speaking. After Feiner ignored a second request to stop, the police arrested him and took him from the scene.

Irv Feiner was tried and convicted for breaking a state law against disorderly conduct. He was sentenced to 30 days in the Onondaga County jail. Feiner claimed that the arrest and conviction violated his First Amendment right to free speech. He appealed through the court system and eventually brought his case to the United States Supreme Court.

Arguments Made for Feiner.

1. The police and the lower court denied Feiner his right of free speech.
2. Political speeches usually create disagreement among the individuals in a crowd. The situation in this case was not dangerous and did not require Feiner's arrest.

Arguments Made Against Feiner.

1. The police acted in a reasonable way to preserve peace and order on the street.
2. Feiner violated a state law and received a fair trial. He was convicted for disorderly conduct, not the content of his speech.

Making Decisions

1. **Understanding Points of View.** Assume that you were one of the following figures in the case: Feiner, the police, the owner of a store near the spot where Feiner spoke. Explain why you acted the way you did under the circumstances. What other actions did you have open to you under these circumstances?
2. **Expressing Problems Clearly.** What do you think was the major problem or issue raised by the Feiner case?
3. **Demonstrating Reasoned Judgment.** The Supreme Court decided the Feiner case in the spring of 1951. If you had been a Supreme Court Justice, what would your position on the Feiner case have been? Why would you have chosen that position? Use the "Arguments For," the "Arguments Against," and "The Decision-Making Checklist" on this page to help you make your decision and develop your answer.

The Decision-Making Checklist

✔	**Clarify the problem.** (What is the issue or conflict?)
✔	**Create a list of possible solutions.** (How might you resolve the problem?)
✔	**Compare the pros and cons of each solution.** (What are the strengths and weaknesses of each solution?)
✔	**Consider your values and goals.** (What is important to you in choosing a course of action, and why?)
✔	**Choose a course of action and evaluate the results.** (What would you decide, and how could you judge the outcome?)

UNIT 2 *The National Government*

Previewing the Unit

By the spring of 1986, William Rehnquist had been a Supreme Court Justice for 14 years. Then came a fresh honor: President Reagan nominated him to be Chief Justice. The nominee knew he would have to survive a "grilling" by the Senate, which has the power to approve all presidential appointments. In hearings that stretched on for three months, Rehnquist fielded questions from the 18 members of the Senate Judiciary Committee. The hearings were not always polite in tone. Sharp questions came from Senators who saw the nominee as an opponent of civil rights, women's rights, and poverty programs. Other Senators, however, regarded Rehnquist as a respected judge and legal scholar. In the end, the nominee survived the test. He was confirmed by the entire Senate later that year.

Conflict between the branches of government is a key ingredient in the balancing act of American political life. In this unit you will learn about how our system of government works at the national level.

Chapters in This Unit

◀ The legislative branch of the national government, housed in the Capitol in Washington, D.C., is said to be the branch "closest to the people."

CHAPTER 5

Making Decisions About Public Policy

Citizens often try to influence government decisions on such public policy issues as Social Security.

Previewing the Chapter

Our republican form of government allows people to have some input into the decisions our lawmakers face. When a majority of the people disagree with the government's plan of action on some issue, public opinion can influence a change in the plan. This chapter describes the process by which the government decides what actions it will take to solve problems.

■ **Before you read,** look up these key terms in the Glossary at the back of this book: *public policy, social welfare, pollute, immigrant, tariff.*

■ **As you read,** look for answers to these questions:
   1. What are some examples of public policy issues?
   2. What are three national issues on which the government has developed a public policy?
   3. Who makes public policy decisions in the United States?
   4. Who influences the public policy decisions made by our government officials?

1 What Is Public Policy?

The countries of the world have many things in common. All countries have a government. All have some way of producing food. All have some method of keeping order. They also have differences. In some countries, for example, cars must be driven on the left side of the road. Some countries consider persons accused of a crime guilty until proven innocent.

In the United States, on the other hand, cars are driven on the right side of the road. Persons accused of a crime are considered innocent until proven guilty. Why do such differences exist? It all has to do with what is known as public policy.

The word **policy** is used in different ways. It is often used to describe a way of doing things. Most school districts have a policy about the number of units or courses required to earn a diploma. In the world of business, companies have hiring policies, promotion policies, and retirement policies. Such policies state how workers can be hired, promoted, or retired.

Public Policy

Any policy prepared by the government is called a public policy. A **public policy** is a plan or course of action made or followed by the government. Sometimes a public policy lasts for a long time. At other times, a policy may be started one year and then dropped the next.

The details of almost any long-term policy will change from time to time. The military draft is an example. From the beginning of our country, our government has followed a policy of calling up men for military service in time of war. Changes have been made in this policy from war to war. Some of these changes have been about the physical requirements, age, and marital status of draftees. Sometimes, persons in war-related civilian jobs were excused. A worker in a weapons factory is an example. At other times persons whose religion forbade them to kill were placed in noncombat positions, such as in the medical corps.

The government has also drafted men in peacetime. The first peacetime draft law was the Selective Service and Training Act passed in 1940. More than 10 million Americans were called. That draft was ended in 1947. A year later, Congress passed the Selective Service Act of 1948. Between 1948 and 1973, about 5 million young men were drafted. Most were called into active service in the Korean conflict and the conflict in Vietnam. Then, in 1973, the military draft was ended. The government announced that the United States Army would be formed entirely from volunteers. Today, the Selective Service Act requires that all American male citizens between the ages of 18 and 26 register for the draft.

Saving the Relics

The scene: Slack Farm, 40 acres of land overlooking the Ohio River in western Kentucky. The time: late 1987. The action: ten men digging in the soft brown earth.

These men were seeking Indian relics—bones and tools that had been buried in the field perhaps a thousand years earlier, when Native Americans occupied the site. The group of diggers had paid the farm owner $10,000 for the rights to dig on the property and sell their findings to rich collectors.

Neighbors noticed the field being torn up and called the authorities. Miles Hart of the Kentucky State Police arrived to investigate. He saw hundreds of holes dug in the field and human bones scattered around. Clearly the diggers were disturbing a burial site—a crime under state law.

The people of Kentucky were shocked and outraged. They soon learned, however, that the law protecting burial sites was far weaker than they knew, calling for a maximum fine of $500 and a year in jail. This did not seem tough enough.

Many area residents marched to protest the Slack Farm looting and the buying and selling of grave relics. In early 1988, as a direct result of these demonstrations, the Kentucky legislature made the crime of desecrating (spoiling) a gravesite a felony. Other states are expected to follow suit.

Since 1980, young men have been obliged to register for the draft at age 18.

What are the reasons for these changes in our government's policy on the draft? There are several. The government has to protect the safety of the country. Not everyone agrees on the best way to do this. As times change, so do policies. In 1940, a peacetime draft was called because of the war going on in Europe. Many people felt that the United States should be fully prepared for anything that might happen. Many people were afraid that Germany, if it was successful in Europe, might attack the United States. In 1948, a second peacetime draft was called because unfriendly actions of the Soviet Union were making our leaders uneasy. President Carter's call for draft registration in 1980 was a reaction to the Soviet invasion of Afghanistan in 1979.

The public mood was one reason for ending the draft in 1973. The American people were tired of war. The Vietnam conflict had dragged on through the administrations of Presidents John F. Kennedy, Lyndon B. Johnson, and Richard M. Nixon. Thousands of American lives were being lost in a land on the other side of the world. There were constant protests against the draft and against the war. Many young Americans fled the country or went to jail rather than serve in the armed forces. Reacting to this, President Nixon announced the return to a volunteer army in 1973.

What if the government had not required persons to register for the draft? Would that have been a public policy? Yes. The decision *not* to do something is still a decision, but such a decision is often misunderstood. People sometimes say a government that makes such a decision has a "do-nothing" policy.

SECTION *1* *Review*

Defining Key Terms

1. Define: policy, public policy.

Recalling the Facts

2. Why does public policy change?

3. How is public policy different from the policy of a company or a school district?

Reviewing the Main Idea

4. Answer "As you read . . ." question 1 on page 78: What are some examples of public policy issues?

Critical Thinking

5. Demonstrating Reasoned Judgment. What situations might call for a "do-nothing" public policy?

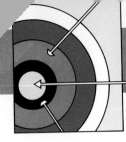

Study Skills

Using Charts and Diagrams

Charts are useful tools for many reasons. Reading a chart, for example, generally takes less time than reading the same material in paragraph form. Some types of information, such as statistics, are easier to absorb in chart form. You're probably already familiar with many kinds of charts. One chart you might have used is the type that shows prime-time television programs.

Some of the data a chart can show include:

- part-whole relationships—how parts fit together to make a whole
- functional relationships—how different things or people work together to accomplish something
- causal relationships—how one thing influences or leads to something else

A chart may present information as a table (an orderly listing of information in rows and columns) or as a diagram (a sketch or drawing explaining relationships among things). The information on pages 83–86 may be organized in a table like the one below.

Similar information might be shown in a diagram. Diagrams often use arrows to show relationships. A diagram of the first column in the table might look like this.

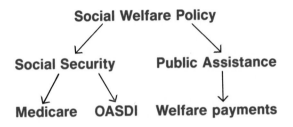

Note the similarities and differences between the first column in the table and the corresponding diagram. The information they present is identical, but the diagram more clearly shows relationships.

Practicing Skills

1. Create a table showing your class schedule for a given day of the week. The table should include the time, subject, and teacher for each class. Then show the same information in a diagram using arrows.
2. **Drawing Conclusions.** What are the advantages of using a chart in place of paragraphs of written material?

Kinds of Public Policy

Social Welfare Policies	Environmental Policies	Other Policies
Social Security (OASDI, Medicare) Public Assistance (Welfare payments)	Water Pollution Air Pollution Solid Waste Disposal	Concerning Students Concerning Immigrants Concerning Foreign Countries

2 Kinds of Public Policy

Public policy reaches out in many directions. It affects workers and employers, consumers and producers, the elderly and the young, rich people and poor people. Public policy also affects the land on which we live, the air we breathe, and the waters that surround us. In fact, there is hardly any part of our lives that is not affected by what our government does. Some examples of public policy are discussed on the next few pages.

Social Welfare Policies

One type of public policy has to do with social welfare. The term **social welfare** refers to any programs that provide assistance (help) to people. Under this policy, the government helps persons with special needs—the disabled, the retired, the unemployed, or the very poor, for example.

An important part of the government's social welfare policy has to do with what is known as social insurance. The word *insurance* is used because social insurance provides protection just as insurance for a car or home does. The Social Security Act of 1935 established the social insurance policy of the government. Its main features are described below.

The Old Age and Survivors Disability Insurance Plan (OASDI). This program sends monthly payments to retired persons 65 years of age or older. Lower payments are made to persons who choose to retire at age 62. In order to be covered by this insurance, workers make monthly payments to the government while they are working. The money is deducted (taken) from their paychecks.

In addition to retired persons, those who become permanently disabled receive payments under the OASDI plan. The plan also provides payments for dependents of disabled workers or for dependents of workers who die before or after retirement. A **dependent** is a person who relies on someone else for support.

Unemployment Insurance. Unemployment insurance is another result of the Social Security Act. This program is run by the states. When a worker loses a job, he or she goes to a state unemployment office and registers for work. If no job for which he or she is qualified is available, the unemployed person is eligible for weekly payments for a limited period of time. These payments usually do not equal a regular paycheck, but they do help meet expenses while the individual tries to find another job.

The national government sets the overall standards for the unemployment insurance program. Chief among these standards is the requirement that employers pay a payroll tax on each worker. Workers do not pay this tax. The money from the payroll tax goes to a trust fund in the United States Treasury. The states then draw on this fund to pay unemployed workers.

Medicare. In 1965, the social insurance program was increased to include medical assistance through Medicare. **Medicare** is a program that provides health care for persons 65 or over. More than 30 million persons are enrolled in Medicare. These people must be covered by OASDI in order to qualify for Medicare. The Medicare program helps pay for doctor bills and hospital bills. Other payments include money for bills for nursing-home care, surgery, X-rays, or artificial limbs.

Over the years, there have been many changes in the original Social Security Act of 1935. Some changes increased the number of workers who are covered by the law. At one time, self-employed workers were not covered. Now they are. Other changes have increased the amount of monthly payments to retired persons and other people who receive benefits. Other welfare programs fall under the heading of public assistance. Public assistance programs provide assistance (money) to certain persons. The money comes from taxes. Individuals do not pay for these benefits. Among the groups who receive public assistance are the aged, the blind, and the disabled who cannot support themselves. The most costly part of the public assistance program is the Aid to Families with Dependent Children (AFDC). Benefits from this program are more commonly known as welfare payments. A typical monthly payment goes to a mother of several children who cannot get a job or has no way to support herself and her family.

Environmental Policies

In 1955, the national government started a program to study ways of stopping air pollution. To **pollute** something means to make it dirty or impure. In 1963 and 1967, laws requiring control of air pollution were passed. Laws to prevent pollution of rivers and lakes and to protect soil were also passed. By the 1970s, the government had a full-scale policy to protect the environment.

One of the main ways the government provides protection against pollution is through the Environmental Protection Act of 1970 and the Environmental Protection Agency (EPA) established that same year.

Water Pollution. The dumping of oil or other harmful wastes into rivers and lakes is forbidden. The EPA also enforces the Safe Drinking Water Act of 1974. This act sets standards of purity for the nation's drinking water.

Air Pollution. The EPA enforces the basic law that is designed to stop pollution of the air, the Clean Air Act Amendments of 1970. This law sets up standards of emission (discharging of waste) for automobiles, power plants, and incinerators (devices for burning waste materials). State governments are required to develop air pollution programs that meet these standards.

An Example of a Public Policy: The Social Security Program

Who is covered?	Form of coverage	Money comes from
Retired persons 62 years of age or older	Monthly payments until death	Payroll taxes, paid jointly by employer and workers
Family of worker who dies	Monthly payments until children reach age 18	
Permanently disabled workers	Monthly payments for life	
Aged persons who need medical care	Specific amounts for doctor and hospital bills	
Unemployed persons	Monthly payments for limited period, usually one year	Payroll taxes, paid by employers
The needy, the aged, the blind, dependent children, disabled persons	Monthly payments until person is able to support himself or herself	Federal income taxes, and other taxes, paid by all citizens of the United States

Solid Waste Disposal. The dumping of solid waste is a serious problem throughout the United States. Solid waste includes anything from old cars to bottles, poisonous chemicals, and tin cans. Every year, there are more than four billion tons of waste that must be disposed of in some way. Dumping of solid waste, especially chemicals, has been a threat to the health of many communities. Starting in 1976, the EPA ordered the states to set rules for the treatment, storage, and disposal of dangerous materials. Federal funds have been made available to help local governments carry out these rules.

Concerning Workers. A minimum wage law protects the earning power of most working people. That wage was 25 cents an hour in 1938. In recent years, it has been about $4.00 per hour. Children who work are protected in certain ways too. Persons under 18 cannot be employed in dangerous occupations such as coal mining. All workers, regardless of sex, age, and race are guaranteed equal job opportunities. This policy is sometimes hard to carry out, because the lack of equal opportunity is difficult to prove. However, the policy is strictly enforced among firms that do business with the national government.

SKILL BUILDER

For how long can an unemployed person usually collect social security payments?

Other Policies

The Environmental Protection Agency enforces the law that is designed to stop pollution of the air. This man is monitoring the air for pollutants.

Concerning Students. By giving aid to school districts, the government has encouraged the growth of educational opportunities for young people. Federal funds have helped school districts provide special programs for handicapped students, for blind students, and for non-English-speaking students. Federal loans have also been made available to students who need money to go to college.

Concerning Immigrants. Persons who come from one country to another country to live are called **immigrants.** The official policy of our government is that 270,000 persons from other countries may enter the United States each year. In some years, however, thousands of special cases increase this number. In the past, some of these have been persons escaping from communist countries. After World War II, about 500,000 homeless persons were allowed to come to the United States without regard to any set limit. During the 1980s, thousands of Cuban and Southeast Asian refugees entered the United States. New regulations on immigration have been set by the Immigration Reform and Control Act of 1986.

Concerning Foreign Countries. In 1948, the national government started a program to help relieve the suffering caused by World War II in many countries. This program cost about $13 billion. Since then, government aid programs have paid out a total of over $284 billion in the form of loans, food, military equipment, advice to farmers, or outright grants of money.

Long lines of immigrants wait outside an Immigration and Naturalization Service Center, hoping to be granted legal status that will allow them to stay in the United States.

SECTION 2 *Review*

Defining Key Terms

1. Define: social welfare, dependent, pollute, immigrant.

Recalling the Facts

2. What are three kinds of policies established by the Social Security Act of 1935?

3. What are three policies in effect on environmental issues?

Reviewing the Main Idea

4. Answer "As you read . . ." question 2 on page 78: What are three national issues on which the government has developed a public policy?

Critical Thinking

5. Testing Conclusions. Some people argue that welfare programs or other government policies that "give" money to people tend to make them lazy. Do you agree or disagree? Explain your answer.

3 Who Makes Public Policy?

Most public policy is written into law. The actions taken by any of our government agencies, whether they inspect coal mines or send astronauts to the moon, must be lawful. Because of this, the role of our lawmaking body, the Congress, is of great importance in forming public policy. Every year, hundreds of bills are passed by Congress and signed into law by the President. All of these measures become public policy.

Congress and Public Policy

Congress does not make public policy overnight. Very often, there are years of discussion and debate before a bill reaches the floor of Congress. Even then, many bills may be rejected. In some cases, a state or territory may adopt a policy before the national government does. The Nineteenth Amendment to the Constitution gave women the right to vote in 1920. However, the territory of Wyoming had given women in the territory the right to vote in 1869. By the time the Nineteenth Amendment was ratified, women had already won the right to vote in 15 states. Child labor laws, which forbid the employment of children in dangerous occupations such as coal mining, also were passed by some states before the national government did so.

The President and Public Policy

The President also makes public policy. Our relationships with foreign countries are an example. Over the years, Presidents have decided to exchange ambassadors (representatives of nations) with countries such as Great Britain and France, but not with others such as Cuba or Albania. In either case, the decision of the President is part of the public policy of the United States.

The President can also change a policy previously approved by Congress. In the case of **tariffs** (taxes on goods brought into the United States), for example, Congress sets the basic policy. It decides which goods are to be taxed and the rates to be paid by countries who ship goods to the United States. But Congress has given the President the power to increase or reduce these rates by as much as 50 percent. If the President ordered a reduction or an increase, the order would change our public policy on tariffs.

Officials within government departments also make public policy. Congress allows the heads of departments and agencies to interpret specific laws. **Interpret** means to explain, or to say, what the law is. One example involves food and drugs. Federal law forbids the sale of food and medicines that are harmful to con-

Before fruit from abroad can be sold in the United States, FDA inspectors test it for possible contamination.

sumers. But what is harmful? Is an artificial sweetener that causes cancer in rats harmful to humans? The law passed by Congress doesn't answer such questions. So, officials within the Food and Drug Administration (FDA) have the authority to decide what is harmful. By making such decisions, they make public policy.

The Courts and Public Policy

Finally, the courts make public policy. This usually comes about because of the power of the courts to interpret laws. The "commerce clause" in the Constitution is an example. Article 1, Section 8, gives Congress the power to regulate commerce among the several states. But what is commerce? The Constitution doesn't say. As a result, the courts have been asked many times to define it. Is a telephone conversation between New York and San Francisco commerce? Is a river running across the boundaries of two states commerce? Is a person walking across a state line commerce? The answer to these questions has been "yes." The courts have said that all traffic among the states, whether human or not, is commerce.

Because of these rulings, the national government has some kind of policy dealing with all phases of interstate activities. Television stations must be licensed by the national government. Trucks going from state to state must follow federal safety standards. Meat shipped from state to state must be approved by federal inspectors. All of these requirements represent public policy.

Defining Key Terms

1. Define: tariff, interpret.

Recalling the Facts

2. How is the executive branch of government involved in making public policy?

3. How do the courts take part in the formation of public policy?

Reviewing the Main Idea

4. Answer "As you read . . ." question 3 on page 78: Who makes public policy decisions in the United States?

Critical Thinking

5. Recognizing Cause and Effect. Why is the Congress often slow in making public policy decisions? In what ways might this slowness be beneficial for the development of public policies? In what ways might it be a drawback?

4 Who Influences Public Policy Decisions?

Government officials differ greatly in the way they come to a decision about public policy. One official may rely heavily on his or her personal beliefs. Another may listen to advisers or personal friends. However, all decision makers are subject to certain influences. Some of the more important influences are discussed below.

The Individual Citizen

As mentioned in Chapter 4, the First Amendment gives all of us the right to petition (write to) our government representatives in order to express our concerns. On the surface, this might not seem to be important. But to our elected officials, it is very important. Letters, telegrams, and telephone calls show that people are interested in what an official is doing—or not doing. At times, a President may receive more than a thousand letters a week. Some legislators, particularly those in positions of leadership, may receive a similar number. Both the President and members of Congress keep a tally (scorecard) of opinions expressed by citizens. In most cases, letters from individual citizens are answered by those who receive them.

A single citizen may greatly influence public policy. In 1905, President Theodore Roosevelt asked Congress to regulate the production of food and drugs. Roosevelt had been advised to do this by a chemist in the Department of Agriculture. Research had shown that dangerous chemicals were being used in the preparation of food and drugs. A year later, Roosevelt's proposal received support in novelist Upton Sinclair's book, *The Jungle.* Sinclair's book described the filthy conditions in the Chicago meat-packing companies. *The Jungle* was widely read. Members of Congress received many letters demanding that something be done. In July 1906, Congress passed a law which required that all meat be inspected and labeled concerning quality. That law is still in force. The next time you visit a meat market, notice the labels on the various cuts of meats. Such labels represent a policy which was put into effect many years ago and which remains in effect today.

In the 1960s, the publication of *Silent Spring* by Rachel Carson had a similar effect. Carson described the effects of pesticides and other harmful chemicals on birds and other animals. Her book attracted wide attention and increased public concern about the state of the country's environment.

Interest Groups

Some people who try to influence public policy are members of **interest groups**. These are groups of persons such as doctors, farmers, or teachers who join together to support a particular

These Native Americans are members of the American Indian Movement, a special interest group.

cause. Conservation-minded people, for example, may push for the passage of laws that will help to preserve places of natural beauty. Others who try to influence public policy are veterans, senior citizens, blind or disabled persons, women, and members of minority groups. The members of all of these interest groups write letters to government officials, make telephone calls, hold public meetings, and sponsor newspaper advertisements in order to gain support for their causes.

The Media

Newspapers often try to influence public policy. At election time, many newspapers endorse (support) candidates who share their views. At other times, editorials (statements by the editor of the paper) express opinions for or against proposed laws or government policies.

Television also plays an influential role. Television programs can reach thousands or even millions of people at a time. These programs can make people aware of public policy issues and make them want to get involved. News analysis and commentary by respected television journalists can sway both public opinion and public policy. Chapter 16 discusses the role of the media in more detail.

SECTION 4 *Review*

Defining Key Terms
1. Define: interest group.

Recalling the Facts
2. How may an individual citizen influence public policy?
3. How did the publication of *Silent Spring* influence public policy on environmental issues?
4. How do different interest groups influence public policy?
5. How do the media have an effect on public policy?

Reviewing the Main Idea
6. Answer "As you read . . ." question 4 on page 78: Who influences the public policy decisions made by our government officials?

Critical Thinking
7. **Demonstrating Reasoned Judgment.** Government officials do not always vote on public policy issues the way their constituents would like them to. Why might this happen?

Government and Law

The War on Drugs

By some estimates, half a million Americans are addicted to heroin. Perhaps 22 million have used cocaine. And 10 to 23 percent of Americans have admitted to using drugs on the job. It is no wonder that some people describe the drug problem in America as an epidemic!

Fighting the war on drugs is a long, uphill struggle. In an effort to win, President Bush created the Office of National Drug Control Policy in 1989, and named William J. Bennett as its director. The office's job is to develop public policy on fighting drugs and to coordinate the efforts of those involved.

Law enforcement. Many people think that the key to winning the drug war is source reduction—stamping out drugs in their source countries, before they enter the United States. Millions of American dollars have been spent, for example, on killing the Central and South American crops that yield cocaine and marijuana.

In addition, Coast Guard and customs officials patrolling the Mexican border and the Florida coast work hard to catch drug smugglers. Millions of dollars worth of new radar devices have been installed on balloons, in aircraft, and along the shore. These devices track suspicious aircraft until they land so that officials can check them for illegal drugs.

A Supreme Court case decided in April, 1989, helped strengthen the federal government's efforts to halt drug smuggling. In this decision, the Court ruled 7-2 that federal agents may stop and question any traveler whose actions arouse "reasonable suspicion" that he or she is transporting

The United States Coast Guard seizes many tons of illegal drugs, such as marijuana, each year.

illegal drugs. Suspicious behavior may include buying expensive airplane tickets in cash, appearing nervous, or traveling under an assumed name.

The government agency charged with waging the war on drugs is the Drug Enforcement Agency (DEA). On city streets around the country, drug enforcement officials try to control the spread of illegal drugs through organized "street sweeps." During these sweeps, officials try to arrest all of the drug traffickers in a given area. Some of these "raids" are successful in disrupting the drug trade, but often the drug dealers who are chased out of one area simply move into another neighborhood.

In an effort to keep drug dealers off the streets, penalties for selling drugs have become increasingly harsh. During the last

months of the Reagan Administration, laws were passed that allowed federal prosecutors to seek the death penalty for drug-related murders of police officers. This law also extends to murders ordered or committed by drug kingpins—leaders in the drug trade.

Sometimes the federal war on drugs gets very personal. For example, police have confiscated the cars, trucks, boats, yachts, and houses of both drug dealers and their clients. This property has then been sold at public auctions. Roadblocks have also been used to stop cars whose passengers might be carrying drugs.

Drug testing. Drug testing is another strategy aimed at discouraging drug use. Many large companies test job applicants or employees who are suspected of drug abuse. In addition, the Supreme Court has ruled that the federal government can test all workers whose duties involve either public safety—such as airline pilots and Amtrak employees—or law enforcement.

People in favor of drug testing point out that the drug user could endanger the lives of others. Other citizens are opposed to drug testing programs, however. They feel that mandatory drug testing violates a person's Constitutional rights. The Fourth Amendment, they argue, protects citizens' right to privacy.

Education. Perhaps the most vital weapon against drug abuse is human intelligence. Concerned school systems nationwide have given drug education programs high priority, often beginning in elementary school. Perhaps there is a drug education program in your own school.

Educators agree that the most effective programs in dealing with drug abuse go beyond classroom talk to include parents and people in the community who work with teenagers. One successful program is run by Alternatives, Inc. in Hampton, Virginia. The organization offers drug education for parents as well as in-school counseling for teens, treatment referrals, and anti-drug clubs for students.

Public education is likely to be the only tactic that will produce a significant, long-term decrease in the use of dangerous drugs. Although the federal government spent $8 billion in 1988 fighting the drug war, the outlay hardly made a dent. The war cannot be won unless human behavior changes. As William Bennett admits, "In the long run, it's a question of values."

Questions to think about

1. Do you support or oppose mandatory drug testing programs for people whose jobs do not endanger the lives of others? Explain your answer.
2. Some people believe that the solution to the drug problem is to make drugs legal. They argue that if drugs were sold on the free market, prices would drop drastically and dealers would not make the enormous profits that now lead to greed and violence. What do you think of legalization as a possible solution?

CHAPTER SUMMARY

Section 1 When government decides to follow a certain course of action, that course of action becomes a public policy. Public policy may be a short- or long-term commitment to a certain way of doing things. The failure to do something is in itself a kind of policy.

Section 2 Over the years, our government has made many kinds of policies. Some of these deal with social welfare—giving aid to the aged, the blind, the sick, or the unemployed. Other policies have been designed to protect the environment from pollution or to limit the number of immigrants who enter the United States.

Section 3 Almost all public policy is set by law. For this reason, the legislatures of our national, state, and local governments are among the chief makers of public policy. In addition, other elected officials and judges make decisions that affect public policy.

Section 4 Many people influence the policy-making process. Individual citizens write letters expressing their views on policy proposals. Authors write books. Newspapers support the candidates they favor. The general public expresses its views through public opinion polls. Special interest groups make telephone calls, meet with legislators, and hire lobbyists to represent them. All are trying to push through a policy they favor, or to change or reject one they are against.

Reviewing Key Terms

Use each of the following terms appropriately in a sentence. Write your sentences on a separate sheet of paper.

1. public policy

2. social welfare

3. pollute

4. immigrant

5. tariff

Understanding Main Ideas

1. What are some reasons for the changes in our military draft policy?

2. What is a social welfare policy? An environmental policy?

3. What groups of people are protected by the government's social welfare policy? How are they protected?

4. Identify three laws passed as part of the nation's environmental policy.

5. Name four ways that government policy affects workers and students.

6. How does Congress make public policy?

7. By what actions can the President make public policy?

8. How do the courts affect public policy?

9. Give two examples of how individuals influence public policy.

10. How do interest groups and the news media influence public policy?

Critical Thinking

1. Demonstrating Reasoned Judgment. Is it possible for a public policy to be popular but not in the best interests of the public? Explain your answer.

2. Identifying Central Issues. Gradually, the United States has been developing a public policy about the frightening AIDS epidemic. With thousands of people dying from the disease and thousands more infected, the government has begun a campaign to educate the public about the causes of AIDS. There are still a lot of decisions to be made. What are some of the central issues that must be considered before a public policy on AIDS can be finalized?

3. Understanding Governmental Relationships. Compare the role of Congress and the President in creating public policy. What is likely to happen if the two branches disagree strongly about certain policies? How can these disagreements be resolved?

Practicing Skills

1. Making a Chart. Make a chart about the public policies described in this chapter.

Write the following headings on a separate sheet of paper: *Social Welfare Policy, Environmental Policy, Foreign Policy.* List as many public policies as you can under each heading.

2. Making a Time Line. Using the information in this chapter or other sources, make a time line showing the development of public policy regarding the military draft, protection of the environment, or immigration. Include at least four events on your time line.

3. Analyzing the News. The editorial pages of daily newspapers often contain political cartoons that comment on current public policy. Bring one of these cartoons to class and explain what the cartoonist is saying about public policy.

Focusing on Citizenship

1. Writing an Editorial. Write an editorial for your school newspaper. In the editorial, discuss who influences policy decisions in your school. Give your opinion about who should have more (or less) of a say in making these decisions.

2. Formulating Questions. Imagine that you have been given the job of determining your community's policy about codes of dress and behavior in the public schools. Who would you contact for information to help you develop a fair policy? What questions would you ask them?

3. Doing Field Research. Choose one of the following areas: the environment, education, or youth employment and training. Find out what policies your state representative or senator supports in your chosen area. In class, discuss whether or not you agree with these policies.

Both Houses of Congress—the Senate and the House of Representatives—meet in the Capitol in Washington, D.C.

The Congress

Previewing the Chapter

One of the causes of the American Revolution was the complaint that colonists did not have adequate representation in Great Britain's Parliament. Proper representation for all citizens continued to be an issue when the Framers began developing the Constitution. The solution: Congress was established as a means of representing all United States citizens in the national government. This chapter discusses the structure of Congress and its method of passing laws.

■ **Before you read,** look up these key terms in the Glossary at the back of this book: *majority party, committee, constituents, seniority system, filibuster, pocket veto,* ex post facto *law, bill of attainder.*

■ **As you read,** look for answers to these questions:
   1. What are the major differences between the House of Representatives and the Senate?
   2. Why is the committee system so important in the way Congress works?
   3. What are the basic steps that a bill must go through before it becomes a law?

97

1 What Is Congress?

The **Congress** of the United States is the lawmaking body of the national government. It is made up of 535 members elected from all of the states of the Union. As you know, it is divided into two parts, or houses—the **Senate** and the **House of Representatives**. Members are known as Senators and Representatives. No idea can become a law unless it is passed by both houses of Congress. Some of the important facts about each house are discussed in this section.

The House of Representatives

Size. The House of Representatives is the larger of the two houses. At present, it consists of 435 members. The number of members, or seats, which a state is given is determined by its population. You will recall that this was agreed upon in one of the famous compromises at the Constitutional Convention. The larger a state's population, the more seats it has in the House of Representatives. If a state's population increases or decreases, it will gain or lose seats. However, the Constitution guarantees every state at least one seat in the House.

Currently, there is one Representative for about every 550,000 persons in our country. Some people argue that, as the population of the United States increases, the total membership of the House should increase. This could happen, but most people do not think it will. The House of Representatives is already one of the largest lawmaking bodies in the world.

Qualifications. A Representative must be at least 25 years old. He or she must have been a United States citizen for at least seven years. Also, the Representative must be a legal resident of the state from which he or she is elected.

Term. Each Representative serves for a term—a period of two years. There is no limit to the number of terms a Representative may serve if he or she is reelected.

Election. Elections for members of the House are held on the Tuesday following the first Monday in November of every even-numbered year. A member's term begins on January 3 following the November election.

Vacancies. Sometimes a Representative dies, resigns, or is expelled from the House before his or her two-year term has ended. The governor of the state must call a special election to fill the vacancy (empty seat) in the House.

Districts. The legislature in each state divides the state into congressional districts. **Congressional districts** are particular areas of a state with clearly defined boundaries and approximately equal populations. The people in each district elect one

Representative to the House. In states which have only one Representative, the whole state is considered a single congressional district. Candidates in states with only one district are said to run "at large."

After each **census** (a count of the number of people in the country), the state legislature is required by law to reshape the state's congressional districts if the state's population has increased or decreased. As a result of the 1980 census, Texas gained three seats in the House of Representatives, but New York lost five seats. The 1990 census could create more changes after 1993.

The Senate

Size. The Senate is a much smaller body than the House of Representatives. It is made up of two Senators from each state. As there are currently 50 states in the United States, there are 100 Senators.

Qualifications. A senator must be at least 30 years old. He or she must have been a United States citizen for at least nine years. The Senator must also be a legal resident of the state from which he or she is elected.

Term. Senators are elected for six-year terms. The terms are staggered, however, so that one-third of the Senators are elected

SKILL BUILDER

What part of the country has states that benefited most from the 1980 census? Why?

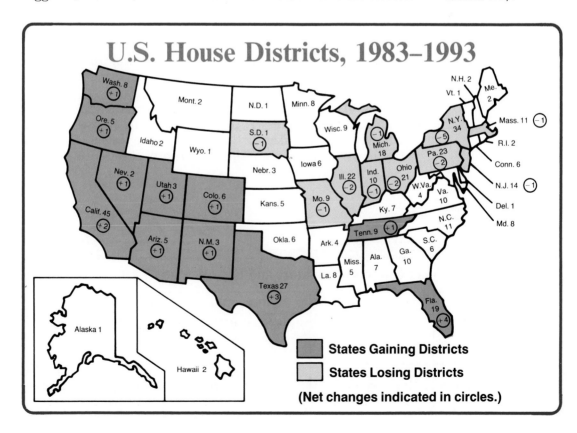

U.S. House Districts, 1983–1993

States Gaining Districts

States Losing Districts

(Net changes indicated in circles.)

every two years. Because of the staggered terms, the Senate is sometimes referred to as a continuous body.

Election. Before 1913, Senators were chosen by the state legislatures. In 1913, the Seventeenth Amendment to the Constitution was adopted. This amendment states that all Senators are to be chosen by the voters in statewide elections. Senatorial elections occur in November of even-numbered years. Only one Senator is elected from a state at any one election, unless the other Senator has died, resigned, or been expelled. Senators are sworn into office when the Congress meets in January following the November election.

Vacancies. If a Senator resigns, dies, or is expelled before his or her term has ended, the governor of the state can do one of two things. He or she can call a special election to fill the vacancy or make a temporary appointment until the next election. In 1989, the governor of Indiana appointed Dan Coats to complete the term of Senator Dan Quayle, who became Vice President of the nation.

Organization of Congress

The Congress of the United States is well organized. It must be well organized in order to carry on the business of making laws. Shortly after each session of Congress begins, each house chooses officers. The Democrat and Republican members each meet in a closed meeting called a **party caucus**. The caucus decides who the party officers will be. The political party with the most members is called the **majority party**. The party with the fewest members is called the **minority party**.

Speaker of the House. The most important and powerful member of the Congress is the Speaker of the House of Representatives. The Speaker of the House is the leader of the majority party in the House. The members of the House elect the

SKILL BUILDER

Why might the age qualifications for Senators and Representatives be different?

Qualifications of Senators and Representatives			
	Minimum Age	**Citizenship**	**Residence**
Senator	30	U.S. citizen at least 9 years	Must be resident of state where elected
Representative	25	U.S. citizen at least 7 years	Must be resident of state where elected

Speaker. Usually, the Speaker is a longtime member of the House who has gained influence over the years. The Speaker is in charge of all House meetings. No member may speak without the permission of the Speaker. The Speaker may also rule a member out of order and require the member to stop speaking. In addition, the Speaker refers all bills (proposals for laws) to appropriate committees, puts questions to a vote, appoints the members of special and conference committees, and signs all bills passed by the House. Of course, as an elected Representative, the Speaker may also vote on any matter before the House.

President of the Senate. The Constitution states that the "Vice President of the United States shall be President of the Senate. . . ." As a presiding officer, the Vice President is much less powerful than the Speaker of the House. He or she may vote *only* to break a tie. The Vice President is often absent because of other duties. The Senate, therefore, elects a member of the majority party to be President *pro tempore.* The **President *pro tempore*** presides when the Vice President is absent. (The words *pro tempore* come from Latin and mean "for the time being.")

Floor Leaders. Next to the Speaker, the most important officers in the Congress are the majority and minority floor leaders in

PEOPLE HELPING PEOPLE

Banking on Kindness

Kelly Leonard owes her life to a stranger. In 1988, 13-year-old Kelly was dying of leukemia. Today she is healthy and strong, thanks to a generous citizen whom she has never met. Kelly benefited from a new medical idea that makes healthy bone marrow—the tissue within bones—available to those in need.

The National Marrow Donor Program, based in St. Paul, Minnesota, was begun in 1987. It works like a blood bank. People undergo a medical operation to donate their bone marrow. The marrow is then stored until a patient with the same tissue type needs it. When that day comes, another operation is performed to remove the diseased marrow from the patient and replace it with the healthy marrow.

So far, more than 25,000 Americans have signed up with the program, and hundreds have already donated. They are matched to patients by computer, and only their first names are revealed.

What motivates donors to give of themselves? For John, a Minnesota engineer, the decision came naturally. "I remember when I was 13 or 14, watching my mother go downtown to give blood," he says. "I learned by example: If you can do something to help, you do it. There's nothing heroic in it at all."

Senator George Mitchell of Maine (center), Democratic majority leader, talks to members of the press. To the left of Mitchell is Senate majority whip Alan Cranston of California.

each house. They are party leaders chosen by the two political parties. The **floor leaders** guide their parties' bills through Congress and plan the order of daily business after consulting with the presiding officer of the House or Senate. The floor leaders in each house are assisted by a **party whip,** who tries to persuade party members to vote as the party leaders wish.

SECTION *1* *Review*

Defining Key Terms

1. Define: Congress, Senate, House of Representatives, congressional district, census, party caucus, majority party, minority party, President *pro tempore,* floor leader, party whip.

Recalling the Facts

2. Describe the makeup of Congress.

3. What are the duties of the Speaker of the House?

Reviewing the Main Idea

4. Answer "As you read . . ." question 1 on page 97: What are the major differences between the House of Representatives and the Senate?

Critical Thinking

5. Demonstrating Reasoned Judgment. Do you think the number of members in the House of Representatives should increase as the population increases? Explain.

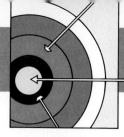

Citizenship Skills

Writing Your Lawmakers

Anyone can write to his or her elected representatives. In fact, some lawmakers' offices receive as many as 10,000 letters a week from the people who put them in office. Most elected officials pay close attention to the opinions that come to them through the mail. Their offices keep a tally (count) of how many "pro" (for) and "con" (against) responses they get on particular bills waiting for a vote. By writing to your lawmakers, therefore, you can directly influence government decision making.

If you need to find out who your representatives are, you can call the League of Women Voters or your local public library. When you write your letter, there are several guidelines to remember.

1. It is not necessary to type. A neatly hand-written letter is just as acceptable.
2. In the upper right corner of your letter, always include the date and your full address (including zip code). That way your legislator can easily reply.
3. Address your legislator as "The Honorable (their name)" at the top of your letter. Then use a more specific title in the greeting: "Dear Representative Gomez" or "Dear Senator Brown."
4. Present your position clearly and sincerely in the body of the letter. Keep your letter as brief as you can, sticking to your major points.
5. If you are writing about a bill that is being considered by the legislature, refer to the bill by its specific number and name. All House bill numbers begin with an *HR* and all Senate bills begin with an *S*. Be sure your letter arrives before the date of the vote.

6. Ask what your lawmaker's position is on the proposed legislation. This indicates that you expect a reply.
7. End your letter with a proper closing (such as "Respectfully yours") and your signature.
8. Make sure you address the envelope properly. The correct addresses in Washington are:

The Honorable Representative __[name]__
United States House of Representatives
Washington, D.C. 20515

The Honorable Senator ____[name]____
United States Senate
Washington, D.C. 20510.

Practicing Skills

1. Which would be a better opening paragraph for a letter to your legislator regarding an upcoming bill? Why?
   a. I am writing in support of S3742, the Clean Water Bill, which would provide funds for cleaning up Lake Boone. I strongly urge you to support this bill.
   b. Please clean up Lake Boone. As you are aware, fishing and swimming have been prohibited at Lake Boone for the past two years due to pollution and health hazards.
2. **Expressing Problems Clearly.** Research the names of your Senators and Representatives. Think about an issue in the news that concerns you and write a letter that you could send to one of your legislators.

2 The Committee System

Thousands of bills come before Congress every year. It would be impossible for all of the members of the House of Representatives or the Senate to study and discuss each bill that is introduced. The task of studying bills and making recommendations about them, therefore, is divided among groups, or **committees**. The chart on this page shows the various committees of Congress.

Kinds of Committees

Both the House and the Senate have a number of permanent committees called standing committees. The **standing committees** are the most important committees. They deal with special matters such as the budget, the armed services, and foreign affairs. Standing committees are often divided into subcommittees. A **subcommittee** is a small group of Representatives or Senators who study in detail a particular part of a subject or problem.

At times, Congress also appoints **select committees** to conduct special investigations and **joint committees** that include

SKILL BUILDER

How do the standing committees allow Congress to study bills more effectively?

Standing Committees of Congress

House of Representatives	Senate
Agriculture	Agriculture, Nutrition and Forestry
Appropriations	Appropriations
Armed Services	Armed Services
Banking, Finance, and Urban Affairs	Banking, Housing, and Urban Affairs
Budget	Budget
District of Columbia	Commerce, Science, and Transportation
Education and Labor	Energy and Natural Resources
Energy and Commerce	Environment and Public Works
Foreign Affairs	Finance
Government Operations	Foreign Relations
House Administration	Governmental Affairs
Interior and Insular Affairs	Judiciary
Judiciary	Labor and Human Resources
Merchant Marine and Fisheries	Rules and Administration
Post Office and Civil Service	Small Business
Public Works and Transportation	Veterans' Affairs
Rules	
Science, Space, and Technology	
Small Business	
Standards of Official Conduct	
Veterans' Affairs	
Ways and Means	

members from both the House and the Senate. In recent years, the Congress has appointed joint committees on atomic energy, defense, and taxation.

One of the most important joint committees is the **conference committee**. A conference committee is formed when the House and Senate have passed two versions of the same bill. Suppose the House passes a bill raising the minimum wage by 12 percent. The Senate, however, passes a bill for only a 5 1/2 percent increase. A conference committee would be formed to work out a compromise on the two versions of the bill. Decisions of a conference committee are usually accepted by both houses.

Committee Selection

Members of Congress want to be on important committees. Publicity, power, and prestige come with assignments to these committees. A seat on the Appropriations Committee is especially sought-after in both the House of Representatives and the Senate. This committee makes many decisions about spending money.

Senators and Representatives also want to be on a committee whose work is of interest to their **constituents** (people they represent). A Representative from a big city, for example, would want to be on the Education and Labor Committees. Both education and labor are of great interest to the voters in the Representative's district. A Representative from a farming district would want to be on the Agriculture Committee.

Not every member of Congress, of course, can be appointed to the committee he or she wants. Who decides the committees on which a lawmaker will serve? The assignments in each house are supposed to be made by all the members of that house. Actually, each political party (Democratic and Republican) holds a caucus to make the assignments. Each party in the House and Senate has a **committee on committees**. This group suggests members of its party who might serve on the standing committees. Then the caucus reviews the suggestions and makes the assignments to the different committees. Party leaders have great influence on the final choices, however. They usually reward hard-working party members by assigning them to the committees they want.

The majority party in each house has a big advantage when it comes to choosing committee members. The number of Democrats or Republicans on a committee is decided by the number of members each party has in each house. If the Senate, for example, has 60 Democrats and 40 Republicans, a ten-member Senate committee would have six Democrats and four Republicans. The majority party sees that party members make a majority on each committee and that the committee chair (head) is also a majority party member. In these ways, the majority party can control much of the work of the committee.

Members of the House of Representatives have many obligations to their constituents. This photo shows John Conyers, Jr., Representative from Michigan.

The Seniority System

Certain customs are connected with congressional committees. For example, once a Senator or Representative has been appointed to a committee, he or she usually stays on that committee. In keeping with another custom, the member of the majority party with the longest service on a committee almost always becomes the committee chair. Such customs are part of the **seniority system**. This system awards both membership on and chairing of committees on the basis of length of service.

Many people are unhappy with the seniority system. There have been several unsuccessful attempts to change it because the chair of a committee has a great deal of power. He or she can call or refuse to call meetings of the committee. The chair sets the rules of procedure for committee meetings and assigns members to subcommittees. Many of the younger members of Congress feel that power should be shared equally between young and old. Under certain conditions, committee chairs are chosen by a secret vote of the majority party in each house.

SECTION 2 *Review*

Defining Key Terms
1. Define: committee, standing committee, subcommittee, select committee, joint committee, conference committee, constituent, committee on committees, seniority system.

Recalling the Facts
2. Describe how a conference committee works.
3. How does the committee selection process work?

Reviewing the Main Idea
4. Answer "As you read . . ." question 2 on page 97: Why is the committee system so important in the way Congress works?

Critical Thinking
5. **Making Comparisons.** Compare the advantages and disadvantages of the seniority system of our government. Are there more advantages? Explain your answer.

3 How a Bill Becomes a Law

As mentioned before, a bill is a proposal for a law. Both houses of Congress must approve a bill before it can become a law. Then it goes to the President of the United States, who can either sign it into law or veto (reject) it.

Actually, passing a law is not very simple. Every year, thousands of bills suggested by individuals or groups are introduced in Congress. Only a few hundred, however, become laws. The rest fail at one of the many steps in the lawmaking process. Those steps are described in this section.

The Basic Steps of a Bill

Drafting a Bill. Before an idea for a new law can be introduced in either house of Congress, it must be put into written form. Writing the idea for a law is called **drafting a bill.** Members of Congress or congressional committees draft most bills. Sometimes members of the President's staff will draft a bill. Once a bill is drafted, it is given to a Senator or Representative who sponsors

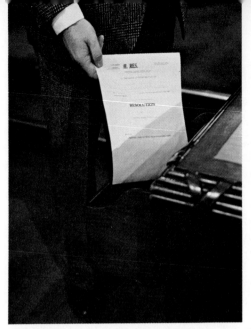
A Representative placing a bill into the hopper. This must be done when a bill is introduced in the House of Representatives.

it in Congress. A bill can be introduced only by a member of Congress.

Introducing a Bill. Most bills may be introduced in either house of Congress. However, according to the Constitution, revenue bills *must* begin in the House. **Revenue** is money raised from taxes. A **revenue bill** is any bill designed to raise money. A bill proposing to increase the amount of federal income tax is an example. This rule was written into the Constitution in order to keep the power to tax in the hands of the voters. This makes Congress directly responsible to the taxpayers. Since members of the House are elected every two years, they must very carefully use their power to raise money. If they do not, they may not be reelected.

When introducing a bill in the House of Representatives, a Representative places the written bill into the hopper (a basket) attached to the desk of the Clerk of the House. In the Senate, a Senator states that he or she wishes to introduce a bill. In both houses, the bill is then given a number and sent to the proper committee. An "S" is placed before the number of a bill introduced in the Senate. An "HR" is placed before the number of a bill introduced in the House of Representatives. A revenue bill in the House may be given the number HR 1018. When the bill is sent to the Senate, it becomes S 1018.

Considering the Bill in Committee. Most of the work in considering a bill is done in committee. The work is long and difficult. The committee may kill (not act upon) the bill, approve it, change it, put it aside (called **pigeonholing** the bill), or draft an entirely new bill. If the committee decides to consider a bill it

In the chamber of the House of Representatives, the Speaker's chair is in front of the flag. Above the Speaker's chair is an electronic voting board.

must hold public hearings, or special meetings. People who are for or against the bill come to the hearing to tell what they think about the bill. The committee then holds private meetings called **executive sessions**. If the committee approves the bill, it is sent to the House (or Senate) for debate.

Voting on the Bill. Once a bill has been approved by a committee, it goes before the entire House (or Senate). At that time, all members have a chance to debate the bill. They may make amendments to it. Then the full House (or Senate) votes on the bill. The bill passes if a majority (one more than half) of the Senators or Representatives votes "yes."

As mentioned earlier, all bills designed to raise money must begin in the House. Usually, money will be needed to carry out a new law. Congress gets this money by passing an appropriations bill. An **appropriations bill** is one that allows the government to use money it has received from taxes or other sources. In many cases, this money is not appropriated beyond the two year term of House members.

Sending the Bill to the Other House. After a bill passes one house, it is sent to the other house where it again goes through the steps described above. It is introduced, sent to committee, and, if accepted, voted on by the full house.

One big difference between the House and the Senate is in the way each debates a bill. In the House, the Rules Committee decides how much time will be spent debating the bill. Debate can be stopped at any time by a majority vote of the membership. In the Senate, however, members may continue to discuss a bill until they wish to stop. Furthermore, they may talk about any subject, whether or not it deals with the bill being debated. On occasion, Senators have been known to read aloud from the telephone book or to recite passages from books of poetry. Such nonstop talking is known as a **filibuster**.

Filibustering is used by Senators to prevent a vote on a bill when they fear the vote will go against them. Filibusters can be stopped through a process known as **cloture** (sometimes called "the gag rule"). Debate on a bill in the Senate can be cut off if 60 Senators vote to do so. A two-thirds vote of the members is required, however, to stop a filibuster involving any rule changes. This rarely happens.

Signing the Bill into Law. If both houses pass a bill, it goes to the President of the United States to be signed. The President has ten days in which to either sign or veto the bill. If the President should veto the bill, it can become a law if it is passed again by a two-thirds majority in each house. If, after ten days, the President has not signed the bill, it becomes law without his or her signature, but only if Congress is in session. If Congress has adjourned within ten days of submitting a bill, the President can **pocket veto** the bill. That is, he or she can simply not sign it, and, after ten days, the bill dies (does not become a law).

As you can see, there are many steps that a bill must go through before it becomes a law. If it fails to clear even one of these steps, it dies. The various steps that a bill must go through are shown in the diagram on page 111.

Who Can Help A Bill Become A Law?

There are many people whose support can help, or whose opposition can hurt, a bill's chances to become a law. They include all of the following.

The President of the United States. As the leader of our country, the President has more opportunity than anyone else to ask for support of a bill. The President can urge the American people to give their support to a bill he or she thinks is especially important. The President can pressure members of Congress to vote for such a bill. The President may hold meetings with individual members of Congress to try to convince them about the merits of a bill. The President might also appear on television to explain a proposed bill and to gain public support for it.

The President can also kill a bill by using the veto power. Remember, though, a bill can become a law if a two-thirds majority of both houses of Congress votes to override (overturn) the President's veto. However, a majority this large is usually difficult to get.

Other Members of Congress. Once a Senator or Representative introduces a bill, he or she needs the support of other legislators to get the bill passed. One way to do this is to get the names of co-sponsors—that is, other legislators—on the bill. Another

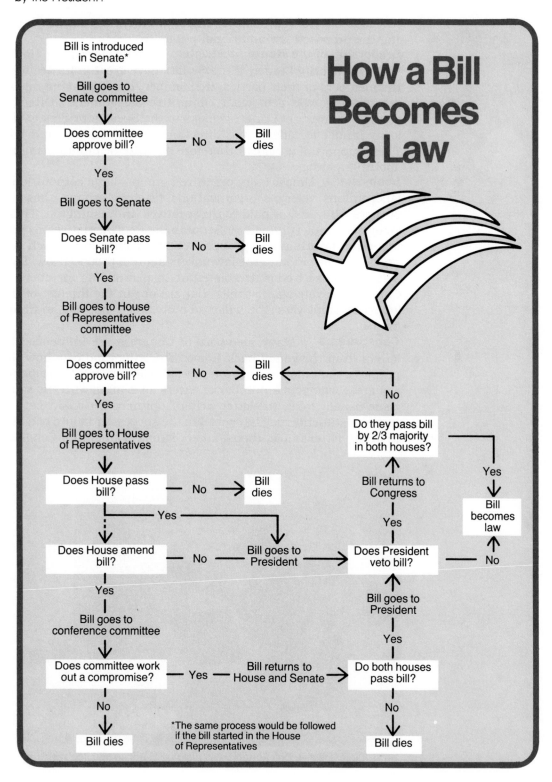

How a Bill Becomes a Law

Bill is introduced in Senate*

Bill goes to Senate committee

Does committee approve bill? — No → Bill dies

Yes

Bill goes to Senate

Does Senate pass bill? — No → Bill dies

Yes

Bill goes to House of Representatives committee

Does committee approve bill? — No → Bill dies

Yes

Bill goes to House of Representatives

Does House pass bill? — No → Bill dies

Yes → Bill goes to President

Does House amend bill? — No → Bill goes to President → Does President veto bill? — No → Bill becomes law

Yes

Bill goes to conference committee

Does committee work out a compromise? — Yes — Bill returns to House and Senate → Do both houses pass bill?

No

Bill dies

Bill goes to President

Yes

No → Bill dies

Bill returns to Congress

Yes

Do they pass bill by 2/3 majority in both houses? — No → Bill dies

Yes → Bill becomes law

*The same process would be followed if the bill started in the House of Representatives

way is to have other members introduce identical bills, thus giving the proposed law additional publicity.

Leadership of the House or Senate. The Speaker of the House and the Majority Leader of the Senate have great influence with the members of their parties. (Remember, they play a big role in determining who gets what committee assignment.) Often, a younger member of Congress looks to the Speaker or Senate Majority Leader for advice and direction on how to vote on a bill. Their support of a bill can therefore be quite helpful in bringing about its passage.

Lobbyists. Almost every organized group—large corporations, labor unions, veterans' organizations, teachers' groups—has one or more lobbyists, or paid representatives, in Washington. These lobbyists contact individual Senators or Representatives to promote laws favoring their groups. Lobbyists often do research and provide information to the lawmakers about a proposed law. Lobbyists also exert considerable effort in persuading members of Congress to vote against bills that are not in the interest of the lobbyists' employers. You will read more about lobbyists in Chapter 19.

Constituents. Many members of Congress are influenced by letters from the voters back home. The letters indicate how the people in their districts or states feel about an issue. A member of Congress who gets a number of letters all dealing with the same issue usually takes the letter writers' opinions seriously. Letters from constituents may be crucial to the success or failure of a bill. In 1989, for example, thousands of letters poured into Congress

Illinois Representative Dan Rostenkowski picks up literature from lobbyists.

to oppose a bill that would have given the members of Congress a huge pay raise. This flood of mail from constituents had a strong effect on the bill's final failure to become law.

The highest law of the land, the Constitution, gives the Congress the power to make laws. However, the Constitution *forbids* Congress to make the kinds of laws discussed below.

1. Congress cannot pass a bill of attainder. A **bill of attainder** is a law which allows a person to be punished without having a trial. The right to a fair, public trial is guaranteed all citizens of the United States by the Constitution. Congress may not pass a law which takes away this right.

2. Congress cannot pass an *ex post facto* law. An ***ex post facto* law** is a law that applies to an act which occurred before the law was passed. For example, it is not against the law today to drive at speeds up to 55 miles per hour on highways. Suppose Congress passed a law tomorrow making the national speed limit 45 miles per hour. People could not be arrested in the future for having driven at a speed of 55 miles per hour today.

3. Congress cannot tax exports. **Exports** are goods that are made in the United States and sent to other nations. Placing a tax on exports would make it expensive for businesses to trade with other countries. They would have to charge higher prices for their goods. However, Congress may tax **imports**, that is, goods coming *into* the United States.

4. Congress cannot pass laws that favor the trade of a particular state. A law which required all states but Alabama to pay a tax on the agricultural goods they produced would be an example of such a law.

5. Congress cannot grant any *titles of nobility.* The Declaration of Independence states that "all men are created equal." This is a basic American belief and ideal.

6. Congress may not take away the writ of *habeas corpus,* except in times of emergency. A **writ of *habeas corpus*** is a court order which requires that a person accused of a crime be brought before a judge. The judge decides whether there is enough evidence to hold the accused for trial. If Congress had the power to take away this writ, a person might be held in jail for years without being formally charged with a crime.

7. Congress may not pass any law that violates the ten amendments that make up the Bill of Rights (see pages 518–520). These first ten amendments to the United States Constitution place definite limits on the lawmaking powers of Congress.

In addition to the above powers that are forbidden to Congress, the Tenth Amendment states that certain powers are "reserved" to the states. This means that they cannot be taken over by the federal government.

Because the Constitution is the highest law of the land, Congress is bound by its laws. Congress may not tax exports, but it may tax imports, such as these goods that have arrived by ship.

SECTION 3 *Review*

Defining Key Terms
1. Define: drafting a bill, revenue, revenue bill, pigeonholing, executive sessions, appropriations bill, filibuster, cloture, pocket veto, bill of attainder, *ex post facto* law, exports, imports, writ of *habeas corpus*.

Recalling the Facts
2. Where do ideas for new laws come from?
3. Who can help or hinder a bill from becoming a law?

Reviewing the Main Idea
4. Answer "As you read . . ." question 3 on page 97: What are the basic steps that a bill must go through before it becomes a law?

Critical Thinking
5. **Predicting Consequences.** How do you think the quality of laws would be affected if one house of Congress had sole power to pass a bill?

Citizenship

Students Go to Congress

"I'll never forget the honor of being elected Boys' State governor," says NBC news anchor Tom Brokaw, who attended Boys' State in South Dakota in 1957. "It taught me, even at that age, that political leadership is easier to criticize than to exercise."

Watching and participating in the processes of government is what Boys' State and Girls' State are all about. These two programs teach the privileges and responsibilities of citizenship to juniors in high school. More than a million students nationwide have graduated from this learn-by-doing school of government. Among them are astronaut Neil Armstrong, who attended Boys' State in Ohio, and Michael S. Dukakis, two-term governor of Massachusetts.

Boys' State and Girls' State are week-long programs that give students first-hand experience of the political process. Using a two-party system, participants hold caucuses, manage campaigns, run for local offices, prepare speeches, and learn how laws are enacted. They carry out the duties of public officials. They learn what is expected of concerned citizens. They consider what issues should influence their voting.

The American Legion, the largest veterans organization in the world, sponsors Boys' State. The American Legion Auxiliary sponsors Girls' State. Both groups understand that by allowing high-school students to become actively involved in government and politics, they are helping to educate America's future leaders.

Each year more than 53,000 young men and women participate in Boys' and Girls' State programs. Of the 50 states, only Ha-

Programs such as Boys' and Girls' State allow students to explore the workings of the American political system.

waii does not have a Boys' State, and only Louisiana does not have a Girls' State.

The week-long programs are usually held on a local college or university campus or at a military base near the state's capital. The number of students in a single program ranges from 25 to 1,400.

Boys' Staters and Girls' Staters come from all over each state. Generally, the young men and women who are chosen to participate have good grades in school, an interest in government, and excellent leadership skills.

Students are assigned to a mock political party—the Federalist or the Nationalist. These parties allow students to learn by participating in a two-party system of government. Students then set up a mock government along the lines of their city, county, or state government.

As in actual elections, the parties nominate candidates for various political offices. Then comes a whirlwind of campaigning. After many hearty handshakes and sincere speeches, elections are held. The mock elections follow the actual election laws of each state. "Citizens" of Boys' State and Girls' State register the voters and count ballots.

Staging elections is not the only activity going on during the week. Many programs offer special classes in law, election officials, or public safety. Some programs produce a newspaper that is written, edited, and printed by the students. Students may also attend lectures given by public officials and other community leaders. And all participants learn parliamentary procedure, a set of formal rules used to keep order in meetings.

At the end of the session, each state selects two participants from its program to act as delegates to Boys' Nation and Girls' Nation. This annual week-long program is held in Washington, D.C.

One American Legion Auxiliary member describes Boys' and Girls' Nation as a "graduate school" for Boys' and Girls' Staters. The students representing their states in Washington form a Senate. They divide into two parties, organize into committees, and debate bills.

The programs may sound like a lot of study and work, but they're also a lot of fun. And students get an "insider's" view of our nation's capital. They visit with elected Representatives and Senators from their home states. They tour national monuments, the White House, and Capitol Hill. They attend meetings held at various government locations, including the Department of Defense and the Supreme Court.

Boys' and Girls' Nation offer a good overview of the workings of national government. The programs give students a chance to better understand how and why laws are made. For many participants, that one week spent in Washington leads to a lifelong fascination with politics.

Questions to think about

1. How could a learn-by-doing program help students to understand better the workings of government?
2. If you were to participate in Boys' or Girls' State, what aspect of the political system would you be most interested in exploring? Why?

CHAPTER SUMMARY

Section 1   Congress is the lawmaking body of our national government. It has two houses, the Senate and the House of Representatives. Senators and Representatives are elected by the people of each state. The House of Representatives has 435 members, who are elected on the basis of their state's populations and serve for a two-year term. The presiding officer, the Speaker of the House, is chosen by the majority party. The Senate has two Senators from each state, or 100 members, who hold office for six years. The Vice President of the United States serves as the presiding officer of the Senate.

Section 2   Both houses of Congress operate through committees. Bills introduced in either house are sent to a committee for study, discussion, and approval. Members of Congress want to be appointed to the most important committees or to committees whose work interests their districts. The majority party controls each committee and chooses the committee chair.

Section 3   Any bill introduced into the House or Senate is sent to the appropriate committee. Bills approved by a majority vote of the committee go to the full house for discussion and voting. A bill must be approved by both houses and signed by the President before becoming a law. The President's veto of a bill can be overridden by a two-thirds vote in both houses. The President, members of Congress, party leaders, lobbyists, and constituents all can exert pressure to pass or defeat a bill. Although Congress has the power to make laws, the Constitution expressly forbids certain kinds of laws.

Reviewing Key Terms

1. Write a paragraph or two about Congress, using the following terms.

majority party	seniority system
committee	filibuster
constituents	pocket veto

2. The Constitution states that Congress cannot pass certain kinds of laws. Here are two such types of laws. Write a sentence about each.

a. *ex post facto* law
b. bill of attainder

Understanding Main Ideas

1. What are the two houses of Congress? What are the members called? Who presides over each house?

2. What is a congressional district?

3. What is the majority party? The minority party?

4. Name six important congressional committees in the House and Senate.

5. What is the purpose of a conference committee?

6. In which house are revenue bills introduced and why?

7. When a committee considers a bill, what different courses of action can it take?

8. When does a committee hold public hearings and why?

9. How does the President affect the lawmaking process?

10. Name five kinds of laws the Constitution forbids Congress to pass.

Critical Thinking

1. Making Comparisons. Compare the two houses of Congress. Include the following aspects: size, qualifications of members, terms of office, organization. How are the two houses alike and how are they different?

2. Demonstrating Reasoned Judgment. Some people have argued that the minimum age requirements for Senators and Representatives is too low. They say it should be raised. Would this be a wise thing to do? Why or why not? If you think so, to what age would you raise the requirement?

3. Recognizing Cause and Effect. A bill must go through many steps before becoming a law. What are the advantages and disadvantages of this long process?

Practicing Skills

1. Writing Your Lawmakers. Read or watch the news to find out about a current national issue that interests you. Then write to your Senator or Representative expressing your views on this issue. Share your letter and its reply with the class.

2. Making a Report. Prepare an oral or written report explaining the term *filibuster*. Refer to some past filibusters. Then discuss whether or not filibusters are a good idea.

3. Formulating Questions. Imagine that you are a reporter assigned to interview two or three members of Congress about their work. Prepare a list of questions that would be important to ask. Then exchange lists with a classmate. Are your partner's questions to the point, important, and clearly phrased?

Focusing on Citizenship

1. Making a Chart. Make a chart identifying who your state's Senators and Representatives are, what party they belong to, what year they were elected, and what their background is.

2. Analyzing the News. Through news articles, trace the progress of a current bill in Congress. What are the arguments for and against it? Would you support this bill? Why or why not?

3. Checking Consistency. Contact your Representative and Senators to find out what positions they support on three issues that are important to you. Then compare their stated positions with their voting records. Are they consistent?

A red carpet of tulips leads to the White House—the President's office and home.

The Presidency

Previewing the Chapter

Thomas Jefferson once called the Presidency a place of "splendid misery." Lyndon Johnson wrote that "no one can experience with the President of the United States the glory and agony" of the office. This chapter takes an in-depth look at the Presidency—one of the most powerful offices in the entire world.

■   **Before you read,** look up these key terms in the Glossary at the back of this book: *natural-born, State of the Union message, treaty, executive agreement, Executive Office of the President.*

■   **As you read,** look for answers to these questions:
   1. What are the Constitutional requirements for a presidential candidate?
   2. What are the chief roles of the President?
   3. Why can the Executive Office be called the "right arm" of the President?
   4. What factors influence presidential decision making?

1 Qualifications and Removal

The citizens of all the states and the District of Columbia vote for the President of the United States. Other public officials are elected by citizens of the community or state in which they live. There have been 41 persons chosen to be President of the United States. Not everyone is eligible for this office, however. Who is?

Qualifications for President

Who Can Be President?   Popular opinion has it that any citizen can be President. The Constitution says only that a President must be:

- 35 years of age
- a natural-born citizen
- a resident of the United States for 14 years

At age 43, John Kennedy was the youngest elected President in American history. On the death of William McKinley in 1901, however, Vice President Theodore Roosevelt became President at age 42. Ronald Reagan, at age 69, was the oldest person to be elected President for his first term.

The phrase **natural-born** means born in the United States. You are considered a natural-born citizen of the United States, even if you were born in another country, as long as one or both of your parents are United States citizens.

There is some question about the reason for the 14-year residence requirement. Some people believe the requirement was included in the Constitution to be sure the first President would be someone who lived in the country before the American Revolution. They did not want any "newcomer" to be President.

Informal Requirements.   There are informal requirements for becoming President that are not stated in the Constitution. These informal requirements have developed as customs or traditions over time. All recent Presidents, for example, have been **candidates** (persons who run for election) of either the Democratic or Republican party. Minor party candidates, such as the Socialists, have never been able to attract many voters. From a practical standpoint, we have a two-party system in the United States.

What do the Democratic and Republican parties look for in a candidate? First, both parties want a winner. Until the end of the 1800s, most candidates had similar characteristics. They were married, Protestant, male, and in good health. They also came from states with large numbers of voters, such as New York or Illinois.

From 1900 on, however, this pattern began to change. In 1928, the Democrats chose a Catholic candidate, Alfred E. Smith, former governor of New York. Smith lost, but John F. Kennedy, also a Catholic, won in 1960.

In 1952 and 1956, the Democrats chose a divorced man, Adlai Stevenson, former governor of Illinois. Ronald Reagan, elected President in 1980 and reelected in 1984, had been divorced and remarried.

Franklin D. Roosevelt, who had had polio, could walk only with the help of heavy braces and crutches. He was elected to the Presidency a total of four times, more than any other President.

In 1940 and 1952, the Republican party chose candidates who had never before run for political office. They were Wendell Wilkie, a businessman, and Dwight D. Eisenhower, a former general. Wilkie lost, but Eisenhower was elected twice to the Presidency.

Some candidates in recent years have been from states with small populations. Senator Barry Goldwater, the Republican candidate in 1964, came from Arizona. Senator George McGovern,

SKILL BUILDER

How many of these Presidents were 55 or older when they were elected?

Backgrounds of Recent U.S. Presidents

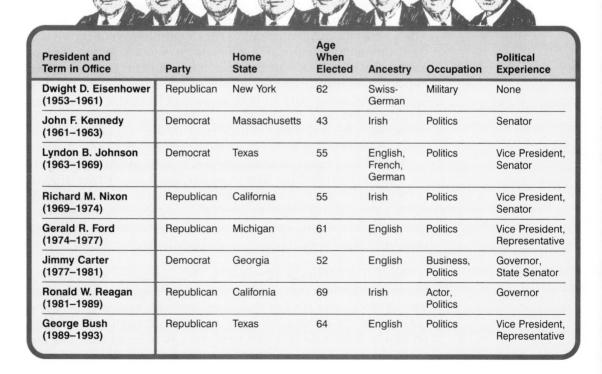

President and Term in Office	Party	Home State	Age When Elected	Ancestry	Occupation	Political Experience
Dwight D. Eisenhower (1953–1961)	Republican	New York	62	Swiss-German	Military	None
John F. Kennedy (1961–1963)	Democrat	Massachusetts	43	Irish	Politics	Senator
Lyndon B. Johnson (1963–1969)	Democrat	Texas	55	English, French, German	Politics	Vice President, Senator
Richard M. Nixon (1969–1974)	Republican	California	55	Irish	Politics	Vice President, Senator
Gerald R. Ford (1974–1977)	Republican	Michigan	61	English	Politics	Vice President, Representative
Jimmy Carter (1977–1981)	Democrat	Georgia	52	English	Business, Politics	Governor, State Senator
Ronald W. Reagan (1981–1989)	Republican	California	69	Irish	Actor, Politics	Governor
George Bush (1989–1993)	Republican	Texas	64	English	Politics	Vice President, Representative

the Democratic candidate in 1972, came from South Dakota. Jimmy Carter, elected President in 1976, came from the state of Georgia.

The Twenty-second Amendment.   The President of the United States serves a four-year term of office. No President except Franklin D. Roosevelt has been elected President more than twice. The Twenty-second Amendment limits the office of President to two terms. If a person becomes President and serves less than two years of an elected President's term, that person could be elected twice and serve as President ten years. However, if the person serves more than two years of an elected President's term, that person may be elected only once. Vice President Gerald Ford became President in 1974 when President Richard Nixon resigned. President Ford served two years and five months of an elected President's term; therefore, Ford could have been elected only once to the Presidency.

Replacing the President

The Twenty-fifth Amendment.   The Presidency is a dangerous job. There have been attacks on the lives of many of our Presidents, as well as on some presidential candidates. Ten Presidents have been shot at with guns. Four, including John F. Kennedy and Abraham Lincoln, have been killed. Ronald Reagan was shot in the chest in 1981, but he recovered from the wound.

As a result of such attacks, many people have worried about who would take over if the President should be killed, resign, or for some reason be unable to perform the duties of the Presidency. The Twenty-fifth Amendment to the Constitution tells us what to do if this should happen. If a President should die in office or resign, the Vice President becomes the President. He or she then appoints someone to be Vice President. The appointment must be approved by a majority in both houses of Congress. If both the President and Vice President die or resign, the Speaker of the House becomes President. Those next in line are shown in the chart on page 123.

What if the President becomes so ill that he or she cannot perform the duties of office? The President must, in writing, inform both the Speaker of the House and the President *pro tempore* of the Senate of the illness. The Vice President then becomes acting President. The acting President performs the duties of the President until the President says in writing that he or she is able to return to work.

What if a President becomes ill, but does not want to stop working? The Vice President may then declare the President unable to work, and take over as President. He or she must get a majority of the Cabinet to agree, however. If the President still refuses to step aside, the Congress, by a two-thirds vote, can approve the Vice President's action.

Removal by Impeachment. A President can also be removed from office by impeachment. You will recall that to impeach someone means to bring charges against that person. A President can be impeached only for "high crimes and misdemeanors," however. Treason (disloyalty to one's country) would be an example of such a "high crime."

The Judiciary Committee of the House of Representatives decides whether a President should be impeached. If the committee brings charges against the President, the full House must then decide whether to accept these charges. If the House accepts the charges, they are presented to the Senate. A two-thirds vote of the Senate is required for the President to be convicted. Only two Presidents in our history have ever been in danger of being impeached and convicted. They were Andrew Johnson in 1866 and Richard Nixon in 1974. Neither was found guilty. The attempt to find Johnson guilty failed by one vote. Nixon resigned before charges could be brought against him in the House of Representatives.

PRESIDENTIAL SUCCESSION

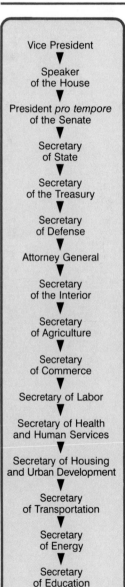

Vice President
▼
Speaker of the House
▼
President *pro tempore* of the Senate
▼
Secretary of State
▼
Secretary of the Treasury
▼
Secretary of Defense
▼
Attorney General
▼
Secretary of the Interior
▼
Secretary of Agriculture
▼
Secretary of Commerce
▼
Secretary of Labor
▼
Secretary of Health and Human Services
▼
Secretary of Housing and Urban Development
▼
Secretary of Transportation
▼
Secretary of Energy
▼
Secretary of Education
▼
Secretary of Veterans Affairs

SECTION *1* *Review*

Defining Key Terms
1. Define: natural-born.

Recalling the Facts
2. What are some of the informal requirements for a presidential candidate?
3. How do the Twenty-second and Twenty-fifth Amendments affect the Presidency?
4. How may a President be removed from office?

Reviewing the Main Idea
5. Answer "As you read . . ." question 1 on page 119: What are the Constitutional requirements for a presidential candidate?

Critical Thinking
6. **Identifying Assumptions.** Is it true that any American child can grow up to be President? Explain your answer.

SKILL BUILDER   Why is it important that the Vice President be an ▶ especially capable leader and politician?

2 The Duties of the President

A writer who visited Calvin Coolidge noted that the President worked only four to five hours a day. Coolidge often spent several hours showing visitors around the White House. That was in the 1920s. Today, such a relaxed presidential workload is not possible. Present-day Presidents work 10 to 12 hours a day, or even more, and often on Saturday and Sunday.

Why is this? One reason is that the duties of the President have increased. The President today supervises many agencies that did not even exist in the 1920s. Some of these agencies were created to deal with problems caused by the increase in our population. Others were created to deal with new developments in science, transportation, or communication. In foreign affairs alone, the President has a full-time job. In a world of continual crises (serious problems), the President shares with the leaders of other nations a duty to keep peace in the world. A second reason is that feelings about the Presidency have changed. In past years, Presidents were not always expected to solve everyday problems. Today this is not so. Whether it be unemployment, inflation, or a lack of decent housing, the President is expected to use the power of office to relieve hardship.

Presidential duties include meetings and negotiations with foreign leaders. Here, President Bush meets with Egypt's President Hosni Mubarak.

Sometimes the President's various duties are called *roles.* Six chief roles are explained below.

Chief Executive. The President is the head of the executive branch of our government. The most important part of this presidential role is to see that the laws of the land are carried out. This role involves a wide variety of tasks, for federal laws deal with almost every part of our lives. They deal with pollution control, delivery of the mail, inspection of foods, airplane safety, banking procedures, and crime control, to name just a few. Along with these tasks, the President watches over a budget that now exceeds $1 trillion.

Naturally, all these tasks cannot be done by a single person. Several million federal employees in numerous agencies assist the President. Some of these persons, such as close advisers, are appointed by the President. The President also appoints Cabinet officers, such as the Secretary of Agriculture. However, most of the workers in the executive branch get their jobs through the Civil Service system (see Chapter 8). Although there are many other workers, the overall responsibility for the daily operation of our government is the President's.

Commander in Chief. In this role, the President is head of all the armed forces of the United States. The President appoints, with Senate approval, the highest ranking generals and admirals. A great deal of authority is usually given to these officers. Only the President, however, may authorize the use of the country's atomic weapons in time of war.

Other military powers of our Commander in Chief include the right to call out the National Guard in a national emergency. The President can order federal troops to put down a riot or to assist victims of floods and other natural disasters. Acting on their own in past years, Presidents have ordered the armed forces overseas to help defend a friendly country against attack or to protect United States citizens. However, a law passed in 1973 now requires the President to check with Congress before sending troops to other countries. (See Chapter 23.)

Chief Lawmaker. The President is not a lawmaker in the usual sense. Only a member of Congress may introduce a bill in the House or Senate. However, the President often can influence the work of Congress. Every year the President delivers a **State of the Union message** to Congress to describe how the country is doing. Special messages are sent to Congress from time to time, too. In these messages, the President may suggest new laws that seem to be needed. Such laws may deal with inflation, crime, or unemployment.

In addition, officials within the executive branch often suggest new laws. The Secretary of Agriculture may propose a bill giving farmers money to experiment with growing new crops. If the bill

Presidential Roles

President Reagan and Soviet leader Gorbachev make history by signing the INF Treaty.

receives the President's approval, it may be introduced into the House or Senate by a member of the President's political party.

The President may also spend a great deal of time with congressional leaders, asking them to support or oppose a bill. Perhaps the President's greatest power as chief lawmaker, however, is the power to veto bills.

Foreign-Policy Maker. "I make American foreign policy," said President Harry Truman in 1948. Presidents do make foreign policy. One of their chief tasks in this role is to direct the relations between the United States and the rest of the world. Only the President has the power to enter into **treaties** (formal agreements) with other countries. Experts in the State Department usually help to work out the details of these treaties. In addition, to become law, all treaties must be approved by a two-thirds vote of the Senate.

The treaty with the Soviet Union to eliminate intermediate-range nuclear-force missiles is one example. The INF Treaty was signed by the Soviet Union and the United States in December, 1987. Ratified in 1988, the INF Treaty called for both nations to destroy all their missiles with a range of about 500 to 5,000 kilometers (300 to 3,400 miles) by 1991.

Presidents also make use of **executive agreements**. These are agreements between the President and the head of a foreign country. Unlike treaties, they do not require Senate approval. Many of our trade relations with other countries are made by means of executive agreements.

As a maker of foreign policy, the President enters into diplomatic relations with another country. This is called **recognizing** the other country. Both the United States and the other country then exchange ambassadors (official representatives of a country). In 1979, the President of the United States established diplomatic relations with the People's Republic of China. The United States had had no diplomatic ties with China since 1949. Cuba is another case in point. Since 1959, no President has agreed to recognize the government of Cuba.

Chief of State.   When meeting with the leaders of other countries at the White House, or greeting important visitors to the United States, a President is Chief of State. In this role, the President is the ceremonial head, or symbol, of our government, and represents our country on many formal and informal occasions.

Party Leader.   The President is head of the political party in power and is sometimes known as "Chief Democrat" or "Chief Republican." This is an honorary position. There are some customary duties which go with the role, however. The President selects the national chairperson of the party and works closely with the chairperson to plan for future elections. At times, the President campaigns for congressional candidates of the same party. Often, the President is able to offer a number of jobs to party members as rewards for faithful service during the election.

SECTION 2 *Review*

Defining Key Terms

1. Define: State of the Union message, treaty, executive agreement, recognize.

Recalling the Facts

2. What does the President do in the role of Chief Executive?

3. What duties does the President perform in the role of Chief of State?

Reviewing the Main Idea

4. Answer "As you read . . ." question 2 on page 119: What are the chief roles of the President?

Critical Thinking

5. Making Comparisons. The President has the power to enter into both treaties and executive agreements with other nations. How do these differ?

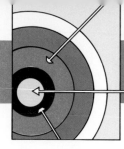
Critical Thinking Skills

Interpreting Pictures

In and out of school, much of the information you get comes from pictures, especially photographs, films, and television. The saying "One picture is worth a thousand words" may be an exaggeration. Yet pictures are useful sources of information about civics topics and issues.

Pictures, however, can be misleading. If you had four photographs taken of yourself on the same day, each one would be slightly different. They might differ in terms of the angle, the amount of light, the distance (close-up or long shot), and your facial expression. As a result, each photo would give a different impression of what you look like. Films can also be misleading when they emphasize some things and leave out others. Therefore, it is worthwhile to develop the skill of careful, critical viewing.

How can you become a more careful, a more critical viewer? Here are some suggestions:

- Read the caption, if there is one. It will help you identify the "who, what, when, and where" of the picture.
- Study the content of the picture. What catches your eye at once? What else do you notice—what objects, people, and actions are shown? How are they related?
- Interpret the picture by identifying its main idea or purpose. What message does the picture send? What impression or feeling does it create? What clues or details contribute to that impression?
- Evaluate the accuracy of the image. In what ways, if any, does the picture distort things? For example, what does it emphasize? What does it leave out? One

way to tell is to compare the picture with other pictures or sources of information on the same topic.

The photograph below shows Walter Mondale and Geraldine Ferraro, Democratic candidates for President and Vice President in 1984. Study the photograph and then answer the questions that follow.

Practicing Skills

1. What scene does the photograph show?
2. How does the photograph create a patriotic impression?
3. **Recognizing Bias.** Does the photograph present a flattering or an unflattering image? Explain.

3 The Executive Office

The office of the President is complex. In order to make decisions, a President must keep in touch with changes in science and technology, business and economics, the arts, education, foreign affairs, and many other fields. Keeping up with these changes takes more than one person. Over the years, several agencies, boards, and commissions (not to mention many key assistant and advisory positions) have been created to help Presidents perform their duties. These helpers are organized in four main groups, the Executive Office of the President, the executive departments (the Cabinet), the independent agencies, and the independent regulatory commissions. The work of the Executive Office will be discussed in the remainder of this section. The Cabinet and the independent agencies and regulatory commissions will be discussed in Chapter 8.

The Executive Office

In 1939, the Congress realized that the President needed additional help. It created the **Executive Office of the President**. This office is made up of many agencies and individuals, including the Vice President, to help the President perform certain tasks.

The Executive Office is sometimes called the "right arm" of the President. Many of the individuals and agencies that make up the office advise the President on important matters. As a result, there is usually a close relationship between the President and the *staff*, as these advisers are often called. The President personally oversees the work of these various advisers and agencies. They, in turn, report only to the President.

The White House Office. Among the agencies in the Executive Office, the White House Office is one of the most important. It is made up of a number of men and women who are close personal and political advisers to the President. Many are specialists who give advice on crime, space exploration, unemployment among teenagers, foreign aid, and other matters. Some workers in the White House Office assist the President by writing speeches, answering mail, or arranging appointments. Aside from the Press Secretary, most of the President's top aides are not generally known to the public. The Press Secretary's meetings with news reporters are often covered in the nationwide media.

In addition to the White House Office, the Executive Office of the President consists of a number of agencies which have a special purpose. These agencies assist, advise, and inform the President in a variety of ways and come under direct presidential supervision. The following are some of the most important additional agencies in the Executive Office of the President.

Executive Office of the President

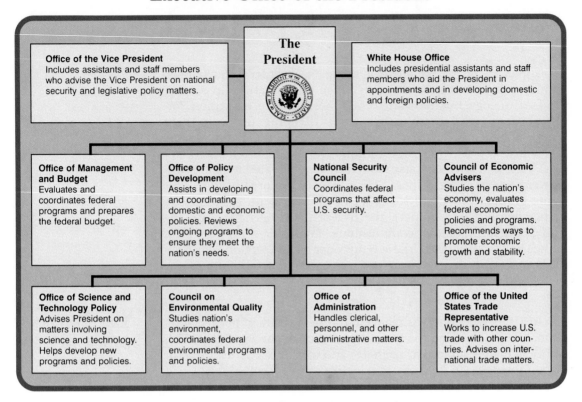

The President

Office of the Vice President
Includes assistants and staff members who advise the Vice President on national security and legislative policy matters.

White House Office
Includes presidential assistants and staff members who aid the President in appointments and in developing domestic and foreign policies.

Office of Management and Budget
Evaluates and coordinates federal programs and prepares the federal budget.

Office of Policy Development
Assists in developing and coordinating domestic and economic policies. Reviews ongoing programs to ensure they meet the nation's needs.

National Security Council
Coordinates federal programs that affect U.S. security.

Council of Economic Advisers
Studies the nation's economy, evaluates federal economic policies and programs. Recommends ways to promote economic growth and stability.

Office of Science and Technology Policy
Advises President on matters involving science and technology. Helps develop new programs and policies.

Council on Environmental Quality
Studies nation's environment, coordinates federal environmental programs and policies.

Office of Administration
Handles clerical, personnel, and other administrative matters.

Office of the United States Trade Representative
Works to increase U.S. trade with other countries. Advises on international trade matters.

SKILL BUILDER

Which office would be most likely to advise the President on a new trade agreement with Japan?

The Office of Management and Budget (OMB). How much will it cost to run the United States for the next year? Should the government spend more money than it takes in? If government spending is going to be reduced, where should the cuts be made? These questions, and others just as difficult, face the President and the budget aides every year. The OMB is responsible for answering these questions in preparing the total U.S. budget. When the budget is finally published, it may consist of as many as 15 volumes. The task is enormous. For this reason, the staff of the OMB is one of the largest in the Executive Office.

Every January, the President sends Congress the proposed budget for the following year. The Congress studies the entire document. Many changes are made by Congress. Adoption of the final budget depends upon approval by the House and Senate.

The National Security Council (NSC). The President is chairperson of this agency within the Executive Office. The members include the Secretary of Defense, the Secretary of State, the Joint Chiefs of Staff, and several others. The job of the NSC is to keep the President informed on all matters that affect the security of the nation. The council is especially active in dangerous times.

When Soviet missiles were discovered in Cuba in 1962, President Kennedy met frequently with this group. In 1980, the movement of Soviet troops into Afghanistan caused President Carter to meet with the NSC. In 1987 and 1988, Iran's threat to attack ships in the Persian Gulf caused President Reagan to meet many times with members of the NSC. The President and the Council decided to use military forces to protect ships in that waterway.

The Office of Policy Development.   This agency assists and advises the President in forming long-range domestic policy. As a sort of "trouble shooter" for the President, the staff may recommend changes in public policy or the creation of new policy.

The Council of Economic Advisers.   This agency consists of three persons who are specialists in the field of economics. The Council also employs a staff that studies wages, prices, profits, and the like. The job of all these persons is to keep the President informed on these matters. They also help the President prepare the economic report to Congress.

The Office of the United States Trade Representative.   This office assists the President in the formation of foreign trade policy. The head of the agency often represents the President in making trade agreements with other countries.

The President's Intelligence Oversight Board.   This group is often referred to as a "watchdog" agency. It keeps the President informed on the work of the Central Intelligence Agency and other agencies that gather information about foreign countries.

The 24-Hour President

Who was President of the United States on March 4, 1849? The question is a tricky one to answer. If anyone held the office on that day, it was probably a senator from Missouri named David Rice Atchison.

You might say that a fluke of the calendar created the question in the first place. Zachary Taylor had been elected to succeed James K. Polk as President. Polk's term of office expired on March 3, a Saturday. Taylor, a strict Episcopalian, refused to be sworn in as President on March 4 because it was a Sunday. He insisted on delaying his inaugural ceremony until Monday, March

5. The United States thus faced a gap of a full day between Presidents. By law, the President *pro tempore* of the Senate—in this case, Senator Atchison—automatically became President in these circumstances.

As it turned out, March 4 was an uneventful day, and Atchison never acted in his presidential role. He was very tired from several nights of staying late at the Senate to put finishing touches on some legislation. As a result, he napped through a large part of his term of office. "I went to bed . . . and I slept most of that Sunday," this easy-going man later confessed.

President George Bush confers with Vice President Dan Quayle in the Oval Office at the White House.

The Central Intelligence Agency (CIA). One of the main jobs of this agency is to gather secret information. The CIA works under the direction of the President or the National Security Council. CIA responsibility includes the gathering of information on political and military activities in foreign countries. The information the CIA gathers helps the President make decisions on what actions to take in trouble spots around the world.

The Office of Administration. This agency provides the Executive Office with services such as data processing, buying supplies, keeping records, library research, printing, and messenger service. The Office of Administration also provides services related to personnel and financial management.

The Council of Environmental Quality. This council advises the President on all matters relating to the environment. The information it supplies generally appears in the President's annual report to Congress on the quality of our environment. As part of its work, the council performs a continuing analysis of trends or changes in the national environment. It reviews and evaluates government programs and conducts studies and research related to environmental issues. This council also makes sure that the National Environmental Policy Act is carried out. The 1980s brought increasing awareness of the threats to our environment, making the work of this council even more important.

The Office of Science and Technology. This last group gives the President advice and information on scientific and technical matters. Most often, its head is a respected scientist.

The Vice President, a member of the Executive Office, takes over for the President at times. For example, if the President is extremely busy, the Vice President might be called on to give a speech at a convention.

Some Presidents have made Vice Presidents traveling ambassadors for the United States. As an ambassador, the Vice President travels to other countries and meets with various officials. Such trips are usually made for the purpose of improving our relations with other countries. In recent years, Vice Presidents have attended Cabinet meetings and been members of the National Security Council. The only job assigned to the Vice President by the Constitution, however, is to preside over the Senate.

John Nance Garner, who was Vice President under Franklin D. Roosevelt, once described his job as "a spare tire in the automobile of government." Others have made similar comments about the position. Fourteen Vice Presidents, however, have become President. This is a good reason to make sure that the Vice President is fully informed about what the President is doing.

SECTION 3 *Review*

Defining Key Terms
   1. Define: Executive Office of the President.

Recalling the Facts
   2. What are some ways in which advisers in the White House office assist the President?
   3. What are some of the kinds of specialized help provided by agencies in the Executive Office?
   4. What is the only official duty of the Vice President? What does the Vice President actually do today?

Reviewing the Main Idea
   5. Answer "As you read . . ." question 3 on page 119: Why can the Executive Office be called the "right arm" of the President?

Critical Thinking
   6. **Demonstrating Reasoned Judgment.** Would it be possible for a President to receive *too much* advice? Explain.

4 The President as Decision Maker

Presidential Decision Making

On a given day, Presidents may make more than a dozen decisions. Some of these decisions may not be of great importance. The President may decide on how many visitors to meet during the day or when to make a trip to another country. Some Presidents allow assistants to decide such matters. On important matters, however, such as the appointment of a federal judge, the President must make the decision. President Dwight Eisenhower once said to his successor, John F. Kennedy: "There are no easy matters that will come to you as President. If they are easy, they will be settled at a lower level."

The President must make many different kinds of decisions. Often, it may take many weeks or months before a final decision is made. Some of the questions that might come to the President for a decision are listed below.
- What bills shall be signed into law or vetoed?
- Who shall be named Chief Justice of the Supreme Court?
- Shall United States troops be sent to aid another country?
- What stand should be taken on a proposed law?
- What action shall be taken if another country seizes a United States Merchant Marine ship?
- How much military aid should be given to other countries?

In times of crisis, making a decision can become very difficult. Delay may serve only to make a bad situation worse. President John F. Kennedy faced a difficult decision in 1961. After only two months in office, he was informed of a proposed invasion of Cuba by a force of 1,300 troops. The purpose of the invasion was to expel the Communist leader of Cuba, Fidel Castro. The invasion had been approved by the previous President, Dwight Eisenhower. The soldiers were Cubans, but they had been trained and supplied by the CIA. In April of 1961 the troops were ready. The date for the invasion was set. All that was needed was a go-ahead from the White House.

Many top advisers told the President that the invasion had a good chance of success. They asked him to give his approval. They argued that delay would weaken the invasion's chance of success. If news of the invasion got out, the whole plan would fail.

The President faced two problems. First, he did not have time to get complete information about the plan. Second, he had not been in office long enough to know very much about the abilities of his advisers. However, since most of his advisers approved of the invasion, the President gave the order to go ahead. The invasion was a failure. Later, Kennedy admitted that he had learned a costly lesson about decision making from this experience.

Congress has a strong influence on presidential decision-making. This is because many decisions of the President require the formal approval of the Congress. If the President proposes a cut in personal income taxes, for example, the Congress must give its approval for the cut. As a result, in order to avoid the embarrassment of failure, Presidents often talk with leaders of Congress before making a decision on public policy. However, if the thinking of Congress is not clear, a President may risk going ahead with a decision. At such a time, the President may seek help from leaders of his or her own party in Congress. The party leaders, in turn, may try to get support for the President's proposal.

Personal beliefs sometimes influence presidential decisions. One President may strongly believe that the possibility of a Communist attack is the greatest danger to the safety of the United States. Another may believe that internal problems such as crime, pollution, or unemployment are a greater danger. A President's beliefs also affect decisions about the spending of public money. Some Presidents favor federal aid to cities. Others feel that the cities should rely on their own resources, not on money from the federal government.

Presidential Decisions

Public opinion polls often affect presidential decisions. Generally, Presidents want to make decisions that the public will approve. This is particularly true of a President who is seeking re-

Public Opinion

Senate leaders Simpson and Dole play an important role in presidential decision-making.

election, because going against the wishes of the people may cost him or her the election. Public opinion polls in recent years have shown that most citizens feel personal income taxes are too high. Therefore, a President calling for a cut in taxes would be taking almost no risk of displeasing the people.

As the 1980s progressed, there was mounting public concern about the problem of illegal drug use in the United States. Many people felt that the government must take stronger, more direct action to combat the drug problem. In response to this (as you read on page 93), President Bush in 1989 appointed William Bennett as the Director of the Office of National Drug Control Policy. Bennett's primary role in his job is to coordinate the efforts of the federal government to push back the rising tide of illegal drug trafficking and use in the United States.

Sometimes a President may try to create favorable public opinion for a particular policy. After World War I, President Woodrow Wilson tried to get the United States to join the League of Nations (similar to the United Nations). Congress would not approve of the idea. Wilson decided to appeal to the people. He spent several months traveling around the country making speeches in favor of joining the League. The appeal failed, however.

SECTION 4 *Review*

Recalling the Facts

1. What are some typical decisions that a President might make?
2. Why was it difficult for President John Kennedy to make a decision about the invasion of Cuba?

Reviewing the Main Idea

3. Answer "As you read . . ." question 4 on page 119: What factors influence presidential decision making?

Critical Thinking

4. **Understanding Anecdotes.** You may have heard the expression "passing the buck," which means giving someone else responsibility for something, such as making a decision. On his desk at the White House, President Harry Truman had a small sign stating: "The buck stops here." What do you think the sign meant?

Government and Law

Presidential Style

When George Washington was President, he always greeted guests by bowing rather than shaking hands. According to one story, a friend once came up to Washington at a party and clapped him on the shoulder. The President responded with such a frosty glare that the man quickly retreated.

There was nothing pompous about George Washington, but he believed his position called for dignity. "Few can realize the difficult and delicate part which a man in my situation had to act," he later said. As the nation's first President, Washington had no models to follow. The Constitution created the position of the President and set minimum legal requirements for the job. But it could not describe *how* to be a President.

Each of our 41 Chief Executives has had a unique presidential style. Just consider the nicknames given to some of these leaders. President Lincoln, famous for his frankness, was dubbed Honest Abe. Andrew Jackson, a man of strong will, was called Old Hickory by his admirers and King Andrew by his critics.

Personality, attitudes toward power, and ability to communicate are all factors that contribute to presidential style. In addition, style is shaped by the unique set of circumstances each President faces. Is the country at war? Is there a slump in the economy? Is some other crisis at hand?

Some Presidents have stayed carefully within the boundaries set by the Constitution. They believed that the President had only limited powers, and they willingly assigned authority to others. James Madison, William Howard Taft, and Dwight Eisenhower exhibited this presidential style.

Many Americans admired the style of President Reagan, who seemed as comfortable in the Oval Office as he was in a saddle. Here he rides with his wife, Nancy, in California.

Other Presidents have exercised more power, leading the country with courage and determination. George Washington, Thomas Jefferson, Abraham Lincoln, Franklin D. Roosevelt, Harry S. Truman, and John F. Kennedy fit this description.

Washington, a well-respected Revolutionary War leader, shaped the Presidency more than any other President. In fact, one reason the Framers of the Constitution included few details about the Presidency is that they knew Washington would be elected to the job and they trusted his judgment. Washington's presidential style was marked by wisdom, courage, and independent action.

Thomas Jefferson, our third President, was another bold and imaginative leader. Without the approval of Congress, Jefferson agreed to buy the Louisiana Territory from France in 1803. This act practically doubled the size of the United States. Nowhere does the Constitution say that the President has the power to buy new territory. By interpreting the Constitution in new ways, Jefferson enlarged the scope of presidential authority.

Abraham Lincoln was President during the Civil War—a time of national crisis. Lincoln rose to the challenge by using the "war power" of the President in ways the Constitution did not specifically state. He took drastic measures to save the Union and the Constitution. Lincoln showed that unusual circumstances may call for unusual presidential leadership.

Franklin D. Roosevelt was also in office during a national crisis—the Great Depression of the 1930s. Roosevelt worked hard to end this severe business slump and to restore America's faith in the democratic system. FDR was a strong legislative leader. He convinced Congress to pass a package of major bills he called his New Deal program. The New Deal created jobs. It got the economy going again. Because of his presidential style, FDR became known as a "mover and a shaker." He was well-loved by many Americans, and he left a strong stamp on the Presidency.

Sometimes, presidential style emerges in response to tough choices. President Harry S Truman was forced to decide whether to use atomic weapons against Japan to end World War II. His decision to drop the bomb demonstrated the authority of the President. Truman took bold action in other foreign policy matters and in domestic affairs as well. A decisive leader, Truman's presidential style is best summed up by the motto on his desk: "The Buck Stops Here."

John F. Kennedy was also a bold decision maker. He stood up to the Soviets when they built the Berlin Wall in the early 1960s and when they sent missiles to Cuba that were aimed at the United States. Kennedy was a popular young President who inspired the nation. He challenged all Americans to "Ask not what your country can do for you—ask what you can do for your country." JFK's presidential style was characterized by charm and wit.

The ability to communicate is a key factor of presidential style. Two popular Presidents were especially skilled communicators. Franklin D. Roosevelt reassured many Americans during the Depression years with his famous radio "fireside chats." Ronald Reagan made masterful use of television. A former actor with a warm manner and a gift for telling anecdotes, Reagan became known as the Great Communicator.

Questions to think about

1. How does presidential style affect political effectiveness?

2. Compare the presidential styles of George Bush and Ronald Reagan.

CHAPTER SUMMARY

Section 1   The President, as head of the executive branch of our national government, has great prestige. Chosen by voters in all of the states and the District of Columbia, the President serves a four-year term of office. No President may serve more than two *elected* terms. A presidential candidate must be a natural-born citizen, at least 35 years of age, and a resident of the United States for at least 14 years. If the President dies or resigns, the Vice President becomes President and appoints a new Vice President. A President can be removed from office by impeachment, but only for a serious crime such as treason.

Section 2   The President has six main roles in the national government. These include being Chief Executive, Commander in Chief of the armed forces, chief lawmaker, chief foreign-policy maker, Chief of State, and party leader.

Section 3   The Executive Office helps carry out the President's duties. Presidential advisers and assistants are grouped into agencies and offices, including the White House Office, the National Security Council, the Council of Economic Advisers, and the Council on Environmental Affairs. The Vice President also assists the President and may serve as a traveling ambassador.

Section 4   Every President must make difficult decisions that often affect the lives of all American citizens as well as people in other countries. These decisions can be influenced by the President's beliefs, public opinion, members of Congress, and the President's personal staff.

Reviewing Key Terms

On a separate sheet of paper, use the following terms to complete the sentences below.

State of the Union message   natural-born
executive agreement   treaty
Executive Office of the President

1. An agreement between the President and the head of another country that does not require Senate approval is an ___?___ .

2. The term ___?___ is used to describe a person who was born within the borders of the United States.

3. A formal agreement between two countries, requiring Senate approval, is a ___?___ .

4. Every year, the President delivers the ___?___ to the Congress and the nation.

5. The ___?___ includes all of the advisers and agencies assisting the President.

Understanding Main Ideas

1. How long is a President's term of office? What is the maximum length of time that a President can remain in office?

2. What are the qualifications for a presidential candidate?

3. What are some of the informal qualifications for presidential candidates today?

4. How can a Vice President become President?

5. Explain the process of removing a President from office.

6. In what ways have the responsibilities of the President increased since the 1920s?

7. How does the President affect legislation?

8. Describe the President's role in making foreign policy.

9. What is the role of the National Security Council? The role of the Council of Economic Advisers?

10. What different kinds of decisions does a President make?

Critical Thinking

1. **Recognizing Cause and Effect.** It often happens that the President belongs to one political party while the majority in Congress belongs to another party. What are some of the advantages and disadvantages of this situation?

2. **Recognizing Bias.** Think about the informal requirements for becoming President. What groups of people are less likely to be elected to the office? Do all natural-born Americans have an equal opportunity to become President? Why or why not?

3. **Testing Conclusions.** Some people say that the President should be limited to one six-year term in office. This would allow Presidents to devote all their energies to the job, rather than spending months campaigning for reelection. Do you agree or disagree with this position? Why?

Practicing Skills

1. **Interpreting Pictures.** Bring to class some newspaper and magazine pictures of the President. Discuss with your classmates what the main idea or purpose of each picture seems to be. How can you tell?

2. **Making a Collage.** Collect pictures showing the various roles of the President. Put the pictures together in a collage for your class bulletin board.

3. **Writing a Biography.** Write a short biography of a minor party candidate for President. One example would be Eugene V. Debs, who ran for President on the Socialist ticket in 1920. Another example is Ron Paul, the Libertarian Party's candidate for President in 1988.

Focusing on Citizenship

1. **Researching Information.** Using the *Readers' Guide to Periodical Literature* as a source, do some research to find out what positions George Bush and Michael Dukakis took on some major issues in their 1988 election campaigns.

2. **Writing to the President.** As a class, choose a topic of national importance that concerns you, such as the nuclear arms race, drugs, higher education, or pollution. Send a letter to the President expressing your views on this topic and asking for a reply.

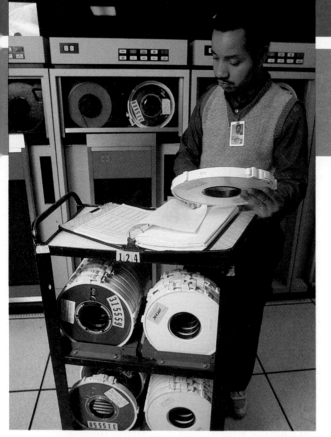

This worker processes computer tapes for the Internal Revenue Service, a part of the Treasury Department.

The Executive Agencies

Previewing the Chapter

How would you feel if companies were allowed to advertise their products with claims that were not true? Would you feel confident depositing your money in a bank if you had no insurance against losing the money? Advertising and banking are just two of the many areas monitored by the executive branch of the United States government. This chapter explores the structure of the executive branch and the services it provides for Americans.

■ **Before you read,** look up these key terms in the Glossary at the back of this book: *bureaucracy, Cabinet, government corporation, spoils system, merit system, diplomat.*

■ **As you read,** look for answers to these questions:
1. What is the President's Cabinet?
2. What are the four types of independent agencies within the executive branch?
3. When and why was the Civil Service created?

141

1 The Cabinet

As mentioned in Chapter 7, the President has many individuals and departments to help with the duties of the Presidency. In the previous chapter you read about the executive office of the President. In this chapter, you will learn about the work of the Cabinet (the executive departments), the independent agencies, and the independent regulatory commissions.

In the early years of the United States, Presidents had only three departments to assist them. They were the Departments of State, Treasury, and War. Several secretaries and clerks made up the rest of the executive branch. Today, about three million persons work in this branch. The number of departments has increased from the original three to 14, and there are now more than 50 separate agencies that employ thousands of people. The various agencies and commissions within the executive branch are sometimes called the **bureaucracy**.

Creating a Cabinet

The **Cabinet** is the name given to the group of persons who head the executive departments within the executive branch. From time to time, the number of departments increases or decreases. Today there are 14 departments—State, Treasury, Defense, Justice, Interior, Commerce, Labor, Agriculture, Housing and Urban Development, Transportation, Energy, Health and Human Services, Education, and Veterans Affairs. The Constitution does not mention a Cabinet. However, Article 2, Section 2 states that the President may "require the opinion, in writing, of the principal officer in each of the executive departments."

Cabinet officers, known as secretaries, are appointed by the President with the approval of the Senate. These officials serve as long as the President wants them. However, Cabinet officials usually stay in office as long as the President. Most Presidents expect Cabinet officers to support presidential policies. Failure to do so may mean dismissal. As a matter of fact, Cabinet officials usually resign if there is a disagreement with the President. In 1980, for example, Secretary of State Cyrus Vance resigned because he disagreed with President Carter over sending soldiers to rescue United States hostages held by the government of Iran.

The Executive Departments

The work of the executive departments is very important in the operation of the executive branch. The secretaries and their staffs keep government running from day to day. A brief summary of each department is given in the following sections.

President Bush congratulates Cabinet members Edwin Derwinski (Veterans Affairs), Samuel Skinner (Transportation), Louis Sullivan (Health and Human Services), and Manuel Lujan (Interior).

Department of State.   Foreign policy presents many problems in today's world. The Secretary of State and a large staff advise and assist the President in shaping and carrying out our foreign policy. The Department of State, therefore, is one of the most important in the Cabinet. Its primary goal in the conduct of foreign relations is to promote the long-range security and well-being of the United States. The Department of State negotiates treaties and agreements with foreign countries and represents the United States at international conferences.

Department of the Treasury.   If you look at a dollar bill, you will find the signatures of both the Treasurer of the United States and the Secretary of the Treasury. The Secretary of the Treasury supervises the collection of taxes and the coining and printing of money. The Secret Service is a part of the Treasury Department. The Secret Service guards the President, the Vice President, and their families.

Department of Defense.   At one time called the War Department, the Department of Defense organizes and trains all United States military forces. It collects information about the military strength of other countries and advises the President and Congress about our country's military needs. The Defense Department also provides military information to nations friendly to the United States.

Department of Justice.   The Attorney General, who heads this department, is the chief law officer of the United States government. The Justice Department enforces all federal law. It supervises the Federal Bureau of Investigation (FBI), our national crime-fighting agency. All federal prisons come under the direction of the Justice Department.

Department of the Interior. The building and operation of dams such as the Hoover Dam in Nevada, the highest dam in the United States, is one way the Department of the Interior works to conserve water, a precious natural resource of the United States. In addition to the conservation of water, the Interior Department carries out programs to protect soil, timber, and other natural resources. It also directs the activities of the National Park Service and the Bureau of Indian Affairs.

Department of Agriculture. Many of the activities of the Department of Agriculture are familiar. There is the purple USDA stamp on meat at the supermarket. This stamp means that the meat has been inspected and approved by the government. There is the food stamp program, which helps needy people buy food. There are grants of money to schools for breakfast and lunch programs. Most of the work of the Agriculture Department, however, is related to providing farmers with information on crop and soil improvement and on animal diseases. This executive department also helps farmers to market (sell) their goods and teaches them about new methods of farming.

Department of Commerce. Every ten years, the federal government takes a count of the people in the United States. This work is done by the Bureau of the Census, one of the agencies within the Department of Commerce. The chief purpose of the Commerce Department, however, is to promote and develop the foreign and domestic trade of the United States. This executive department also gives various kinds of help to small business firms and supervises the activities of the United States Merchant Marine.

Department of Labor. When created by Congress in 1913, the purpose of this department was described as "promoting the welfare of wage earners of the United States." To carry out this purpose, the Labor Department enforces federal laws that deal with the safety of workers, child labor, minimum wages, unemployment insurance, and worker's compensation (pay for workers injured on the job). The Labor Department also publishes a cost-of-living index which describes prices for the same items in different parts of the country.

Department of Housing and Urban Development (HUD). This executive department was created in 1965. Its goal is to help cities and other communities deal with the problems of housing and urban (city) living. To carry out this goal, HUD supervises the distribution of federal money for such things as rebuilding run-down parts of cities and replacing urban sewage systems. Special assistance is given to the elderly and also to low-income families to help them purchase homes.

Department of Transportation. This executive department assists the states in the development of a safe and efficient national transportation system—on land, air, and water. One agency within the department, the Federal Aviation Administration (FAA), is responsible for the safe operation of all private and commercial aircraft.

Department of Energy (DOE). The Department of Energy is one of the newest executive departments. It was established in 1977 to deal with the problems created by a shortage of oil, natural gas, and other sources of energy. It encourages the development of solar (sun) power and other different energy sources. The Energy Department also enforces federal laws relating to producing and distributing gasoline, oil, and natural gas.

Department of Education. This department was created in 1979. It was formerly part of the Department of Health, Educa-

SKILL BUILDER

Which executive departments were created in the same year the Constitution was adopted?

The Executive Cabinet

Department of State (1789)	Department of the Treasury (1789)	Department of Justice (1789)	Department of the Interior (1849)	Department of Agriculture (1862)
Department of Commerce (1903)	Department of Labor (1913)	Department of Defense (1949)	Department of Housing and Urban Development (1965)	Department of Transportation (1966)
Department of Energy (1977)	Department of Education (1979)	Department of Health and Human Services (1980)	Department of Veterans Affairs (1989)	

tion and Welfare. The Department of Education funds and administers programs dealing with a wide variety of educational matters. It also collects and distributes information about schools and colleges in the United States.

Department of Health and Human Services. This department was originally the Department of Health, Education, and Welfare, which was created in 1953. It directs social security, public health, welfare, and other programs. One agency within the department, the Food and Drug Administration (FDA), checks food, drugs, and cosmetics for possible dangers to health. Other agencies in the department provide services for physically or mentally handicapped people, alcoholics, drug addicts, and the poor.

The Department of Veterans Affairs. This department was established in 1989. The Department of Veterans Affairs employs about 240,000 people and serves the needs of more than 27 million veterans and their dependents. It also supplies services and benefits to survivors of veterans who have died. This department supervises a nationwide system of hospitals, medical clinics, and homes for disabled and aged veterans. In 1989, the Department of Veterans Affairs administered benefits totalling about $30 billion.

SECTION *1* *Review*

Defining Key Terms
1. Define: bureaucracy, Cabinet.

Recalling the Facts
2. How are Cabinet officials chosen?
3. What is the function of the Department of Labor? The Department of Energy?
4. How has the function of the executive departments grown and changed since the 19th century?

Reviewing the Main Idea
5. Answer "As you read . . ." question 1 on page 141: What is the President's Cabinet?

Critical Thinking
6. **Drawing Conclusions.** Should a Cabinet officer resign if he or she disagrees with the President over a public policy? Why or why not?

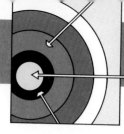

Sharpening Your Skills

Critical Thinking Skills

Making Comparisons

Suppose you wanted to understand the President's Cabinet today. In order to gain a better understanding of how it grew into what it is now, you might go back in history and read about the President's Cabinet in 1800. You might research the number of departments in each Cabinet, their functions, and their influence on decisions. You would thus be comparing the past Cabinet with the Cabinet today.

When people make comparisons, they identify the similarities and differences between two or more items. Making comparisons is one way people make sense of things. By placing items into categories (in the case of the Presidents' Cabinets, above, the categories are "past" and "present") and looking at how those categories are alike or different, we begin to see how items are related. Two things that may have appeared very similar at first may turn out to have important differences. Items that once seemed unrelated may turn out to be alike in many ways.

The following are some guidelines for making comparisons:

1. Choose the items you plan to compare carefully. The items being compared should be similar enough to warrant a comparison. Trying to compare an apple pie to a tiger will not give you much useful information.
2. Ask yourself: What is my reason for making this comparison? When making a comparison, it is important to know why you are comparing two or more items. If your purpose is clear you can then formulate questions to ask about the items being compared.
3. Ask the same questions about each item you are comparing. For example, it would not make much sense, when comparing two movies, to compare the theme song of one with the story line of the other.
4. Note the answers to your questions. Look at the ways in which the answers to each question are similar or different. When you are doing research it is sometimes helpful to write your answers down in list form. Another possibility is to place the information on a chart.
5. Draw conclusions based on your comparison. This is the final stage in making a comparison. Evaluate the similarities and differences that you have identified between items. Your conclusions may give you insight into a particular situation. In studying the President's Cabinet in 1800, for example, you may gain a more complete understanding of the President's Cabinet today. Your conclusions may also help you make choices. If you were comparing two candidates running for office, your findings about the candidates would help you decide whom to vote for.

Practicing Skills

1. Make a chart that compares three Cabinet departments. Set up columns with the headings *Department*, *General Purpose*, and *Specific Functions*. Then fill in appropriate information.
2. **Identifying Central Issues.** Make a list of five items that would be important to you when comparing candidates running for President.

2 The Independent Agencies

The **independent agencies** are another group of governmental units within the executive branch. These agencies, like the executive departments, help the President carry out the duties of the Presidency. The independent agencies are part of the executive branch, but they are separate from the executive departments. There are four types of independent agencies: the independent executive agencies, the independent regulatory commissions, the government corporations, and the Civil Service. The Civil Service will be described in Section 3 of this chapter.

The President appoints the heads of the independent agencies with the approval of the Senate. The independent agencies do not come under the control of the Cabinet, and most are largely free of control by the President. They perform special tasks outlined in laws passed by Congress. Many of the heads of independent agencies cannot be dismissed if they differ with the President. This gives them greater freedom of action than the secretaries of the executive departments.

Independent Executive Agencies

This group includes over 30 administrative units, some with billion dollar budgets and thousands of employees. Each agency provides a special service. Like Cabinet secretaries, the heads of the independent executive agencies serve as long as the President wants them.

Congress set up independent executive agencies because it wanted certain services to get special attention. *The Environmental Protection Agency* (EPA), for example, was created in 1970 to repair the damage that our smokestacks, exhaust pipes, and chemicals have caused to the nation's air, land, and water. *The National Aeronautics and Space Administration* (NASA) directed the program that placed astronauts on the moon. Today, NASA conducts research on space flights, develops space vehicles, and directs space flights.

Among the other independent executive agencies that provide important services to the people of the United States are the following:

The Federal Election Commission (FEC) administers and enforces the laws relating to all aspects of elections and campaigns, including financing.

The Commission on Civil Rights (CCR) works to bring about equal opportunity for all persons in voting, jobs, education, and housing. The commission investigates reports of discrimination and reports its findings to Congress and the President.

The National Mediation Board helps to settle disputes between airline and railroad workers and management.

The National Transportation Safety Board (NTSB) works to promote transportation safety.

The General Services Administration, sometimes called the "housekeeper" for the executive branch, purchases government supplies, manages federal buildings, and keeps public records.

The Small Business Administration (SBA) provides loans up to $500,000 to small businesses. These loans may be given to buy machinery or supplies, to assist in the building of a new

NASA launches the space shuttle Discovery from the Kennedy Space Center in Florida.

plant, or in some cases, to help a firm move to a better location. The SBA also helps minority businesses and businesses owned by women.

The *National Science Foundation* (NSF) promotes research in science. Sometimes the NSF provides grants of money to universities so that they can carry on specific research projects.

Some of the independent agencies are small and rarely heard about. Examples include the *Migratory Bird Conservation Commission* and the *American Battle Monuments Commission.*

Independent Regulatory Commissions

These commissions are called "regulatory" because they have the power to enforce national laws. Officials of the independent agencies are appointed by the President for periods of from four to fourteen years. Congress set the long-term appointments to prevent Presidents (during their four-year terms) from filling the agencies with only their appointees. Congress wanted these agencies to be free of presidential control.

Congress created the independent regulatory commissions because it felt there was a need to control certain activities in trade, business, science, and transportation. The congressional lawmakers believed that neither the courts nor they themselves could control these activities. They believed that specialists were needed who were trained in the activity that was to be regulated.

Congress sets down the general rules of regulatory policy for each independent regulatory commission, but it gives the directors of the commissions power to set standards based on the general rules. For example, a law passed by Congress forbids "false or misleading advertising." However, the law does not define the words "false" or "misleading." Definition of these words is left to the Federal Trade Commission (FTC), the independent regulatory commission created to enforce the law. The FTC has ruled, for example, that cigarettes may not be advertised as being "kind" to your throat. Such advertising is false and would mislead the public.

The decisions of the independent regulatory commissions have the force of law. A decision to fine or otherwise punish a lawbreaker may be challenged in a federal court, however. Some of the most important regulatory commissions are described below.

The Interstate Commerce Commission (ICC), established in 1887, was the first of the independent regulatory commissions. It was set up to regulate freight and passenger rates charged by the railroads. The demand for regulation came from farmers and other groups who objected to unfair practices and favoritism on the part of the railroads. Today the ICC supervises all transportation that crosses state lines. This includes transportation on trains, trucks, buses, and ships. A major goal of this commission is to ensure good service at fair rates.

The Consumer Products Safety Commission (CPSC) enforces regulations that forbid the sale of products harmful to buyers. For example, a recent ruling of the CPSC prevents the use of flammable material in clothing for children. The CPSC also conducts research on the safety of various products.

The Federal Communications Commission (FCC) gives licenses to all television and radio stations. It also rules on the rates that may be charged for interstate telephone and telegraph service.

The Farm Credit Administration (FCA) regulates bank loans and provides dependable credit to farmers, ranchers, and harvesters of fish and shellfish.

The Securities and Exchange Commission (SEC) makes rules for the buying and selling of stocks and bonds. These rules protect people who invest their money in stocks and bonds.

The Nuclear Regulatory Commission watches over the use of nuclear energy. It sets safety standards for the building and operation of nuclear power plants.

The Federal Energy Regulatory Commission (FERC) sets rates and charges for the transportation and sale of natural gas, for the transmission and sale of electricity, and for the licensing of hydroelectric power projects.

The Federal Reserve System serves as the central bank of the United States. It administers and sets policies for the nation's credit and monetary affairs.

The Federal Maritime Commission watches over rates, services and labor practices of United States ships taking part in foreign and offshore ocean commerce. The commission also runs an academy to train officers for the Merchant Marine.

The Federal Trade Commission (FTC) carries out a program to prevent unfair practices by business firms. It tries to prevent false or misleading advertising of consumer products. The FTC requires, for example, that packages be labeled correctly and that banks state the interest rate they charge to lend money. The FTC can prevent the merger (combining) of two or more large businesses if the merger will be harmful to other businesses or the public.

Government Corporations

Some of the independent agencies are government corporations (also called government authorities). A **government corporation** is a business that is owned and operated by the national government. Government corporations are largely self-directing, that is, they do not depend upon annual grants of money from Congress.

The TVA operates a system of power plants in the valley of the Tennessee River. TVA dams such as this one produce electricity and help to control floods.

One of the largest government corporations is the Tennessee Valley Authority (TVA). The TVA built and now operates a system of power plants in the valley of the Tennessee River. The United States government owns the dams and plants and sells the electricity they produce. Residents of areas in and surrounding the Tennessee Valley may buy electric power directly from the TVA. In addition to their usefulness in producing electricity, the TVA dams are also useful in controlling floods.

Other government corporations are the United States Postal Service and the National Passenger Corporation, otherwise known as Amtrak. Amtrak is responsible for the operation and improvement of railroad service between cities. Amtrak's 38,400-kilometer (24,000-mile) system serves more than 500 station locations. About 21 million people traveled on Amtrak trains in fiscal year 1987. The Postal Service is committed to providing swift and reliable mail delivery both within the United States and to and from foreign countries. The Postal Service handles more than 153 billion pieces of mail each year.

Ten Independent Regulatory Commissions

Interstate Commerce Commission (ICC)

(created in 1887, 11 members, 7-year term)

Regulates rates and services of interstate carriers—highways, railroads, waterways.

Federal Communications Commission (FCC)

(created in 1934, 7 members, 7-year term)

Regulates interstate and foreign communications— radio, TV, telephone, telegraph, and cable; grants licenses.

Federal Reserve System

(created in 1913, 7-member Board of Governors, 14-year term)

Establishes banking policies; influences use of credit in economy.

Federal Maritime Commission (FMC)

(created in 1936, 5 members, 5-year term)

Controls rates and services of water carriers, both foreign and domestic commerce.

Federal Trade Commission (FTC)

(created in 1914, 5 members, 7-year term)

Seeks to prevent unfair business practices, price fixing, false advertising.

Consumer Product Safety Commission (CPSC)

(created in 1972, 5 members, 5-year term)

Establishes safety standards for consumer products.

Farm Credit Administration (FCA)

(created in 1933, 3 members, 6-year term)

Regulates bank loans and provides dependable credit to farmers, ranchers, and harvesters of aquatic products.

Nuclear Regulatory Commission (NRC)

(created in 1974, 5 members, 5-year term)

Licenses and regulates civil and military uses of nuclear power.

Securities and Exchange Commission (SEC)

(created in 1934, 5 members, 5-year term)

Regulates buying and selling of stocks and bonds (securities).

Federal Energy Regulatory Commission (FERC)

(created in 1977, 5 members, 4-year term)

Sets rates and charges for the transportation and sale of natural gas and the transmission and sale of electricity and the licensing of hydroelectric power.

SECTION 2 *Review*

Defining Key Terms
    1. Define: independent agency, government corporation.

Recalling the Facts
    2. What are some of the differences between independent executive agencies and regulatory commissions?

    3. What are three examples of government corporations?

Reviewing the Main Idea
    4. Answer "As you read . . ." question 2 on page 141: What are the four types of independent agencies within the executive branch?

Critical Thinking
    5. Testing Conclusions. Do you agree or disagree that the United States has too much government regulation? Explain your answer.

3 The Civil Service

What is a government worker? Perhaps you think of a mail carrier or a clerk or janitor who works in a government office. Actually, the federal government employs almost every kind of worker that private industry does. The United States Forest Service, for example, hires botanists, biologists, and other specialists in science. The Department of Veterans Affairs hires nurses and physical therapists for its hospitals and medical centers. The Bureau of Indian Affairs hires teachers for reservation schools. All together, there are more than 2,000 different jobs available in the federal government.

A Civil Service Is Formed

More persons work for the federal government than for any other employer in the country. These government workers get their jobs in different ways. The President and members of Congress, of course, are elected. Several thousand workers are appointed by the President, including high officials such as Cabinet officers and ambassadors. Nearly 90 percent of those who work for executive branch agencies, however, receive their jobs through the Civil Service System. The Civil Service is made up of persons employed by the federal government who are not members of the military service.

PEOPLE HELPING PEOPLE

Skid Row Samaritan

Michael Greenberg's dad was a baker in Brooklyn, New York, more than 50 years ago. He used to tuck a coffee cake or a sandwich into a customer's bag without the customer knowing. This was his secret gift.

The father's generous example has guided the son. Greenberg, now in his sixties, is a retired advertising executive who has made a habit of handing out free gloves to poor people since 1965. Each year in late fall he buys 300 pairs of gloves with his own money. Then he sets out on the streets of New York City to find the most deserving men and women to get them.

Greenberg finds his people among the down-and-out drifters of Manhattan's Bowery, a rough neighborhood long-known as Skid Row. He may come across an old man muttering on a bench. He will then hold out a pair of woolen gloves and say, "Take them, please. They're free. They're a gift. No strings attached."

Why did Greenberg pick gloves as a gift? Gloves are a powerful symbol, he says, "because being warm is being well-off and being cold is being poor."

The Civil Service was created by the Pendleton Act of 1883. This law was passed to replace the spoils system. Under the **spoils system**, government jobs were given to party workers as rewards for their loyal service. Most of these persons kept their jobs only as long as their political party was in power. A change of President meant that these workers would be replaced by other workers as the new presidential administration made its own appointments. With the creation of the Civil Service System, however, this practice was changed. Workers no longer have to depend upon political favors as a way of getting government jobs. They can go to work for the government as a lifetime career.

Today, the Office of Personnel Management and the Merit Systems Protection Board make sure that federal hiring and promotion are based on merit. A **merit system** is one in which people are hired for a job and/or promoted because of the ability to perform, not because of their personal contacts. The ability to perform is often determined by a test. For example, a typist will take a speed test, and translators of foreign languages will be tested on their knowledge of languages.

Federal workers have paid vacations, sick-leave benefits, and a retirement plan. Furthermore, the government has an excellent record as an employer of minorities. As of 1989, more than 26 percent of all federal employees were members of minority groups.

The Civil Service Commission is in charge of federal jobs. This Civil Service employee is inspecting damage caused by a hurricane.

Federal Workers

Most people who work for the federal government intend to make a career of it. A change in the national administration does not affect them. Many hold clerical, secretarial, or other minor positions. Many others are highly trained in law, science, mathematics, or other fields. The work of all these employees usually does not involve policy making. They perform a number of required tasks, but they do not make decisions about government policy.

Among other government career workers are the several million persons who have chosen the military services as their life's work. The opportunities for advancement in the armed forces are similar to opportunities in other government jobs. All the military services provide education and training.

There are also career jobs in the foreign service. **Diplomats** are persons such as ambassadors or consular officials who represent the United States in other countries. Other jobs in the foreign service are for clerks, typists, drivers, mechanics, and office workers. The top diplomatic officials are appointed to their positions by the President. However, many others prepare for jobs in the foreign service by studying foreign languages and other helpful subjects at a university. After graduation and after passing an examination, they take a three-month course at the Foreign Service Institute in Washington, D.C. Once on the job, promotion is based on performance.

Ambassadors represent the United States to other nations. Here is Vernon Walters, United States Representative to the United Nations.

SECTION 3 *Review*

Defining Key Terms

1. Define: spoils system, merit system, diplomat.

Recalling the Facts

2. What are some of the jobs government workers do?

3. What law ended the spoils system?

4. What are two fields often chosen by people who plan to make a career in government?

Reviewing the Main Idea

5. Answer "As you read . . ." question 3 on page 141: When and why was the Civil Service created?

Critical Thinking

6. Demonstrating Reasoned Judgment. War veterans are given five extra points on Civil Service exams. Wounded veterans are given ten. Explain whether or not you think this policy is fair, and why.

Government and Law

Federal Aid to Farmers

Farming is a gigantic business in the United States. In 1987, farm income totaled more than $42 billion. About half of all the land in the United States is used for farming. Much of the world's farm output, including 25 percent of the beef and 15 percent of the grain, milk, and eggs, comes from the United States.

These figures might suggest that the picture of American farming today is a rosy one. But, although today's farmers are making more money than ever before, they owe more money, too. Farmers today are facing a debt crisis. The question of what the federal government should do about it has raised considerable debate.

These farm workers are harvesting a carrot crop in California.

The origin of federal aid. Government plays a major role in our nation's agriculture. The Department of Agriculture (USDA) is one of the largest departments in the executive branch. The USDA runs programs and services for farmers.

Through the USDA, the federal government gives a great deal of financial aid to the farming industry. In 1987, farmers received more than $23 billion in aid. In the same year, the government loaned another $158 billion that farmers must repay.

The federal government hasn't always provided aid to farmers. Federal aid to farmers began only during the 1930s. Before that, the USDA limited itself largely to research. The need for farmers' aid, however, had been building up since about 1914, the year World War I began.

During World War I, foreign demand for American-grown food skyrocketed. This forced prices to rise. Eager to sell food to our allies, farmers produced more. Many borrowed a lot of money to enlarge their farms.

Then the war ended. Demand from overseas quickly dried up as European countries rebuilt their own farms. As demand fell, so did prices. Many American farmers were left with huge debts to repay and not enough earnings.

The Great Depression of the 1930s brought more trouble to the farming industry (see page 404). Prices for farm goods dropped so low that many farmers were not able to make their mortgage payments. The banks that had loaned them money took over their farms. By 1932, American farmers were earning less than one-third what they had earned in 1919.

The federal government stepped in to help. President Franklin D. Roosevelt created several agencies within the USDA to help farmers. For example, one agency gave financial aid to farmers who agreed to cut production. It worked on the assumption that when supply falls, demand rises. So do prices.

Roosevelt also created USDA programs designed to provide farmers with low-interest loans. For example, the Farmers Home Administration was created for small farm owners who might not qualify for a loan anywhere else. The Commodity Credit Corporation also made loans to farmers. These federal aid programs did much to get America's farmers back on their feet.

The state of farming today. The federal government continued to allow farmers to borrow a tremendous amount of money. An unfortunate result has been the most recent chapter in the farm crisis—the debt crisis.

The current farm crisis bears eerie similarity to the problem in the 1930s. During the 1970s, food prices rose partly because overseas countries wanted more American-grown food. Farmers borrowed huge sums of money to increase their output.

In the early 1980s, however, foreign demand for American products fell. Thus, food prices fell. Interest rates on borrowed money rose. The result was that farmers were getting less money for their goods —money they needed to pay back loans.

Hundreds of small farmers fell deeply into debt and ended up losing their farms to their creditors. Many rural banks were hurt because they lost the money they had loaned to the farmers. In 1985, 42 rural banks went out of business. Farmers who sold their farms lost money, too. In the early 1980s, the value of farmland fell by as much as 60 percent in parts of Iowa, Nebraska, and Minnesota.

The farmers' debt crisis of the early 1980s caused the most problems for farmers and bankers since the Great Depression. Many farmers blamed the Reagan Administration for reorganizing federal aid programs and proposing financial cuts.

By the late 1980s, life on the farm had improved a bit. Congress approved $28 million of federal aid for farmers in 1985. Crop prices rose slightly. Land values improved. Debt costs dropped slightly. An increase in farm exports to foreign countries caused farm income to rise by 30 percent from mid-1986 to mid-1987.

Most politicians now believe that the cost of federal farm programs is too high. They believe that the programs are not helping the farmers who need help most —the family farmers. They say most federal aid ends up in the hands of large farming companies. Critics say that the nation's agricultural policy badly needs a major overhaul. But how do you cut back federal aid without driving farmers into bankruptcy and hurting rural banks?

Questions to think about

1. Do you think that the federal government should continue to aid farmers? Explain your answer.
2. How does the national and world economy affect farmers?

CHAPTER SUMMARY

Section 1   In addition to the Executive Office, the executive branch of the federal government also includes the Cabinet, the independent agencies, and the Civil Service. The Cabinet is a group of persons who head the 14 executive departments. The Cabinet members, called secretaries, give the President advice and help in the daily operation of the government. The executive departments include State, Treasury, Defense, Justice, Interior, Agriculture, Commerce, Labor, Housing and Urban Development, Transportation, Energy, Education, Health and Human Services, and Veterans Affairs.

Section 2   There are four types of independent agencies within the executive branch: independent executive agencies, independent regulatory commissions, government corporations, and the Civil Service. These agencies are largely free of control by the President or the Cabinet. The independent executive agencies provide special services and programs, such as protection of civil rights and loans to small businesses. The independent regulatory commissions enforce laws in areas such as trade, business, science, and transportation. Government corporations are businesslike operations that are owned and directed by the federal government.

Section 3   Most federal workers are hired through the Civil Service system. The Civil Service's merit system replaced the spoils system of hiring government workers. Workers are now hired and promoted based on their ability and performance.

Reviewing Key Terms

On a separate sheet of paper, use the following terms to complete the sentences below.

merit system	government corporation
Cabinet	bureaucracy
spoils system	diplomat

1. Under the ___?___, most federal workers are hired or promoted on the basis of their ability to do the job.

2. The Tennessee Valley Authority (TVA) is an example of a ___?___.

3. A large group of agencies and government workers is called a ___?___.

4. The system of giving federal jobs to loyal party workers was called the ___?___.

5. The group of 14 heads of executive departments is called the ___?___.

6. A ___?___ works in the foreign service.

Understanding Main Ideas

1. What officials make up the Cabinet?

2. Who appoints Cabinet members? How long do Cabinet members hold office?

3. What does the Attorney General do?

4. Which department helps the President develop foreign policy?

5. Which department works to conserve water and other natural resources?

6. Which department helps cities manage their special problems?

7. What are two examples of independent executive agencies?

8. Why has Congress created independent regulatory commissions?

9. Why are regulatory commission officials appointed for long terms?

10. Which regulatory commission supervises the building and operation of nuclear power plants?

11. Which regulatory commission tries to prevent false or misleading advertising?

12. What is the Civil Service?

Critical Thinking

1. **Testing Conclusions.** Give evidence for or against this conclusion: Some kinds of jobs can be done better by the federal government than by private industry.

2. **Predicting Consequences.** Unlike other workers, federal employees are not allowed to strike. Should they be? What might happen if they were?

3. **Demonstrating Reasoned Judgment.** One federal agency, the National Aeronautics and Space Administration (NASA), spent about $25 billion to put astronauts on the moon. Some people argue that the money should have been spent to provide decent housing, jobs, medical service, and other needs on earth. What do you think?

Practicing Skills

1. **Making Comparisons.** Contact your state employment office. Ask for job information about clerical workers or hospital workers in both the federal government and private industry. Make a chart comparing wages, benefits, and other working conditions.

2. **Analyzing the News.** Find at least eight news stories about issues or events involving independent executive agencies, departments, or regulatory commissions. For each story, write a paragraph telling the role of the federal agency or department in this event.

Focusing on Citizenship

1. **Doing Field Research.** Visit the closest Civil Service office and ask about federal job opportunities. List the qualifications needed for the most interesting jobs.

2. **Having a Guest Speaker.** Invite a local business leader to your class to discuss the ways in which the government aids and/or regulates his or her firm.

3. **Writing to a Cabinet Member.** Write to the head of an executive department that interests you. Ask for information about what type of work the department does.

CHAPTER 9

The Federal Court System

This impressive building has been the home of the Supreme Court since 1935.

Previewing the Chapter

The Supreme Court today is a highly respected branch of government, entrusted with the job of evaluating complex Constitutional issues. The original Court, however, had little work and was actually housed in a large broom closet! The Supreme Court is the highest level in the federal court system of the United States. This chapter explains the structure and function of this federal court system.

- **Before you read,** look up these key terms in the Glossary at the back of this book: *court, suit, plaintiff, defendant, appeal, jury, verdict, brief.*

- **As you read,** look for answers to these questions:
  1. What kinds of cases are heard in federal courts?
  2. What is the difference between a civil case and a criminal case?
  3. What are the three main divisions of federal courts?
  4. What is judicial review, and what case established this procedure?

1 The Jurisdiction of Federal Courts

In our society, conflicts and disputes often occur. These disputes may be between individuals or between groups of people. Our court system has been established to allow the peaceful, legal settlement of these disputes. Thus, when individuals or groups of people cannot agree about solutions to serious disputes, they turn to the courts.

Courts are places where disputes or arguments about the law are settled. In one kind of dispute, a person is accused of breaking a law, but he or she denies the charge. In another kind of dispute, one person accuses another of wrongdoing. Each of these kinds of dispute is called a court case, or **suit**. The word *suit* is used because one person or group of persons is suing another.

The Work of the Courts

Courts are unfamiliar places to most of us. Many people, in fact, have never been inside a courtroom. They get their information about the courts from newspapers, books, magazines, movies, or television programs. As a result, they believe that most courts deal with sensational cases involving murder or wrongdoing by public officials. However, such cases are only a tiny part of the workload of the courts. Most court cases deal with helping ordinary citizens settle disputes with other people. Sometimes they deal with cases involving the government. For example, many people have raised questions about some of the things that are going on in the schools. People have asked the courts to decide whether schools legally can start the day with a school prayer. In the above example, parents objected to the reading of a daily prayer in the public schools of New York City. When school officials refused to stop reading the prayers, the parents took them to the courts. The parents and school officials each presented arguments for or against the prayer reading. In time, the United States Supreme Court ruled that the reading of a prayer went against the constitutional principle of separation of church and state. The justices on the Court ruled that the reading of a prayer was a religious ceremony. They said that because it was a religious ceremony, prayer reading should not take place in a public school.

Jurisdiction of the Courts

Disputes about practices in the school system are not the only cases heard in federal courts. Many other kinds of cases are heard as well. Article 3 of the Constitution sets the jurisdiction of the federal courts. **Jurisdiction** refers to the types of cases

Federal courts may hear cases involving ships on the open sea or along U.S. coastal waters. The Soviet ship on the right is shown being taken into custody.

a court can hear and decide. Federal courts may hear cases which deal with certain subject matter, that is, all cases that:

- come under the provisions of the United States Constitution
- come under any of the laws passed by Congress
- involve treaties made by the United States government
- involve ships on the open sea or along the coastal waters of the United States

Federal courts also hear all cases involving persons if the cases deal with:

- two or more states
- the United States government and a state
- the United States government and a citizen of any state
- two or more citizens of different states
- ambassadors, consuls, or public ministers

In most of the cases listed above, the federal courts are said to have exclusive jurisdiction. **Exclusive jurisdiction** means that the case can be tried only in a federal court. For example, a federal court has exclusive jurisdiction in any dispute involving the ambassador of another country. No state or local court can hear such a case. Likewise, crew members accused of bringing drugs into the United States aboard a ship must be tried in a federal court.

In some of the above cases, however, there is concurrent jurisdiction. **Concurrent jurisdiction** means that the right to try certain cases is shared by both federal and state courts. Many such cases deal with disputes between citizens of different states. The amount of money involved determines whether the case is heard in a federal or state court. Thus, if a citizen of Maine is suing a citizen of Texas over a debt of $2,000, either a Maine or Texas

It is against federal law to smuggle drugs into the United States. These customs agents are examining containers in which they found drugs.

court can have jurisdiction. However, if the amount is over $10,000, a federal court has jurisdiction.

A case involving kidnapping is another example of concurrent jurisdiction. Kidnapping is a violation of state law, but if a kidnapped person is taken across a state line, a federal as well as a state law is broken. It is possible for an accused kidnapper to be tried in both a state and a federal court. People who break certain drug laws can also be tried in both federal and state courts.

Some people feel that trying a person in both a state and a federal court is double jeopardy. The courts have ruled, however, that trial by both a federal and a state court (for the same crime) is not double jeopardy.

SECTION 1 Review

Defining Key Terms
1. Define: court, suit, jurisdiction, exclusive jurisdiction, concurrent jurisdiction.

Recalling the Facts
2. What kinds of cases are the major work load of courts?
3. What cases fall under the jurisdiction of several courts?

Reviewing the Main Idea
4. Answer "As you read . . ." question 1 on page 162: What kinds of cases are heard in federal courts?

Critical Thinking
5. **Demonstrating Reasoned Judgment.** Could a modern society exist without a court system? Explain.

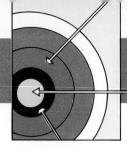

Sharpening Your Skills

Critical Thinking Skills

Distinguishing Fact from Opinion

Lawyer: Where were you on the night of May 12?

Witness: I was at home, watching television with my brother.

Is the statement made by this witness a fact or an opinion? How can you tell the difference between facts and opinions? In a courtroom trial, facts are crucial to the outcome of the case. The judge and jury must base their decisions on facts, not opinions. Facts and opinions are also a part of everyday citizenship. Knowing how to tell them apart can help you to become a fully informed citizen. Whether you are reading news articles or listening to political speeches, this is a valuable skill.

A fact is something that actually happened or can be proven true. The information that proves a fact is called evidence. A fact is true regardless of whether or not people believe it or know about it. An opinion, on the other hand, is something that a person or a group of people believes. An opinion may be true—if it is based on facts—or it may be false—if it is based mainly on wishes or prejudices.

There are certain clue words that can help you to recognize a fact or an opinion. A statement that contains the words *I think, should,* or *ought to* is probably an opinion. A statement that begins with words such as *Studies show that* or *From the evidence it is clear that* is probably a fact. Of course, you must always be prepared to investigate and interpret the evidence for yourself if you want to be sure that something really is a fact.

Consider the following statements:

1. Sandra Day O'Connor is the first

woman to serve on the Supreme Court.

2. The Supreme Court should have at least four women justices.

How could you prove that the first statement is a fact? One way would be to check a list of all the Supreme Court Justices appointed before O'Connor. If none are women, the statement is a fact. Indeed, evidence does show that O'Connor is the first woman on the Supreme Court. Therefore the statement is a fact.

The second statement, however, is not based purely on facts. It expresses a personal opinion about how many women *ought to* be on the Supreme Court. Therefore, the statement is an opinion.

Practicing Skills

Using what you have just read, answer the following questions on a separate sheet of paper.

1. Determine whether the following statements are facts or opinions. If you decide that a statement is a fact, tell how you would prove it.
   a. Washington, D.C., is located between Virginia and Maryland.
   b. Washington, D.C., is the most beautiful city in the United States.
2. **Distinguishing False from Accurate Images.** Based on what you have read so far in this chapter, tell which statement below is a false image of the kinds of cases courts handle:
   a. Courts deal mostly with cases involving murders or political scandals.
   b. Courts deal mostly with relatively minor disputes among citizens.

2 The Courts and the Law

As mentioned in Chapter 1, a law is a rule or regulation passed by Congress or by a state legislature. A law places certain limits on people or tells them how to behave. When courts settle disputes, they often must interpret, or explain, the law.

Interpretation of the Law

Why is it necessary to interpret the law? The chief reason is that the meaning of some laws is not very clear. The Eighth Amendment to the Constitution, for example, forbids the use of cruel punishment. People, however, disagree over the exact meaning of the word "cruel." Some say that the death penalty is a cruel punishment. Others say that torture is the only punishment that is truly cruel. In the case of *Furman* v. *Georgia* (1972), the Supreme Court ruled that the death penalty may be used as a punishment for certain crimes. As part of this decision, the Court also warned that the provisions of the law (providing for a death penalty) must apply equally to all persons.

Many times the laws passed by Congress are purposely stated in very general, not exact, terms. The income tax laws are an example. Congress passed the laws which state how personal income taxes are to be collected. However, officials of the Internal Revenue Service (IRS), the tax collection agency, are allowed to make decisions about carrying out the details of the laws. In practice, officials of IRS say exactly what the income tax laws mean. If a taxpayer disagrees with the IRS officials, then it may be up to the courts to settle the disagreement.

Kinds of Laws

The courts must deal with different kinds of laws. Many laws are statutory laws. **Statutory laws** are passed by a federal, state, or local legislature, and then written down. Laws that forbid the sale of certain drugs are examples of statutory laws.

A second type of law is **constitutional law**, law based on the United States Constitution. Supreme Court decisions which interpret the Constitution are considered part of constitutional law. The Court actually says what the Constitution means about the crime of treason, for example.

There is a third kind of law called **common law**. Common law developed many centuries ago in England. It is often called judge-made law because rulings made by judges in the past are used to decide present cases. Such past rulings are called **precedents**. These rulings have been made over and over again so that they become common ways of explaining how laws apply in particular cases.

Fourth and finally, there is **administrative law**. It is made up of the various rules and regulations of governmental agencies. A ruling by the Department of Agriculture that forbids the use of a certain pesticide (chemical) in farming would be an example.

Civil and Criminal Law

The four kinds of law discussed above are used in courts to settle disputes. For the purpose of court procedure, however, these four types of laws are broken down into two main categories—civil law and criminal law. Cases in **civil law** deal with disputes between private persons or between citizens and their government. Divorce laws are one example. In a civil case, the person making the complaint is called the **plaintiff**. The other party is the **defendant**.

Cases in **criminal law** deal with crimes. Laws related to robbery of the mails, murder, or kidnapping are examples. In a criminal case, the government is always the accuser, or the **prosecution**. The person being charged with a crime is the defendant, or accused.

Due Process of Law

In our system of justice, protection of individual rights is a major goal. The Fifth and Fourteenth Amendments contain a clause (or part) that describes this protection by the words **due process of law**.

Accused persons are guaranteed the right to a public trial.

The due process clause has two meanings. One meaning is that the government cannot take away a person's life, liberty, or property except according to the rule of law. Another meaning refers to **procedural rights**. These are the rights that apply to the steps, or procedures, in the trial of persons accused of a crime. For example, accused persons are guaranteed the right to be informed of the crime they are charged with. They are guaranteed the right to a public trial and the right to remain silent during the trial if they wish to do so. They are entitled to confront their accusers and to question them. They are entitled to have witnesses appear in their behalf as well as to an impartial (fair) judge and jury. Accused persons also have the right to have lawyers who will defend them. The court must provide a lawyer, without charge, for those who cannot afford one. Taken together, all of these rights are meant to guarantee a fair trial.

A fair trial is a goal that is not always reached. As in any other human activity, mistakes can happen in court proceedings. A mistake by a judge or other court official can lead to an unfair trial for the accused. For this reason, the system of justice in the United States allows for appeals. An **appeal** is a request to have a decision by a trial court reviewed by a higher court. Those who make the appeal hope to have the trial court decision reversed and a new trial ordered.

SECTION 2 *Review*

Defining Key Terms
1. Define: statutory law, Constitutional law, common law, precedent, administrative law, civil law, plaintiff, defendant, criminal law, prosecution, due process of law, procedural rights, appeal.

Recalling the Facts
2. What are four kinds of law?
3. What kinds of guarantees are given to a person accused of a crime?

Reviewing the Main Idea
4. Answer "As you read . . ." question 2 on page 162: What is the difference between a civil case and a criminal case?

Critical Thinking
5. **Making Comparisons.** How does statutory law differ from common law?

3 Organization of the Federal Court System

Article 3 of the United States Constitution created the federal court system. In 1789, Congress passed the Judiciary Act, which provided for 13 district courts. Later, other district courts were added.

Today, the federal court system has three main divisions—the district courts, the appellate, or appeals courts (including the United States Supreme Court), and a number of special courts.

The District Courts

The **district courts** are the federal trial courts. They are placed around the country in 91 districts. Each state has at least one district court, and the larger states have three or four. The District of Columbia has one, as does Puerto Rico. Each district court has one judge or more, depending upon the number of cases that are heard each year.

District courts are generally known as courts of **original jurisdiction** because most federal cases begin there. Such cases include criminal suits involving counterfeiting or kidnapping, or civil cases involving bankruptcy or copyright laws.

Decisions are made in the district courts by either a judge or a jury. A **jury** is a panel of citizens, usually 12, who come to a **verdict** (decision) of guilty or innocent based on the evidence presented to them during a trial.

Appellate Courts

The **appeals courts** are said to have **appellate jurisdiction** because they hear cases appealed from the district courts or other courts. There are no juries in appeals cases. It is common practice for three judges to review a case. The judges reach a decision by vote. In the process of review, the judges look only for errors of law that may have happened during the original trial. Errors of law occur when rules of trial procedure are not followed correctly. The refusal of a judge to allow any witnesses to testify in behalf of a defendant would be an example of an error of law. Another would be the failure of a court to allow a defendant to question his or her accuser.

The United States is divided into 11 judicial districts, or **circuits.** Several district courts are assigned to every circuit. For each circuit there is a court of appeals. There is also one appeals court for the District of Columbia. The final court of appeals in the United States is the Supreme Court. It is the highest court in our land. The Supreme Court is discussed in Section 4 of this chapter.

A jury is a panel of citizens who come to a verdict of guilty or innocent based on the evidence presented to them during a trial.

These courts are called "special" because they hear only particular types of cases. The special courts include:

U.S. Claims Court. Persons wishing to sue the United States may do so in this court. Suits against the government arise for a variety of reasons. An example would be damage to a person's property by an Air Force plane or a truck of the Postal Service. When money must be paid for the damage, Congress has to approve of the amount. Usually, approval is given as a matter of course. There are 16 judges assigned to the claims court.

U.S. Tax Court. This court handles only civil cases involving disputes over how the tax laws are to be applied. For example, if the heir to a family fortune felt that the federal inheritance tax was figured incorrectly, the case could be taken to this court. There are 19 judges assigned to this tax court.

U.S. Court of International Trade. This court handles cases involving imports. For example, the decision of a customs agent to classify imported ceramic dishes as works of art rather than as ordinary plates might be challenged in this court. All cases involving "dumping" are also handled by the Court of International Trade. Dumping is a practice in which one country ships products to another country and offers them at a price below the current market price. Dumping is unfair because it makes it difficult for local producers of the product to compete in the marketplace. The court has a chief judge and eight judges, not more than five of whom may belong to any one political party.

Special Courts

U.S. Court of Military Appeals. This court reviews court-martial (military trial) convictions in the Army, Navy, or other armed services. Its jurisdiction is limited to criminal cases. The court consists of three civilian judges appointed by the President. Since it is usually the final appeal of cases under military law, the court is sometimes called "the soldier's Supreme Court."

Territorial Courts. these are courts located in the United States territories of Guam, the Virgin Islands, and the Northern Mariana Islands. The work of these courts is similar to that of local courts in the 50 states.

The Judges

Judges are in charge of court hearings. It is their job to see that court procedures are orderly. They make sure that both sides have a fair chance to present their cases. Judges also give the final approval (or disapproval) of each person called to serve on a jury. While a trial is going on, judges may explain a law to the jurors or to one of the lawyers. After both sides have presented their cases, the judge instructs the jurors about how the law ap-

SKILL BUILDER What are the benefits and drawbacks of appointing judges to lifetime terms?

The Federal Court System

Court	Number of Courts	Number of Judges	Term of Judges
District Courts	91	563	Life
Appeals Courts	12	168	Life
Supreme Court	1	9	Life
Claims Court	1	16	15 years
Tax Court	1	19	12 years
Court of International Trade	1	9	Life
Court of Military Appeals	1	3	15 years
Territorial Courts	3	4	10 years

plies to the trial. This instruction is an important part of the procedure, since jurors are expected to make a decision based on law rather than on feelings or opinions.

Judges have other duties. Sometimes they are asked to issue search warrants. They also issue injunctions. An **injunction** is a court order that forbids (or directs) some course of action. For example, judges sometimes issue injunctions ordering striking workers back to their jobs until the strike is settled in court.

Federal judges are appointed by the President, subject to approval by the Senate. The Constitution set no qualifications for federal judges. Almost all Presidents, however, have chosen judges who are members of their own political parties.

Judges serve for life or for as long as they exhibit good behavior. "Good behavior" means that a judge is honest and fair in the performance of her or his duties. Lifetime appointments mean that judges cannot be dismissed if they make decisions unpopular with the administration in power.

Judges can be dismissed from their positions only by the process of impeachment. (See Chapter 3.) Up to the present, only nine federal judges have been impeached, and only four of these have been found guilty.

The salary of federal judges ranges from $89,500 per year in the district courts to $115,000 per year for the Chief Justice of the United States Supreme Court. A judge's salary cannot be reduced during her or his term of office—another requirement designed to preserve the independence of judges. Congress cannot use salary as a means of influencing court decisions.

Constance Baker Motley, a judge of the U.S. district court in New York.

After 191 years and 101 male justices, President Ronald Reagan appointed a woman to the Supreme Court. In 1981, Sandra Day O'Connor became the first woman to serve on the Court. Justice O'Connor served on the Arizona court of appeals before her appointment to the Supreme Court.

Judges are assisted in their work by court officers. Each federal court has a clerk who keeps a record of the court proceedings. There are secretaries, probation officers, and court reporters. United States marshals make arrests, serve legal papers, and hold accused persons until their trial.

SECTION 3 *Review*

Defining Key Terms
1. Define: district court, original jurisdiction, jury, verdict, appeals court, appellate jurisdiction, circuit, injunction.

Recalling the Facts
2. What types of cases are heard in the special courts?
3. What are some of the duties of a judge?

Reviewing the Main Idea
4. Answer "As you read . . ." question 3 on page 162: What are the three main divisions of federal courts?

Critical Thinking
5. **Demonstrating Reasoned Judgment.** The Constitution does not set any definite qualifications for federal judges. What qualifications do you think they should have?

4 The United States Supreme Court

The United States Supreme Court (often called the High Court) is the only court created by the Constitution. The High Court is made up of a Chief Justice and eight Associate Justices. The justices are appointed by the President (upon approval of the Senate) for life. From time to time, Congress has increased or decreased the membership of the Court. But the present number (nine) has remained the same since 1869. In 1937, President Franklin D.

Roosevelt urged Congress to increase the membership to 15. FDR's reason for this proposal was that the Court had declared some of the President's favorite legislation unconstitutional. By appointing new members who agreed with his way of thinking, FDR hoped to change the direction of Court rulings. The Congress refused.

Jurisdiction of the Court

Article 3 of the Constitution defines the jurisdiction of the Supreme Court. Two types of cases come within the original jurisdiction of the Supreme Court—first, all disputes between two or more states; second, all cases involving ambassadors or ministers of other countries. Both types of cases are rare, however; they form only a small part of the caseload of the High Court.

In all other cases, the Supreme Court has appellate jurisdiction. Appeals come to the Court from federal, district, appellate, and special courts. Appeals also may be made to the Supreme Court from the highest state courts.

Most cases reach the Supreme Court through a request for a **writ of *certiorari*** (a Latin word meaning "let us be informed"). The High Court is requested to review a decision made by a lower court. This happens if it seems that an error was made in the trial proceedings in the lower court. If the Supreme Court agrees to the request, a writ of *certiorari* is issued. In effect, this writ means: "Send us a record of the case." The Court hears only a fraction of such appeals. Whatever the source, the Supreme Court is the last court of appeal. Its decisions become the law of the land.

Early in our history, one question of Supreme Court jurisdiction was not quite clear. Some years after the adoption of the Constitution, a question arose: Does the Supreme Court have the power to nullify (cancel) a law passed by Congress? The year was 1803. Thomas Jefferson, who was President at the time, had a firm belief that the answer to that question was no. However, others in positions of power were just as firm in believing that the answer was yes. One of these was John Marshall, Chief Justice of the Supreme Court.

The question of jurisdiction involved an action of President John Adams. In his last night at the White House, Adams stayed up late signing commissions for jobs for members of his party. Some of these papers were lost, including one that made a man named William Marbury a justice of the peace. Thomas Jefferson, who followed Adams as President, refused to give Marbury the job. Marbury took his case directly to the Supreme Court, stating that a part of the Judiciary Act of 1789 gave the Court original jurisdiction in cases like his. Marbury didn't get the job, but his name will always be remembered because of the case, *Marbury* v. *Madison* (1803).

In his decision, Chief Justice John Marshall held that Marbury did not have a right to the job. He stated that the part of the Judiciary Act of 1789 on which Marbury based his case was not in keeping with the Constitution. The rest of that law which created new courts, however, was in keeping with the Constitution. Even so, in *Marbury* v. *Madison* the Supreme Court had used its power to declare an act of Congress unconstitutional.

Judicial Review

The Court's decision in *Marbury* v. *Madison* established the procedure known as judicial review. **Judicial review** is the power of the appellate courts and the Supreme Court to review laws to determine whether or not they are in keeping with the Constitution. In *Marbury*, Marshall reasoned that, since the Constitution is the basic law of the land, it can be changed only by amendment. Therefore, any law that goes against the provisions of the Constitution must be declared null and void. Who has the power to declare a law null and void? That power, according to Marshall, rests with the courts. "It is their right," he wrote, "to say what the law is."

Although *Marbury* v. *Madison* involved a law passed by Congress, the right to judicial review also covers laws passed by state legislatures. In time, the power of judicial review has come to include the right to review any action by the legislative or executive branches of our federal or state governments. It should be noted, however, that appeals courts do not look around for cases to review. Someone must bring the matter to the attention of the courts by making a formal request for a review.

Ranking the Justices

In 1971, law professors Albert Blaustein and Roy Mersky wanted to know which Supreme Court Justices were considered the best in United States history. They polled 65 lawyers, law school deans, judges, and scholars. The following list shows the top ten responses.

Justices are listed from top to bottom by degree of excellence. The dates indicate years of service on the high bench. John Marshall was the only unanimous choice.

1.	John Marshall	1801-1835
2.	Oliver Wendell Holmes	1902-1932
3.	Louis Brandeis	1916-1939
4.	Earl Warren	1953-1969
5.	Hugo Black	1937-1971
6.	Felix Frankfurter	1939-1962
7.	Benjamin Cardozo	1932-1938
8.	Harlan Stone	1925-1946
9.	Charles Evans Hughes	1910-1916, 1930-1941
10.	John Marshall Harlan	1877-1911

In a given year, several thousand lower court decisions may be sent to the Supreme Court on appeal. Out of this number, the justices of the Court will accept slightly more than 100. The decision of whether or not to hear a case is decided by a vote of the entire Court. Four "aye" (yes) votes ensure a hearing.

Why is one case accepted and another refused? It depends upon the nature of the case. Some cases are refused because the subject matter is purely local and belongs in the state courts. Thus, a suit challenging a state law setting the legal age for marriage would be rejected by the Court. The right to set the age of marriage is a legal power of each state. However, some years ago a married couple challenged a Maryland state law forbidding marriage between black and white persons. The Supreme Court accepted this case and ruled against the Maryland law. The reason was that such a law denied persons the "equal protection of the laws" guaranteed by the Fourteenth Amendment. As a general rule, the Supreme Court will accept only those cases in which the subject matter is related in some way to the United States Constitution.

The Supreme Court is in session from October to June. During the hearing of a particular case, lawyers from both sides give oral arguments. Written arguments, or **briefs**, may also be presented to the Court by interested parties. These briefs, which are sometimes several hundred pages long, are studied carefully. Then, when all the arguments are finished, the justices vote.

A simple majority vote (for example, 5 justices for, 4 justices against) decides the outcome of a case. Because of illness or previous contact with one of the parties to a case, one or more justices sometimes may decide not to vote. Six justices, however, must be present to decide a case. Four must agree on the decision. A tie vote has the effect of upholding the previous court ruling.

Usually, after the Court reaches a decision, one or more of the justices explain the reasons for the decision. In a split decision, the arguments of the winning side will be explained in a **majority opinion**. A **dissenting opinion** explains the minority vote.

Decisions of the Supreme Court are final. There is no higher court of appeal. There are two ways by which a particular ruling of the Court can be changed. Congress can pass a law overturning the Court's ruling or the Constitution can be amended.

Let us use the personal income tax as an example. In 1895, the Supreme Court ruled that a federal tax on income was unconstitutional. The reason for the ruling was that the tax was based on a person's ability to pay. (The more income a person earned, the more tax he or she had to pay.) The Constitution, however, states that all taxes must be uniform. So, in 1913, the Congress and the states approved the Sixteenth Amendment, which made it legal to

The Supreme Court at Work

Checking the Supreme Court

Pictured above are Chief Justice William Rehnquist (front row, center) and the Associate Justices of the Supreme Court. To the left is the official seal of the Court.

tax personal incomes. A similar attempt was made to override the Supreme Court ruling on prayer in the public schools. However, in that case, the proposed amendment failed to get the required vote in Congress.

The Warren Court

Beginning in the early 1960s, the Supreme Court made some decisions that caused a great deal of debate. These were the years of the "Warren Court" (1954–1968). Earl Warren, former governor of California, was Chief Justice.

Some of the decisions of the Warren Court protected the rights of persons accused of crimes. Two of the most important decisions were *Escobedo* v. *Illinois* (1964) and *Miranda* v. *Arizona* (1966). In both of these rulings, the Court held that persons suspected of crimes must have a lawyer present before police can question them. The Court also held that suspects should be warned that they have a right to remain silent before any questioning begins.

Throughout the nation, many police departments put the Miranda Warning (as it came to be called) on a printed form. In this way, officers could have suspects sign the form as proof that they had heard and understood their rights. Suspects must be told that any statements they make to police may be used against them at a later trial. What is more, even if suspects agree to answer police questions, they may stop answering the questions at any time. If the police fail to warn a suspect, the police may lose the case. For instance, if an officer gets a signed confession of guilt with no lawyer present, the confession is worthless. From

A police officer reads the Miranda Warning to a suspect. Suspects must be guaranteed the right to a lawyer and the right to remain silent. A confession is worthless unless a lawyer is present.

the standpoint of the law, the confession is "illegally seized evidence." Such evidence cannot be used in a court trial.

Many people spoke out against these rulings. Police and other law enforcement officials said that the Supreme Court had made it very difficult for them to capture criminals. Others blamed the Court for being soft on criminals and ignoring the victims of their crimes. Newspaper articles blamed the increasing crime rate of the 1970s in part on these regulations.

There were a number of persons in favor of the Court's decision, however. They pointed out that the *Miranda Warning* is simply a statement of the constitutional rights of a person accused of a crime. Why, they asked, should it be necessary for police to use illegal methods to catch criminals? The job of police is to uphold the law, they said, not to break it.

The Burger Court

By the 1970s, the nature of the Supreme Court had changed. Earl Warren had retired in 1969. President Richard Nixon appointed Warren Burger Chief Justice. In time, Mr. Nixon also appointed three other justices to the Court.

The Burger Court made some changes in the field of criminal justice. One Court decision withdrew the right of a suspect to have a lawyer during questioning at the police station. At present, this decision applies only after a judge has made a formal charge against an accused person. The Court has allowed the use of illegally seized evidence in certain court cases. One ruling allowed police to search suspects without a search warrant. In another decision, the Court held that a unanimous guilty vote by a jury is not necessary in a criminal case. Nine out of twelve jurors are enough to convict a person who has been tried for a crime.

In the 1980s, President Reagan appointed three new justices (when others retired) who tended to have more conservative views than those expressed by the Burger Court. When Burger retired in 1987, Reagan appointed Associate Justice William Rehnquist to be Chief Justice.

The Rehnquist Court

In 1988 the Rehnquist Court said that school officials may censor student newspapers that are part of the school's learning program. In 1989 the Court ruled that a program in Richmond, Virginia, that set aside 30 percent of its public works funds for minority-owned construction companies was unconstitutional. The Court said this discriminated against non-minority-owned companies.

Following the trend of the Richmond decision, the Court struck down a Michigan affirmative action law in March, 1989. In June, the Court reheard and weakened an earlier civil rights ruling, *Runyon* v. *McCrary*, that had protected minorities from harassment and discrimination on the job. Some see these rulings as backward steps in the area of civil rights.

SECTION 4 *Review*

Defining Key Terms
1. Define: writ of *certiorari,* judicial review, brief, majority opinion, dissenting opinion.

Recalling the Facts
2. How does one become a Supreme Court Justice?
3. What were two major decisions made by the Rehnquist Court?

Reviewing the Main Idea
4. Answer "As you read . . ." question 4 on page 162: What is judicial review, and what case established this procedure?

Critical Thinking
5. **Drawing Conclusions.** Should Congress, by a two-thirds vote of both houses, be able to overturn a decision of the Supreme Court? Why or why not?

Government and Law

Equality Under the Law

How has the federal court system influenced public policy? Two landmark Supreme Court cases—*Plessy* v. *Ferguson* (1896) and *Brown* v. *Topeka Board of Education* (1954)—illustrate the important role that the federal courts have played in determining the connection between public policy and skin color.

For much of this country's history, racial segregation was a way of life. Blacks and whites went to separate schools, hospitals, and movie theaters. They used separate drinking fountains and public washrooms and sat in separate sections of buses, trains, and restaurants.

Homer Plessy, a black man living in New Orleans, knew "the rules." But on June 7, 1892, Plessy boarded a train heading north and took a seat in a car labeled "White Persons Only." After a short time, the conductor told Plessy that he would have to move to the section of the train reserved for blacks. Plessy refused. At the next stop he was arrested and jailed.

In suing for his freedom, Plessy lost in the Louisiana courts. Louisiana, like many nearby states, had so-called Jim Crow laws that made separation between races legal. The only exception was that black women taking care of white children could sit in the "whites only" section of trains.

A lawyer appealed the Louisiana decision to the United States Supreme Court. In 1896, the Court upheld the legality of Jim Crow laws by a vote of 7 to 1. That decision has been called the "separate but equal" doctrine. It said, in effect, that the separation of blacks and whites in public places was legal as long as the separate facilities

Linda Brown made headlines when she and her parents began a court battle to end segregation in public schools.

for black people were equal to those provided for white people.

The one vote disagreeing with the decision came from Justice John M. Harlan. Harlan made a statement worth remembering: "Our Constitution is colorblind, and neither knows nor tolerates classes among its citizens."

For more than 50 years, however, *Plessy* v. *Ferguson* protected state laws that turned black Americans into second-class citizens. Such laws required separate schools for black and white children, separate seating in public libraries and parks, and separate areas in cemeteries.

Were separate schools really "equal"? Studies made in the 1940s and early 1950s showed that in black schools:

- textbooks often were ones thrown away by white schools
- teacher qualifications were lower than in white schools
- student test scores were on the average lower than in white schools

Perhaps most important was the finding that segregated schools created feelings of inferiority among black students.

By 1950, black leaders were ready to challenge the *Plessy* decision. Among those leaders was Thurgood Marshall, chief legal counsel for the NAACP (National Association for the Advancement of Colored People) and later a Supreme Court Justice.

The challenge to the *Plessy* decision came from Mr. and Mrs. Oliver Brown, black residents of Topeka, Kansas. The Browns wanted to send their eight-year-old daughter, Linda, to a school five blocks from their home. When Mrs. Brown tried to enroll her daughter, school officials reminded her of the Kansas law that required black and white children to attend separate schools. The closest black school to the Browns' home was 21 blocks away. The Browns decided to appeal to the courts.

In Kansas, the Browns had no success. The lawyer for the school board said that the Topeka schools for blacks were equal to those for whites. The school board attorney noted that *Plessy* v. *Ferguson* had already settled the question of the legality of separate schools for black and for white children. Mr. and Mrs. Brown then appealed the decision to the United States Supreme Court.

The Supreme Court accepted the case. In 1954, it overturned the *Plessy* decision in its ruling in *Brown* v. *Topeka Board of Education*. The vote was unanimous. The justices concluded that "in the field of public education, the doctrine of 'separate but equal' has no place." The following year, the Court ordered school districts in 17 states to develop plans that would end segregation in the schools. The plans were to be made with "deliberate speed."

Some states responded with deliberate slowness, however. They tried to find ways to get around the Court ruling. In time, though, all the segregation laws were repealed. Progress has been made in bringing all students together in our country's schools. But almost as important as the ruling itself was the effect of *Brown* on other kinds of segregation. The decision inspired a movement to put an end to segregated lunch counters, buses, theaters, and other public places. Some people have called the *Brown* decision the most important Court ruling of the 20th century.

Questions to think about

1. What is the meaning of the words "Our Constitution is colorblind?"

2. Why might the *Brown* decision be one of the most important rulings of the century?

CHAPTER SUMMARY

Section 1   The federal courts make up the judicial branch of our federal government. The courts interpret the law, settle disputes and arguments, and try persons accused of breaking the law. Article 3 of the Constitution defines the jurisdiction of the federal courts.

Section 2   The courts interpret our laws by explaining what they mean. The courts deal with different kinds of laws, including statutory law, constitutional law, common law, and administrative law. These four types of law may be classified as either civil or criminal law. Civil law deals with disputes; criminal law deals with crimes. Due process of law ensures each person's right to a fair trial.

Section 3   The United States district courts are the federal trial courts. Decisions of the district courts may be brought to an appeals court. The United States Supreme Court is the highest court of appeals in our land. There are also several special courts that hear only particular kinds of cases. These include the U.S. Claims Court, the U.S. Tax Court, and the Court of Military Appeals. Judges are in charge of all court hearings. Federal judges are appointed by the President with approval by the Senate. Because federal judges are appointed to lifetime terms, they cannot be removed from office for unpopular decisions.

Section 4   The Supreme Court has one Chief Justice and eight Associate Justices. Generally, the Supreme Court hears only cases involving the Constitution. Only the Supreme Court and the federal appeals courts can decide whether laws are Constitutional. This is called the power of judicial review. The decisions of the Supreme Court are final.

Reviewing Key Terms

Match the following terms with the definitions below. Write your answers on a separate sheet of paper.

court   defendant   verdict
suit   appeal   brief
plaintiff   jury

1. a written statement presented by a lawyer to a court

2. another word for a court case

3. the decision of a judge or jury

4. the person charged with a crime

5. the person making a complaint in a civil case

6. the place where legal disputes are settled

7. a request to have a trial court decision reviewed by a higher court

8. a group of people selected to decide the guilt or innocence of a person in court

Understanding Main Ideas

1. What is the *jurisdiction* of a court?

2. Name four kinds of cases in which the federal courts generally have jurisdiction.

3. How do civil and criminal law differ?

4. Name at least four rights guaranteed to a person accused of a crime.

5. What is the purpose of an appeals court?

6. How do federal judges get their jobs? How long do they keep them?

7. What is the power of judicial review?

8. How does the Supreme Court decide the outcome of a case?

Critical Thinking

1. Recognizing Cause and Effect. Federal judges are appointed to lifetime terms. Do you think this helps or hurts the judiciary system? Explain your answer.

2. Drawing Conclusions. Former Chief Justice Charles E. Hughes made the following statement: "We are under a Constitution, but the Constitution is what the judges say it is." What does this mean?

3. Determining Relevance. In your own words, explain *due process of law*. Then, explain how due process helps to protect individual rights and liberties.

Practicing Skills

1. Distinguishing Fact from Opinion. Determine whether the following statements about the courts are facts or opinions.

   a. The district courts are the federal trial courts.

   b. The Eighth Amendment to the Constitution forbids the use of cruel and unusual punishment.

   c. It would be a good idea to have more women judges.

   d. Federal court judges are overpaid.

2. Analyzing the News. Find two or three news stories in which the Supreme Court or other federal courts are involved. For each story, write a paragraph explaining the role of the federal courts in this issue or event.

Focusing on Citizenship

1. Staging a Mock Trial. Have a mock trial of some well-known historical person. Possible subjects include Aaron Burr (treason), Alexander Wirz (war crimes after the Civil War), and General Billy Mitchell (criticism of U.S. Army policy, 1925).

2. Visiting a Courtroom. Make arrangements to visit a courtroom near your school. Most judges welcome visits by student groups and will usually explain what is taking place.

3. Doing a Research Project. Use the *Readers' Guide to Periodical Literature* to locate information about the case of *Tinker* v. *Des Moines* (1969). This Supreme Court decision involved a teenager's right to engage in nondisruptive protest in a public high school. Write a short paper about your findings.

The federal government, like individual citizens, needs money to survive.

Paying for Our National Government

Previewing the Chapter

If you want to buy something that costs more than you can afford, you can probably borrow the money and promise to pay it back over time. The federal government has been borrowing money for many years, and its debt has been mounting. But how much is too much? Is it realistic to expect to pay off a debt of millions of dollars? Billions of dollars? In 1989, our national debt approached *$3 trillion* ($3,000,000,000,000). This chapter focuses on how the government acquires and spends its money.

- **Before you read,** look up these key terms in the Glossary at the back of this book: *income tax, estate, fiscal year, national debt, deficit spending, tax loophole.*

- **As you read,** look for answers to these questions:
  1. What are the main sources of money for the federal government?
  2. What are the two items on which the federal government spends most of its money?
  3. What four goals would a fair system of taxation meet?

1 What Are the Sources of the Government's Money?

Each year, the national government spends a huge amount of money for defense, aid to our cities, help to elderly people, and many other things. The federal government may be paying some of the cost of the lunches served at your school. Some of the highways you ride on or the national parks and forests you may have visited have been built and maintained by federal money. The water you drink may come from a reservoir built at federal expense. In 1988, the government spent more than $1 trillion. This was an average of over $4,000 for every citizen. The government obtained most of this money in various types of taxes.

Taxes

What is a tax? A tax is a payment that people and businesses are required by law to make to government. The amount that different individuals and groups pay is based on their total income from wages, rent, interest, and other sources. The most important taxes collected by the national government include individual income, Social Security, corporation income, excise, estate, gift, and import taxes. Individual income taxes give the federal government almost half the money it takes in. (See the graph on page 187.) Social Security taxes provide the second largest amount. Together, these two taxes provide about three-fourths of the federal government's income.

Income Taxes. An **income tax** is a tax on the money a person earns. Income includes salaries, wages, interest on bank accounts, tips, rent from property, profits made from selling things, and money won in gambling. Today, people in the United States take it for granted that by every April 15 they will have to pay income taxes. However, this was not always the case. Although the Constitution gave Congress the power to levy federal taxes in 1788, it was not until 1913 that the first modern income tax took effect. President Franklin D. Roosevelt's New Deal program in the 1930s drastically increased federal services and activities. Many of the programs established by the New Deal still exist in some form today, and income taxes help to pay for them.

The amount of federal income tax people must pay depends on how much they earn. The more a person earns, the more she or he must pay in taxes. Taxpayers in the United States pay a graduated or **progressive income tax.** Not only the amount of tax in-

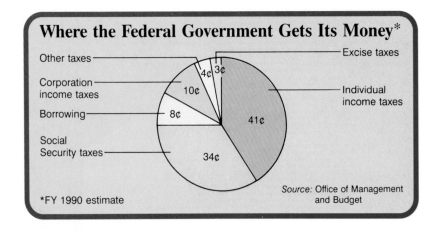

Where the Federal Government Gets Its Money*

- Other taxes
- Corporation income taxes — 10¢
- Borrowing — 8¢
- Social Security taxes — 34¢
- Excise taxes — 3¢
- Individual income taxes — 41¢
- 4¢

*FY 1990 estimate

Source: Office of Management and Budget

SKILL BUILDER

From what source does the federal government gain most of its revenue?

creases with income; the percentage also increases. In 1988, a single person who earned $10,000 a year paid a tax of $761, about 8 percent of his or her earnings. A person who earned $30,000 a year paid a tax of $4,701, about 16 percent of her or his earnings.

Although most people earn enough income to have to pay taxes, some do not. A single person who had a yearly income of less than $4,950 in 1988 was not required to pay any federal income taxes. A married couple with two children could earn up to $12,200 before they had to pay any income tax.

The federal government requires employers to take money for income taxes from the paychecks of their employees. The employers then turn the tax money over to the government. Self-employed people are required to figure their yearly taxes and send one-fourth of what they owe to the government every three months. A taxpayer reports his or her income between January 1 and April 15 of each year on an income tax form. Each taxpayer figures out how much tax he or she must pay by taking deductions from his or her total income. A **deduction** is an expense that can be subtracted from a person's total income. Examples of deductions include home mortgage payments, interest paid on bank loans, and large medical expenses. After deductions have been subtracted, the income on which a person pays taxes is smaller, so the tax paid is smaller.

The Internal Revenue Service (IRS) collects income taxes. IRS is a part of the Treasury Department. Its offices in thousands of cities give information and advice to taxpayers. Every year, IRS workers mail out the tax forms on which taxpayers report their incomes. They also check people's tax reports carefully.

Excise Taxes.   An **excise tax** is a tax placed on certain items and services. These taxes are added to the price people must pay for these goods and services. Excises on tobacco and liquor bring in the most money.

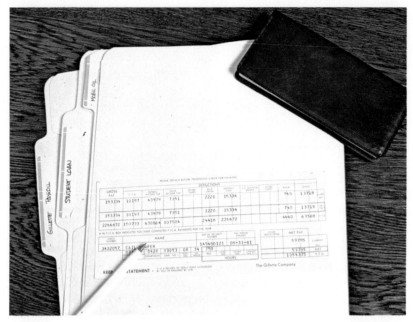

This payroll stub shows the amount of tax money an employer takes out of an employee's pay. This tax money is turned over to the government.

Corporation Income Taxes.   A **corporation income tax** is a tax that corporations have to pay on their yearly profits. Such a tax is similar to the personal income tax paid by individuals. It is a graduated tax. The taxes a company must pay increase as company profits increase. Each year, some corporations pay millions of dollars in income taxes.

Social Security Taxes.   A **Social Security tax** is a payment people make into a government retirement fund. Both employees and employers pay an equal amount into this fund. In 1989, a person paid a Social Security tax on all income up to $48,000 a year. Like income taxes, Social Security taxes are taken out of workers' paychecks.

Workers can retire at age 62 or older. When people retire, the government pays them a monthly amount out of the Social Security fund if they have paid Social Security taxes for at least ten years. The amount of money a person receives depends on how much he or she paid into the fund while working.

Estate Taxes.   A person's **estate** is the total amount of money and property he or she has. An **heir** is a person to whom an estate is left when the owner of the estate dies. When the owner dies, his or her heirs must pay an **estate tax** on everything worth more than $600,000.

Gift Taxes.   A person who gives a gift worth more than $10,000 to any one person in any one year must pay a gift tax on the amount over $10,000. The person may give many gifts to different people and not pay a tax, if each gift is less than $10,000. The person who receives the gift does not have to pay a tax.

Tariffs

As mentioned before, tariffs are taxes placed on goods imported (brought) into the United States. The companies that import the goods must pay this tax. They usually add the tax onto the price they charge when they sell the goods. Thus, people who buy the imported goods really pay this tax.

A high tariff can discourage business firms in other nations from sending goods to be sold in the United States. They have to sell their goods at a higher price to cover the tariff. Companies in the United States, since they do not have to pay the tariff, can sell similar goods they make at lower prices. Such tariffs are said to "protect" United States companies. For this reason, they are often called **protective tariffs.**

Manufacturers in this country often ask the government to place or raise tariffs on imported goods to make these products too expensive for consumers. They hope people in the United States will then buy products made here. Steel companies in the United States, for example, have asked Congress to raise tariffs

A Shrinking Security Blanket?

Money for the Social Security program comes largely from the taxes paid by workers and employees. In the summer of 1988, though, the government got some extra income from a surprising source. Ann Roselle Hunley Hayne, a Florida resident who died in June at the age of 87, chose to pay back a part of the monthly Social Security benefits she had collected during the last 20 years of her life. Hayne left the Social Security Administration more than $30,000 in her will.

As generous as this gift was, it represented little more than a drop in the bucket of Social Security costs. The government

has for many years been paying out more money than it has been bringing in. In the early 1980s, the Social Security program was, in fact, on the brink of collapse.

Congress stepped in to try to rescue Social Security in 1983. Congress passed a bill that will gradually raise the age at which retired citizens can collect full benefits. Beginning in the year 2000, that age will be 67.

Some doubts linger about the security of Social Security. The number of people collecting benefits is expected to double by the year 2035. Costs, meanwhile, may jump 25 times, to more than $5 *trillion.*

on imported steel. They hope U.S. customers will then buy steel products made in this country.

Protective tariffs can work to the disadvantage of the United States, however. Other countries can raise their tariffs on goods from the United States being sent to them. Some U.S. manufacturers want to sell their products in other countries. Since the 1930s, such companies have pressured the national government to use protective tariffs less and less.

Customs Duties

A **customs duty** is a tax people must pay when they bring certain products into the United States. Every year millions of United States citizens travel to other countries. They often bring back items they buy in those countries. The law requires them to report many of these items to Customs Service inspectors when they come back to the United States. The Customs Service is a part of the Treasury Department. It has inspection stations at airports, harbors, and along the borders of the United States. A duty must be paid on any goods a person brings in worth $400 or more. A person can, however, bring in goods worth $800 or less from a United States territory without paying a customs duty.

Borrowing

The federal government also gets money through borrowing. It borrows money in several ways. One way is by selling savings bonds. For example, you might buy a $50 savings bond. You pay only $25 for this bond. After 12 years you can cash the bond and receive the full $50 face value of the bond because of the interest that has accumulated.

The U.S. Customs Service checks luggage of people returning to this country.

Most of the money borrowed by the government comes from the sale of Treasury bills, notes, and bonds. Individuals and companies loan money to the government by buying these certificates. The prices range from $1,000 to $10,000. As with savings bonds, the federal government uses the money for a certain period of time and then pays back the purchase price plus any interest that has accumulated.

Insurance companies, banks, investment companies, savings and loan companies, other businesses, and foreign governments usually buy treasury certificates. Their price is higher than most individuals can afford. The government has never refused to pay back a loan, so these certificates are safe investments.

In 1986, the government owed $411 billion to holders of T-bills, $897 billion on T-notes, and $242 billion on T-bonds. These totals equaled about 75 percent of the national debt. That year, the government owed $86 billion, or 4 percent of its debt to savings bond holders. These are usually citizens who have small amounts of money to save.

SECTION 1 *Review*

Defining Key Terms
1. Define: income tax, progressive income tax, deduction, excise tax, corporation income tax, Social Security tax, estate, heir, estate tax, protective tariff, customs duty.

Recalling the Facts
2. What determines the amount of federal income tax a person must pay?
3. What are some examples of tax deductions? How do they affect the amount of taxes paid?
4. What does the Internal Revenue Service, or IRS, do?
5. What are some ways the federal government borrows money?

Reviewing the Main Idea
6. Answer "As you read . . ." question 1 on page 185: What are the main sources of money for the federal government?

Critical Thinking
7. **Checking Consistency.** Taxes allow the government to provide services that most people want. Yet almost everyone complains that taxes are too high. How would you explain this?

2 How the Government Spends the Money It Collects

How does the federal government spend the money it collects? The graph on this page shows that direct benefit payments such as Social Security are the largest items on which federal money is spent. Defense is the second largest. The federal government spends over half the money it collects on just these two items. Some of the other ways the government spends our money are listed below.

- It provides pensions and medical care for elderly and disabled people, veterans, widows, orphans, and retired government workers.
- It purchases military equipment and weapons and pays salaries for people in military service. It maintains bases and equipment, and supplies money for research to develop new weapons.
- It maintains our national parks, forests, and other recreational areas.
- It pays government employees to check on the purity of foods, drugs, and cosmetics.
- It gives money to cities and states to improve old neighborhoods.
- It pays the salaries of FBI agents, federal lawyers, and judges.
- It maintains our courts and prisons.
- It provides money for space exploration.
- It provides money for scientific and medical research.

SKILL BUILDER

How does this graph show the economic importance of reducing the national debt?

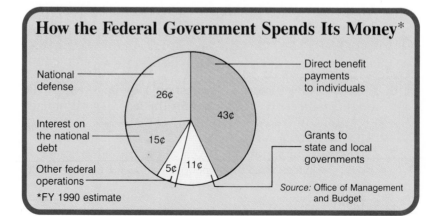

How the Federal Government Spends Its Money*

National defense — 26¢

Interest on the national debt — 15¢

Other federal operations — 5¢ / 11¢

43¢ — Direct benefit payments to individuals

Grants to state and local governments

Source: Office of Management and Budget

*FY 1990 estimate

- It pays for highway construction.
- It gives money and food to other nations.
- It helps victims of floods, earthquakes, and fires.

The national budget tells how the government spends its income each year. The budget of the United States was an estimated $965 billion in 1989. The budget is based on what is called a **fiscal year.** *Fiscal* means "having to do with money." A fiscal year is a period of 12 months during which financial matters are settled. The federal government's fiscal year begins October 1 and ends September 30.

The President must prepare a budget proposal each year and submit it to Congress. The President meets with the heads of the executive departments and other advisers to draw up the budget. In recent times, defense has been considered very important. Social Security also has been an important item.

Interest on the national debt is another costly item. The **national debt** is the amount of money owed by the government.

The President and the advisers must make many decisions about how much money the government should spend on each budget item. Should more money be spent on national defense?

The National Budget

National Debt of the United States

SKILL BUILDER

By about how much did the national debt increase between 1950 and 1970? Between 1970 and 1990? What does this trend indicate?

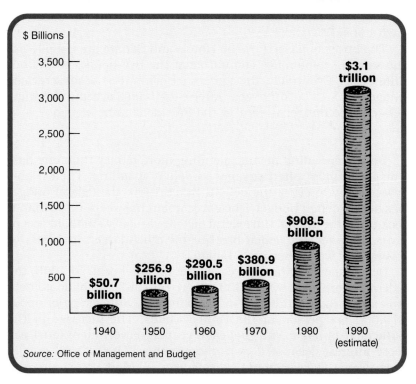

$ Billions

3,500 —

$3.1 trillion

3,000 —

2,500 —

2,000 —

1,500 —

$908.5 billion

1,000 —

$380.9 billion

500 — $256.9 billion · $290.5 billion

$50.7 billion

| 1940 | 1950 | 1960 | 1970 | 1980 | 1990 (estimate) |

Source: Office of Management and Budget

More money for defense could mean less money for programs that give aid to poor people or provide job training. These are very difficult decisions to make. Pressure from interest groups (see Chapter 19), members of Congress, and the President influence budget preparation, as do arguments by the President's advisers about where money is most needed.

People who actually write the budget are in the Office of Management and Budget (OMB). All federal departments send their spending requests to the OMB. The OMB then places these requests in reports for the President's advisers to study. The Director of the Budget also suggests what he or she thinks the government's income will be. Requests are often changed because of priorities (order of importance) and the amount of money available. The final budget proposal, which contains hundreds of pages, is then given to the President.

The President presents the proposed budget to Congress, usually in January. He explains to Congress how he believes the government should spend its money in the coming fiscal year. He then asks Congress to approve the budget.

Congress usually takes several months to study and discuss the budget. Budget committees in each house of Congress hold hearings on the budget. The President's advisers and the heads of many departments attend these hearings to give their views. Each budget committee then sends a revised budget to its house of Congress. More revisions may occur as a result of debate in each house.

The budgets passed by the House and Senate are usually not the same. A conference committee of the two houses works out differences. Eventually, the conference committee sends a revised budget back to both houses. After each house accepts the same version, the budget is sent to the President to be signed.

Deficit Spending

Deficit spending means spending more money than one has. The government often engages in deficit spending. Then it borrows money to cover the deficit. Since 1960, the federal budget has been a deficit budget. The government has spent more than it took in. In the 1960s, the federal deficit was fairly small. In recent years, however, the deficit has become much larger. In 1989, for example, it was about $130 billion.

Deficit spending has increased the national debt. In 1965, the federal government owed $323 billion. By 1987, the national debt was about $2.35 trillion. This amounted to an average of about $10,000 per person in the United States. The increase in the national debt has meant that each year the government must pay more interest because it owes more money. The interest is paid from taxes the government collects from all of us.

Federal spending has increased drastically since 1960. The increase is due, in part, to rising costs. For example, payments to people on Social Security have increased. Prices of materials and salaries of government workers have also increased in recent years, causing a higher cost for government projects.

The President and Congress often announce that balancing the budget is an important goal. A **balanced budget** is one in which government spending is exactly equal to the income government receives from taxes or other sources. Candidates for public office frequently criticize the government for spending too much money and for deficit budgets. However, if those candidates are elected, they soon learn that balancing the budget is a difficult goal to achieve.

SKILL BUILDER

In what year did federal spending first exceed $1 trillion?

Federal Spending, 1962–1989

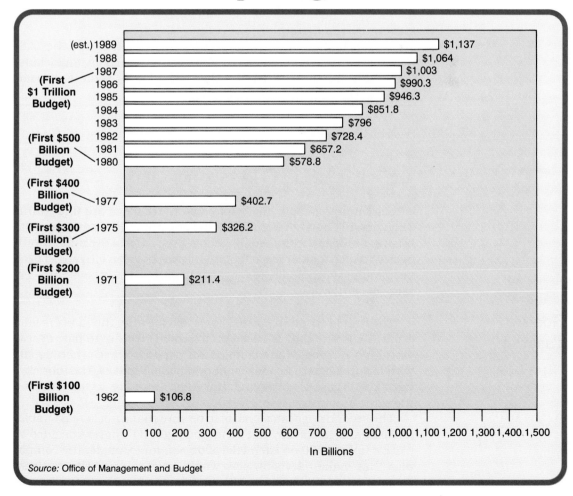

Source: Office of Management and Budget

Defining Key Terms

1. Define: fiscal year, national debt, deficit spending, balanced budget.

Recalling the Facts

2. What are some specific ways the government spends the money it collects?
3. Why has federal spending increased rapidly since 1960?

Reviewing the Main Idea

4. Answer "As you read . . ." question 2 on page 185: What are the two items on which the federal government spends most of its money?

Critical Thinking

5. **Evaluating Government Policy.** Do you think the U.S. government should give money to young artists, musicians, and athletes to develop their talents, as some European governments do? Explain your answer.

3 Taxation

Few, if any, people like to pay taxes. Yet taxes are important. They provide most of the money the government needs to run its business. Nevertheless, some people argue that government officials should consider the effect high taxes have on citizens. These people suggest that lawmakers should write the tax laws with certain goals in mind.

Goals of Taxation

The first of these suggested goals is to be sure that a tax is fair. A fair tax is one that is based on a person's ability to pay. People with high incomes, for example, can pay more taxes than people with low incomes. The more money a person makes, the more tax he or she is capable of paying. It would not be fair to tax everyone the same amount.

The second suggested goal is to be sure that a tax is reasonable. A reasonable tax is one that is not too high. If Congress decided to place a tax of $300 on each television set, for example, the companies that make television sets would have to raise their prices. Sales of television sets would probably go down, some makers of television sets would go out of business, and workers would lose their jobs.

A third suggested goal is to be sure that goods which all of us need for our health and safety are not taxed. Taxes on medicines, food, or artificial limbs would be examples of such goods.

A fourth suggested goal is to be sure that taxes do not discourage individuals and companies from investing. Individuals **invest** money in real estate, stocks and bonds, jewelry, and other things. They hope that the value of these things will increase and that they will make a profit. Corporations often invest their profits to improve their businesses or to start new ones. When taxes are high, however, people and companies may feel that trying to earn more money to invest is not worth the effort. As their income increases, they say, taxes take it away.

By allowing **tax loopholes** (ways to earn more money to invest), the federal government tries to encourage people and companies to make investments. Oil companies, for example, do not have to pay taxes on some of their profits. The federal government also permits companies to deduct a certain amount from their income for depreciation of such things as buildings and equipment. To **depreciate** means to decrease in value. Buildings and equipment decrease in value as they become worn from being used. Individuals owning their own businesses are permitted to deduct such business expenses as travel and entertainment from their incomes. People who sell property after keeping it more than a year pay federal income taxes on only half of the profit they make. Tax loopholes like these, however, benefit only a few people. Most taxpayers do not have any loopholes to help them reduce their taxes.

ROTHCO

SKILL BUILDER

Do you think that this cartoon expresses the way many people feel about paying taxes? Explain.

Federal Grants-in-aid

Many people are worried about the rising cost of government. They point out that the federal government's tax collections in 1987 were over nine times more than they were in 1960. In that 27-year period, the federal income tax of the average taxpayer rose from about $507 to over $3,629. Much of the money from this increase has been used to help people by means of food programs, job retraining, and unemployment or welfare payments. Another part of the money from increased taxes has been used to pay increased government pensions.

Money from the increase in taxes also has been used to provide federal grants-in-aid. A **grant-in-aid** is money given by the federal government to state and city governments to pay for programs that improve life. For example, grants-in-aid have helped to rebuild old neighborhoods, to provide job training for members of minority groups, to build roads and parks, to pay for medical care for old people, and to hire more police. State and city governments can receive grants-in-aid if they follow federal rules telling how to use the money. In some cases, the state or city governments must match the grants with their own money.

Requests for grants-in-aid have been growing in recent years. They are an important source of badly needed money for many state and city governments. Mayors, governors, and other city and state officials often ask the federal government for such grants. Federal officials, however, point out that the growing federal deficit puts limits on the amount of money available.

SKILL BUILDER

What does the man lying under the "snowman" in this cartoon represent? Why is he pictured this way?

Critics argue that grants-in-aid are not a good way to use our tax money. They argue that these grants often cause many cities to undertake programs they do not really need and cannot afford. They also believe that state and city officials could do more with less money if they did not have to follow federal rules. Such rules are often complex and require filling out many forms.

Many of those who criticize high taxes argue that lowering taxes will increase production and jobs. Money spent on taxes might be spent to build more plants and make more products. These people have urged Congress to pass a Constitutional amendment to prevent deficit spending, forcing the federal government to cut its spending.

Supporters of federal spending and higher taxes believe that government has a duty to take care of those who need help. They argue that high taxes are necessary to pay for Social Security and other programs. Federal grants, these people explain, provide services that state and city governments by themselves could not offer. The real problem with taxes, in their view, lies in the way they are collected. In the opinion of these critics, corporations and wealthy individuals should pay more for taxes, and poorer people should pay less.

Two Views on Rising Taxes

SECTION 3 *Review*

Defining Key Terms
1. Define: invest, tax loophole, depreciate, grant-in-aid.

Recalling the Facts
2. What are some of the tax loopholes for businesses? For individuals?
3. What are some reasons for continuing federal grants-in-aid? Why are some people against it?

Reviewing the Main Idea
4. Answer "As you read . . ." question 3 on page 185: What four goals would a fair system of taxation meet?

Critical Thinking
5. **Predicting Consequences.** Imagine that the federal government has decided to reduce all income taxes—on individuals and corporations—by one-half for a period of three years. What do you think would happen as a result of this policy?

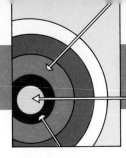
Study Skills

Using Graphs

Every day, lots of information comes your way in the form of statistics. One of the clearest ways to present such information is to use graphs. Graphs can help you see trends and relationships and make comparisons quickly.

Every graph should have a brief title that tells what the graph is about. A graph should also have a note giving the source and date of the information.

Circle Graphs. Circle graphs (sometimes called pie graphs) show how parts combine to make up a whole. The entire circle represents 100 percent. Each sector of the graph (each slice of the pie) shows a percentage of the whole.

Look at the circle graph on page 187. The graph shows the six sources of federal income. They are represented by the six sectors of the circle. The largest sector on the graph, individual income tax, is therefore the largest source.

Bar Graphs. Bar graphs show numerical information in amounts or in percentages. The horizontal and vertical axes (the left and bottom edges of the graph) should have labels indicating the measurements being used (such as millions of people, thousands of dollars, or years). Bar graphs can be drawn with the bars going vertically (bottom to top) or horizontally (left to right).

Look at the bar graph on page 195. The vertical axis is marked with amounts from 0 to 1,500 in $100 billion intervals (the distance between each mark). Each horizontal bar represents the federal spending for that year.

Line Graphs. Line graphs are similar to bar graphs because they also use vertical

Federal Revenue and Spending

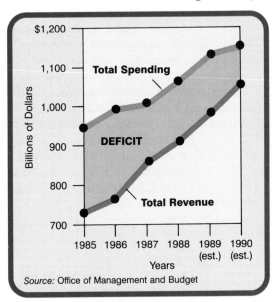

Source: Office of Management and Budget

and horizontal axes. Rather than use bars, however, a line graph connects points with an indicator line. Look at the graph on this page. It allows you to compare government revenue (income) and spending from 1985 to 1990. Study the graph and then answer the questions that follow.

Practicing Skills

1. What is the title of the graph? What is the source of the information? What is shown along the horizontal axis? In what interval is the vertical axis drawn?
2. About how much money did the government spend in 1987? About how much income did it receive that year?
3. **Recognizing Cause and Effect.** According to this graph, what is the result of the government's spending compared with its revenue?

Government and Law

The Internal Revenue Service

Every year from January to April, tax lawyers and accountants begin to work at top speed. Millions of Americans sharpen their pencils and get out their calculators. As April approaches, the Post Office is flooded with mail. The reason for all this activity? April 15 is "Tax Day," the day when tax returns must be mailed to the Internal Revenue Service (IRS). The IRS is the government agency that collects federal income taxes.

For much of the history of the United States, tariffs (taxes on imported goods) provided the government with most of its revenue. The first federal income tax was passed in 1861 to help pay for the Civil War. It was discontinued during the 1870s, but another income tax was passed in the 1890s. That tax was almost immediately declared unconstitutional. (At that time, the Constitution forbade direct taxes based on income.) It took an amendment to the Constitution, passed in 1913, to allow an income tax. But it wasn't until World War II that income taxes became the essential source of government revenue that they are today.

The IRS was established as part of the Treasury Department in 1862. Its mission is to collect the proper amount of income tax from each American citizen. IRS employees provide tax forms and booklets, answer questions, help people who need assistance in filling out tax forms, and check completed returns for errors. About 3 out of every 100 returns are audited, or double-checked, by a tax examiner.

The IRS has information centers across the nation to answer citizens' questions about taxes.

No one likes to pay taxes, but taxes keep the government running and provide Americans with essential services. As former Supreme Court Justice Oliver Wendall Holmes once said, "Taxes are what we pay for a civilized society."

Questions to think about

1. All income tax returns in the United States may be checked for errors. What might happen if the IRS changed its policy and did not check any returns?
2. What do you think would happen to the American economy if people stopped paying their taxes?

CHAPTER SUMMARY

Section 1   Running the United States government costs a lot of money. The money to support the government comes mainly from taxes—personal income taxes, corporation income taxes, Social Security taxes, excise taxes, gift taxes, estate taxes, and import taxes. The personal income tax provides the greatest source of government revenue. This tax is called a progressive tax because the percentage a person must pay increases as his or her income increases. In addition to taxes, the federal government obtains money through tariffs, customs duties, and borrowing. Most of the money borrowed by the government comes from the sale of Treasury bills, notes, and bonds.

Section 2   The federal government spends more money on the Social Security program than on any other single item. Defense is the second highest item. Each year the President, the executive staff, and Congress develop a budget, or plan, for the amount of money to be spent on each federal program. Since 1960, the government has had to borrow money to cover its costs, thus increasing the national debt. Many people want the government to reduce federal spending and maintain a balanced budget.

Section 3   Though taxes are necessary, they are rarely popular. Suggestions for improving tax laws include having fair and reasonable taxes, encouraging investment, and not taxing things we need for health and safety. Many people say that too much federal money is given back to state and city governments in grants-in-aid programs. They argue that lower taxes will increase production and jobs. Other people believe that higher taxes are needed to provide money for essential services.

Reviewing Key Terms

Use each of the following terms appropriately in a sentence. Write your sentences on a separate sheet of paper.

1. income tax

2. estate

3. fiscal year

4. national debt

5. deficit spending

6. tax loophole

Understanding Main Ideas

1. What is the largest source of the federal government's money?

2. Name three kinds of taxes most people pay in the United States.

3. Why is the income tax called a progressive tax? What are two kinds of taxes that are not progressive?

4. Give three examples of income tax deductions to which taxpayers are entitled.

5. What does the IRS do?

6. What does the Social Security tax pay for?

7. Who pays an employee's Social Security tax?

8. How does the government borrow money?

9. Name at least five things on which the federal government spends money.

10. What is the national debt? Where does it come from?

11. What are two examples of tax loopholes?

12. In what different ways have grant-in-aid money been used by cities and states?

Critical Thinking

1. **Identifying Alternatives.** Can a country exist without taxes? If you think it can, how would the government operate?

2. **Testing Conclusions.** Some people argue that there are some services the government should *not* provide. Do you agree? If not, why? If so, which services could our government eliminate?

3. **Expressing Opinions Clearly.** Should taxes on so-called harmful items such as cigarettes and alcohol be higher than taxes on other items? Why or why not?

Practicing Skills

1. **Making a Bar Graph.** Look at the circle graph about where the federal government gets its money (page 187). Change this graph into a bar graph.

2. **Making a Line Graph.** Make a line graph showing how much the federal government has spent on national defense since 1980. Find this information in the current *Statistical Abstract of the United States* in your local library.

3. **Making Decisions.** Suppose you are a candidate for President of the United States. As President, you would like to balance the budget. Choose two ways to accomplish this goal. Write a short explanation of your decision-making process.

Focusing on Citizenship

1. **Recognizing Ideologies.** As you have read, many American manufacturers favor high protective tariffs that encourage citizens to buy American-made goods. Do you think Americans should avoid buying foreign products? Why or why not?

2. **Researching Excise Taxes.** Find out how much federal excise tax is charged on the following items: (a) a gallon of gasoline, (b) a five-minute telephone call, (c) four radial tires, (d) two airplane tickets to your state capital, (e) a package of cigarettes.

3. **Completing Tax Forms.** Suppose you earn $15,000 and have no dependents. Obtain federal income tax form 1040EZ and the information booklet that goes with it. Fill out the form and compute your tax.

4. **Holding a Debate.** Here are two viewpoints on cutting the federal budget deficit: 1) increase taxes on wealthy individuals and maintain services; 2) lower taxes on wealthy individuals and cut services. Divide into teams to research the arguments supporting each position. Then hold a debate on this question.

Should English Become the Official Language of the United States?

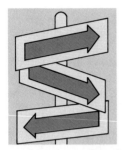

"We can speak any language we want to at the dinner table, but English is the language of public discourse, of business, and of the voting booth."

The Issue in Question

S. I. Hayakawa, a former United States Senator from California, made the above statement in 1981. That year Senator Hayakawa, himself an immigrant, proposed an amendment to the Constitution that would make English the official national language. In 1983, Hayakawa helped form a national organization called "US English" to promote the English language movement at the state and national level.

Currently the federal government prints many documents, such as voting ballots and social security forms, in different languages. Some 50 different languages are used yearly in federal court cases. And to meet the needs of students with limited skills in English, the federal government and many state governments provide funds to school districts for programs taught in more than 70 languages.

The English language amendment would represent a major change in public policy. It would make English the official language for public documents, government operations, voting ballots, and schools. Many government programs and practices would be affected.

Background on the Amendment

Since its introduction in 1981, the English language amendment has gained steady support. During the past decade, moreover, about one-third of the states have passed laws or amendments to state constitutions that make English the official state language. In 1986, voters in California approved such a state amendment by a margin of nearly three to one. Voters in Florida and Colorado approved similar measures in 1988.

Supporters of the English amendment note that a knowledge of English is already a requirement for becoming an American citizen. Since this is the case, they say, there is no need for bilingual ballots for voters. Nor is there any danger of violating the right to free speech. Because people will not be required to speak English in business or personal matters, the English language amendment is consistent with the First Amendment.

Critics of the English language amendment know that good English skills are important for success in this country. But they believe there are already many economic and educational incentives encouraging immigrants to learn English. They point to the fact that thousands of foreign-language speakers are currently enrolled in English classes.

Critics of the English language amendment also argue that it would have the effect of discriminating against many immigrant groups and denying them basic government services. They fear that without multilingual ballots, for example, many foreign-speaking citizens would be discouraged from voting.

Arguments for the Amendment.

1. The amendment will encourage the greater use of English, a trend that will help immigrants advance and participate more fully in American culture.
2. Multilingual government and school programs foster division rather than national unity.
3. The increased use of English will unify Americans.

Arguments Against the Amendment.

1. Non-English speakers need multilingual programs to help them participate fully in our society and suceed in school.
2. The proposed amendment promotes discrimination against non-English speakers.
3. Diversity of languages enriches American culture and life.

Making Decisions

1. **Distinguishing Fact from Opinion.** Review the arguments for and against the English language amendment. Which arguments are based on fact? Which are based on opinion?
2. **Predicting Consequences.** If the proposed amendment were approved, what changes in public policy might result? What would be the impact on non-English speaking Americans?
3. **Demonstrating Reasoned Judgment.** If you were a member of Congress and had to vote on the English language amendment, what position would you take? Why would you take that position? Use the "Arguments For," the "Arguments Against," and "The Decision-Making Checklist" on this page to help you make your decision and develop your answer. Be sure to think about the ethnic makeup of your state and the wishes of your constituents, as well as your own views.

The Decision-Making Checklist

✔	**Clarify the problem.** (What is the issue or conflict?)
✔	**Create a list of possible solutions.** (How might you resolve the problem?)
✔	**Compare the pros and cons of each solution.** (What are the strengths and weaknesses of each solution?)
✔	**Consider your values and goals.** (What is important to you in choosing a course of action, and why?)
✔	**Choose a course of action and evaluate the results.** (What would you decide, and how could you judge the outcome?)

3 State and Local Governments

Previewing the Unit

Until late March, 1989, the waterway known as Prince William Sound in Alaska was a largely unspoiled wonderland. Bald eagles and snow geese soared above seas teeming with fish. Sandpipers flocked to the beaches, and seals and otters swam offshore. By the end of March, though, Prince William Sound was a blackened disaster area—the victim of the worst oil spill in American history. State and local officials called for immediate action. "There's going to have to be a plan that satisfies our specialists," said Governor Steve Cowper. Through the summer, work crews tried to clean up the shoreline and save wildlife. At the same time, legislators worked for tougher measures to protect Alaska's natural beauty.

States and towns alike are responsible for what happens within their borders. In this unit, you will study how these smaller units of government manage their affairs.

Chapters in This Unit

11   States and State Legislatures
12   Governors and State Agencies
13   State Courts
14   Local Governments
15   Urban Problems

◀ Local government in the form of town meetings, like this one in Vermont, dates back to New England's colonial days.

207

11

States and State Legislatures

The Maryland State Senate, pictured above, is in Annapolis, the state's capital.

Previewing the Chapter

The Constitution is the "supreme law of the land," but many matters are left to the states to regulate. And laws and public policies sometimes vary from state to state as much as the landscapes and the local accents do. This chapter explores how state governments work and how they influence the lives of their citizens.

 Before you read, look up these key terms in the Glossary at the back of this book: *unicameral, bicameral, initiative, referendum, recall, sunshine law.*

 As you read, look for answers to these questions:
1. How does state government affect your daily life?
2. What is the main purpose of a state constitution?
3. What happens in a state legislature?
4. How can citizens take part in lawmaking at the state level?
5. What do state legislators do?

1 The States and You

Do you listen to the evening news on a nationwide television or radio program? If so, you may have noticed that most of the news about American government has to do with the President, members of the Congress, or some other officials in the federal government. This is also true of the news in most of our daily newspapers. Most of the news on the front pages has to do with the activities of the federal government. News about a governor or a state legislator or a state agency is sometimes hard to find. At times, people may wonder what the state governments are doing.

Actually, the state governments are doing a great deal. State governments, for example, provide services that touch the lives of every citizen. Consider your own life as a citizen of one of the 50 states. When you are born, your state issues a birth certificate. As you grow up, your state provides an education for you if you are one of the thousands of students attending public schools. While you are still in school, your state will issue you a license to drive a car. If you go to work after high school, your state sets the safety standards that apply to your job. If you go to college, you may attend a state college or a state university. Should you decide to become a barber, a lawyer, a veterinarian, or a teacher, your state will issue you a license to work at your job. Should you eventually decide to get married, your state will issue you

Every State Provides Services

The state sets safety standards that apply to student jobs after school.

One of the many ways in which the states help citizens is by providing an education for everyone. These students have just graduated from a public high school.

a marriage license. Should the marriage fail, a state court will handle the divorce proceedings. When you die, your state may decide who will inherit your property if you have not left a will.

State governments also provide many services to people with special needs. They provide pensions and medical care for persons over 65 who are not covered by the Social Security program. They operate hospitals for persons who are mentally ill or who are addicted to drugs or to alcohol. They provide schools and jobs for the blind. They set up free vaccination clinics. With laws that forbid discrimination on the part of employers, they promote the welfare of women and members of minority groups.

The State Justice System

The nation's criminal justice system is largely under state control. About 90 percent of all people in law enforcement work for state and local governments. As of 1989, for example, New York City had slightly less than 27,000 police officers. This was almost equal to the total number of law enforcement workers in the federal government. The states are responsible for most prisoners too. At any given time, only about 10 percent of all prisoners are held in federal prisons. The remaining 90 percent are held in state prisons or local jails. Most criminal cases end up in state courts. Juvenile courts and reformatories (prisons for juveniles) are operated by the states.

The State Political System

Qualifications for voting are set by state law. All elections, including those for President and Congress, take place in the states. Both of our major political parties rely on state groups to manage and provide workers for their political campaigns. All of the elected officials of this country are elected by voters in the states. Many members of Congress receive their first experience as lawmakers in state legislatures.

Congressional candidates often focus their campaigns on state issues when campaigning for the House of Representatives or the Senate. After being elected, many members of Congress spend a great deal of time working for their home districts or states. Finally, every four years, party delegates from the states make one of the most important decisions in our political system—they select party candidates for President of the United States.

You can see that state governments influence our lives in many ways. Each state does so in a different manner, however. There are great differences among the states in the laws that reg-

SKILL BUILDER

Which state in this chart has the fewest people per square mile?

How Some States Compare In Land Area and Population

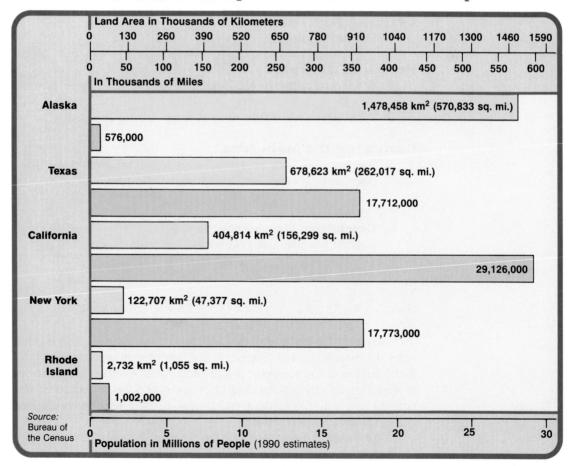

Land Area in Thousands of Kilometers
0, 130, 260, 390, 520, 650, 780, 910, 1040, 1170, 1300, 1460, 1590

0, 50, 100, 150, 200, 250, 300, 350, 400, 450, 500, 550, 600
In Thousands of Miles

Alaska — 1,478,458 km² (570,833 sq. mi.)
576,000

Texas — 678,623 km² (262,017 sq. mi.)
17,712,000

California — 404,814 km² (156,299 sq. mi.)
29,126,000

New York — 122,707 km² (47,377 sq. mi.)
17,773,000

Rhode Island — 2,732 km² (1,055 sq. mi.)
1,002,000

Source: Bureau of the Census

0, 5, 10, 15, 20, 25, 30
Population in Millions of People (1990 estimates)

ulate such activities as marriage, education, and employment. Some states allow marriage at age fourteen with parental consent. The requirements for graduation from high school or college differ from one state to another. All states set a minimum wage that must be paid to workers, but the amount set differs from state to state. There is even variety among the states in saying what crimes are and how they should be punished.

Since 1790, Congress has admitted 37 states to the Union. The last two to be admitted were Alaska in January 1959 and Hawaii in August of the same year. Today, most citizens live in one of the 50 states. The exceptions are people who live in Washington, D.C. or in territories such as Puerto Rico. A **territory** is land owned by the United States. People who live in Washington, D.C. have their own local government, apart from any state.

SECTION *1* *Review*

Defining Key Terms
1. Define: territory.

Recalling the Facts
2. What are some of the services that a state government provides?
3. What are some differences in laws among the states?

Reviewing the Main Idea
4. Answer "As you read . . ." question 1 on page 208: How does state government affect your daily life?

Critical Thinking
5. **Developing Arguments.** Develop an argument for or against making the District of Columbia a state.

2 State Constitutions

Each of the 50 states has a written constitution. Just as the federal Constitution is the supreme law of our country, a state constitution is the supreme law of each state. A state constitution is superior to any law passed by a state or local legislature. No part of any state constitution, however, may conflict with the United States Constitution.

State constitutions are similar to the federal Constitution. Most contain a preamble, a main body, and a bill of rights.

The preamble is an opening statement that usually describes the purpose of the state's government. In several state constitutions, the bill of rights is called a **declaration of rights**. The protections are similar to those in the United States Constitution. The state guarantees certain freedoms that the government cannot take from the people. Freedom of speech and religion are such freedoms. Some of the rights that are listed, however, differ from those in the federal Bill of Rights. The right of the people to move from state to state, the right to be free from being jailed for debt, and the right to self-government are a few examples.

In the main body of a state constitution, the legislative, executive, and judicial branches of the state government are usually described. The powers of the state, especially the state's power to tax, to spend, or to borrow money, are also described.

State constitutions vary greatly in length. A few are about the same length as the United States Constitution—about 7,000 words. Most contain between 15,000 and 35,000 words. The constitution of Louisiana is the longest; it has more than 200,000 words.

The Preamble and Bill of Rights

The Main Body

Organization of State Government

LEGISLATIVE BRANCH
Senate
House of Representatives (sometimes called the Assembly)

EXECUTIVE BRANCH
Governor
Lieutenant Governor, Secretary of State, Attorney General, Other elected officials
Heads of Departments or State Agencies
(many are appointed by the Governor)

JUDICIAL BRANCH
State Supreme Court
Court of Appeals
Trial Courts, Probate Courts, Juvenile Courts, Family Courts, and others

SKILL BUILDER

Who has the same position in a state government that the President has in the federal government?

Amendment Procedures

Too much detail in a constitution leads to problems. As times change, new ways of doing things are sometimes necessary. Because of this, many states have to amend their constitutions to make them into working documents. In fact, several states have amended their constitutions more than 100 times. Both Louisiana and California have amended their constitutions more than 300 times. In contrast, the United States Constitution has been amended only 26 times!

All state constitutions allow for change or amendment. The most common method for adding amendments is for the state legislature to make a proposal for a constitutional change. The vote required for approval ranges from a simple majority to two-thirds or three-fifths of the lawmakers. After a proposal is approved by the legislature, it is put on the ballot at the next election. If a majority of the people of the state votes to approve the amendment, it becomes part of the state constitution. Delaware is the only state that does not require approval of amendments by the people of the state.

SECTION 2 *Review*

Defining Key Terms
1. Define: declaration of rights.

Recalling the Facts
2. What are some ways in which state constitutions are similar to the United States Constitution?
3. How do the lengths of state constitutions compare to the length of the United States Constitution?
4. How may state constitutions be amended?

Reviewing the Main Idea
5. Answer "As you read . . ." question 2 on page 208: What is the main purpose of a state constitution?

Critical Thinking
6. **Expressing Problems Clearly.** As you have read, state constitutions are amended much more often than the United States Constitution. Explain why you think this is true, listing all of the possible reasons why state constitutions need more frequent amendment. Think about the areas of law covered by a state constitution as you answer.

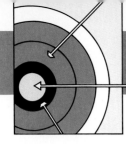

Citizenship Skills

Registering to Vote

A government "for the people and by the people" means little when Americans do not exercise their right to vote. When each eligible voter casts a vote, he or she makes a difference in shaping the future. Consider this: In the 1960 presidential election, John F. Kennedy beat Richard Nixon by only 118,550 popular votes. That works out to about 40 people from every county in the United States. If these voters had not registered and had stayed home from the polls, imagine how different history might have been!

The process of registration usually involves filling out a form like the one shown below, giving your name, address, and date of birth. You may be asked to list other information as well, such as your political party affiliation or your social security number. And while most states do not require identification when you register, they do require you to sign an *affidavit* (a written statement swearing that information you provided for them is true).

In about half the states, you can register by mail. In other states, you must appear before a *registrar,* or voting official at a town or city hall. Still other states allow voters to register at the local offices of agencies such as the Department of Motor Vehicles. You can contact your town clerk or county board of elections for more specific information about the procedure in your state.

Practicing Skills

1. All states have residence requirements for voters. That is, they require voters to have lived in the state for a certain period of time—usually at least 30 days before the election. Whom would you contact to find out about your state's residence requirements?

2. **Predicting Consequences.** What do you think would happen if voter registration was not required?

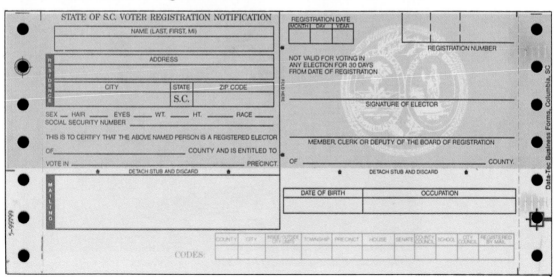

3 State Legislatures and How They Work

The state legislature is the lawmaking body of each state. In all states, except one, the legislature is made up of two houses. The one exception is Nebraska, which has a **unicameral**, or one-house legislature. In different states, the lower house is called by different names such as the House of Representatives or the Assembly. The upper house is called the Senate.

The members of a state legislature are called **legislators**. In most states, they are elected by the people of the state for either a two-year term or a four-year term. The legislators meet in the capitol building, located in the capital city of their state.

The Size of Legislatures

The size of state legislatures varies greatly. In most cases, the total membership is 200 or less, but a few are larger. Members are elected to both houses of the state legislature on the basis of state voting districts. Each of the states having a **bicameral** (two-house) legislature is divided into districts. The more people there are living in an area, the more districts that area has. There is one set of districts for the Senate and another set for the lower house. Each district has about the same number of people living within it. But there are always more districts for the lower house than for the Senate. For this reason, the lower house always has more

The Nebraska state legislature, shown above, is unicameral.

members than the upper house. Each Senate district sends one person to the Senate and each lower house district sends one person to the lower house.

In Nebraska, there is only one set of districts for the single legislative body, which is called the Senate. There are 49 members in the Nebraska Senate. The members are elected every two years.

Qualifications for Legislators

Residence in the state is required in all cases. By law or by custom, members must also reside in the district that they represent. Age requirements differ. A few states allow 18 year olds to serve in the legislature. In all other states, representatives must be at least 21. Many states set 25 as the minimum age for senators. Terms of office also differ. In most cases, members of the lower house serve two years, while senators serve four-year terms.

State legislatures are busy places. In those states with large populations, more than 8,000 bills may be entered into the legislature in a single year. At the most, only about 30 or 35 percent of these bills will become law.

The Lawmaking Process

In general, the lawmaking process in a state legislature is similar to the process in Congress. A bill is entered into the upper or lower house. After that, it goes to a committee for study and debate. Amendments or other changes can be made in committee. A public hearing is often held on an important bill. At the hearing, people have a chance to speak for or against the bill. In most cases, the committee vote on a particular bill takes place in a closed (secret) session. A majority vote in favor of the bill sends it to the entire house for discussion, debate, and vote. Most states require that all revenue bills start in the lower house.

If a bill passes one house, it is then sent to the other. In general, the bill goes through the same steps in the other house. In some states, however, there are rules that allow the commitee hearings to be skipped.

Delays are frequent. Amendments must be discussed and voted upon. Sometimes delay is caused when there are similar bills in each house but neither house will accept the wording of the other's bill. At such times, both bills are referred to a conference committee which tries to use wording that both houses will accept. If both houses approve the new wording, a single bill is then sent to the governor to be signed.

Elected leaders play an important part in the state lawmaking process. The two most important leaders are the Speaker of the lower house and the Majority Leader of the Senate. Both are selected by the majority party in each house. As in Congress, the selection usually takes place at a private meeting of party members. In many states, the Speaker and the Majority Leader appoint the chairpersons of all committees. They also make important decisions about rules of procedure during a debate. Getting the support of the Speaker or the Majority Leader is often the first step toward the passage of a bill.

The lieutenant governor, in states that have one, presides over the Senate. The position is similar to that of the Vice President in the United States Senate. That is, the lieutenant governor is not actually a member of the legislature and has little lawmaking power.

Other Duties of State Legislatures

In addition to making laws, state legislatures have other duties to perform. They review the governor's appointments. Final approval of appointments is made by the Senate. The legislatures also judge the work of the state agencies, noting especially how they spend money. Since the budget of each state agency must be approved by the legislature, it is important that lawmakers know how state money is being used.

State legislatures are usually given higher marks for doing their jobs than is the Congress of the United States. Recent polls show that many people think the state legislatures are less wasteful and better at day-to-day governing.

Quiz on the States

1. Which of the 50 states has the smallest population?
2. Which New England state was once owned by another New England state?
3. Where in the United States does sunlight first touch land every morning?
4. Which eight states are named after Indian tribes?
5. Which three states are named after famous women?
6. What is the only state to have existed under six different national flags?
7. Which state is sometimes called the Flickertail State?
8. In what state did the first "cowboys" ride?
9. Which is the Blue Hen State?
10. Which two states are bordered by the greatest number of states?

Answers: 1. Alaska. **2.** Maine. In 1677 the state of Massachusetts bought Maine from the family who owned it. **3.** Mt. Katahdin, Maine. **4.** Alabama, Arkansas, Illinois, Iowa, Kansas, Michigan, Missouri, and Utah. **5.** Maryland, for Henrietta Maria, wife of England's Charles I; Virginia, for Queen Elizabeth I, the "Virgin Queen"; and West Virginia, also for Queen Elizabeth I. **6.** Texas. **7.** North Dakota, which has a large population of flickertails, a kind of squirrel. **8.** New York. During the Revolution, Tories were called "cowboys" because they often hid in bushes ringing cowbells to trap patriots who went looking for their cows. **9.** Delaware. **10.** Missouri and Tennessee—each is bordered by eight other states.

SECTION 3 *Review*

Defining Key Terms
1. Define: unicameral, legislator, bicameral.

Recalling the Facts
2. What are the general requirements for election to a state legislature?

3. How do bills become laws in states?

Reviewing the Main Idea
4. Answer "As you read . . ." question 3 on page 208: What happens in a state legislature?

Critical Thinking
5. Formulating Questions. Is it better for a state legislature to have one or two houses? Create a list of specific questions that you would need to have answered before you could reach a conclusion on this issue.

4 The People as Decision Makers

Under our system of government, the people rely entirely on their elected representatives to pass laws, to amend the Constitution, or to impeach high officials. That is why our system is called a representative democracy. At the state level, however, the people have a chance to take a direct part in these activities. The people in some states are allowed to take a direct part in passing or vetoing laws, or in removing an elected official from office. They do so in statewide or local elections by means of initiative, referendum, or recall.

Some states allow voters to amend the state constitution by **initiative.** In 21 states the voters take part in making laws by this method. Each of these 21 states allows the use of the initiative at both the state level and the local level. About a dozen other states allow its use only at the local level.

The number of voters who must sign an initiative petition varies. In some states, the requirement is eight percent of the number of votes cast for governor in the last election. In a state with many voters, this can mean as many as 300,000 signatures.

Initiative

This young voter is adding his signature to an initiative petition. Some states allow voters to amend the state constitution by this means.

Referendum

Another form of direct legislation is the **referendum**. It is used in about half of the states. In a referendum, a bill passed by the legislature is referred to the people to be voted on before the bill can become law. Many referendums are in the form of proposals, for example, a proposal to levy (pass) an increase in state taxes. In its most common form, the referendum is known as the "people's veto."

Some states have a **mandatory referendum**. Certain bills *must* be referred to the voters before they can become laws. Some states require that a bond issue for school construction or a proposal to call a constitutional convention be referred to the voters.

The **popular referendum**, the most common type, allows people to oppose or reject bills passed by the legislature and signed into law by the governor. Again, signatures of registered voters must be obtained. Then at a general election, the people vote on the bill.

Voters vary in their response to initiative and referendum proposals. There is often very little interest when the proposal involves a technical matter, such as a plan to reorganize state government. However, voter turnout is usually heavy when the bill involves something that people feel strongly about, such as legalized gambling or the use of marijuana. Matters of health also attract voters. Thus, in many states, the issue of putting fluoride in drinking water has been put to the voters. Dentists argue that the use of fluoride helps to prevent tooth decay. Others say that fluoride could be harmful to health. This issue is almost always a heated one, and there is usually a large turnout. Bills which have to do with taxes also bring out the voters.

Recall is a method by which voters may remove an elected official from office. Only 15 states allow recall. The first step, again, is to obtain a petition signed by a certain number of registered voters. The number of signatures is usually 25 percent of the votes cast in the last election. After the required number of signatures has been gathered, a special election is held. The name of the person being recalled, along with his or her replacement, is on the ballot. A majority vote keeps or removes the elected official. Recall elections do not have a high rate of success. Only one governor has ever been removed by recall.

Recall

SECTION 4 *Review*

Defining Key Terms
1. Define: initiative, referendum, mandatory referendum, popular referendum, recall.

Recalling the Facts
2. How many voters must sign a petition in order to get an initiative measure on the ballot? Is the number the same in all states?
3. How does a referendum differ from an initiative?
4. How can an elected official be removed from office?

Reviewing the Main Idea
5. Answer "As you read . . ." question 4 on page 208: How can citizens take part in lawmaking at the state level?

Critical Thinking
6. **Drawing Conclusions.** Explain why you think the methods of initiative, referendum, and recall would or would not work well at the national level.

5 The Job of a State Lawmaker

There is a high rate of turnover among state legislators—a much higher rate than among members of Congress. One reason for the high turnover is the low salary. In most states, legislators say that they cannot survive on the pay without taking another job. Several states pay salaries below $10,000 a year. Also, legislative sessions are often scheduled at odd times. In some cases, legislators must go back and forth to the capital city three or four times a year.

In states with large populations, the work of the legislators is sometimes exhausting. This is especially true at the end, or adjournment, of a session. Many bills still have not been thoroughly studied in the final weeks before adjournment. To finish their work, lawmakers must work late hours. In one state legislature, the clock was stopped before midnight so that time would not "run out." This allowed the members legally to vote on all unfinished measures.

Complaints of Legislators

Over the years, legislators have made many complaints about their jobs. Here are a few: (1) Terms of office should be longer, particularly in the lower house. With only a two-year term of office, a newly elected member must start campaigning immediately for reelection. (2) The workload of the various committees should be made equal. Some committees have very few bills to consider, while others have too many. (3) Certain committees have too many members. When there are more than 20 persons on a committee, discussion by every member is difficult. (4) All committee hearings should be scheduled in advance, so that the public may know the time and place of each hearing. One effort that has been made in this regard is the passage of **sunshine laws**. These are laws that forbid committee hearings to be held in secret behind closed doors.

Legislators' complaints vary from state to state. One complaint of legislators from all 50 states, however, has to do with publicity. All feel that their work is too often ignored by the media. While the activities of the President and Congress are in the news almost every day, the activities in the state capitol are often given little or no publicity.

Legislators in the Home District

The job of a state legislator is a busy one. Back in the home district, legislators are asked to attend breakfasts, lunches, banquets, funerals, and many other public functions. To refuse such

In the state capitol, legislators spend a great deal of time attending committee hearings and being on the floor of the legislature. This photo shows the New Jersey state legislature.

invitations is to risk the bad feelings of the voters. A lawmaker usually tries to meet and talk to as many voters as possible. Personal contacts are often very important in getting reelected.

Legislators in the State Capitol

In the state capitol, most legislators spend most of their time visiting with people, attending committee hearings, and being on the floor of the legislature. In one day, a state legislator might answer several telephone calls, meet many visitors, and dictate numerous letters in his or her office. Committee work involves a heavy schedule of studying and discussing proposed laws. Outside opinions must be heard, amendments must be considered, and discussions must be held before the final vote.

To some legislators, however, the most difficult part of the job is not the meetings, the telephone calls, or the long hours. Rather, it is deciding how to vote.

Should legislators vote in accordance with the wishes of their constituents or according to their personal standards or conscience? As you read on page 16, there are several possible answers, depending on how a legislator views his or her role. One is that a legislator is merely the representative of the voters in his or her district and should vote according to their will. Another answer is that a legislator is chosen because of constituents' confidence in his or her ability to make proper decisions for them. He or she should vote as conscience and beliefs dictate.

The answer to this question is very important to legislators. Voting against the wishes of the people back home can mean defeat in the next election. At the same time, a lawmaker may have excellent reasons (the good of the entire state, for example) for voting according to personal beliefs.

Fixing a Constitutional Flaw

Sometimes a dare is just a dare, and nothing comes of it. Other times it can lead to a great surprise. This was certainly the case in 1987 when Arizona State Representative Jim Green paid a visit to his son's junior high class in Tucson.

Green was there to speak about political life and the beauty of the American system of government. As part of his talk, he urged students in the class to examine the state constitution. If they could find anything unfair in it, Green promised to work to have those parts corrected.

The class took the challenge seriously. To everyone's amazement, the students found that the constitution limited the state's top offices to men only. The restriction applied to the offices of governor, secretary of state, treasurer, and attorney general. This was especially surprising news since the governor in 1987 was a woman named Rose Mofford.

A group of students made a trip to the capitol to present their findings. Red-faced legislators promptly voted to eliminate the ban against women.

SECTION 5 *Review*

Defining Key Terms
1. Define: sunshine law.

Recalling the Facts
2. What are some of the duties of a state legislator while at home in his or her district?
3. What are the duties of a legislator while the legislature is in session?

Reviewing the Main Idea
4. Answer "As you read . . ." question 5 on page 208: What do state legislators do?

Critical Thinking
5. **Identifying Alternatives.** What should a legislator do when his or her personal beliefs conflict with the wishes of constituents on an issue? Does your answer depend on the particular issue involved?

Government and Law

State Lotteries

A 29-year-old truckdriver won $23 million in New York. A Florida resident took home a whopping $55 million. Fourteen lucky ticket-holders split $115 million in Pennsylvania. All of these people were big winners in state lottery games.

Twenty-eight states and the District of Columbia run public lotteries. The idea is not new. The 13 original colonies and many of the early states had lotteries. Money raised by these drawings was used to build bridges, canals, roads, and schools. A number of American universities, including Harvard, Yale, Brown, Columbia, and Dartmouth, were also supported with state lottery funds. Then scandals came to light about the use of lottery revenues, and the drawings were stopped during the 1800s.

New Hampshire was the first state to set up a modern lottery. Other states, in urgent need of money, soon turned to lotteries as well. If your state runs a lottery, you may have seen tickets for sale at local convenience stores or gas stations. These tickets usually cost a dollar or two. Prizes range from a free game or a few dollars to thousands and even millions of dollars. Some states also run daily or weekly drawings. In these games, players choose a combination of four to six numbers. A ticket-holder who selects the winning combination is entitled to the money in the jackpot.

Despite the publicity surrounding the "big winners," the chances of winning the jackpot in any of the lottery games are very slim, usually one in several million. It's the state that ends up the real winner.

Across the nation, a wide variety of lottery games can be played—each with its own specific ticket.

In most lottery states, the money collected from the games can be spent for any purpose. Sometimes the money is reserved specifically for public education. A few states earmark lottery money for other purposes. In Pennsylvania, for example, the funds go to support programs for the elderly. In Massachusetts, the money is distributed to local governments. Colorado spends its lottery revenues on parks and recreation.

State lotteries are popular, but they are also controversial. Supporters point out that lotteries are voluntary—people play because they want to. Some supporters even see state lotteries as a form of entertainment provided by the state. Many supporters also argue that people will gamble no matter what the law says, so the state may as well get its "piece of the action." The money raised from this "gambling" can then be used for good purposes that benefit the general public, rather than filling the pockets of casino owners.

Some critics of state lotteries argue that any form of gambling is morally wrong. Studies have not shown a direct link between lotteries and compulsive gambling. Nevertheless, playing the lottery is easy and not very time-consuming. Because of these characteristics, some experts fear that lotteries can have a negative effect on people, especially teenagers, who otherwise would not gamble but could get "hooked" on playing lottery games.

Other opponents worry that it is the poor who spend the largest portion of their income on playing state lotteries. The poor have the most to gain if they win big. But they often spend money on lottery tickets that they cannot well afford, usually without ever winning their money back. Studies in California have found that the poor spend 2.1 percent of their income on lottery tickets, compared with the rich, who spend 0.3 percent.

Those who have studied lotteries warn that states should not become too dependent on money from lottery sales. California, for example, was able to raise large sums of money for education when its lottery first began. Public schools and colleges began to count on lottery funds to help pay teachers' salaries and buy "extras" like computers and lab equipment. But income from lotteries is not always steady. After the initial excitement wears off, fewer people play the games. A state that depends on lottery sales may not get all the money it had counted on. Such shortages of expected revenue can lead to unbalanced state budgets.

States raise extra money in a number of ways. When you pay a fee to get your driver's license or when you buy a fishing license, you are contributing to state revenues. Fines for speeding or littering also help fund state treasuries. Some states sell alcoholic beverages at state-run stores and many states operate toll roads and bridges. State lotteries have become another way for many states to raise extra revenue. Whether lotteries continue to be an important source of funds or go the way of the lotteries of the past remains to be seen. For the time being, though, the dream of hitting the lottery jackpot stills attracts many enthusiastic players.

Questions to think about:

1. Do you support or oppose state lotteries? What arguments do you find the most persuasive for or against a state lottery?
2. What stand do you suppose advocates for senior citizens might take on state lotteries? Explain.

CHAPTER *11 REVIEW*

CHAPTER SUMMARY

Section 1 State governments influence our lives in many ways. All 50 states provide services such as education, medical care, and law enforcement. The right to perform certain jobs requires a license from a state. State officials also direct the criminal justice system and organize elections.

Section 2 The basic law of each state is the state's constitution. No part of any state constitution may conflict with the United States Constitution. State constitutions guarantee civil liberties and describe the framework and powers of the state government. Most state constitutions are quite long and have been amended many times.

Section 3 Each state legislature, except Nebraska's, has a lower house and a Senate. The size of the legislatures varies from one state to another. Seats in both the upper and lower houses are based on population, with more members in the lower house than in the Senate. Usually, legislators serve two-year terms in the lower house and four-year terms in the upper house.

Section 4 The lawmaking process in state legislatures is similar to the one in Congress. The Speaker of the House and the Majority Leader of the Senate play important roles in this process.

Section 5 Almost half the states give voters direct power over the lawmaking process through the initiative and the referendum. Fifteen states allow voters to recall elected officials.

Section 6 Both at home and in the state capitol, legislators have many obligations. Many legislators think that terms of office should be longer and committee workloads more manageable. Legislators are often torn between following the wishes of their constituents and voting in accordance with their own beliefs.

Reviewing Key Terms

Match the following terms with the definitions below. Write your answers on a separate sheet of paper.

unicameral   initiative
bicameral   referendum
sunshine law   recall

1. a vote by the people to approve a bill before it becomes a law

2. term for a legislature with two houses

3. term for a legislature with one house

4. a method for voters to remove elected officials from office

5. a law that forbids secret committee hearings

6. a method for voters to amend the state constitution or take part in making laws

Understanding Main Ideas

1. Name at least five ways in which your state government influences your life.

2. What limitation is placed on all state constitutions?

3. What three parts do most state constitutions have?

4. Name three ways that many state constitutions differ from the U.S. Constitution.

5. What is the difference between a bicameral and a unicameral legislature?

6. Briefly describe the lawmaking process in a state legislature.

7. What is the difference between a mandatory referendum and a popular referendum?

8. What are three complaints made by state legislators about their jobs?

Critical Thinking

1. Recognizing Cause and Effect. In some states, there are more registered lobbyists in the state capital than there are members in the legislature (over 200 lobbyists in some cases). What effect might this have on the legislative process?

2. Demonstrating Reasoned Judgment. No state has educational requirements (such as a high school diploma) for members of the legislature. Should there be such requirements? Why or why not?

Practicing Skills

1. Registering to Vote. Have your local voter registration office send copies of the forms needed to register. Have your teacher or parents help you complete these forms.

2. Researching State Laws. Find out what your state laws say about (a) the age at which a person may get a driver's license, (b) the minimum wage for minors, (c) the legal age for marriage, and (d) the age at which a person can run for the state legislature. Ask your librarian to help you research.

Focusing on Citizenship

1. Staging a Mock Committee Hearing. Select a bill under discussion in the state legislature. Find out as much as you can about the pros and cons of this bill. Get the information from local newspapers, special interest groups supporting and opposing the bill, and your state legislators' offices. Then hold a mock session of a committee hearing to discuss and vote on the bill.

2. Talking with a Legislator. Invite a state legislator to visit your class to discuss problems in your district.

3. Doing Field Research. Choose an issue or activity that interests you, such as the arts, teen health care, or pollution control. Contact a group that lobbies for legislation in this area. Find out what kinds of legislation the group supports and opposes. Ask how citizens can become involved.

4. Making a Chart. Prepare a chart showing some basic facts about your state government, such as when elections are held, how many legislators there are, what the qualifications for legislators are, and how the constitution may be amended.

CHAPTER 12

Governors and State Agencies

The governor of Alabama lives in the beautiful Governor's Mansion in Montgomery, the state capital.

Previewing the Chapter

The governor of a state holds a powerful and prestigious position. Five governors have been elected President, and others have become United States Senators. This chapter outlines the qualifications and duties of governors and describes how the many types of state agencies help keep state governments running smoothly.

■ **Before you read,** look up these key terms in the Glossary at the back of this book: *pardon, reprieve, special session, item veto, regressive tax, property tax.*

■ **As you read,** look for answers to these questions:
1. What qualifications must a candidate for governor have?
2. What major types of duties do governors perform?
3. What are the major state offices?
4. What are some of the ways states raise money to run their governments?

1 Qualifications and Requirements

The governor is the most powerful leader in state government. In an emergency he or she is the only official who can speak for the entire state. Governors have some powers that allow them to influence public policy. As head of the executive branch of state government, the governor has much prestige.

The executive branch is organized along similar lines in all state governments. The governor is the chief executive officer. In some states, the governor is assisted by a lieutenant governor. The rest of the executive branch is made up of elected or appointed officials and a number of executive agencies.

Governors

Most governors have served in their state legislatures or other state offices. Many have held important positions, such as Speaker of the House or Majority Leader, in their state legislatures. Once in a while, people with no previous political experience have been elected governor. Nelson Rockefeller of New York and Ronald Reagan of California are two such people.

Qualifications. To be elected governor, a woman or man must be a United States citizen and have lived in a state for a certain period of time. In most states, the candidate must be at least 25 to 30 years old. In Oklahoma, however, the minimum age required is 35.

In 43 states, a lieutenant governor is the second highest state official. The qualifications for this office are the same as those for governor. The only formal duty of the lieutenant governor is to preside over the state Senate. However, she or he may serve on boards or commissions as an informal representative of the governor.

A typical governor is a white male and has been a lawyer. As of 1989, there have been eight women governors. At times, a governor's wife has been appointed to take her husband's place. Miriam "Ma" Ferguson of Texas and Nellie Ross of Wyoming became the first elected women governors in 1925.

Selection. All governors are now elected by the people. A majority vote is required in all but four states. In these four states, a candidate may win by a plurality. In a **plurality**, the person with the largest number of votes wins, even if the largest number is not a majority of all the votes cast.

In some states, candidates for governor are nominated in primary elections. In several states, however, the two major candidates are selected at state conventions of the Democratic and Re-

Madeleine Kunin, Governor of Vermont, served as lieutenant governor and in the state legislature before being elected governor.

publican parties. In about half of the states, voters cast a single vote to elect a governor/lieutenant governor "team." In other states, votes for the two offices are separate. In these states, the governor and the lieutenant governor sometimes belong to different parties. When this happens, the two often disagree about state policy.

Term. In New Hampshire, Vermont, and Rhode Island, the governor serves for only two years. In all other states, the term is four years. In three states, the governor is allowed by law to serve only one term. In 26 states, governors cannot serve more than two terms in a row.

Succession. Each state constitution provides for someone to take the place of the governor if the office becomes vacant. In most states, the lieutenant governor is next in line of succession. In Maine, New Hampshire, New Jersey, and West Virginia, the president of the state Senate succeeds. In Arizona, Oregon, and Wyoming, the secretary of state succeeds.

Vacancies in the governor's office happen fairly often. Usually this happens because governors sometimes resign to run for the United States Senate or because they are appointed to the President's Cabinet.

Removal. Fifteen states allow the voters to recall the governor. Only one governor has ever been removed by recall, however (Lynn Frazier of North Dakota in 1921). All states except Oregon provide for removal by impeachment. In an impeachment,

Governors and State Agencies   231

charges of wrongdoing against the governor are drawn up by the lower house of the state legislature. The Senate sits as a court to hear the charges. In 1988, Governor Evan Mecham of Arizona became the first governor in over 60 years to be impeached.

Salary. The average salary of governors is about $75,000 a year. However, the gap between the lowest and highest is great. Salaries range from $35,000 a year in Arkansas to about $130,000 a year in New York. In most states the governor is also given a residence, usually called the governor's mansion. Money for travel and entertaining are also a part of a governor's income.

SECTION 1 *Review*

Defining Key Terms
1. Define: plurality.

Recalling the Facts
2. How are governors elected in various states?
3. What is the only formal duty of a lieutenant governor?

Reviewing the Main Idea
4. Answer "As you read . . ." question 1 on page 229: What qualifications must a candidate for governor have?

Critical Thinking
5. **Demonstrating Reasoned Judgment.** What do you think are some of the advantages and disadvantages in limiting the governor's term to two years? To two terms?

2 What Does a Governor Do?

As the chief executive of a state, a governor's job is often compared to the job of the President of the United States. A governor is leader of his or her political party at the state level. She or he is also the symbol of state government at public ceremonies. Like the President, a governor has many other duties. Some are executive duties. Others are judicial, legislative, and military.

Executive Duties

State constitutions make it the duty of the governor "to see that the laws are faithfully executed." This is a large order. In addition to a great number of criminal laws, there are numerous other state laws that must be enforced. Many states have more than 35 separate agencies within the executive branch which deal with different branches of state law. Any one of these agencies (the Department of Motor Vehicles, for example) may be responsible for carrying out thousands of laws. The governor must see that all of these agencies do their jobs properly.

The power to appoint helpers is important. Like the President, no governor can carry out all the duties that go with the job. He or she depends on many other individuals or groups for help.

In most states, the governor may appoint a number of personal assistants without getting the approval of the legislature. Among these assistants are a press secretary and aides who work with the legislature, the courts, and state agencies. The appointment of a person to be the head of a department usually requires approval by the Senate. Many states place other limits on the power of appointment. The governor of these states must appoint members of both political parties to state boards and commissions. This limitation is meant to prevent control of state boards and commissions by a single political party. Another limitation on a governor's appointment power requires that vacancies be filled with persons from different regions of the state.

Many top officials in the executive branch of most states are not appointed by the governor. These officials include the state attorney general, the state treasurer, and the superintendent of public education. These officials are usually elected, so they cannot be removed from office by the governor. Furthermore, these elected officials share executive power with the governor, and they are largely free of his or her control. Thus, you can see that

The Department of Motor Vehicles is an important state agency.

the governor is the chief executive officer of the state, but not the only one.

The preparation of the state budget is an important executive duty. The governor works closely with department heads and financial experts to decide how money will be spent in the fiscal year. Working out the details of the budget may take many months.

The state legislature must give final approval to the budget. However, the governor usually has a big say in who gets how much of the state's money. Having a balanced budget is important to any governor. As mentioned in Chapter 10, this is a budget in which spending does not go beyond income received from state taxes and other sources. By keeping state spending in line with income, the governor can take credit for being careful with the state's money.

What happens if there is a shortage of money? If this happens, taxes must be raised, state services (for example, health care) must be cut, or the amount of money given to state agencies must be reduced. Any of these choices is bound to create enemies. Balancing the budget is one of the most difficult tasks for any governor.

Judicial Duties

A governor also performs judicial duties. He or she may issue a **pardon**, which releases a person from prison. In most states, pardons cannot be granted to persons convicted of treason (acts of disloyalty to one's country) or to those who have been impeached and convicted by the legislature. A governor may grant a **reprieve**, an order which delays punishment for a crime. Reprieves are often granted in death-penalty cases. The delay allows the convicted person time to appeal to a higher court. A governor may **commute** a sentence, an order which reduces a sentence—a death sentence to life imprisonment, for example. Finally, a governor may grant a **parole**, an order releasing a prisoner before his or her sentence is completed. When a parole is given, the person reports regularly to a parole officer.

In many states there are limits to the governor's powers discussed above. That is, the governor shares these powers with a state board or commission. A pardon may be granted, for example, if it is approved by a board of pardons.

Legislative Duties

A governor also performs legislative duties. Although lawmaking is chiefly the job of the state legislature, all governors have some legislative powers. Every state constitution gives the governor power to call special sessions of the legislature. Some legislatures have a regular meeting for a certain number of months every year. Some legislatures meet every other year. A **special session** is a meeting other than the regular one.

A governor, like the President, must play many roles. Pictured above are Governor Bob Martinez of Florida (left) and Governor Evan Bayh of Indiana (right).

The governor may call a special session because she or he feels the legislature should reconsider an important bill that failed to pass in a regular session. Also, in some states the regular session is short. It does not allow legislators enough time to finish all the work to be done. In such states, special sessions are called fairly often.

Every year (usually in January) governors deliver a message to the legislature. The purpose of this annual message is to suggest needed legislation. Governors also deliver other messages to the legislature. They may deliver a budget message or a special message about an emergency. The success of "the message power" depends upon the personality and popularity of the governor.

In every state except North Carolina, the governor may veto laws passed by the state legislature. The governor's veto power is similar to the President's. The veto may be reversed by a two-thirds vote of the legislature. The governor does not have to reject an entire bill. In 43 states, governors have the **item veto**. This gives them the power to veto one or more parts of a bill. The President, on the other hand, must veto an entire bill.

Military Duties

A governor also has military duties. Each state constitution makes the governor the commander in chief of the National Guard. The National Guard may be called up by the governor for different purposes—to deal with prison outbreaks and riots or to help the victims of floods and disasters, for example. The Guard may also be called into federal service by the President.

**Ceremonial
Duties**

A governor has many ceremonial duties. When the President or another high official visits a state, the governor greets him or her. Governors open state fairs, give speeches at public ceremonies, and attend funerals of important people. Almost every day, the governor performs ceremonial duties such as these.

Duties of a Governor

Carries out the laws of the state. Supervises the work of the executive branch.	Appoints and removes officials in the executive branch.
Prepares the state budget. Sends it to the legislature for approval.	Pardons criminals. Commutes sentences.
Suggests new laws to the legislature. Calls special sessions of both houses.	Calls out the National Guard in emergencies.
Signs bills into law.	Meets important visitors and represents the state at public functions.

SKILL BUILDER

Review the information in Section 2 of Chapter 7 and compare the duties of a state governor with those of the President.

SECTION 2 *Review*

Defining Key Terms

1. Define: pardon, reprieve, commute, parole, special session, item veto.

Recalling the Facts

2. What limits are placed on the governor with regard to selecting top officials in the executive branch?
3. What are some of the judicial duties of a governor?

Reviewing the Main Idea

4. Answer "As you read . . ." question 2 on page 229: What major types of duties do governors perform?

Critical Thinking

5. **Determining Relevance.** How might serving as a governor prepare a person to be President?

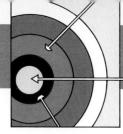

Sharpening Your Skills

Critical Thinking Skills

Formulating Questions

Asking questions comes naturally to all of us. We may need to ask for directions to a place we've never been before. When we are reading and studying, we may ask ourselves questions to help clarify the material. And we have all watched professional question-askers interviewing other people on television.

Well-formulated questions—ones that are carefully thought out and remain focused on the subject—help us to get clear and informative answers. In other words, effective questions require the type of answers that lead us to the information we are looking for.

Effective questions have at least three characteristics:

- They are *relevant*, or related to what you want to know.
- Effective questions are *significant*. This means that their answers will provide information that is worth knowing and remembering.
- Effective questions are *clearly phrased* so that they are easy to understand. They are also very specific. A complicated question with many parts may be easier to understand if it is broken down into shorter, more direct questions.

If your questions are not relevant, significant, and clear, the answers you get may provide interesting information, but they will not be the answers you need.

Use the following three questions as a guide to help you determine whether or not the questions you create are relevant, significant, and clear.

- What do I want to know? (Relevance)

- Why is this information important? (Significance)
- Will the person I am speaking with understand me? (Clarity)

The questions above will help you master the skill of formulating questions. You will discover that knowing how to create effective questions will help you with any kind of research you may do.

Practicing Skills

1. Imagine that you are interviewing a candidate for the office of governor of your state. Your purpose is to learn about her past political experience and what she would like to accomplish in office. Analyze each of the following questions. Then explain why you think it is either an effective or an ineffective question for your interview:
   a. What are your political views?
   b. What political experience do you have that qualifies you for the position of governor?
   c. Are there any particular bills that you would support as governor?
   d. Do you think that our state flower truly represents the character of the state?
   e. Where were you born?
2. **Formulating Questions.** Plan an interview of a famous person whom you admire or whom you find especially interesting. Write a clear sentence that explains the purpose (what you want to find out) of your interview. Then make a list of the questions you would ask the person.

Governors and State Agencies　237

3 State Officers and Agencies

All state governments have a number of officers and agencies in the executive branch. The heads of the state executive departments—attorney general, treasurer, secretary of state, and others—often serve as the governor's cabinet, or advisory group. However, in some states, only those persons who are appointed by the governor serve in the cabinet.

Secretary of State

The secretary of state guards the public records of the state. He or she often supervises elections. The secretary is keeper of the Great Seal of each state. This seal is attached to all official papers the governor signs. Almost all the duties of secretary of state are set by law. Because of this, he or she can do little to influence the public policy of the state.

Attorney General

The attorney general is the state's chief legal officer and chief prosecutor. The attorney general also acts as the chief legal adviser to the governor, other state officials, and the different state agencies. In a court suit against the state, the attorney general serves as the state's defense lawyer.

The attorney general is often asked to give a legal opinion. An **opinion** is a written statement that explains a part of the state constitution or a law passed by the state legislature. Any agency of the state may ask for a legal opinion. Thus, a secondary school district may ask the attorney general if it is legal for students to smoke on campus. An attorney general's opinion can be challenged in court, and the court can reverse the opinion.

Auditor

The auditor (also known as the comptroller or controller) controls all money paid out by the state. The state auditor has to approve a payment before it is made. He or she also examines all spending to see that it is in accordance with state law.

Treasurer

The treasurer is the state's banker. He or she is often called the "custodian" of state money. Very often, he or she makes the payments out of the state's treasury after these payments have been approved by the auditor. In some states, the treasurer is also the chief collector of state taxes.

Superintendent of Education

This state official supervises the state school system. The superintendent of education usually shares authority with a state board of education. In 18 states the superintendent is elected. In

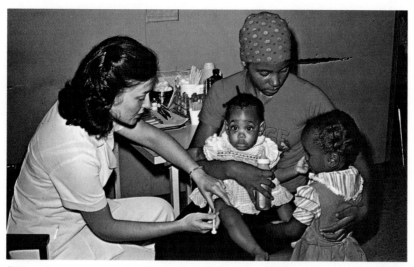

States offer many public health services through their departments of public health. This child is being vaccinated against disease. The state pays for this important service.

the other states, the governor or the board of education appoints someone to the job.

All states have agencies that serve a number of purposes. Some states, for example, have a department of public health to supervise hospitals for the mentally ill, drug addicts, and alcoholics. Within the past ten years, many states have created fair employment practices commissions within the executive branch. Such agencies help enforce state laws against discrimination in the hiring and firing of workers.

Departments of Public Health. All states have at least one agency that deals with public health problems. Many activities are carried on under the director of public health. The director is usually a doctor. Local health agencies often work under the guidance of the state health department.

States offer many public health services through such departments. School districts receive help in providing physical and dental examinations for students. Most states require school children to be vaccinated against measles, polio, and other diseases. In these states, vaccination is paid for by the state. Clinics for free or low-cost medical care are set up in cities. Free X-rays to detect tuberculosis are sometimes given in these clinics. Public health nurses visit homes to help people who need special care.

Specialists perform many different tasks to protect public health in the states. They test milk, water, and different foods. They inspect the kitchens of restaurants and hospitals. Factories, mines, and workshops are inspected to make sure there is protection for the health and safety of workers. Many states also inspect meat and poultry where there is no federal inspection. (Goods that are not shipped across state lines are not inspected by federal officials.)

Fair Employment Practices Commissions.   As you know, these are agencies that enforce state laws meant to protect workers. These laws govern the hiring, promotion, and firing of workers. In particular, the laws forbid discrimination against workers because of race, age, sex, or religion. Many of the laws apply to labor unions as well as to employers. The top officials of the fair employment commissions are usually appointed by the governor. Many staff workers, however, are hired through civil service. There are still several states which do not have fair employment practices commissions.

When a worker has a complaint, he or she files it with the local commission office. A commission official investigates the complaint and arranges for a conference with the employer. If no law has been broken, the worker will be told. If a law has been broken, the employment commission issues an order to obey the law. Commission orders may be challenged in the courts.

Public Utilities Commissions or Boards.   A **public utility** is a privately owned company that provides people with a product or a service. Public utilities provide electricity, natural gas, water, and telephone service. These companies are often legal **monopolies**. That is, they are the only firms that provide certain services or products. The states allow the utility monopolies, but have public utilities commissions or boards that regulate rates, hours of service, and working conditions. The purpose of these boards or commissions is to make sure that the utility companies provide the people with good service at fair rates.

Private ownership of utilities is not the rule. At the local level, many cities and other units of government now operate such utilities as water systems, sewage plants, and garbage-collection companies.

Licensing Agencies.   Most states have many agencies that issue licenses or that serve as examining bodies. Thus, a fish and game commission issues licenses to fish or hunt within the state. Certain types of workers—lawyers, teachers, pilots—must be examined and licensed by the state in order to carry on their professions.

Civil Service and Unions.   All states have some sort of civil service for state employees. Under this system, a worker is hired on probation, usually for a period of about six months. After that period, the worker can be fired only for cause, that is, for a good reason. What makes a good reason is open to debate. A worker usually has the right to a hearing, however, to challenge any dismissal.

In many states, a fish and game commission issues licenses to fish or hunt within the state. Here a member of the department stocks a lake with fish.

During the 1970s, many state workers joined unions. In some states, workers have gone on strike for higher salaries or better working conditions. In other states, strikes are forbidden by state law. In those states, unions usually deal only with personnel problems, such as hiring, promotion, or firing procedures.

SECTION 3 *Review*

Defining Key Terms
1. Define: opinion, public utility, monopoly.

Recalling the Facts
2. What are the duties of the major state officers?

3. What is the purpose of a fair employment practices commission?

Reviewing the Main Idea
4. Answer "As you read . . ." question 3 on page 229: What are the major state offices?

Critical Thinking
5. Demonstrating Reasoned Judgment. Do you think civil service workers should be able to join unions or have the right to strike? Support your answers.

4 Paying for State Government

Running the government of a state is expensive. Recent figures show that, altogether, the 50 states spend about $400 billion each year. Costs continue to increase. Many states have been in serious trouble due to lack of money. Some have been close to **bankruptcy** (having no money to pay their debts).

Some people see these financial problems as a simple matter of poor use of state money. Others blame inflation that continues to send the costs of goods and services higher and higher. There is also the problem of population growth. As population increases, more services are needed—improving downtown areas, pollution control, sanitation, and public housing for low-income and elderly people. Crowded areas bring about the need for more workers to deal with traffic problems and crime control. Where do the states get the money to pay for these services?

Sales Tax

Most states use some kind of sales tax to raise money. A **sales tax** is a tax you pay on an item when you buy it. The tax may be a general tax, one that is placed on almost all goods; or it may be a selective tax, one placed on only certain items. Stores collect the tax for the government. One reason the sales tax is popular with state governments is because it is easy to collect. By means of a sales tax, all citizens contribute to the support of government.

The sales tax is considered a **regressive tax**. That is, it is not based on a person's ability to pay. Low-income people pay more of their total salaries in sales taxes than high-income people. A sales tax is a heavy burden on low-income people because they have to pay the same amount of tax on clothing, for example, as high-income people. To reduce this unfair burden, some states do not tax food, clothing, and other goods that are considered necessities. All states place a tax on gasoline, cigarettes, and alcohol.

Personal and Corporate Taxes

The personal income tax is another major source of income for most state governments. The amount of money states can raise from personal income taxes is limited because of the amount that workers pay in federal income taxes. State personal income taxes are usually progressive. The taxable income is based on the amount paid in federal income tax.

A business pays a state corporate income tax on a fixed percentage of income the business earns. Only a few states tax on a progressive basis. States want to attract businesses. Therefore, they do not want to make corporate income taxes too high.

PEOPLE HELPING PEOPLE

Sticking Their Necks Out

Outside a tiny office in the tiny town of Langley, Washington, hangs a sign that reads "The Giraffe Project." Founded in 1983 by the husband-and-wife team of John Graham and Ann Medlock, the Giraffe Project recognizes people who "stick their necks out for the common good."

The organization operates on a shoestring. It honors winners with certificates praising their courage. That's it. No cash prizes, no awards ceremony. To date, several hundred Giraffes have been named. They include a battered wife in New Jersey who started a group to help other women in her situation. Another winner was a North Carolina teacher who shut down a local incinerator that produced toxic fumes.

"Each of these individual acts teaches the rest of us important lessons," says Graham, a former diplomat. "There's something each of us can do to make the world a better place."

Estate and Gift Taxes

All states except Nevada and California have an inheritance, or estate tax. In Arizona, Texas, California, and a few other states, all property a married couple acquires after marriage is considered **community property.** This means that the property is owned equally by both husband and wife. Property owned by the woman or man before marriage remains separate. Any property either one receives as a gift or an inheritance also remains separate. Community property is subject to estate tax when either the husband or the wife dies.

The states also tax gifts to prevent people from trying to avoid estate taxes by giving their property away before they die. About 3 to 5 percent of a state's income comes from these taxes.

License Fees

States earn 5 to 10 percent of their income from license fees that are really taxes. Doctors, dentists, lawyers, plumbers, real estate brokers, hairdressers, and other people in business have to pay a license fee in order to do business.

Property Tax

A **property tax** is a tax on things people own. This tax can be placed on property such as land or buildings. The tax may also be on movable property such as machinery or furniture. A government official decides the value of the property and then decides the amount of tax that should be paid on it. Property taxes are the chief source of income for cities and towns. Less than 2 percent of the income of most states, however, is raised by property taxes. In recent years, property owners have protested the

© 1977 by Chicago Tribune-N.Y. News Synd. Inc.
All Rights Reserved

SKILL BUILDER

What factors might cause property taxes to rise?

amount of taxes they have to pay. Several cities and states have taken steps to limit the amount of taxation.

The different kinds of taxes the states collect have one purpose—to raise money. State governments need money to provide services for their citizens. Recently, some state governments have cut back on their spending. Of course, such cuts lead to a reduction in services. They also mean that some state workers who provide the services lose their jobs.

SECTION 4 *Review*

Defining Key Terms

1. Define: bankruptcy, sales tax, regressive tax, community property, property tax.

Recalling the Facts

2. What kinds of taxes are collected by state governments as well as by the federal government?

3. Who receives the money raised from property taxes?

Reviewing the Main Idea

4. Answer "As you read . . ." question 4 on page 229: What are some of the ways states raise money to run their governments?

Critical Thinking

5. Identifying Assumptions. You have read that many states do not collect sales tax on food or clothing but do tax items such as cigarettes. What could be the reason for this choice.

Citizenship

Helping Youth and the Environment

"Hard work, low pay, miserable conditions." That's how the California Conservation Corps (CCC) advertises its program. Doesn't sound very appealing, does it?

Yet that's what the state of California offered its youth when it introduced the CCC. The idea for this new state agency came from a successful program that existed during the Depression. President Franklin Roosevelt started the original CCC—the Civilian Conservation Corps. That program put more than 2.5 million people to work building trails and parks in the early 1930s.

The California Conservation Corps was founded by Governor Jerry Brown in 1976. Brown and other government leaders conceived of the CCC as a way to meet two needs. One was to manage and protect California's *natural* resources; the other was to develop the state's *human* resources. Thus, the CCC was set up to hire young people to work in conservation.

The idea worked. Today the California Conservation Corps is the nation's oldest and most successful state-run public service program for young adults. Since 1976 more than 40,000 California residents have joined the corps. The CCC has a waiting list of applicants, and its success has encouraged at least 12 other states to set up similar programs.

Just what do members of the CCC do? Some of their assignments echo the work of the original CCC. Much like the original CCC workers, the California crews build parks, clear trails, plant trees, fight forest

On a hillside above San Francisco, members of the California Corps work to preserve the environment.

fires, and dam waterways. They also work in cities and towns, restoring historic buildings and helping build or maintain neighborhood centers.

The work can be hard and physically demanding. Corps members may be outside for hours in rain, high winds, snow, mud, or intense heat. Yet teamwork makes the job a little easier. Men and women work together in groups of 12 or 14, doing the same tasks and wearing the same uniform —high-topped boots, cotton pants, tan shirt, and a hard hat.

Almost any California resident between the ages of 18 and 23 is eligible to join the CCC. About 2,000 applicants are accepted into the program every year. More than one-third of these are women, and some are people with disabilities.

New members start out by spending two weeks at the CCC's training academy. They learn such skills as how to use tools safely, how to control floods and fires, and how to give first aid. Then they are assigned to one of 17 centers throughout the state—home base for the next 4 to 12 months.

Those months will be a time of community service and camaraderie. They will also be a time of self-development. Corps members spend a few evenings a week taking classes to earn a high school diploma or learn job-hunting skills. They can also receive specialized training to match their interests. For example, they may choose to learn about construction, energy conservation, landscaping, or food service. The corps also requires that members keep a daily journal of their experiences and that they register to vote.

The CCC pays its workers about $10,000 for a term of one year. Only two of ten workers stay a full year, with the average worker leaving after six months. Many leave to take full-time jobs or attend college. Members who work a year are rewarded with a $500 bonus or a $1,000 educational scholarship.

Because it is a public service program, California taxpayers pay for the CCC. In 1989 the program cost $55 million, up from $37 million in 1982. Although expensive, the program has been praised because, unlike many other youth programs that have failed, the CCC is a success. It provides jobs to young adults who need work. It also promotes citizenship. In a world of scarce labor, the program supplies services that might not otherwise be provided. And the services bring lasting benefits to the community, such as newly planted forests.

Perhaps most importantly, the CCC has a lasting impact on its members. Members develop self-discipline and learn to work as part of a team. This gives them a sense of pride in what they accomplish and a sense of belonging. Their self-confidence soars to new heights as well. Once they leave the corps, many go back to school or use their experience to find jobs.

Questions to think about

1. Suppose the governor has appointed you to head up a job corps in your state. What kind of work would you want its members to do? How much would you pay its workers?
2. The CCC costs California taxpayers about $23,000 per corps member, based on an average of 2,000 workers each year. Do you think programs like the CCC are worth the money? Would you support one in your state? Explain your answers.

CHAPTER SUMMARY

Section 1   The governor is the most powerful leader in state government. In many states the lieutenant governor is the second highest elected official. All governors are elected by the voters. Qualifications for the job are set by state constitutions. Terms of office tend to be from two to four years. Some states limit the number of terms a governor may serve. Recall of the governor is allowed in 15 states, and all states but Oregon allow for removal by impeachment.

Section 2   Governors have many kinds of duties—executive, judicial, legislative, military, and ceremonial. Some executive powers are shared with elected officials (such as the attorney general and secretary of state) and with state boards and commissions. The governor appoints and removes high officials. The governor prepares an annual budget, grants pardons and reprieves, and commands the National Guard. Legislative powers include vetoing bills and sending messages to the legislature.

Section 3   Every state has a number of elected officials who head state executive departments. These generally include the attorney general, secretary of state, treasurer, and superintendant of education. In some states, these officials form the governor's cabinet, while in other states the cabinet is made up of appointed officials. All states have many agencies that help the governor provide services or perform regulatory duties.

Section 4   Each state collects a variety of taxes to pay for running the government. These include sales taxes, income taxes, estate and gift taxes, license fees, and property taxes.

Reviewing Key Terms

On a separate sheet of paper, use the following terms to complete the sentences below.

reprieve	property tax	pardon
item veto	special session	regressive tax

1. If necessary, a governor can call the legislature into a ___?___ .

2. Some governors have great power over legislation through their use of the ___?___ .

3. A ___?___ is not based on a person's ability to pay.

4. Governors may set a prisoner free by granting a ___?___ .

5. Governors may postpone punishment for a crime by granting a ___?___ .

6. A ___?___ is based on the value of things people own.

Understanding Main Ideas

1. What are the qualifications for candidates for governor in most states?

2. How are governors elected?

3. In most states, who can the governor appoint without approval by the Senate?

4. What are two limitations set on the governor's power of appointment in some states?

5. How does the governor prepare the state budget?

6. Describe three judicial duties of a governor.

7. What powers do governors have over state legislation?

8. Identify three other chief officers in state government and describe their duties.

9. What is the purpose of a state department of public health?

10. Name two other kinds of agencies found in the states and describe what they do.

11. Why is the sales tax considered a regressive tax?

12. On what kinds of things do people pay property taxes? Where does most of this money go?

Critical Thinking

1. **Determining Relevance.** Make your own list of qualifications you think a governor should have. Are there any characteristics you think a governor should *not* have?

2. **Evaluating Public Policy.** Most state universities charge out-of-state students higher tuition than they charge state residents. Is this fair? Why or why not?

3. **Demonstrating Reasoned Judgment.** As you have read, in some states the governor and lieutenant governor are elected as a team; in other states they are elected separately. Which system do you think is better? Why?

Practicing Skills

1. **Formulating Questions.** Suppose you are governor of your state and you must decide whether to grant parole to a prisoner. Write five questions that you would want answered to help you make this decision. Discuss your questions with the rest of your class.

2. **Making Comparisons.** Compare the duties of a state governor with the duties of the President. How are they alike and how are they different? Put your comparison in the form of a short written report or a chart.

Focusing on Citizenship

1. **Researching Information.** Find out the background of the governor of your state. What education and work experience did he or she have before becoming governor?

2. **Making a Bulletin Board Display.** Collect news clippings showing the activities of the governor and other state officials in a two-week period. Display them on a bulletin board.

3. **Giving a Campaign Speech.** Imagine you are running for governor of your state. Give a speech outlining what it takes to be a good governor and why you think you can do the job. After you deliver your speech, ask for reactions from the class.

CHAPTER 13

In state courtrooms like the Lowell Superior Courthouse in Massachusetts, all cases dealing with state laws are heard.

State Courts

Previewing the Chapter

Since each state has its own constitution, it needs its own court system to interpret and apply the laws set down in the state constitution. State courts are often overloaded with cases involving both serious crimes and minor disputes. This chapter explains the structure of the state court systems and describes how they work to ensure justice for all.

- **Before you read,** look up these key terms in the Glossary at the back of this book: *misdemeanor, felony, grand jury, reasonable doubt rule, cross-examination, plea bargaining.*

- **As you read,** look for answers to these questions:
  1. What types of cases are heard in state courts?
  2. What are the three levels of courts within a state court system?
  3. How is the judicial process different for minors than for adults?
  4. What are some court procedures that some people consider unfair?

1 The Work of the State Courts

Each state has its own system of courts. The purpose of each of these court systems is defined in a state's constitution. From state to state, the names of the courts that make up the system are different, but the basic pattern of justice is the same in all states.

State courts hear almost all the same kinds of cases that federal courts hear. However, certain cases cannot be heard in state courts. A dispute between two citizens of two states, for example, must be heard in the federal courts.

Criminal and Civil Cases

State courts hear criminal and civil cases. In a criminal case, a person is tried for committing a crime. Criminal cases involve two kinds of crimes—misdemeanors and felonies. A **misdemeanor** is a minor criminal offense, such as speeding, petty theft, or disorderly conduct. The punishment for a misdemeanor may be a fine or a short jail sentence. Serious crimes are called **felonies**. Some examples are kidnapping, robbery, murder, and arson (deliberately setting fire to a building). The punishment for a felony may be a long prison sentence or even death.

State courts also hear civil cases. As you learned in Chapter 9, civil cases are disputes between two or more persons or between citizens and governments. A civil case might involve a store owner suing for payment of a bill, a person seeking a divorce, or the victim of an accident suing for payment of medical bills. Most civil cases result in the payment of money to one of the parties involved.

Courts Influence Public Policy

Deciding legal issues between two parties is only one part of the work of the judges in state courts. The rulings of these judges also often have a strong influence on public policy. Consider the use of local property taxes to pay for the public schools. In some states, schools are supported almost entirely by these taxes.

In 1971, the California State Supreme Court ruled that it was unconstitutional to depend only on local property taxes to pay for education. Because the people living in some school districts paid high property taxes, the schools there would be better than schools where property taxes were lower. The education of students in different districts would be unequal. This went against the equal rights guarantee in the Constitution. Other state courts have made similar decisions.

In 1973, the United States Supreme Court ruled differently in *San Antonio* (Texas) *School District* v. *Rodriguez*. This ruling said that the use of local property taxes to pay for public schools does not go against the Fourteenth Amendment. The Court said that the local property tax could be used as the chief way of paying for public schools.

State court decisions can also affect public policy on the use of nuclear power. In recent years, groups of citizens have sometimes stopped the building of nuclear power plants by means of court decisions. Arguments against the building of such plants have been based on possible dangers to people who live nearby or to the environment.

Judicial Review

The higher state courts have the power of judicial review. In using this power, the courts review a state law to see whether it conflicts with the state constitution. Laws which conflict with the constitution are declared **null and void** (not binding).

Workload

State courts are extremely busy places. California has about 256 state courts and about 1,200 judges, more than the total number of judges in the entire federal court system.

It is very difficult for state courts to keep up with their heavy workloads. In one large city, the average waiting period for a civil case to come to trial is two years. The delay for criminal trials still may be four to six months. Studies of criminal cases show that some persons have waited for more than a year before their cases came to trial.

An arbitrator, trained in the law, helps to settle a dispute.

The long delays have many causes. Some trials take several weeks. The increasing crime rate adds to the number of criminal cases in the courts. Individuals also go to court to protect their rights. A conservation group sues to stop construction of a nuclear power plant or a dam. Workers sue employers over hiring practices, promotion policies, or working conditions. Automobile accidents, too, result in a large number of lawsuits at the state level.

Relief for the Courts

Some states are trying different methods for relieving the courts of the great number of auto accident disputes. One method is to turn such cases over to an **arbitrator** (a person who settles a dispute). The arbitrator is not a judge, but he or she is trained in the law that applies to auto accidents. The hearing takes place in an office. Both sides are present. After arguments are heard, the arbitrator makes a decision that is final.

Some people feel that the only way to reduce the number of cases in state courts is to change our criminal laws. They argue that there are too many laws trying to control personal behavior, such as laws against gambling or public drunkenness. These offenses are sometimes called "victimless crimes" because, it is said, they do not harm other persons.

SECTION 1 *Review*

Defining Key Terms
1. Define: misdemeanor, felony, null and void, arbitrator.

Recalling the Facts
2. Give one example of a state court decision that has influenced public policy.
3. What are some causes of the heavy workload of the state courts?

Reviewing the Main Idea
4. Answer "As you read . . ." question 1 on page 249: What types of cases are heard in state courts?

Critical Thinking
5. **Predicting Consequences.** Some people have suggested removing divorce and child-custody cases from the jurisdiction of the courts as a way to reduce the workload. These cases would be handled by an arbitrator. Explain whether or not you think this would be a good idea.

2 The Organization of the State Courts

From state to state, the courts are organized in a similar way. Courts are often described as being lower or higher. You might compare the organization of state courts to a ladder. The supreme court is a state's highest court, and the highest rung on the ladder. Lower courts are the lowest rung on the state court ladder. They have limited jurisdiction.

Lower Courts

Justice Courts. These courts are presided over by a justice of the peace. Most justice courts are located in rural areas. The only cases that come to justice courts are minor civil cases and cases involving misdemeanors. Only civil cases involving $100 or less are heard by a justice of the peace. Misdemeanors include traffic violations and charges of public drunkenness. In addition to hearing such cases, a justice of the peace can perform marriage ceremonies and serve as a witness to the signing of public papers.

Not all states have justice courts, and even in states that do, their numbers have been decreasing in recent years. One reason for this is that some justices of the peace have not studied law.

Police Courts. The similarity of these courts to justice courts lies in the kind of cases they handle. They are usually located in small cities and towns. Police courts are known as magistrate courts in some areas.

A justice of the peace hears some civil cases and performs marriages.

Municipal Courts. These courts are located in the larger cities of our states. Both civil cases and misdemeanors come within their jurisdiction. One type of civil case is heard in the family court, which deals with divorce suits and child-custody cases. Another type of municipal court is the small claims court which hears disputes over amounts of money less than a given amount. The amount varies, from $300 in Georgia to $5,000 in Virginia and Tennessee. Misdemeanors are handled in several different kinds of municipal courts. The most common ones are the traffic court, which deals with violations of the traffic laws, and the juvenile court, which hears cases involving young offenders.

Higher Courts

Some higher state courts are a rung above the lower courts. **General Trial Courts.** These courts are known as district, county, common plea, circuit, and superior courts in different states. Most states are divided into political districts. In each district, there is at least one general trial court.

These courts hear felony cases and civil disputes involving amounts of money over the amount allowed in a small claims case. In many states, general trial courts judges are elected to terms of from four to ten years. Juries are used in both civil and criminal cases.

Appellate Courts. These courts hear cases on appeal. A person who disagrees with the verdict of a general trial court or a lower court may ask an appellate court to review the case. The appeals court checks to see whether the original trial was conducted according to law. If the original trial judge makes an error, the appeals court can reverse the verdict. Three to nine judges serve on appellate courts. A majority vote of the judges decides the outcome of the case. Juries are not used.

State Supreme Courts

On the highest rung of the state courts ladder are the state supreme courts. These courts review cases appealed from the appellate courts. Three to nine justices make up a state supreme court. Decisions of a state's highest court may be appealed to the United States Supreme Court. It should be remembered, however, that there is no guarantee that the Supreme Court will hear an appeal. As noted in Chapter 9, the United States Supreme Court grants an appeal only if a federal question is involved. The subject matter of the case must be related to some part of the United States Constitution or to a law passed by Congress. If the appeal is refused, the decision of the state supreme court is final.

Selection of Judges

Judges for the state courts are chosen in three ways: (1) election by the people, (2) appointment by the governor, and (3) appointment by the legislature.

The Court System in the States

State Supreme Court
(Last court of appeals at the state level)

State Courts of Appeals
(These courts hear appeals from the lower courts.)

General Trial Courts
Also known as District, County, Common Plea, Circuit, or Superior Courts. (These courts hear felonies and civil cases of $500 or more.)

City Courts:
Traffic, Family, Small Claims, and Juvenile Courts
Justice of the Peace and Magistrate Courts
(These courts hear only minor civil cases and misdemeanors.)

SKILL BUILDER

If you had paid a repair shop $85 to fix your bicycle and it still did not work properly, to what court could you take your complaint?

In several states, judges can be chosen only by the vote of the people. In other states, a majority of the judges are chosen by the voters, and the others are appointed. Judges are usually elected on a **nonpartisan** (no party-label) basis. In Pennsylvania, however, state judges run as Republicans or Democrats.

In almost all states, the governor can fill vacancies by appointment. When a judge dies or retires between elections, the governor appoints a replacement. Once a judge has been appointed, it is fairly easy for her or him to keep the job. Voters usually reelect a judge who is already in the position.

What is the best method for selecting judges? Lawyers in the American Bar Association (ABA) are against appointment of judges by the legislature or election by the voters. These lawyers say that judges should be free from outside pressures. The ABA opposes appointment by the legislature because it gives lawmakers too much power over the court system. As for the *election* of judges, ABA argues that the ability to win votes has little to do with a person's qualifications as a judge. Whether a judge is elected or appointed, he or she is likely to owe a debt to those who helped.

Many lawyers approve of the method of selecting judges which is used in Missouri, California, and some other states. In this method, a committee of regular citizens, lawyers, and judges submits names to the governor when a vacancy occurs. From this list of names, the governor selects a judge to fill the vacancy. Then, after about one year of service, the judge's name appears on a statewide ballot. If the voters approve of the judge by a majority vote, he or she stays on the job.

SECTION 2 *Review*

Defining Key Terms
1. Define: nonpartisan.

Recalling the Facts
2. What are three kinds of lower courts in most states?
3. How does an appeals court differ from a trial court?

Reviewing the Main Idea
4. Answer "As you read . . ." question 2 on page 249: What are the three levels of courts within a state court system?

Critical Thinking
5. Determining Relevance. What qualifications do you think a judge in a state court should have?

3 Court Procedures

As noted earlier in this chapter, state courts deal with civil and criminal cases. A criminal case usually starts with the arrest of a suspect by police. At the police station, the suspect may be booked. His or her name and other information are recorded. If the crime is minor, the suspect might be released on bail. Bail, a payment of money to the court, allows a person to stay out of jail until the trial. Bail also increases the likelihood that an individual will appear at the trial. Sometimes a person who is well-known in the community will be released without bail.

Before a court trial can begin, an accused person must be brought before a judge. The judge must tell the accused of the charges against him or her. The accused must also be given an explanation of certain Constitutional rights, such as the right to a lawyer or the right to remain silent.

Above, a suspect is being fingerprinted at the police station.

If a person is accused of a felony, there is usually a formal charge by a grand jury or a charge by information. A **grand jury** usually has more jurors (up to 23) than an ordinary trial jury. The grand jury examines the evidence. If there appears to be enough evidence to hold a person for trial, the grand jury issues an indictment. An **indictment** is a formal notice of a charge. If there is not enough evidence, the suspect is released. **Information** is also a formal charge against an accused. It is issued by a district attorney. The word *information* is used because the written statement contains information reported by police, eyewitnesses, or others.

An accused person is always given a chance to enter a **plea** of guilty or not guilty.

In some countries, a person accused of a crime is thought to be guilty until proven innocent. In our system of justice, however, a person accused of a crime is always considered innocent until he or she is proven guilty. If the accused pleads guilty, the judge may sentence the person to prison or probation. **Probation** sets the accused person free, but requires that he or she make regular visits to a probation officer. In most cases, a jury trial will be called if the accused pleads not guilty. Any person accused of committing a crime has the right to a jury trial in our country.

Formal Charges Against the Accused

Before a trial begins, a jury must be selected. The **trial jury** is a group of 12 persons who make a decision about the evidence presented during the trial. In federal criminal cases, the verdict (decision) of the jury must be **unanimous** (all jurors must agree on the verdict). In noncapital cases the Supreme Court has upheld the validity of less than a unanimous jury verdict—9-12 (*Apodaca* v. *Oregon*, 1972).

The Trial Jury

The jury must decide the facts in a case. The jurors must decide what actually happened. Then they must decide whether the evidence proves the accused guilty or not. In making this decision, jurors are expected to follow the **reasonable doubt rule**. If there is any question about the guilt of the accused, the jurors should vote *not guilty.* A jury that cannot agree on a verdict is known as a *hung jury.* A hung jury is dismissed. A new trial with a new jury is then called, or sometimes the case is dropped.

Misdemeanor cases and civil suits are often heard by a judge without a jury. In traffic courts, for example, there is no jury. A judge presides. Civil suits over small amounts of money are also usually heard only by a judge.

Taking Part in a Trial

Many people take part in a criminal trial. The lawyer for the state is called the **prosecuting attorney**. He or she prepares the case against the accused and attempts to prove guilt. The lawyer for the defendant is called the **defense attorney**. He or she attempts to disprove the charges against the accused. The judge must keep the trial moving in an orderly fashion. The judge must also make sure that each side has a fair chance to present its case.

SKILL BUILDER

In a criminal trial, does the judge decide whether an accused person is innocent or guilty? If not, who does?

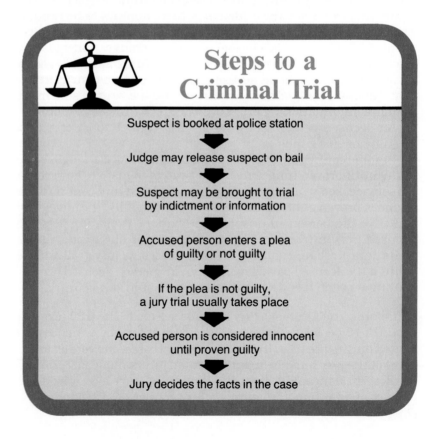

Steps to a Criminal Trial

Suspect is booked at police station

Judge may release suspect on bail

Suspect may be brought to trial by indictment or information

Accused person enters a plea of guilty or not guilty

If the plea is not guilty, a jury trial usually takes place

Accused person is considered innocent until proven guilty

Jury decides the facts in the case

SKILL BUILDER What dilemma about selecting a jury does this cartoon point out?

Witnesses are persons who are called up to give sworn testimony about some part of the case. They are asked questions by the prosecuting and defense attorneys.

Many people take part in a civil case too. A civil case starts with an accusation by one person (the plaintiff) against another (the defendant). Here are some examples: a store owner accuses someone of not paying a bill or a car owner accuses another of damaging his or her car in an accident. The two lawyers in a civil case are the attorney for the defense and the attorney for the plaintiff. Civil cases can be held with or without juries. Very often, in order to save time and money, the two sides in a dispute will agree to have the case heard without a jury.

The evidence presented by the plaintiff must show clearly that the defendant is in the wrong. Witnesses play an important part in giving evidence. They are usually questioned first by the lawyer for the plaintiff. Then the attorney for the defense asks them questions. Either attorney can check the accuracy of the evidence given by a witness. This is called a **cross-examination**.

Juvenile Courts

Minors (persons under the age of 18) are usually tried in juvenile courts. A minor accused of breaking the law is usually taken to a detention home. A first hearing of the case takes place in a room of that home. A hearing officer presides, and a probation officer assigned to the case is present. The hearing officer is not a judge. She or he is usually someone experienced in working with juveniles. A parent or guardian may be present, but visitors are not allowed. Proceedings are informal. Everyone in the room may speak freely.

At the end of the session, the hearing officer makes a decision about the case, for example, to send the youth to a state camp. If

In many cases, young offenders are assigned to report to a probation officer. The officer takes on the role of counselor, and works closely with parents and school authorities to help the young offender.

the parents object to the decision, they may appeal. If they appeal, the case goes to a special court assigned to juvenile cases. The person presiding will be a regular court judge. Some states do not allow any further appeals.

In many cases, a young offender will be assigned to report to a probation officer. A probation officer takes on the role of counselor. He or she works closely with parents and school authorities to help the young offender.

One juvenile case that reached the United States Supreme Court has had a lasting effect on juvenile proceedings. The case was *In Re Gault* (1967). Gerald Gault, age 15, a resident of Arizona, was found guilty of making an "obscene" telephone call to a neighbor. He was sentenced to six years in the State Industrial School. For an adult, the punishment for this offense would have been a fine or a jail sentence of a few months.

At his trial in juvenile court, Gerald did not have a lawyer. He did not have the chance to question his accuser. There was no record kept of the police questioning or of the proceedings in juvenile court. The boy's parents did not receive written notice of the charges against their son.

For all these reasons, the Supreme Court reversed the decision of the juvenile court. As a result of the ruling in the Gault case, minors now must have lawyers in juvenile courts. If the family cannot afford a lawyer, the court must provide one. Also, the police must advise a minor of his or her right to remain silent.

Written notice of the charges must be sent to the youth and the parents.

The Supreme Court did not, however, say that minors have all the legal rights of adults. For example, the Court later decided that juveniles are not entitled to jury trials.

SECTION *3* *Review*

Defining Key Terms

1. Define: grand jury, indictment, information, plea, probation, trial jury, unanimous, reasonable doubt rule, prosecuting attorney, defense attorney, witness, cross-examination.

Recalling the Facts

2. What is the function of a grand jury?
3. What is a hung jury?

Reviewing the Main Idea

4. Answer "As you read . . ." question 3 on page 249: How is the judicial process different for minors than for adults?

Critical Thinking

5. **Recognizing Bias.** Why might it be difficult to find a fair and impartial jury in some cases?

4 Justice and the State Courts

Some people feel that the courts do not carry out the promise of "equal justice under law." They think that certain court procedures are basically unfair. One of these procedures is plea bargaining. Other court practices that cause disputes are bail, the selection of jurors, and sentencing.

Plea bargaining is an agreement between a judge and a person accused of a crime. If a defendant agrees to plead guilty, the charges against him or her will be reduced. For example, if a person who is charged with robbery and assault agrees to plead guilty, the charge will be reduced to robbery. The punishment for robbery alone is much less than for robbery and assault. If the

Plea Bargaining

defendant faces a three- to five-year sentence, a lighter sentence may be promised in return for a guilty plea.

Plea bargaining makes the workload of the courts lighter. A guilty plea takes only five minutes or so of the court's time. The judge passes sentence and the case is over. A criminal trial, on the other hand, takes weeks or months. It is also expensive, sometimes costing hundreds of thousands of dollars.

Many judges and lawyers defend plea bargaining. They say it is the only practical way to solve the problem of overcrowded courts. Those who oppose plea bargaining say it is too often used to help persons of wealth or influence escape the disgrace of prison. Confessing to a lesser charge can mean probation instead of a prison term.

Bail

The amount of bail set by judges varies greatly. It may be $1,000 to $5,000 or more. Whatever the amount, many persons cannot pay it. Those who can afford bail go free until their trial. Those who cannot afford bail stay in jail.

Consider what happens to someone who cannot afford bail. He or she may have to wait weeks or months in prison for trial. Studies have shown that some people spend up to nine months in prison before their trials begin. They may face the loss of jobs and families. Also, the lawyers for such people are often appointed by

AMERICAN ALMANAC

A New Legal Twist

With court systems across the nation backed up, sometimes for years, people who want a legal question resolved are turning another way. Rather than waiting in line outside the courtroom, they are renting private (usually retired) judges to decide their cases.

It's not a solution for everyone. Hiring a judge usually costs between $150 and $300 an hour—prices that are out of reach for many people. But when a city the size of Los Angeles is clogged with about 150,000 new civil cases each year, those who can afford

it are often finding it worthwhile to pay a freelance judge to settle things.

The rent-a-judge idea started in California in 1976 and has since gone national. In 1988, a Philadelphia-based network of judges heard almost 800 cases in 34 states.

Critics charge that this new legal twist lets the rich sidestep the nation's judicial system. For this reason, the rent-a-judge system has been called "Cadillac justice." Whatever its name and whatever its flaws, it does help lighten the caseload in the courts.

the court and paid by the state, not by the client. This fact may or may not make a difference in the kind of defense the lawyers prepare. As a general rule, however, court-appointed lawyers have only limited time to spend with each client.

The Jury System

Selecting 12 jurors is often a slow and difficult process. One reason is that lawyers on both sides question possible jurors carefully. The purpose of the questioning is to select jurors who have not already formed an opinion about the case. The lawyers also try to select jurors who will not be influenced by racial or other kinds of prejudice. Sometimes it takes several weeks before a jury is formed.

Lawyers on either side of a case may reject a possible juror in a peremptory challenge or a challenge for cause. A **peremptory challenge** is one in which each lawyer can reject a juror without having to give a reason. State laws differ in the number of these challenges that the presiding judge can allow.

Other jurors may be excused for cause. **Challenge for cause** means that a juror is dismissed for a particular reason. Suppose a defendant is a Native American. A person who admits to being prejudiced against Native Americans would be challenged for cause and excused. There is no limit to the number of jurors who can be excused for cause.

Sentencing

Studies have shown that judges give greatly different sentences for the same crime. One person convicted of robbing a bank may be sentenced to ten years in prison. Another may be put

A person found guilty of a serious crime must go to prison.

on probation. Some people claim that judges give lighter sentences to wealthy individuals than to low-income people.

The states have tried to deal with the problem of sentencing in different ways. Some make use of the **indeterminate sentence**. The convicted person is sentenced to prison without a date for release. The length of the sentence is decided by a parole board or officials within the prison. Their decision is based on the behavior of the convicted person while in prison. Many prison officials do not like this type of sentence. They feel it causes conflict among the inmates.

Other states now have the mandatory sentence. A **mandatory sentence** requires judges to give a prison sentence (rather than probation) if the convicted person used a gun in committing a crime. Many judges are not in favor of mandatory sentences. They feel they are not given a chance to distinguish between a first offender and a repeater. They argue they should have the right to decide whether prison or probation is more likely to bring about a change of behavior in persons convicted of crimes.

SECTION 4 *Review*

Defining Key Terms
1. Define: plea bargaining, peremptory challenge, challenge for cause, indeterminate sentence, mandatory sentence.

Recalling the Facts
2. What are the advantages and disadvantages of the bail system?
3. What are some arguments for and against plea bargaining?
4. How does a challenge for cause differ from a peremptory challenge during jury selection?

Reviewing the Main Idea
5. Answer "As you read . . ." question 4 on page 249: What are some court procedures that some people consider unfair?

Critical Thinking
6. **Evaluating Fairness.** Do you think our judicial system should have mandatory sentences for all people convicted of the same crime? Explain why you believe this practice would be more or less fair than indeterminate sentences.

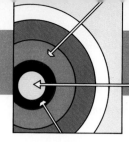

Citizenship Skills

Finding Legal Advice

"You must be out of your apartment by May 1," read the letter from the landlord. Bonnie and her parents had lived in their cozy apartment since she was born. Now the landlord wanted to gut the building, redo the interior, and charge rents higher than her family could afford.

Bonnie wondered, "Can the landlord actually do this to us? Is this legal?" Bonnie knew her parents could not afford a lawyer. Where could they go for advice?

Legal Services. Low-income families, like Bonnie's, can get advice through local legal services programs. Such programs go under various names. Your local phone book may list them as the Legal Services Center, the Legal Services Corporation, or the Legal Aid Society.

These agencies give free legal advice on civil cases and provide court representation to people who cannot afford private lawyers. Tenants' issues are common in legal services offices. These offices also handle job-related complaints, such as unfair firing. In addition, they help people get government benefits they deserve, such as Social Security payments.

Protecting People's Rights. If anyone violates your civil rights (for example, if you are turned down for a job because of your race or sex), there are other organizations you can turn to for help. One is the American Civil Liberties Union (ACLU), which is mainly concerned with protecting freedom of expression, equality before the law, and due process. Another resource is the National Association for the Advancement of Colored People (NAACP), an organization that works for racial equality.

The Attorney General's Office. If you believe a business has cheated you, you can call the Consumer Protection Division of the state Attorney General's Office. Free of charge, the office will try to settle disputes between businesses and customers who have complaints.

Private Lawyers. Private lawyers tend to be more expensive than the other resources mentioned here. However, many do not charge for the first meeting with a client. Others will sometimes offer inexpensive advice and services through "legal clinics." Legal clinics are most often located in metropolitan areas. They serve people with middle-level incomes who do not qualify for free legal services.

The American Bar Association (ABA). This organization is made up of lawyers, judges, law students, and law teachers. Their goal is to ensure high standards within the legal profession. Because they keep listings of licensed lawyers of all kinds, they can match you with an appropriate legal resource. If you have any kind of legal problem and don't know where to go for help, the ABA or your state bar association is a good place to start.

Practicing Skills

1. A mechanic has put defective parts in your car. From what government office could you seek legal advice?
2. **Identifying Alternatives.** Suppose Bonnie suspected that her landlord wanted to evict her family from their apartment because they were black. Where else, besides legal services, could Bonnie go for legal help?

Government and Law

The Juvenile Justice System

Juveniles, like adults, must be read the Miranda Warning if they are arrested.

A 16-year-old boy named Joel goes out one Saturday night with some friends. On a dare, Joel breaks into a soda vending machine. Joel is caught and taken to the local police station.

Thirteen-year-old Alice is referred by her teacher to a social worker. Her teacher suspects that Alice is being neglected, and possibly abused, by her parents.

Because both of these cases involve minors, they will be heard in juvenile court. Juvenile courts handle two types of cases —cases of neglect and cases of delinquency. Cases of neglect involve minors whose parents do not care for them properly. Cases of delinquency involve young people who are accused of breaking the law.

Protecting minors. Alice's case will be heard in juvenile court because she needs the care and protection of the law. If her case is found to be serious, she might be made a ward of the court—placed under the legal control of the courts rather than her parents. The court can then decide how best to help her. In some instances, young people are placed in foster homes to be taken care of by families other than their own.

Dealing with juvenile offenders. Joel's case involves delinquency. Perhaps a simple warning from the judge will be enough to keep him out of trouble. Or Joel might be placed on probation. He will then have to follow certain rules, such as being home by a certain time every night. He might not be allowed to drive a car or loiter near areas where he could get into trouble. He will probably have to meet with a probation officer once a week. If he does not follow these rules, his probation officer can take him back to court.

Some judges might assign a young offender to community service, such as working in a hospital or picking up litter. Others might try to make the punishment fit the crime. For example, Joel could be sentenced to work after school for the vending company whose machine he had robbed.

In more serious cases of juvenile crime, offenders are assigned to a youth correctional facility. Juveniles are sent to these facilities only after other attempts to help them have failed. Most offenders are held in these reform, or training, schools for six to nine months. Institutions where juveniles are held for a shorter time are called juvenile detention centers. Both types of facilities emphasize helping juvenile offenders to improve their behavior.

Comparing adult and juvenile courts.
When sentencing adult criminals, the courts have several goals. One is to punish those who have broken the law. Another is to deter criminals from committing more crimes. Yet another goal is to remove dangerous people from the community.

In juvenile cases, the aim is to help young offenders return to their communities, rather than to punish them. Juvenile courts recognize that young people sometimes get into trouble because of immaturity and vulnerability to peer pressure rather than criminal intent. The courts try to offer compassion, discipline, and supervision.

Juvenile courts differ from courts for adults in several important ways. The emphasis is on ensuring the young person's privacy. Not only are the proceedings held in private, but the minor usually is not photographed and is rarely fingerprinted. The media are discouraged from publicizing the names of young offenders. Records are kept confidential and often destroyed when the minor legally becomes an adult. This way, he or she will not have a criminal record.

How well does it work? Recently the juvenile justice system has come under increasing criticism. Many people feel that in trying to protect young offenders, the courts are too lenient and fail to do a good job of stopping juvenile crime. Some juvenile crimes are extremely serious— burglary, dealing drugs, arson, even murder. Teenagers charged with such crimes often already have a long history of arrests. Because their records were kept private, though, police and judges did not know about past offenses.

Now some communities are giving police full access to juveniles' records, enabling them to keep a close watch on repeat offenders. In addition, many states have laws that allow juveniles accused of the most serious crimes to be tried in adult courts.

Perhaps the greatest problem is how to get delinquents to change their behavior. Some states have started programs that emphasize employment counseling for offenders. That way these young people can return to the community with job skills that can help keep them out of trouble. Many offenders, however, also need help fighting drug or alcohol addiction. Because treatment programs are overcrowded, they are often unable to get the help they need.

The front pages of newspapers from Honolulu to New York are filled with stories about crime. Keeping teenagers from adding to the statistics will depend partly on whether society can come up with innovative approaches that reform and deter young offenders.

Questions to think about

1. Statistics show that in any given year, about 1 out of 25 young people between the ages of 14 and 18 will appear in juvenile court. Why do you think this figure is so high?
2. What do you think is the best way to deal with juveniles who commit crimes?

CHAPTER SUMMARY

Section 1   Each of the 50 states has its own system of courts. State courts hear all cases, both civil and criminal, that deal with state law. State court decisions sometimes influence public policy. The higher state courts have the power of judicial review. Due to an increasing crime rate and an increasing number of automobile accidents, it is hard for state courts to keep up with their heavy workload. To relieve the courts, some people favor appointing more judges, changing the criminal laws, or giving some cases to arbitrators instead of judges.

Section 2   All 50 states have lower courts that hear minor civil cases and misdemeanors. General trial courts hear most of the major civil and criminal suits. State appellate courts hear cases on appeal from lower courts. A state supreme court hears appeals from the appellate courts and interprets the state constitution. Appeals from this court must go to the United States Supreme Court. State judges are chosen in three ways. They can be elected by the people, appointed by the governor, or appointed by the legislature.

Section 3   A criminal case begins with a formal charge by the state against the accused person. After both sides present witnesses and evidence, a jury must decide what happened and whether the accused is guilty. A civil case starts with an accusation by a private citizen. The case is decided by either a judge or a jury. Proceedings against a young offender may be heard by a hearing officer or a judge of the juvenile courts. A minor must have a lawyer present in juvenile court.

Section 4   Some people believe that certain court practices are unfair. These include plea bargaining, the setting of bail, the selection of juries, and sentencing by judges.

Reviewing Key Terms

Choose the term that best completes each of the following sentences. Write your answers on a separate sheet of paper.

1. A (felony/misdemeanor) is a more serious crime than a (felony/misdemeanor).

2. (A grand jury/The reasonable doubt rule) is used to decide if there is enough evidence to hold a person for trial.

3. Witnesses in a court trial usually have to undergo a period of (plea bargaining/cross-examination) by the attorney for the opposing side.

Understanding Main Ideas

1. How do civil cases differ from criminal cases?

2. Give two examples of how the courts influence public policy.

3. What are two causes of the increasing workload of state courts?

4. What types of state courts exist?

5. What kinds of cases do the lower courts hear? General trial courts?

6. How can a decision by a state supreme court be appealed?

7. What are three ways of selecting judges?

8. What are the main steps in a criminal trial? A civil trial?

9. Why did the Supreme Court reverse the *In Re Gault* (1967) decision?

10. Why do some people oppose the use of plea bargaining?

Critical Thinking

1. **Predicting Consequences.** Some people believe laws against "victimless crimes" such as traffic violations or gambling should be changed to reduce the caseload of the courts. What effects could this have?

2. **Drawing Conclusions.** When might a trial by a judge be better for an accused person than a trial by jury?

3. **Demonstrating Reasoned Judgment.** In most states, juvenile court hearings are held behind closed doors. Only the family, a judge, and a defense lawyer are present. Is this a good idea? Why or why not?

Practicing Skills

1. **Finding Legal Advice.** Investigate the resources available in your community for helping citizens with legal problems. Make a list of names, addresses, and telephone numbers.

2. **Formulating Questions.** Almost all adult citizens are eligible for jury duty, and many are called to serve on a jury. What questions do you have about jury duty? Write three or four clearly worded questions about the information you want. Then find answers with the help of a librarian.

3. **Researching Information.** Find out how judges are selected in your state. Do you think this is a good method? Why or why not? Write a report explaining the process and your views on it.

Focusing on Citizenship

1. **Talking with a Lawyer.** Invite a lawyer to your class to discuss the operation of the courts in your state. Find out what problems the courts have and how they are trying to solve them.

2. **Interviewing Jurors.** Interview two or more adults (your parents or their friends) who have served on a jury. Write a short report summarizing their experiences and their reactions to jury duty.

3. **Doing Field Research.** Visit a court in your area. If possible, attend a jury trial. Give a short talk describing your experiences.

4. **Learning About Traffic Violations.** Penalties for traffic violations vary in all states. Find out the penalties in your state for the following violations: drunk driving, reckless driving, and driving without a license.

CHAPTER 14

Local Governments

City halls, like this one in Alexandria, Virginia, are the centers of power and decision making for local governments.

Previewing the Chapter

Suppose you were looking for the nearest public tennis courts or library or police station. If you needed any of these services, you would probably call your local government. There are more than 83,000 units of government on the county, city, town, or district level. This chapter describes these governments—what they are, what they do, and who influences them.

■   **Before you read,** look up these key terms in the Glossary at the back of this book: *county commission, ordinance, charter, home rule, council member at-large, mayor.*

■   **As you read,** look for answers to these questions:
1. What are some units of local government in the United States?
2. What are the main features of each of the three forms of city government?
3. Who are the most important officials in local government?

1 Units of Local Government

When we talk about government, we often talk about the powers which the federal government and the state governments share. The 50 state governments, in turn, share some of their powers with local governments. The state governments give these local units the power to pass laws and to levy taxes.

There are many types of local government. Counties and townships are units of local government in rural areas. In some states, counties are mainly court districts. Cities, towns, and villages are units of government in urban areas.

Towns and Villages

Towns are important units of local government in the six New England states. A town is an area in a state; it is smaller than a city and larger than a village. In most cases, towns include rural and urban areas within their boundaries.

The town meeting is a familiar event. In colonial days, such meetings were often held in a church or other central building. Today, town meetings are held in town halls. It is difficult to find a building large enough for a town meeting in an area with a large population. In these areas, town meetings have been abolished. A town meeting is direct democracy in action. The people themselves meet to discuss and solve their common problems.

A town meeting is an example of direct democracy in action.

The local governments of many New England towns still operate through town meetings. These meetings are usually held once a year. All registered voters may attend. At a town meeting, the voters make decisions on the town's policies on traffic control, sanitation, road building and repair, and taxes. An important part of the meeting is the election of town officials. The most important officials are called **selectmen**. A board of selectmen manages the town between meetings. Other elected officials include an assessor, a tax collector, a constable, and members of the school board.

Villages are the smallest units of local government in the United States. A village is usually, but not always, small in size. Some villages are larger than medium-sized cities.

Each village has a lawmaking body consisting of a board of trustees. The board is elected by the entire village. The executive officer, also elected, is usually called the president or the mayor. Other elected officials include a village attorney, a treasurer, and a village clerk.

The powers of a village government are limited. Rarely does a village board of trustees have the power to tax or to borrow money. Because of these limits, when the population of a village increases, it may be necessary for it to become a city. The change from village to city can be made by a vote of the people or by an act of the state legislature.

Counties and Townships

A **county** is another unit of local government in the United States. All states except Connecticut and Rhode Island have some county governments. In Louisiana, the local unit is called a **parish**. In Alaska, it is called a **borough**. In New England, counties are used chiefly as court districts. In other words, state courts are placed in various counties. In the Northeast and the Midwest, counties share the government of rural areas with other units of government. In the South and the West, counties are the main form of government in rural areas.

There are over 3,000 counties in the United States. The number varies from three in Delaware to 254 in Texas. Counties also vary in size. San Bernardino County in California is the largest in the nation. It covers more than 52,000 square kilometers (20,200 square miles). Arlington County in Virginia is one of the smallest. It covers only about 68 square kilometers (26 square miles). County populations also vary. There are many with more than 80,000 people, and some with populations in the hundreds.

Powers of County Governments.   Counties are governed by a **county board** or a **county commission**. The number of members is usually between three and 15. They are chosen by the voters, usually for a term of four years.

The powers of a county government vary from state to state. County boards have both lawmaking and executive powers. Thus,

A county is a unit of local government in the United States. Counties provide many services, such as the maintenance of highways. This photo shows highway maintenance in Texas.

a board may pass **ordinances** (laws) regulating the use of camping grounds in a county park. The board may also direct the county sheriff to see that these laws are carried out.

County boards also have control over land use. They can decide upon the location of a golf course, a public transit system, or a sewage treatment plant. Many airports come under county control.

The counties provide many services. The sheriff runs county jails, juvenile homes, and other correctional institutions. Counties also maintain courts, highways, schools, and welfare agencies.

County Officials.   The makeup of the county board varies from state to state. The *assessor* decides the value of all taxable property within the county—land, buildings, equipment, and furnishings. The *treasurer* is the keeper of county funds. He or she pays the county's bills. The *auditor* approves those payments if they are in keeping with state law.

The *clerk* keeps records of births, deaths, marriages, and divorces within the county. He or she is also the guardian of legal documents such as mortgages (loans for the purchase of homes).

The *district attorney* is the chief prosecutor for the county. School districts and other county agencies often seek legal advice from the district attorney. Criminal investigation is another important duty of the district attorney.

The *coroner* investigates all suspicious deaths. Most states require the coroner to investigate deaths that happen when no doctor is present. This county official is often called into court to testify to the cause of death.

The *superintendent of schools* is responsible for running the elementary and secondary schools within the county.

Townships. In the East and Midwest, many counties are divided into **townships**. Townships were created many years ago to deal with problems in areas far away from the center of county government. Townships today handle mostly rural matters—roads, weed control, drainage, or traffic control.

Special Districts

In all 50 states, there are about 25,000 *special districts.* They often provide services not available through a city, county, or other unit of local government. Thus, for example, a special district may be organized to provide fire protection in a remote area of a state.

The governing body of a special district usually consists of an elected board of from three to five members. The board has the power to tax and to make decisions that are necessary for the operation of the district.

SECTION 1 *Review*

Defining Key Terms
1. Define: selectmen, village, county, parish, borough, county board, county commission, ordinance, township.

Recalling the Facts
2. Who are the most important officials in a typical town government?
3. What specific problems might lead the people of a village to vote to form a city?
4. What powers does a county government have?
5. What positions make up a county board?

Reviewing the Main Idea
6. Answer "As you read . . ." question 1 on page 270: What are some units of local government in the United States?

Critical Thinking
7. **Predicting Consequences.** What kinds of conflicts might arise between a Superintendent of Schools and a School Board?

2 City Government

What is a city? Some years ago, the United States Bureau of the Census (the government agency that counts the population every ten years) defined a city as a place with 2,500 people. Today, that number is much too low. We see the continued growth of **urban** (city) centers such as Dallas and Los Angeles. An urban center and its surrounding suburbs make up a **metropolitan area**. Chicago and New York are large metropolitan areas with several million residents. They are also centers of trade, industry, and culture.

Cities

In most states, the unit of local government known as a city must draw up a charter. A **charter** is similar to a constitution. It defines the boundaries of the city, its powers, and its responsibilities. Charters are approved by state legislatures.

Home rule gives cities the power to write their own charters and to manage their own affairs. Home rule limits interference of the state legislature in city matters. Texas, Nebraska, and Missouri allow home rule for all cities with more than 5,000 people. In 36 states, including Oklahoma and Ohio, municipal home rule has been established in the state constitution. In eight other states, such as Indiana and Vermont, home rule must be granted to a city by the state legislature.

PEOPLE HELPING PEOPLE

Opening Hearts and Pocketbooks

Early in 1989, the community of McKeesport, Pennsylvania, was faced with a budget crisis. When the town police were awarded a pay increase of 4 percent, the town's budget was at its limit. Mayor Louis Washwich announced that he had no choice but to lay off 21 of 50 police officers. Faced with the loss of nearly half of its police force, the residents of the town reached deep into their pockets.

Community response came fast. The town's ambulance service gave $15,000 of its own money to launch a "Save Our Police" fundraising drive. Collection cans were placed in local businesses, and a special offering was taken during church services. The town barber chipped in $100. Gas stations, furniture stores, car dealerships, restaurants, and banks all contributed to the emergency fund.

Within a week, over $100,000 had poured into City Hall. The police officers' jobs were saved. And McKeesport had restored its sense of community in a tough time.

City government follows a pattern. There is a legislative (law-making) body called by different names—the city council or the board of commissioners. There is usually a chief executive officer. There are a number of municipal (city) courts. City officials are elected on a nonpartisan basis (no political parties). In spite of this, candidates are generally known to be either Democrats or Republicans. Rarely are they members of minor parties.

Three Forms of City Government

Mayor-Council Form.   This is the oldest form of city government in use today. More than half of the cities in the United States have this form of government. The mayor-council plan provides for the separation of powers—the executive and the legislative. The mayor is the chief executive officer. The city council is the lawmaking body. Both the mayor and the council are elected by the people. Atlanta, Chicago, and Omaha are among the many cities using a mayor-council form of government. Does your city have a mayor and a council?

SKILL BUILDER

According to this chart, what power does a strong mayor have that a weak mayor does not?

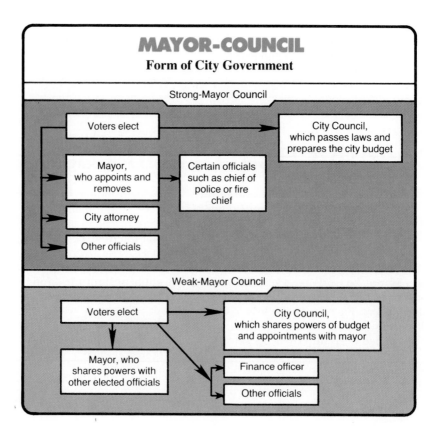

MAYOR-COUNCIL
Form of City Government

Strong-Mayor Council

Voters elect → City Council, which passes laws and prepares the city budget

Mayor, who appoints and removes → Certain officials such as chief of police or fire chief

City attorney

Other officials

Weak-Mayor Council

Voters elect → City Council, which shares powers of budget and appointments with mayor

Mayor, who shares powers with other elected officials → Finance officer

Other officials

The mayor's job is usually full-time. He or she works on a day-to-day basis with the heads of the police, fire, public transportation, and other departments. Many mayors have assistants to help them run the city.

The city council is almost always unicameral (one house), made up of members elected for terms of from two to six years. The most important job of a city council is to consider and pass or reject city ordinances.

Mayor-council governments have either weak mayors or strong mayors. In a weak-mayor type of government, the mayor has little real power. He or she shares the power of appointment or removal with the city council. The mayor also shares executive duties with other elected officials, such as the chief of police and the city treasurer. A so-called weak mayor with strong leadership ability may exert a great deal of influence on city government.

Under the strong-mayor plan, a mayor has a great deal of power over city affairs. The mayor's power includes the preparation of the city budget and the right to hire and fire certain officials. He or she can veto city ordinances. In many cities, however, a two-thirds vote of the council can override the mayor's veto. The power of a strong mayor may be reduced by a city council that frequently opposes his or her ideas.

Council-Manager Form. A second form of city government is found mostly in medium-sized or small cities. However, four large cities—Phoenix, Dallas, San Antonio, San Diego—have the council-manager form of local government. The city council is the lawmaking body. The job of running the city is turned over to a professional city manager hired by the city council. He or she is usually a specialist in business administration. This council-manager form of government was first used in Dayton, Ohio.

In some cities that have this form of government, mayors are elected. More often, though, they are members of the council and are appointed mayor by the other members. In many cities, one councilor is chosen to serve as mayor each year.

Commission Form. In 1901, Galveston, Texas was the first city to form a commission type of government. In 1900, a hurricane destroyed part of Galveston. The city's weak-mayor government could not handle the emergency. The Texas state legislature provided for five commissioners to run the city. Galveston later abandoned the commission form.

Under the commission form of city government, three to nine elected commissioners run the city. As a group, the commissioners pass laws, and each commissioner serves as the head of the public works, police, finance, or other city departments. In many cities, one commissioner is chosen mayor, either by popular vote or by the vote of commission members. In either case, the office of mayor is largely honorary. The mayor has no power beyond that of a commission member.

Commissioners are usually elected for terms of from two to four years. They are elected by the entire city on a nonpartisan basis. Their jobs are usually full-time.

The commission form of city government became popular in the first 20 years or so of this century. In 1920, about 500 American cities had the commission form. Fewer cities have chosen the commission form of government in recent years, however—today there are just a few more than 100 cities that use it. One reason is because, in this form, there is no separation of legislative and executive authority. Therefore, there is no way for citizens to keep a check on spending. The lack of an executive officer makes it difficult for voters to fix responsibility. Another flaw in the commission form is the fact that it tends to create "empire-building," in which each commissioner tries to draw as much of the city's money and power as he or she can to his or her own department. Tulsa, Oklahoma, and Portland, Oregon, are two cities that still have a commission form of government.

SKILL BUILDER

According to these diagrams, which form of city government concentrates power in the hands of just one group of people?

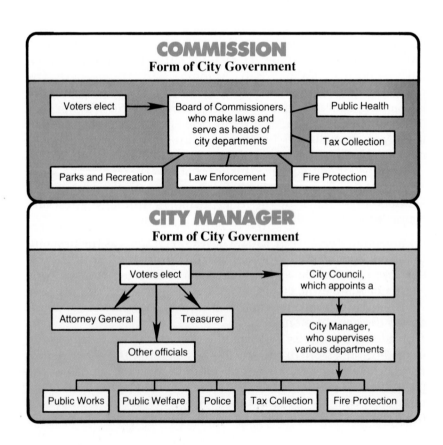

Defining Key Terms
1. Define: urban, metropolitan area, charter, home rule.

Recalling the Facts
2. What are the three forms of city government?
3. How do weak-mayor and strong-mayor plans differ?
4. What drawbacks are there in a commission form of city government?

Reviewing the Main Idea
5. Answer "As you read . . ." question 2 on page 270: What are the main features of each of the three forms of city government?

Critical Thinking
6. **Testing Conclusions.** "The commission form of city government is best because the commissioners can make decisions and carry them out quickly and efficiently." Explain why you agree or disagree with this conclusion.

3 Key Decision Makers in Local Government

There are many important officials in local government. City managers are appointed to office. Mayors and city council members are elected. All elected officials run on a nonpartisan basis in order to keep local government free from the control of political parties. These local government officials often make decisions which affect the lives of all citizens. It is felt that nonpartisan elections will encourage citizens to take a greater interest in their local governments.

A specially trained **city manager** is hired by the city council. He or she is responsible for running the entire city. He or she is also responsible to the city council. A city manager is not usually well-known in the community. Very often he or she comes from a part of the state far away from the city, or even from another state.

City Managers

As chief executive officer, the city manager must make sure that all city ordinances are enforced. The city manager must also supervise city services such as police and fire protection, water supply, and public transportation.

Another important duty of the city manager is in the area of finance. Throughout the year, the city council must be kept informed of the financial condition of the city. How much money does the city have on hand? How has money been spent? Some city charters do not allow deficit spending. (As mentioned in Chapter 10, deficit spending means that a government spends more money than it takes in from taxes and other sources of income.) The city manager also prepares the annual budget and submits it to the city council for its approval.

City managers do not have an easy job. They may not have to deal with the public, but the city council is often a very demanding employer. The decisions of the council must be carried out by the city manager, whatever she or he thinks of such decisions. Although the city manager attends all council meetings, he or she has no vote and cannot veto council decisions.

City Councils

The **city council** is the lawmaking body for a city. Four years is the most common term. In most cities, there are from five to nine members on the council, although the Chicago city council has 50 councilors. In recent years councils have become smaller. The smaller size makes it easier for citizens to follow the voting record and other activities of each councilor. A councilor's pay is generally low, so most city councilors have another job or source of income.

Cities differ in their methods of electing city councilors. In some cities, voters elect **council members at-large**, that is, from the city as a whole. In other cities, they are elected from **wards**, or voting districts. The voters of each ward are allowed to elect one city councilor.

Both methods of electing councilors have advantages and disadvantages. Those who favor the at-large system argue that each councilor should represent the entire city. He or she should work for the good of all the people, not just those in a single ward. One disadvantage of this system is that it leads to large numbers of candidates running for a few council seats.

The chief argument in favor of the ward system is that it is the only way to ensure fair treatment to all parts of the city. Low-income sections or those with large numbers of minorities are often ignored by city councils. The citizens living in these wards need someone to speak for them. One argument against this system is that councilors put all their efforts into helping their own wards. They may ignore the needs of the city as a whole.

Besides being the lawmaking body of a city, the council sets local tax rates and reviews the city budget as prepared by either the mayor's office or the city manager's office. The council gives final approval of the budget before it is passed into law. At times, the council might be called upon to give approval for spending money on a project not included in the city budget.

Councils pass resolutions as well as ordinances. A **resolution** is a statement of opinion. An example would be a resolution praising a city official for a long career in city service.

Council members work hard. In the morning, they usually meet with voters and other people in their offices. Twenty or more telephone calls a day is not an unusual number for a city councilor to receive. A caller may ask to have a traffic signal installed at a busy corner near her or his home. Another caller may complain about the noise from a neighborhood tavern late at night. Many callers ask for help in finding jobs or getting loans.

Formal city council meetings are held both during the day and at night. In recent years, many councils have scheduled important meetings in the evening so that working people can attend. At these meetings, proposed laws are discussed. Citizens are given time to express their opinion for or against a measure. As a result, these meetings often go on for many hours. An example of the kind of question which might be discussed is, "Shall the fares on the city transit system be increased to help pay for operating costs?"

The city council makes laws, sets tax rates, and reviews the budget.

Mayors

The **mayor** is the chief executive of a city. The mayor sees that all laws are carried out. Almost all mayors of large cities admit that they have a tough job. One reason is that cities tend to be the center of national problems. Racial tension, strikes, unemployment, pollution, crime—these and other national problems are usually centered in the cities. Dealing with these problems is an extremely difficult task. Because of this, some mayors have been known to quote President Lyndon Johnson. When the President's job was going badly, Johnson was reported as saying: "Things could be worse. I could be a mayor."

Strikes are one example of the problems mayors face. In past years, cities have been the scene of walkouts by police, fire fighters, sanitary workers, teachers, and other city employees. Such strikes often cause great anger among city residents because a vital service is stopped. Many people look to the mayor to do something, even though he or she has no power to force a settlement.

What should a mayor do? On the one hand, he or she is expected to look after the welfare of city employees. To do otherwise is to invite charges of being against working people. On the other hand, a mayor's primary duty is to keep the city running at all times. This is particularly true when the health and safety of the people are concerned. Faced with a possible strike, a mayor will try to persuade workers to compromise on their demands. If the strike continues, however, the blame falls on the mayor's shoulders.

Being in the middle of opposing groups is not always a handicap. Suppose, for example, a mayor proposes higher taxes in

Xavier Suarez, mayor of Miami, Florida, poses near the city's scenic harbor.

order to increase fire and police services. Such an increase will mean higher tax rates and will bring an immediate reaction from at least one group in the city. The reaction may come from a taxpayer's league, a group formed to fight tax increases. The argument of the league—namely, that taxes are already too high—would appeal to many of the voters. The mayor can challenge the argument, stressing that the value of human life and property cannot be measured in money.

The job of a mayor has often been compared to the job of a promoter or salesperson. There are several reasons for this comparison. One is that, in many cities, the mayor leaves the daily running of the city to assistants and other city officials. This gives the mayor time to work as a promoter of special programs and projects—anything from tax reform to crime control to sewage disposal. Whatever the program or project, there is usually a job of selling to be done, for a mayor cannot simply order a program to be passed into law. He or she must spend a lot of time and effort convincing the city council, elected officials, and the voters that the program is worthwhile.

Many mayors also spend a great deal of time promoting their programs in Washington, D.C. The federal government gives financial aid to cities for many different purposes. The amount of such money is limited. Cities must therefore compete with one another for federal money. Thus, a mayor must work hard to sell a particular program such as a subway or a hospital to federal officials who will decide which city gets the money.

SECTION 3 *Review*

Defining Key Terms
1. Define: city manager, city council, council members-at-large, ward, resolution, mayor.

Recalling the Facts
2. What are some of the duties of a city manager?
3. What are some of the problems that mayors face?

Reviewing the Main Idea
4. Answer "As you read . . ." question 3 on page 270: Who are the most important officials in local government?

Critical Thinking
5. **Making Comparisons.** Compare the advantages and disadvantages of electing city council members by districts and at large. Which system do you think is more fair?

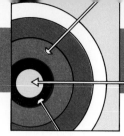

Citizenship Skills

Locating Government Resources

If you want information about government procedures or services, you should know how to identify and contact the appropriate government office or official. By doing so, you can learn more about how each level of government works and what services it provides. You can also get help in solving problems connected with traffic laws, mail delivery, garbage disposal, or other matters involving government.

Before you can obtain information or help from government offices and officials, you need to find out who "they" are. A good place to begin is in the white pages of your phone book under the heading "Government." Usually, there are complete listings of names, addresses, and phone numbers of the offices for each level of government (federal, state, local). In addition, a general information number for each level of government is often listed.

Suppose you have a question or problem related to local government. You have identified the office or official you need to contact. The next step is to make a phone call and request the information or assistance you want. When you call:

- Introduce yourself, giving your name and the town or city where you live. ("My name is Marty Dodds, and I'm a resident of Sunnyvale.")
- Explain the purpose of your call. (Be specific and brief.) If you need to talk to another department or person, you will be told now.
- Be polite, patient, and, if necessary, persistent.

- Thank the person for helping you. (Be sure to get the person's name in case you have to call again or follow up with a letter.)

Below are typical listings of government resources.

Frequently Called City, County, State, and Federal Government Numbers

City Hall or Town Hall
Fire Department
Health Department
Library
Parks and Recreation
Police Department
Public Works Department
School Department
U. S. Postal Service
Veterans' Services

Practicing Skills

Using the information you have just read, answer the following questions on a separate sheet of paper.

1. Copy the list of government offices above. Fill in the correct phone numbers for your community.
2. **Identifying Alternatives.** Which of the above government offices would you call if a water pipe burst on your street? If you wanted to know where you could play softball?

Citizenship

Community Recycling Programs

"City officials in Seattle still cannot forget the Thanksgiving Day a few years ago when nine persons had to be evacuated from their home—turkey dinner and all—because of methane.

The gas was seeping from one of the city's landfills into homes and had reached explosive levels. Two weeks earlier, two families and employees of an insurance office had been evacuated. Eventually, an entire neighborhood was forced to move at the city's expense."

So began a story in the *Boston Globe* on October 9, 1988. Headlined "Seattle recycles its way to the top," the story went on to explain that the methane leak motivated Seattle officials to take a good, hard look at their waste disposal problems.

One result is that today Seattle has one of the most sophisticated and most successful recycling programs in the country. Recycling is the process of turning waste into usable materials. Materials that can be recycled include newspapers, glass, plastics, aluminum cans, rubber, and steel. In the Seattle program, 2,200 tons of cans, bottles, and newspapers are recycled every month.

Seattle is not alone. Other cities across the United States have invested heavily in recycling as well. Austin, Texas; Minneapolis, Minnesota; and San Jose, California, all recycle thousands of tons of waste each month.

The idea of recycling trash is not new. It was popular with environmentalists in the 1970s. Yet little recycling was actually done at that time. Why is the practice catching on now?

Young volunteers in Woodstock, New York, bundle newspapers at a community recycling center.

One reason is that the quantity of trash and garbage material keeps increasing. The amount of waste generated by homes and businesses in the United States has more than doubled since 1960. This increase has overloaded waste disposal programs using the traditional methods of landfill and burning. Communities that use landfill as a method of disposal find that available land is becoming scarce. Communities that burn trash find that their plants cannot keep up with the mountains of garbage piling up. To make matters worse, incinerators produce large amounts of polluting smoke that can endanger people's health. Many incinerators have been closed down because they do not meet federal air quality standards.

Local Governments   285

Continued

The price of dumping has increased as well. Although prices vary from community to community, the trend everywhere is sharply upward. Today the cost per ton of dumping ranges from less than $35 to $55 or more. And it is estimated that the price will soon climb over $100 a ton. Anything, therefore, that cuts down on the amount of waste saves money. And recycling is one of the most effective ways of reducing the amount of waste to be dumped.

As a result, many states have passed laws that require residents to recycle newspapers, glass, aluminum cans, and plastics. In some states, residents who do not recycle must pay a penalty. In other states, trash collectors will not pick up trash that contains recyclables.

Many communities have set up recycling centers where residents can drop off their recyclables. Typically, residents bring their used bottles, jars, plastic milk jugs, newspapers, and magazines to the recycling center. There, these items are separated into different containers. Residents of some communities also take part in paper pick-ups. Corrugated cardboard from local businesses may be collected, as well as newspapers and computer print-out paper.

For recycling to be successful, consumers need to be educated. They need to know which products are made from recycled materials. They need to know that recycled products generally cost less. And they need to get in the habit of buying recycled products. Although the public has been slow to change old habits, media coverage of the "trash crisis" has helped to encourage citizens to take action. More and more individuals are realizing how fragile the environment is and deciding to do what they can.

Communities across the country are also discovering that recycling waste materials makes economic sense. Recycling centers across the nation process hundreds of tons of garbage every year. Since disposing of a single ton of garbage would ordinarily cost an average of $45, that adds up to savings of thousands of dollars per year for taxpayers. For example, the recycling project in Seattle is saving that city more than $1 million every year.

No community can afford to turn its back on this kind of savings. In the end, though, it is up to the citizens of a community to support recycling efforts. Citizens who recycle not only help the community save money, they also help protect the environment and preserve our natural resources.

Questions to think about

1. How do you think recycling paper goods, plastic, glass, and aluminum can help protect the environment and preserve our precious natural resources?

2. Despite all the benefits of recycling, many people oppose mandatory recycling laws and refuse to recycle material. Why do you think this is so?

CHAPTER SUMMARY

Section 1   There are many types of local government, including counties, cities, towns, townships, villages, and special districts. Towns are the main units of local government in New England. Many towns govern by direct democracy through town meetings. Villages, the smallest units of government, have elected lawmaking bodies and executive officers. In the West and South, counties are the main form of government in rural areas. They are governed by an elected county board and other officials. Townships are rural governments that deal only in matters involving land use. Special districts provide services not furnished by any other units of government.

Section 2   A city government consists of a lawmaking body, a chief executive officer, and a number of municipal courts. The mayor-council plan has an elected mayor and city council. It provides for the separation of the legislative and executive powers. Some cities have council-manager governments. An elected city council hires a professional city manager to carry out their laws. In the commission form, voters elect a group of commissioners who pass laws and carry them out. In these plans, there is no separation of legislative and executive powers.

Section 3   There are many key officials in city government. City managers are appointed by city councils to supervise the daily operation of the city. City councils are the elected lawmaking body of city government. The mayor is the elected chief executive of a city. Most mayors have hard jobs because cities are the center of many national problems.

Reviewing Key Terms

Match the following terms with the definitions below. Write your answers on a separate sheet of paper.

council member at-large   home rule
charter   county commission
mayor   ordinance

1. a city's basic law, similar to a constitution

2. the governing body of a county

3. the chief executive of a city

4. a councilor elected from the city, not the voting districts

5. a law

6. powers given to cities to manage their own affairs

Understanding Main Ideas

1. What is meant by the term *local government?*

2. What is a town meeting?

3. Name five kinds of services that county governments provide.

4. What are the three forms of city government in our country today?

5. In which kind of city government are the legislative and executive powers separate?

6. Compare a strong and weak form of mayor-council government.

7. What is a city manager? Why is a city manager's job difficult at times?

8. In what two ways are city council members elected?

9. Describe at least four duties of city council members.

10. Describe at least two kinds of problems that mayors of large cities must solve.

Critical Thinking

1. **Demonstrating Reasoned Judgment.** Because of overcrowding in many cities, should the use of city parks be restricted to the people who live within ten square blocks of those parks? Why or why not?

2. **Making Comparisons.** Compare the advantages and disadvantages of the two methods of electing city council members.

Practicing Skills

1. **Locating Government Resources.** Identify a problem in your community—traffic control, lack of parks and recreation areas, or another problem. Then look in your telephone book under "Government." Find the appropriate number and call to get information about why this problem exists and what steps are being taken to solve it.

2. **Writing a Letter to the Editor.** Some people take part in local affairs by writing letters to the editor. These letters express the writers' opinions on current issues. Choose an issue in your community that you feel strongly about. Send a letter about the issue to the editor of your local newspaper.

3. **Organizing Information.** Make a chart showing the vital statistics about your local government. Include number of voters, type of government, elected and appointed officials, terms of office; and make up of your city or town government by sex and age.

Focusing on Citizenship

1. **Talking to a Local Official.** Invite a member of your city council (or other local lawmaking body) to talk to the class about problems in city or local government.

2. **Attending Local Government Meetings.** Attend a meeting of your local city council or school board and write down what you observe. Report your findings to the class.

3. **Understanding Student Government.** See how your school government is organized by studying a copy of its constitution or bylaws. What qualifications are needed to run for office? How are student officers elected? What powers do officers have? How can they be removed from office?

4. **Staging a Mock Town Meeting.** Imagine that you live in a town governed by town meetings. Decide what issues should be discussed at the next meeting. Then hold a mock town meeting and choose someone to preside over the discussion and voting.

CHAPTER 15

Urban Problems

Bumper-to-bumper traffic is typical at rush hour in most large American cities.

Previewing the Chapter

The pages of the local newspapers in major American cities are filled with descriptions of urban problems. Each day, city officials face difficult decisions about handling crime, pollution, poverty, housing shortages, health issues, and transportation. There simply are no easy solutions. This chapter explores some of the ways that governments on all levels are attacking these problems.

■ **Before you read,** look up these key terms in the Glossary at the back of this book: *city planner, zoning, smog, public housing project, urban renewal.*

■ **As you read,** look for answers to these questions:
   1. What problems are addressed by a city planning commission?
   2. What are four major problems facing cities today?
   3. What are some of the partial solutions to urban problems that cities are trying today?

1 City Planning

To plan something is to think about how you want it to turn out. A **city planner** is a person who thinks about how a city should be. He or she suggests ways to make a city a better place in which to live. Many cities have a city planning commisson whose job is to think about the city's future.

City Planning in Colonial Times

Some of the early cities in the colonies were designed with great care. In 1688, William Penn, the Founder of Pennsylvania, revealed his plan for the city of Philadelphia. One part of the plan provided for five large squares, or civic centers.

Washington, D.C., our nation's capital, also began as a planned city. Congress gave the job to a French engineer, Pierre L'Enfant. He submitted his plans to Congress in 1791. L'Enfant designed Washington so that there would be plenty of open space. Some of the streets were 46 meters (150 feet) wide, with 3 meters (10 feet) of sidewalk on either side. L'Enfant's plan provided for the planting of trees and a number of circles and beautiful parks.

Over the years, L'Enfant's original design has been followed fairly closely. Today, the National Capital Planning Commission supervises further developments and improvements in the city.

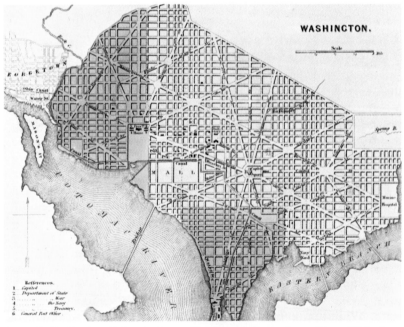

Above is Washington, D.C., as planned by the French engineer, Pierre L'Enfant.

The work of the early designers was the exception rather than the rule. There was little or no attempt to develop an orderly plan for most cities. Boston and other "walking cities" of the early 1800s were examples. People who lived in these cities could walk quickly and easily from one place to another. To keep this walking time short, however, homes, factories, public buildings, schools, stores, and offices were all crowded together. The distance around many of these cities was only about three to five kilometers (two to three miles). In the later 1800s, the invention of the streetcar led to an increase in the size of cities. Growth continued to take place without any plan, however.

Our cities of the 1800s were not pleasant places in which to live. Visitors from foreign countries have written about unpaved streets "filled with mud." One writer, Jacob Riis (an immigrant from Scandinavia) shocked many people with his description of the rat-infested slums of New York. In many cities, poor sewage and sanitation led to dangerous epidemics. Outbreaks of malaria, typhoid, and yellow fever caused the death of thousands of city people. Crime became so widespread that it was unsafe to walk in most city streets at night.

Toward the end of the 1800s, some of the problems of the cities had been solved. Main streets were paved. Street lights were provided. Sewers were installed. Many cities passed laws against dumping garbage into the streets. The building of hospitals and clinics helped to solve health problems. Police and fire departments were created.

These improvements were needed, but they were only a beginning. By 1900, new problems arose. Increases in city populations led to two, three, or more families living together in small apartments. More and more factories were built. Automobiles crowded city streets and polluted city air. Dumps, filled with heaps of old cars, were often located near city outskirts. Many houses were built without schools or parks nearby. New streets and highways were built without any thought of future needs.

The city of Hartford, Connecticut, became the first city to think about planning for its future. In 1907, Hartford created a planning commission to think about the city's future. About seven years later, some of the commission's plans were carried out. In 1918, the city of Detroit also set up a planning commission.

Today, most large cities have planning commissions. The members are usually appointed by the mayor and must be approved by the city council. The number of members on a planning commission varies. They are often trained in architecture and engineering. In many cities such commissions have come up with a master plan for the city. A **master plan** gives a detailed outline of

Most large cities have planning commissions such as the one meeting in the photo to the left. In many cities these commissions prepare a master plan for the city. They conserve some old buildings, while adding new ones.

present and future needs of a city. Some of the problems with which city planning commissions have to deal are discussed in the following paragraphs.

Land Use.   A planning commission makes decisions about how the land of a city can be used. **Zoning** is the practice of dividing a city into districts or zones, and then deciding how each zone is to be used. There are usually three kinds of zones in most cities. Residential zones are for homes, commercial zones are for stores and offices, and industrial zones are for factories. Each zone is divided into subzones. A residential zone, for example, may contain one section for large apartment houses, and another where only single-family houses may be built.

Today, almost all large cities are zoned. Zoning often gets a lot of opposition from citizens, however. The main argument against zoning is that it denies people the right to use their property as they wish. In many cities, for example, zoning laws require all new buildings to include space for parking. The courts, however, have upheld the right of cities to enforce zoning laws.

Transportation.   The first recorded sale of an automobile was on April 1, 1898. It was a one-cylinder Winton. Today, there are millions of cars on our roads and highways.

The rapid growth in the number of automobiles has caused many problems for city planners. The planners must see to it that a city has enough streets so that the cars will avoid traffic jams. One common solution has been to design highways that allow through traffic to bypass (drive around) the center of the city. Highways are often planned so that motorists may move freely around the city, thus avoiding the downtown area. City public transportation systems also help to reduce the number of cars.

Public Health. As late as 1950, many large cities dumped raw sewage into nearby rivers and other bodies of water. Such dumping caused many health problems in these cities. Since 1950, many city planning commissions have included the building of sewage disposal plants in their master plans. Planning has also led to the moving of garbage dumps away from the center of cities.

Many city planning commissions pay close attention to improving the beauty of their cities. Overhead wires have been placed underground. The parking of cars on streets has been prohibited during certain hours so that street cleaning can take place. Trees have been planted along downtown streets. Boston, St. Louis, Los Angeles, and other cities have rebuilt downtown and waterfront areas, making them attractive locations.

SECTION 1 *Review*

Defining Key Terms
1. Define: city planner, master plan, zoning.

Recalling the Facts
2. What major city has tried to follow its original plan? Who designed it?

3. What is meant by a "walking city"?

4. What are some of the steps taken by city planning commissions to improve public health conditions?

Reviewing the Main Idea
5. Answer "As you read . . ." question 1 on page 289: What problems are addressed by a city planning commission?

Critical Thinking
6. Determining Relevance. Many city planning commission members are architects or engineers. In view of today's problems, what other professionals might be selected?

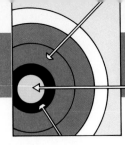

Study Skills

Making an Outline

Think of a skeleton, with all those bare bones. An outline could be said to be a bare-bones summary of ideas. Written in list form, an outline provides a structure on which a writer can build. Writers, in fact, sometimes "flesh out" an idea, or make an outline come to life, by creating full sentences and paragraphs.

All writing begins with either a mental or a formal outline. Mental outlining is something people often do automatically. When you wake up on a Saturday morning, for example, you might "outline" your day by listing to yourself what you will do first, what will follow that, and so on. A formal outline is a written list organized into main ideas and supporting facts or examples. Each entry in a formal outline should be brief—just a few words that identify an idea or topic.

Look at the outline on this page, which covers the information in Section 1 of this chapter. Notice that it uses roman numerals to identify main ideas, capital letters for subtopics, and Arabic numerals for supporting facts. Also notice that the outline has a title that gives the main idea of the outline as a whole.

City Planning

I. City Planning in Colonial Times
- A. Philadelphia
  1. William Penn
  2. city squares
- B. Washington, D.C.
  1. Pierre L'Enfant
  2. open space
  3. wide roads and sidewalks
  4. city circles and parks
  5. tree planting

II. The Walking Cities
- A. Unplanned Cities
  1. Boston
  2. New York
- B. Solving City Problems in the 1800s
  1. paving city streets
  2. installing street lights
  3. installing sewers
  4. passing garbage laws
  5. building hospitals
  6. creating police and fire departments

III. Planning Commissions
- A. Land Use
- B. Transportation
- C. Public Health

An effective outline is a wonderful tool for studying as well as for writing. A student can take written material and break it into its basic parts. In this way, a student can quickly review and remember what has been written.

An outline can be short and simple or long and complicated. An outline does not necessarily have to follow a format like the one shown on this page. An outline written in note form, using short sentences instead of numbered items, can also be a useful tool for classifying information.

Practicing Skills

1. Why are outlines useful to writers?
2. **Writing Outlines.** Reread the material in Section 1 under the heading "Planning Commissions." Then, on a separate sheet of paper, recopy the outline shown on this page and add supporting facts under the letters *A*, *B*, and *C*.

2 Problems That Cities Face

The cities of the United States have many problems. Some of these problems have been around for a long time. Others are more recent. In the rest of this section, you will learn about some of the most difficult city problems.

Housing

Each of us needs a place to live. The right to choose where we want to live is one of our basic freedoms. Unfortunately, we may find it difficult to make that choice, particularly in our larger cities.

First, there is a shortage of homes. Since the end of World War II, the population of our cities has increased sharply. More and more people have moved to cities in search of jobs. The building of new homes has not kept up with this increase.

Second, many homes are in poor condition. When there is a shortage of places to live, people have to take whatever is available. According to recent studies, one out of seven families lives in substandard dwellings in our cities.

Most substandard housing is in slum areas. A **slum** is a section of a city where the homes are in rundown or poor condition. The buildings are firetraps. Often they lack heat, water, and even toilets. Overcrowding is common. The people who live in slums

A slum is a section of a city in which the homes are in poor condition.

are poor. Often they are members of minority groups who are living in crowded buildings.

Many landlords take advantage of tenants who live in slums. Although the slum landlords pay a lower property tax, the rents they charge are often just as high as those in other parts of the city. Lower taxes may be the reason that landlords refuse to make repairs to slum property. Putting a slum building in first-class condition would cause property taxes to go up, and so the owner does not improve the building. There is little that tenants can do, except move. For many poor people, there is no place to go. The cycle of poverty is hard to escape. Housing costs have risen dramatically in recent years, making it even more difficult to move out of a slum to a better location.

Slums are a burden to any city. Because slums have high crime rates, they require additional police protection. Firefighting services are also called upon more often than in other parts of the city. Many people in the slums receive welfare payments because a large number are unemployed. At the same time, people who live in slum areas cannot pay very much tax money to support city services.

Poverty

Who are the poor in our country? The federal government tells us that more than 13 percent of our people are poor. Poor persons do not have enough money to support themselves. Not all poor people live in cities. About 20 percent live in the suburbs. Another 20 percent live in rural areas. As a general rule, though, the cost of living is higher in cities than in the suburbs or rural areas outside the cities.

A serious problem for many cities is the cost of welfare programs. More and more people have been receiving welfare in the United States. Welfare is a payment from the government to a person who cannot earn enough money to live. Cities share the cost of welfare with the federal government. The growing number of people who receive welfare payments has increased the money problems of cities.

A typical welfare family is a mother and three small children without any way to support themselves. The amount of the welfare payment to such a family is based on the number of children. Many poor families who have had to go on welfare have several children. In recent years, more than 11 million persons have been receiving welfare payments.

Crime

Crime is one of the most serious problems in most cities. Recent public-opinion polls show that a majority of people are afraid to walk the streets in their own cities at night. In many cities, stores close before it gets dark. Bus drivers carry no money. Many people take lessons in self-defense or carry weapons for protection.

This fear is not without reason. Annual figures released by the Federal Bureau of Investigation (FBI) show that most robberies, burglaries, and assaults on people occur in metropolitan areas with populations over 100,000. FBI studies show that violent crime increased about 44 percent between 1977 and 1986.

Juvenile delinquency is also on the rise. One out of every six persons arrested in 1987 was under the age of 18. School districts have to spend millions of dollars every year repairing damage done to school buildings by young people. Violence inside schools is another serious matter. Some city school districts have had to hire police to patrol school grounds and hallways. Shoplifting and automobile theft are other common juvenile crimes.

Why is there so much crime in the cities? Experts cite many causes—increasing drug use, high unemployment, inadequate police protection, poor schools and neighborhoods, a decline in religion and moral values, broken homes, and the failure of parents to teach their children proper behavior. Some people think that poverty and crime go hand in hand. Studies do show that more crimes are committed by low-income people than by middle-income or wealthy people. Yet the problem is clearly not limited to the poor.

PEOPLE HELPING PEOPLE

Saving the Next Generation

In the inner cities of the United States, just walking the streets can be a dangerous game. In Detroit, Michigan, 365 children under the age of 17 were shot during 1986—one for every day of the year. Among the victims were Derik Barfield, age 16, and his younger brother Roger. The two unarmed boys were shot by a teenager on a playground. Roger was wounded; Derik died.

Derik's mother, Clementine Barfield, had to do something. In January, 1987, she formed a citywide organization called Save Our Sons and Daughters, or SOSAD. The group now has nearly 1,000 members.

SOSAD is active in lobbying for a ban on handguns. It also promotes anti-drug rallies. Recently the organization has taken counseling programs into city schools, stressing nonviolent ways of handling conflict. SOSAD members also offer more personal services. They may give comfort to grief-stricken parents who have lost a child and help with such nitty-gritty matters as funeral arrangements.

Clementine Barfield remains upbeat about the future. "Derik was tall, dark, and handsome, and he was good-spirited," she says. "He had planned to be a minister. Through SOSAD, I feel I am carrying on his ministry."

Pollution is a serious problem in most cities. Exhaust from cars, trucks, and buses, as well as pollutants from factories cause irritating smog, such as that seen in this photo.

Pollution

Almost all large cities have to deal with some form of pollution. Exhaust fumes from millions of automobiles, trucks, and buses in city streets are among the greatest polluters. These fumes add millions of tons of pollutants to the atmosphere each year. In some cities, factories produce almost equal amounts of air pollution. The resulting **smog** (unclean air) is an irritation to city dwellers' eyes and throats. Pollution may cause serious damage to the lungs or other parts of the body after several years.

In most cities, noise is often as much of a problem as waste disposal. Most large urban centers have airports close to residential areas. Many people complain about sleepless nights and jangled nerves because of the noise of airplanes landing and taking off. Some residents have sued their city government for damages of one kind or another.

The problems of many cities

Shortage of low-cost housing

Slums

Unemployment

Air pollution

Crime

Poverty

Inflation

Juvenile delinquency

Noise pollution

SKILL BUILDER   Have you seen any evidence of these problems in your area or in a city you have visited?

SECTION 2 *Review*

Defining Key Terms
1. Define: slum, smog.

Recalling the Facts
2. Why do many landlords not make an effort to improve their buildings?

3. Why are slums a financial burden on any city?

4. Why are many people in cities afraid to walk in the streets after dark?

5. What are some of the causes of increasing crime rates in America?

6. What is one of the chief causes of air pollution?

Reviewing the Main Idea
7. Answer "As you read . . ." question 2 on page 289: What are four major problems facing cities today?

Critical Thinking
8. Recognizing Cause and Effect. Do you see any connections between various urban problems (such as between crime and poverty)? Explain how some urban problems may cause others.

3 Finding Solutions

City Ordinances

Solving the problems of cities is not a simple matter. Some cities have passed ordinances that try to deal with the problems. The federal and state governments, too, have made such laws. For example, there are laws requiring auto makers to install anti-pollution devices in automobile exhaust systems. There are also laws that forbid discrimination in the sale or rental of homes and apartments.

Laws may or may not solve a city's problems, however. Some cities have improved air quality by passing laws forbidding apartment owners to burn trash in their furnaces. Laws requiring automobile anti-pollution devices have not worked. Exhaust fumes are still a serious health problem in many cities.

Public Housing Projects

Many cities have made some progress in dealing with their shortage of housing by the construction of **public housing projects**. These are large groups of apartment buildings for low-income families. Rents are often based upon family income. Many housing projects are built in areas that were once slums. The run-down homes and other buildings were torn down. New housing was built with funds provided by the government. About four million households receive federal housing assistance today.

Urban Renewal

Another plan for slum clearance is called **urban renewal**. A city clears out a number of slum properties and then sells the land to private contractors. The contractors use the land (according to an approved plan) for hotels, office buildings, convention centers, apartments, or shopping centers.

In the past, urban renewal came under severe criticism. The criticism was that, in some cities, the homes of people in slum areas were torn down and replaced with housing that the former residents could not afford. At present, urban renewal projects must include housing for those who are displaced at prices they can pay.

Money

Money, of course, would help to solve urban problems. Many cities, however, do not have the money they need, and they are limited in their ability to raise money. Most of the income of cities comes from the property tax only. State and federal governments place heavy income taxes on individuals. Any attempt by cities to place other taxes on the people is strongly resented and opposed. There has been a movement to reduce property taxes. Where such a movement has been successful, the reduction has cut deeply into the income of the local governments. The lack of money is serious. Many cities do not have enough money to pay for adequate police and fire protection.

A money crisis started in 1970, when officials in Newark, New Jersey announced that the city treasury was almost empty. In 1975, political leaders announced that New York City was running out of funds, too. Then, in 1978, Cleveland, Ohio came close to financial collapse. At the present time, all three cities are operating and continuing to try to solve their basic money problems. New York City was helped by loans from the federal government. In spite of the loans, however, the city continued to spend more money than it had.

Why are local governments having money problems? One observer noted that New York City "had been trying to do too much for too many with too little." Over one ten-year period, the city's spending grew at a rate of 12 percent. However, the money it collected in taxes during the same period increased by only 5 percent. This difference amounted to a loss of millions of dollars over the ten years. Some people blame the money problems of cities on high salaries and high pensions (retirement payments). They also say that there are too many persons on city payrolls.

PEOPLE HELPING PEOPLE

Cleaning Up "Death Valley"

With rakes and shovels in hand, and a determined look in their eyes, 300 residents of south Houston, Texas, gathered in early 1989 to clean up their neighborhood. The area was a scene of frequent drug dealing and had earned the nickname of "Death Valley" for the number of killings that had occurred there in recent years.

People who lived in the neighborhood were fed up with the situation. "I'm getting sick and tired of being awakened at night by sirens and being scared to come out at night," said one resident.

Houston police and neighborhood leaders joined hands in the cleanup effort. First the police led a sweep through the neighborhood, raiding empty apartments that drug dealers had taken over for their deals.

Next came the physical cleanup. The crew of volunteers, who included homemakers, senior citizens, and a troop of Boy Scouts, worked their way through the mess. They picked up garbage and placed it in dumpsters. They swept the walks and cut down the weeds.

By taking strong action, the volunteers reclaimed their own neighborhood. "I wanted to come out and show my support," explained a 35-year-old woman. Said another member of the cleanup crew, "Everybody can do something. That's the whole deal."

City Income Tax

City governments have tried to deal with their money problems in different ways. Some cities collect money through a tax that guests pay on hotel rooms. Some cities have placed a personal income tax on all working residents. The tax is generally about one percent of a worker's total income. A few cities have considered putting a special tax on those who work in the city but live in the suburbs. There is some doubt, however, that such a tax would be legal.

Federal Aid

Almost all city governments ask the federal government to help them deal with their money problems. This is because the problems that cities face often require more funds than the city budget can provide.

In recent years, the federal government has given such help in the form of grants-in-aid.

Federal Grants-in-Aid. As mentioned in Chapter 10, a grant-in-aid is money given to state and local governments to help pay for their different programs. The governments are required to match the amount of money they receive. Since the 1930s, Congress has set up hundreds of grant-in-aid programs. More than 500 are now in operation. Over the years, state and local governments have received billions of dollars from the national government.

Grants-in-aid provide money for such things as highways, airports, education, and health. Money given to school districts, for

Federal grants-in-aid provide money for health care. These people are being innoculated against the flu.

Grants-in-aid also provide money for maintaining highways. This includes beautifying them.

example, may be for school lunch programs or special classes for handicapped children. Other grants-in-aid have been used for welfare, school buses, and job training for young people. The federal government provides guidelines that must be followed in using this money. A disadvantage of grant-in-aid money is that it transfers some state and local decision-making power to the federal government. However, many states continue to take advantage of grant-in-aid money rather than cut back on programs and services.

Before 1987, the federal government helped state and local governments by giving them federal funds. The states and local governments could set their own guidelines on the use of the money. Under President Reagan's "New Federalism," however, this type of aid became much more limited. The federal government cut or abandoned many former programs, forcing the states to pick up the slack. This trend has often meant higher state taxes and/or cutbacks in services. The services that have been cut include many social services, such as low-income housing projects, programs for the elderly, and health care programs.

SECTION 3 *Review*

Defining Key Terms
1. Define: public housing projects, urban renewal.

Recalling the Facts
2. How has the government helped with the problem of a housing shortage?
3. What is one criticism of urban renewal projects that replace slums with better-quality housing?
4. Why might local governments be reluctant to accept grants-in-aid?

Reviewing the Main Idea
5. Answer "As you read . . ." question 3 on page 289: What are some of the partial solutions to urban problems that cities are trying today?

Critical Thinking
6. **Demonstrating Reasoned Judgment.** Should persons who work in the city but live outside it pay a special tax to help raise money for city problems? Give reasons for your answers.

Citizenship

The Housing Shortage

Volunteers from Habitat for Humanity work together to build a home in Georgia.

What do subway tunnels, dumpsters, church doorways, and telephone booths have in common? Believe it or not, these are all places that some Americans call "home." In the book *Rachel and Her Children*, Jonathan Kozol paints a frightening picture of the homeless in the United States. He writes, for example, about a boy in Florida who ran away from home at the age of nine and spent the next five years living in a cardboard box. Equally vivid is the image of a family of three asleep on their feet in a New York City phone booth.

These are only two examples of a problem that is becoming more serious every day. It is estimated that there are as many as 3 million homeless people in the United States today—more than at any time since the Great Depression of the 1930s. Who are the homeless? Why are there so many in the United States? And what is being done to help them?

The nature of the problem. The homeless come from all kinds of backgrounds. Recent research has shattered the stereotype that all homeless people are lazy drifters, mentally ill, or addicted to drugs or alcohol. Some people, of course, do fall into these categories. But as many as one-third are families with children. Twenty percent are young mothers with children. These people have not always lived on the streets. Many different circumstances can lead a family down the road to homelessness.

About 2.5 million Americans lose their homes every year. Some make low wages. Some are on welfare. Some have had a drop in their income due to loss of a job or unexpected medical bills. All are people who can no longer keep up with their rent or mortgage payments. The lucky ones find new homes with lower rent, or friends or family who are willing to take them in. Those who cannot find shelter end up on the street.

The situation is not getting better. Rents have been rising. At the same time, there have been cuts in welfare benefits. In addition, in recent years federal funding to build low-income housing has been cut back. As a result, poor people have a harder time finding a place they can afford.

Tackling the problem. What is being done to solve the housing crisis? In 1987, Congress passed the Stewart B. McKinney Homeless Assistance Act. Some of the money from this act was used to turn government buildings into shelters. Then in 1988, President Reagan signed the Housing and Community Development Act. This measure helped some 152,000 needy families and renovated 10,000 run-down public housing units.

Still more needs to be done. Private citizens and groups concerned for the homeless are working to come up with solutions. Such groups have set up shelters in cities across the country, where people in need can find a dry bed and a hot shower. Experts say, however, that what is needed is permanent, affordable housing.

One group that is making this goal a reality is Habitat for Humanity, a Georgia-based nonprofit organization. The aim of Habitat is to work with low-income families to build decent, affordable housing.

Habitat houses are built or renovated using as much volunteer labor and donated materials as possible. Then they are sold to families too poor to qualify for bank loans. The homeowners must agree to help build their new home and to help other would-be homeowners.

The success of Habitat is a result of the joint efforts of many people in a community. For example, in Charlotte, South Carolina, where Habitat built 14 houses, more than 350 builders sawed boards, drilled, hammered, toted bricks, and fitted windows. The volunteer builders ranged from college students to retirees. Among them were former President Jimmy Carter and his wife Rosalyn, who are active volunteers in the Habitat program. Money for the land and for building materials was raised by a local citizens' group. Donations also came from corporations and church groups, and building professionals volunteered their skills.

Campus Charters is a Habitat program aimed at making high school and college students aware of the housing problem. Campus Charters groups across the United States raise money, recruit volunteers, and help on local building projects. Some student groups have raised enough funds to build whole houses.

Habitat makes no profit on the homes it builds, and it does not charge interest on the mortgages. The $25,000 or so that it takes to build a house is repaid over 15 or 20 years. The monthly payments go into a local fund and are recycled to build more homes in the community.

By working together, citizens across the nation have made a difference. More than 2,000 families in the United States have received new or renovated houses since Habitat began operation in 1976. In 1987, more than 1,000 Habitat houses—three a day—were built. By 1996, if things go as planned, Habitat will have built homes in 2,000 American cities.

Questions to think about

1. It is estimated that there are over 500,000 homeless children in the United States. What problems do you think these children face from day to day as a result of not having permanent homes?

2. Many of the homeless refuse to stay in city- and state-run shelters because they consider these places dirty, dangerous, and crowded. What do you think could be done to make the shelters acceptable to the homeless?

CHAPTER SUMMARY

Section 1   Most colonial cities were not built according to a plan. They grew up in a disorderly fashion. The buildings and streets were crammed into a small area, making it easy to walk quickly from one place to another. As a result, cities became overcrowded, unhealthy, and unsafe. Although some improvements came in the 1800s, increased population, automobiles, and factories brought new problems. Today, almost all cities have a planning commission that works to beautify the city and control zoning, land use, sanitation, traffic, and sewage disposal.

Section 2   Cities are faced with many problems. There is a shortage of housing, particularly for poor people. Many people live in slums where they pay high rents for substandard buildings. Slum areas require many city services, but the people who live there do not pay enough in taxes to cover the costs of those services. Poverty puts many people on welfare rolls. Crime and juvenile delinquency cause many people who live in cities to be afraid. Noise is often constant. Waste must be disposed of. Despite many laws to prevent air pollution, many cities still suffer from smog.

Section 3   Solving the problems of cities is not easy. Laws may be passed to reduce pollution or housing discrimination, but the problems still remain. A shortage of money has brought several cities close to bankruptcy. In past years, the federal government has given money to cities to build housing, highways, and parks and to improve city living in general.

Review Key Terms

Use each of the following terms appropriately in a sentence. Write your sentences on a separate sheet of paper.

1. city planner

2. public housing project

3. urban renewal

4. zoning

5. smog

Understanding Main Ideas

1. Describe a typical colonial city.

2. What is the purpose of city planning?

3. How are members of planning commissions usually selected?

4. Into what three kinds of zones do planners usually divide the land of a city?

5. What are two common solutions for transportation problems in modern cities?

6. Why is it difficult for many people to find decent housing in our country today?

7. How do slum landlords contribute to the housing problem in cities?

8. What are welfare payments and how are they funded?

9. Why are smog and other forms of pollution growing problems in many cities?

10. What are some of the ways in which local governments have tried to deal with their money problems?

Critical Thinking

1. **Predicting Consequences.** Some people are opposed to the federal government giving money to cities. They feel that federal grants will lead to federal control of local governments. Is this a possibility? Explain.

2. **Making Decisions.** Some people have suggested getting rid of the complex welfare systems of the state and federal governments. They propose, instead, a Family Assistance Plan. Under this plan, all persons, working or not, would be guaranteed a certain income. If their earnings were below the guaranteed income, the federal government would pay the difference. What would be the advantages and disadvantages of this idea? Would you favor such a plan? Explain.

3. **Identifying Alternatives.** You have read that exhaust from automobiles, trucks, and buses is a leading cause of air pollution—a problem in most cities. Gather information about this problem and discuss possible solutions. What steps might cities and individual citizens take to reduce air pollution?

Practicing Skills

1. **Making an Outline.** Reread the material in Section 2, "Problems That Cities Face." Then outline the section following the guidelines found on page 294. Your outline should include the headings "Housing," "Poverty," "Crime," and "Pollution" as main ideas, along with subtopics.

2. **Expressing Problems Clearly.** Find out more about the growing problem of homelessness in the big cities. How much has the homeless population grown in the last 15 years? Why are people becoming homeless? How are federal, state, and local governments trying to solve this problem? Ask your librarian to help you find sources of information. Report your findings to the class.

Focusing on Citizenship

1. **Identifying Local Land Use.** Draw a zoning map of your local community. Show all three kinds of zones and recreational land. Then discuss the drawing with other class members. What zones take up the most space? Do you see places that could be better used for parks and recreation? How far are residential zones from industrial and commercial zones? Is there adequate transportation between them?

2. **Making Comparisons.** Investigate the standards for auto exhaust systems in your state. Make a comparison of these standards with the federal standards.

3. **Researching Information.** Find out how much state aid your local government has received in the past year. Consult a librarian for help in finding this information.

Focus on Decision Making

Should We Build More Prisons?

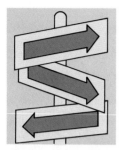

"Every day, laws are passed to put people in jail longer. Then people are surprised when the jails are crowded. Before, they worried about getting [criminals] there. Now they worry about whether [criminals] should be there."

The Issue in Question

Carl Holmes, the chief deputy public defender from Orange County, California, made the above statement in 1987. Like many other places across the nation, Orange County faces a serious new problem: overcrowded prisons. To solve this problem, county and state governments must choose between building expensive new jails or finding alternative programs for their prisoners.

The United States has one of the highest crime rates in the world. The criminal justice system has responded with stricter law enforcement and more aggressive prosecution of suspected criminals. Many states are also setting stiffer penalties for crimes like drunk driving and drug sales.

More arrests and convictions mean that the nation is locking up more prisoners than ever before. Since the early 1970s, the number of inmates has tripled to more than 750,000. The United States now has the world's third highest per capita prison population, ranking right behind the Soviet Union and South Africa. If present trends continue, it is estimated that the total American prison population will reach nearly 1.5 million by the year 2000.

During the past two decades, jail construction and operating expenses have skyrocketed. It now costs between $15,000 and $40,000 yearly to keep a prisoner in jail.

Background on the Issue

In 1978, a United States federal judge ordered Orange County to end overcrowding in the central men's jail in Santa Ana. Seven years later, the same judge fined the county's Board of Supervisors $50,000 for failing to obey his order. In light of this ruling, the Orange County sheriff had no choice in early 1987 but to let six arrested men go free. Jailing these men would have pushed the central jail's population over the legal limit of 1,296 inmates.

As a result of these events, the Orange County Board of Supervisors began to discuss a proposal to build a new jail with 6,000 beds. If built, it would be among the largest prison complexes in the nation. The construction costs were estimated at over $450 million, an expense that equaled more than a third of the county's entire 1987 budget. The proposed jail immediately became the subject of heated debate.

Supporters of new jails believe that the threat of imprisonment discourages people from committing crimes and encourages law and order. In their view, tough jail sentences for criminals and reduced opportunities for parole make society a safer place.

Other people oppose the construction of new jails. They believe that we should continue to keep dangerous criminals behind bars. But they argue that there are many less expensive options for prisoners who pose little danger to society. These include drug and alcohol treatment centers and work release and early release programs.

Arguments for Building More Jails.

1. Jails help prevent crime by keeping criminals apart from society and by discouraging law breakers.
2. Expanded police enforcement and stricter sentencing create a need for more jail space.

Arguments Against Building More Jails.

1. Alternative treatment and sentencing programs are more suitable and effective than jail for some criminals.
2. The growing expense of building and operating jails is putting a great strain on state and local governments.

Making Decisions

1. **Recognizing Cause and Effect.** What factors have contributed to the rapid growth of the prison population? What new problems have resulted from that rapid growth? Which of these new problems do you think is most serious?
2. **Identifying Alternatives.** List three possible punishments, other than prison, that could be used for people convicted of drunk driving. Which alternative do you think is the best choice? Explain your answer.
3. **Demonstrating Reasoned Judgment.** If you had been a member of the Orange County Board of Supervisors in 1987 and had to vote on the proposal for a new prison, what position would you have taken? Why would you have taken that position? Use the "Arguments For," the "Arguments Against," and "The Decision-Making Checklist" on this page to help you make your decision and develop your answer.

The Decision-Making Checklist

✔	**Clarify the problem.** (What is the issue or conflict?)
✔	**Create a list of possible solutions.** (How might you resolve the problem?)
✔	**Compare the pros and cons of each solution.** (What are the strengths and weaknesses of each solution?)
✔	**Consider your values and goals.** (What is important to you in choosing a course of action, and why?)
✔	**Choose a course of action and evaluate the results.** (What would you decide, and how could you judge the outcome?)

4 *Influencing Government*

Previewing the Unit

The United States Congress has been called "the nation's town meeting." Beneath the shining white dome of the Capitol, the viewpoints of Americans from coast to coast are heard. Sometimes the voices of the 535 men and women elected to the House and Senate are angry and passionate; other times, reasoned and cool; but they are the mingled voices of America. Everything political comes together here. Lobbyists wait in the marble hallways to pluck the sleeves of Congress members and try to sway their votes. Interest groups wave signs and chant slogans on the Capitol steps, where television cameras and microphones are never far away. And individuals, too, make their presence felt. People arrive daily from every corner of the nation to add their voices to the din.

Electing men and women to office and then seeing that they respond to our opinions ensures that we have a truly representative government. In this unit you will read about the many forces that shape political life in the United States.

Chapters in This Unit

◀ Against a backdrop of the Washington Monument in Washington, D.C., Margaret E. Kuhn, founder of the Gray Panthers Organization, addresses a rally.

CHAPTER 16

Public Opinion

The constant presence of the mass media greatly influences Americans' beliefs.

Previewing the Chapter

Most Americans are not experts in government. That doesn't mean, though, that Americans don't have strong views on political issues and politicians. What factors have shaped *your* opinions? Has your family played a role? School? Newspapers and television? This chapter takes a look at how public opinion is formed and how it influences the actions of government leaders.

- **Before you read,** look up these key terms in the Glossary at the back of this book: *sample, campaign, propaganda, news media, syndicated.*

- **As you read,** look for answers to these questions:
  1. How do government officials learn what people think about issues?
  2. What are the major influences in forming our opinions about government?
  3. In what ways do the media try to influence public opinion?

1 What People Believe About Government

Most of us hold certain beliefs in common about government and politics. We believe in the Constitution and the system of government it created. We believe our government should serve and protect us. We believe government officials should do as the people wish. We believe those in government should be honest and efficient.

There are other ideas about which people in the United States differ, however. Here are some responses to one recent survey of public opinion. How do your beliefs compare with these?

- Thirty-three percent said the country would be governed better if more women held government offices. Eighteen percent said it would be governed worse.
- Sixty-seven percent said that workers in government do not work as hard as they would if they held nongovernment jobs.
- Sixty-seven percent felt that the federal government employs too many people to do the work it needs to do.
- Sixty-five percent thought it very important for the federal government to spend no more money than it takes in.
- Sixty percent said that the most important reason they had for voting for their candidate for President was the candidate's stand on issues. Twenty-one percent said they selected a candidate because of personal qualities.
- Sixty-four percent said they would not want their children to go into politics.

How Public Opinions Are Expressed

How do those in government find out what people think? Here are some of the methods they use.

Mail and Telephone Calls.   Elected officials receive thousands of telegrams, mailgrams, letters, and telephone calls. Members of their staffs count the number of people who are on each side of an issue. The actions which officials take often depend on the number of messages they receive for or against a particular issue.

Questionnaires.   Members of Congress and state legislators send out questionnaires to their constitutents a few times each year. The legislators want to know what the people think about issues they are considering.

Public Meetings.   Members of a community are frequently invited to speak at meetings of city councils, school boards, and other agencies of local government. Sometimes they speak before national and state legislatures and government agencies. Since it is difficult for most people to travel to the national and state capi-

Public meetings are important forums for expressing opinions. A meeting of the school board provides excellent opportunities for this purpose.

tals where such meetings are often held, representatives of special interest groups are most likely to attend and speak. The head of a parent organization once told the members, "If we want a special tutor program, we have to ask the Board of Education. At the next meeting, we need to fill the auditorium to show support. When the board sees lots of people, it may vote for our program." Elected officials are often influenced by a large turnout at a public meeting.

Obtaining Public Opinion

A poll attempts to find out what people think. Taking a poll involves asking people questions (either on paper or orally) and recording their answers. There is much interest in polls involving presidential elections.

People who take public opinion polls are called **pollsters**. They use computers to select samples from which they obtain important information about people—age, income, occupation, education, religion, political party, sex, race, and community size.

There are several well-known poll-taking organizations. They include those of George Gallup, Elmo Roper, and Louis Harris. Over many years, these organizations have developed methods to obtain accurate measures of public opinion. These pollsters:

1. Ask carefully-thought-out questions that will not influence a person's answers.
2. Train their interviewers carefully so that the way they ask questions and record responses will not influence how people respond.
3. Select a group of people who make up a representative sample of the whole population. A **sample** is a small group taken from a larger group. A **representative sample** is a small number of people who together have all of the characteristics of the population from which the sample was taken.

A person who takes public opinion polls is called a pollster. Some polls are conducted through written questionnaires. Others survey people at random.

Polling a representative sample will usually tell quite accurately how the public feels about a candidate or an issue. Here, for example, is the Harris Poll's prediction of the 1988 presidential election as compared with the actual outcome of the election.

Harris Poll Prediction		Actual Election Results
George Bush	50%	53%
Michael Dukakis	46%	43%
Undecided	4%	

SECTION 1 *Review*

Defining Key Terms
1. Define: pollster, sample, representative sample.

Recalling the Facts
2. How is public opinion expressed?
3. What do pollsters do?

Reviewing the Main Idea
4. Answer "As you read . . ." question 1 on page 312: How do government officials learn what people think about issues?

Critical Thinking
5. Demonstrating Reasoned Judgment. Most people get their information about news events from television. Give some reasons why this should not be the only source used to form an opinion about current events.

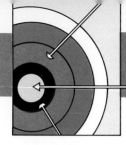

Sharpening Your Skills

Citizenship Skills

Conducting Opinion Polls

Imagine that you are working as a campaign manager for your best friend Sam Hunt, who is running for student body president. The election is a month away and you want to know what the chances are that Sam will win. To get an idea, you might conduct an opinion poll of the students in your class. As you read in Section 1, opinion polls find out what people think about a given issue. Use the following four steps to help you design your own poll.

Step 1: Decide which people to poll. It is rarely possible to survey the entire group of people whose opinions you seek. Therefore, selecting a representative sample is necessary. A survey for a national election, for example, should include Democrats, Republicans, and Independents; men and women of different ages; and people from various regions and backgrounds. For your purposes, it will be important to poll boys and girls from different "crowds" in different classes.

Step 2: Prepare the questions. Survey questions should not suggest a particular bias (a particular slant) and thus influence the respondents' answers. "Don't you think Sam Hunt would make a great class president?" is a biased question. A better question is: "Which candidate for class president would you vote for if the election were held today?"

Questions should be direct and call for specific answers, as in the last question above. Multiple-choice questions are also useful. (You are probably familiar with this type of question from tests you have taken.)

Step 3: Ask the questions. Polls taken by telephone are time-consuming because you can get only one response at a time. Opinion polls sent by mail that require a written response are often not returned. Passing out (and then collecting) a written poll can save time because many people can answer questions all at once. Of course, this method works best when your sample is relatively small.

Step 4: Analyze the results. Tally your results and look for patterns or relationships between answers. For example, you might find that students who think the student body president should focus on social events usually said they would vote for Sam's opponent. Knowing this, Sam could explain to his classmates why he believes other projects are more important.

Well-designed polls measure public opinion fairly accurately, but remember that there is always a small chance of error. Polls reflect, at best, a general direction in which the population may be heading. Thus, they are not foolproof measures.

Practicing Skills

1. If you were Sam Hunt's campaign manager, list two important questions you would want on your opinion poll (other than the examples given on this page).
2. **Recognizing Bias.** Which of the following is the better question to include in an opinion poll? Why?
   a. "What do you think is the most important environmental issue today?"
   b. "Since pollution is among the most important environmental issues today, don't you think we should elect a candidate who will make pollution a priority?"

2 How Beliefs Are Formed

Each of us holds certain beliefs about governments and the problems governments face. Many people and things influence what we believe.

Important
People

Parents. Parents influence the beliefs of their children. Children hear their parents express views on candidates or issues and on what they think the government should do. It is not surprising that, when most young people register to vote for the first time, they register with the political party their parents belong to.

Some young people are influenced by their parents' participation in politics. They come to believe that taking part in government is a good thing to do. Others, hearing their parents say such things as, "The politicians do as they please" or "The little guy can't do anything," come to believe that taking part in government will not solve their problems.

Teachers. Students obtain knowledge and hear opinions in the school courses they take. Often they are influenced by what they hear and read in these courses. A teacher's goal is to inform and to stimulate the students to think.

Government Leaders. In 1980, President Jimmy Carter influenced public opinion when he stated that United States athletes should not go to the Olympic Games in the Soviet Union. Many citizens agreed with the President. In 1981, President Ronald Reagan convinced both Democrats and Republicans to support

PEOPLE HELPING PEOPLE

Students Get a Helping Hand

When Eugene Lang graduated from high school in 1941, he knew what the future held—a job as a busboy in a restaurant. After a few months, however, one of the customers took an interest in young Lang and helped him win a scholarship to college.

In 1981 Lang, by now a successful business leader, found a way to repay the favor. He launched the "I Have a Dream" program, currently thriving in 30 cities across the country and benefitting some 8,000 junior high and high school students.

Under the program, disadvantaged young people receive financial aid and special counseling to help them succeed in school and, later, college. Just as important, says Lang, they receive the knowledge that "someone believes in them."

him in his plans to cut back on federal spending and to lower the federal income tax.

Television News Reporters.   Millions of people watch news reporters on television every day. They believe things are the way these reporters describe them. Surveys taken in the 1970s revealed that many people trusted Walter Cronkite, a well-known newscaster, more than they did many government officials.

Events.   The Gallup, Harris, and Roper polls show that the popularity of Presidents and other government leaders changes. In November of 1986, only 29 percent of the people in one poll said they disapproved of the way President Ronald Reagan was handling his job. In the months that followed, however, the public learned that members of Reagan's staff had arranged to sell arms to Iran to secure the release of American hostages in the Middle East. The money from these sales was used to support the contras, a group of rebels fighting the communist government of Nicaragua. Reagan's role in the Iran-contra affair was unclear, but four months after the original poll, 53 percent of the people said they disapproved of his work.

Campaigns.   Beliefs about candidates often change during campaigns. A **campaign** is a contest for political office. Well-known candidates are often rated highly at the beginning of a campaign. As the campaign continues, lesser-known candidates sometimes become better known and begin to gain support.

In the early months of the 1988 election campaign, Jesse Jackson was the front-runner for the Democratic nomination. However, as the Democratic national convention approached and the American people became more familiar with the views of all the candidates, Jackson's popularity declined. Governor Michael

Students active in student government often become involved citizens.

Dukakis of Massachusetts, who was virtually unknown in many parts of the country at the start of the race, gradually gained in popularity as he campaigned throughout the 50 states. Dukakis was finally nominated to head the Democratic ticket.

Experience. People's experiences and interests often influence their ideas and opinions. Many people who lived during the Great Depression of the 1930s blamed the Depression on the Republicans who were in power at the time. When the Democrats took office in 1933, President Franklin Roosevelt started many programs to try to bring the country out of the Depression. Some people felt that Roosevelt saved the country. They became lifelong Democrats. On the other hand, many people resented the regulations the Roosevelt government established. Many became Republicans and remained Republicans.

Many schools have student governments. Students who become involved in student government often become involved citizens. They may come to believe that government can be used to promote the people's interests. Other students who do not participate may believe that government cannot help them.

Propaganda. Efforts to persuade people to believe something or act in a certain way are called **propaganda**. Propaganda appeals to people's emotions rather than to their minds. Propaganda is spread by means of television, billboards, movies, car bumper stickers, pamphlets, speeches, books, and magazines. Advertising agencies spend millions of dollars a year to persuade us to buy certain products. Candidates for public office also spend millions on election advertising. Candidates and government officials often use propaganda to try to shape public opinion. Here are seven of the most common propaganda techniques.

Association. This propaganda technique attempts to associate a product (or a person or an idea) with something or someone that is well-known. A certain brand of running shoes or tennis racquet, for example, may be linked with a well-known athlete. The advertisers hope that buyers will think, "If this famous person uses Brand X, it must be good."

Bandwagon. This type of propaganda tries to convince people that "everybody" uses a certain product or supports a certain candidate. It suggests that you should go along with what "everyone else" is doing. The name of this propaganda technique suggests a circus bandwagon that attracts people to follow the parade. Using the bandwagon technique in a campaign speech, a politician might say, "A majority of the people supports me. My victory is certain. Join a winner! Vote for me!"

Card Stacking. Someone who uses this type of propaganda slants or stacks ideas or facts to get others to reach a certain

Propaganda Techniques

ASSOCIATION
"Vote for Jones. The President is in favor of his election."

BANDWAGON
"My victory is assured. Join a winner, vote for me."

CARD STACKING
"Vote for Roth, she'll reduce your taxes."

GLITTERING GENERALITIES
"I am in favor of the American way."

NAME CALLING
"My opponent represents communists and criminals."

PLAIN FOLKS APPEAL
"My parents were poor. I know what it is like to be hungry."

TESTIMONIAL
"I always use Brand X," says Dana Product.

SKILL BUILDER

Can you give examples of any of these propaganda techniques from a recent election or a product advertisement?

conclusion. Also, speakers may use different tones of voice to give listeners different feelings about an event. A television station that broadcasts a candidate giving a major speech but does not give the opponent's comments on the speech is stacking the cards.

Glittering Generalities. In this technique, propagandists use words that sound good but have little or no meaning. The words often suggest patriotism, pride, safety, or strength. No explanation, however, is given as to how these things are to be brought about. For example, a mayor running for reelection states: "I am in favor of the American Way."

Name Calling. This technique uses names or labels that bring bad feelings to mind. For example, a candidate for senator may tell an audience: "My opponent's law office has represented many communists and well-known criminals," suggesting negative things about the opponent. Usually, no proof or evidence is given to support what the statement suggests.

Plain Folks. A person using the plain folks propaganda technique hopes to win public confidence by describing himself or herself as one of the common people. The intent is to have voters believe he or she shares and understands their problems. Using a plain folks technique, a presidential candidate may state: "My parents were poor. They had to struggle to put food on the table. I know what it is like to be hungry."

Testimonial. Companies or candidates using this technique have a well-known person such as a movie star or athlete speak for them, hoping the famous person will influence others.

SECTION 2 *Review*

Defining Key Terms
1. Define: campaign, propaganda.

Recalling the Facts
2. What are some propaganda techniques?
3. Explain the bandwagon propaganda technique.

Reviewing the Main Idea
4. Answer "As you read . . ." question 2 on page 312: What are the major influences in forming our opinions about government?

Critical Thinking
5. **Drawing Conclusions.** Should government officials use propaganda techniques to develop support for their policies? Why or why not?

3 The Role of the Media in Shaping Beliefs

Will Rogers was a well-known humorist of the 1920s. He told many jokes about government officials. In response to a question about events in Washington, he once said, "I only know what I read in the newspapers." An updated version of that statement might be, "I only know what I see on television." Approximately two-thirds of the people of the United States receive their knowledge of what is happening in the world from television. Fewer people read newspapers and news magazines. Television, radio, newspapers, and news magazines are known as the **news media**.

Television. Candidates for public office are well aware of television's effect on shaping the opinions of people. Buying television time is one of the largest expenses of candidates for national office. Candidates for the Presidency spend thousands of dollars to bring their messages to the people on television prime time. **Prime time** is from 7:00 P.M. to 10:00 P.M.

Some people believe that television played an important role in the 1976 presidential election. Jimmy Carter and Gerald Ford debated each other. The election was close. Jimmy Carter was not as well known as Gerald Ford, the President. Many observers believe Carter gained more from the debates than Ford. They say exposure on television helped Carter win the election. The same was true in 1980. Many political experts think that Ronald Reagan's television presence helped him to be elected President.

Television and newspapers play important roles in campaigns for the Presidency.

Newspapers play an important part in shaping public opinion. These students study the newspaper as part of their class work.

Newspapers and News Magazines.   Newspapers and news magazines as well as television do more than present news. They also can influence people's thinking. They can be powerful in shaping public opinion. The **editorial section** of a newspaper presents editors' personal opinions on issues and events. Newspapers also print letters to the editor. In these, people express their opinions.

Columns written by nationally syndicated writers are also printed on the editorial page. **Syndicated** means that newspapers all over the country buy and reprint these columns. The writers of the columns are trained journalists who study issues and events and present their views of them. News magazines also have a page or two for comments written by their staffs as well as a section for letters from readers.

Just before an election, newpapers usually name the candidates they support. The newspaper gives its reasons for endorsing these candidates. In a close contest, such endorsements can influence the outcome of an election.

Reporting.   Every day thousands of events happen throughout the world. National television networks, large city newspapers, and news magazines have reporters stationed in Washington, D.C., the state capitals, and in major cities of the United States, places where important news is likely to happen.

Reporters are also assigned to the capital cities of foreign countries. When important events take place, reporters are sent quickly to the scene. In less than 24 hours, a news team can be anywhere in the world. Local television companies and newspapers assign their reporters to the mayor's office, city council meetings, school board meetings, and the police and fire departments. Their reporters and camera crews rush by automobile and helicopter to report the news.

The Media Affect Public Opinion.   The media shape people's ideas and beliefs in several ways. Television brings the world into people's homes. It helps people to feel they are present at the scene of an important news event. It makes events seem real. In 1963, almost the entire nation sat in front of television sets to watch the events following the assassination of President John F. Kennedy. They saw the place where he was shot. They saw the man arrested for the assassination be assassinated himself. They saw the dramatic funeral ceremonies. Television coverage enables us to be eyewitnesses to history as it is being made. In 1989, people listened and watched as George Bush was inaugurated as our forty-first President.

SECTION 3   *Review*

Defining Key Terms
1. Define: news media, prime time, editorial section, syndicated.

Recalling the Facts
2. What does the editorial section of a newspaper contain?
3. How has television influenced the outcome of recent presidential elections?

Reviewing the Main Idea
4. Answer "As you read . . ." question 3 on page 312: In what ways do the media try to influence public opinion?

Critical Thinking
5. **Identifying Assumptions.** What responsibilities do you believe the news media have in reporting and commenting on the news?

Citizenship

Campaigning Against Drinking

Drunk drivers in the United States account for an average of 2.7 deaths every hour. They speed out of control and hit other cars, people, trees, or telephone poles. They drive the wrong way down busy interstates. Or they fail to stop soon enough for a red light. By some estimates, half of all highway deaths—about 25,000 deaths each year—involve alcohol.

Drunk drivers often have blood alcohol levels greatly exceeding their state's legal limit—sometimes by as much as 50 or 100 percent. (In most states, the legal limit for blood alcohol content is .10 percent.) Many of these drivers have been convicted of drunk driving before, and some have even attended state alcoholism programs.

For a long time, many people believed that "driving while under the influence" was socially acceptable. They often joked about having "one more for the road." During the early 1980s, however, citizen groups began working to change public attitudes toward drinking and driving. These groups have pushed for tougher drunk driving laws and stiffer penalties for offenders. Two of the most widely known groups in the fight against drunk driving are MADD (Mothers Against Drunk Driving) and SADD (Students Against Driving Drunk).

MADD was founded in 1980 by Candy Lightner after her daughter was killed by a hit-and-run drunk driver. SADD was founded a year later with the specific goal of educating teenagers and young adults about the dangers of drinking and driving.

Both SADD and MADD have focused their attention on the group most likely to

Winners of a contest co-sponsored by MADD display their artwork against drunk driving.

be involved in drunk driving accidents—16 to 24 year olds. SADD, for example, has organized peer counseling programs to help students avoid alcohol abuse. Students are also shown how to plan ahead of time to cope with, or avoid, drunk driving incidents. Discussion is particularly directed at prom nights and graduation, times often associated with teenage drinking.

One important part of the SADD program is the SADD contract. This is a formal agreement that both parents and teenagers sign. In it, teenagers agree that they will call their parents to provide transportation if they ever find themselves facing a drunk driving situation. Parents agree that they will provide safe transportation at any time, with no questions asked until later. Parents also agree that they will not place themselves in a drunk driving situation.

Largely as a result of public pressure and the efforts of organizations like MADD and SADD, many states have begun to crack down on drunk drivers. Many states have raised the legal drinking age from 18 or 19 to 21. Some states now seize cars or license plates belonging to drunk drivers. In some states, drivers who fail or refuse a breathalyzer test (which measures a person's blood alcohol level) can lose their driver's licenses. Repeat offenders in states like Massachusetts receive mandatory jail sentences.

New state laws have also been enacted and are being upheld in courts that hold individuals, restaurants, and bars liable for accidents that result from serving alcoholic beverages. For example, in some states, if a guest is involved in a crash after leaving a party, the host or hostess can be held responsible.

Activists against drunk driving would like to have these measures extended to all states. In addition, many would like to see more highway checkpoints where police stop drivers to check for evidence of drinking. Many activists also argue that the legal limit for blood alcohol content should be lowered to .08 or even .05 percent.

Everywhere there is evidence that public opinion about drinking and driving has changed. Perhaps you have seen public service announcements on television that warn against drunk driving. Or you might have watched a situation comedy that included dialogue about safe driving habits. The term "designated driver" has become commonplace. It refers to people who pledge in advance that they will not drink alcohol at a party so that they can drive friends home safely.

The movement to alert people to the dangers of drunk driving has also spread to various consumer industries. Some car makers, for instance, have installed devices that take a "breathprint" before the car can be started. If the device picks up a trace of alcohol, or if it is not used, the car cannot be started. Some greeting card companies have stopped making cards that emphasize drinking on occasions like graduations and New Year's Eve. Beer and alcohol companies often end their advertisements with a plea against driving drunk.

Drunk driving fatalities decreased between 1981 and 1986. But statistics since then have shown an increase in drunk driving deaths. Penalties for drunk driving will probably continue to become harsher. And public awareness campaigns against drunk driving by groups like MADD and SADD will intensify their efforts.

Questions to think about

1. Do you think that the SADD contract for teenagers and parents is a good idea? Why or why not?

2. What measures do you think are most effective in stopping drunk driving? Why?

CHAPTER SUMMARY

Section 1   Most citizens of our country have definite opinions about the purpose and operation of our government. Elected officials are interested in these opinions. They find out about them through letters, telephone calls, questionnaires, personal contacts, and public meetings. Public opinion polls are a major source of information for all persons in government. To obtain accurate measures of public opinion, pollsters must choose a representative sample of the population and ask questions that do not influence the response. The decisions of elected officials are often influenced by all these sources of information.

Section 2   People's opinions are influenced by many factors —by parents, teachers, government leaders, news reporters, and campaign speeches. Events and experiences, such as a war or a depression, can have long-lasting effects on people's beliefs. Several propaganda techniques can be used to shape public opinion. These techniques include association, bandwagon, card stacking, glittering generalities, name calling, plain folks, and testimonials by celebrities.

Section 3   The media play an important role in influencing Americans' beliefs. Today most people get their information from television. Presidential candidates usually spend thousands of dollars to buy time on national television networks. Newspapers and news magazines influence opinion by presenting editorials and syndicated columns that express the views of editors and writers. These media also endorse candidates before elections. By covering news events, reporters tell people what is happening around the world and bring them closer to important events.

Reviewing Key Terms

Use each of the following terms appropriately in a sentence. Write your sentences on a separate sheet of paper.

1. campaign
2. sample
3. propaganda
4. news media
5. syndicated

Understanding Main Ideas

1. Describe three ways that elected officials find out about public opinion.

2. What three steps do pollsters follow to make sure that their results accurately measure public opinion?

3. Identify three groups of people who influence what we believe.

Public Opinion   327

4. Give an example of how political beliefs were influenced by the Great Depression.

5. What is the purpose of propaganda?

6. What does the bandwagon type of propaganda try to do?

7. Give an example of a "glittering generality."

8. In what two kinds of propaganda techniques are famous people linked with products or ideas?

9. Which of the media do most people use to find out about news?

10. How can the news media be helpful to candidates?

Critical Thinking

1. Recognizing Bias. Find three newspaper or magazine advertisements that use propaganda techniques. Cut them out and bring them to class. Explain what propaganda technique(s) each uses.

2. Identifying Assumptions. Both television newscasters and government officials inform us about issues in our country. What assumptions do we make about these news reports? What kinds of information can we get from each of these sources? What kinds of information might be missing?

3. Identifying Alternatives. Should certain propaganda techniques be banned from use in election campaigns? If so, which ones? How could this be monitored?

4. Testing Conclusions. Jim has watched several television debates involving the two Presidential candidates. He has concluded that the candidate who is most at ease in front of the cameras will make the best President. Do you agree with Jim's conclusion? How important do you think image is for elected leaders?

Practicing Skills

1. Conducting an Opinion Poll. Join with several students to conduct a public opinion poll of teachers and students in your school. Ask the following questions: (a) "What is the main source from which you obtain news—television, radio, newspapers, or news magazines?" (b) "Which of the media do you believe does the best job in reporting the news—television, radio, newspapers, or news magazines?" Summarize all the responses and report your findings to the class.

2. Analyzing the News. Read an article about an important national or world event in the latest issue of a weekly news magazine. Read about the same event in your local newspaper. In what ways were the two articles similar? In what ways were they different? Which was more detailed? Easier to understand? More interesting?

Focusing on Citizenship

1. Understanding Propaganda. Imagine you are running for a student-government office. Create a campaign poster that uses a propaganda technique.

2. Identifying Influences. Rearrange the list below to show how different people influence your thoughts about government and events. List the most influential person first: (a) your parents, (b) your friends, (c) government leaders, (d) television news reporters, (e) your teachers. Compare your list with those of others in the class.

CHAPTER

17

Political Parties

The conventions of the Republican and Democratic Parties are generally lively and colorful events.

Sections in
This Chapter

1 Political Parties
2 Party Structure
3 What Do Political Parties Do?

Previewing the Chapter

Political parties are not mentioned in the United States Constitution. Ironically, though, the debate over adopting the Constitution led to the formation of the first parties: the Federalists, who supported the Constitution, and the Anti-Federalists, who opposed it. Today, the two dominant parties in the United States are the Democrats and the Republicans. This chapter describes those parties and the structure and functions of political parties in general.

■ **Before you read,** look up these key terms in the Glossary at the back of this book: *two-party system, third party, precinct, ward, Independent, register, party vote.*

■ **As you read,** look for answers to these questions:
1. What are the two major political parties in the United States today?
2. What are the levels of organization in a political party?
3. What are some of the goals of political parties?

1 Political Parties

In the United States, the people choose their leaders from two parties. A **political party** is an organized group of people who have similar ideas about what they want the government to do. A party suggests candidates for political offices.

There are two major political parties in the United States today—the Democratic Party and the Republican Party—as well as a number of other, smaller parties. Since 1860, every President of the United States has been either a Democrat or a Republican. In the United States Congress, the majority party usually has between 50 and 65 percent of the membership. Having a choice between the candidates of two major parties is an important part of our democratic system of government. Political parties did not exist when our country began, however.

The Beginning of Political Parties

There were no political parties in the United States when George Washington was elected President. Small groups of delegates began to discuss ideas at the Constitutional Convention in 1787. Delegates with the same interests and views tended to vote the same way.

One group of delegates was made up of merchants, shippers, bankers, and other business people. They wanted a strong central government to protect their business interests. They feared that a weak government could not require debts to be paid or could not hold the 13 new states together as a united country. They became known as Federalists. They were called Federalists because they favored a strong federal government. They worked for adoption of the new Constitution.

Alexander Hamilton, President Washington's Secretary of the Treasury, was a leader of the Federalists. He developed a program to help business. Hamilton believed that if business people did well they would provide jobs for others. The country would benefit because many people would earn money. On the other hand, Hamilton was not very helpful to the farmers. His program called for taxes that would take money from the farmers to pay for government efforts to help business.

Many members of Congress supported Hamilton's program. They wanted to pass laws to carry out his ideas. Hamilton urged these members of Congress and others who favored his program to form a political party. He wanted people who shared his views to win future elections for President and Congress. The party they formed became known as the Federalist party.

Another group with common interests was made up of farmers, workers, people in debt, and pioneers. These people wanted strong state governments rather than a strong national government.

They felt that state governments would be easier to control. They feared a strong central govenment would tax them heavily to pay its debts to wealthy people who had loaned money to the government. These people were known as Anti-Federalists because they opposed a strong central government. They were against the adoption of the Constitution.

Thomas Jefferson, Washington's Secretary of State, was the leader of the Anti-Federalists. They were afraid of Hamilton's program so they formed a political party to oppose it. This party was called the Democratic-Republican party. By the time Washington's term of office had ended, both the Federalists and the Democratic-Republicans were well organized. Both parties supported candidates for President and Congress in the election of 1796.

The United States has had only two *major* parties throughout its history. A major party is one that has many supporters. The political system of the United States is often called a **two-party system**. The roots of today's Democratic Party go back to the Democratic-Republican party. The roots of today's Republican Party go back to the Federalist party.

The Two-Party System

This portrait shows Thomas Jefferson, Washington's Secretary of State.

Alexander Hamilton, Washington's Secretary of the Treasury, is shown above.

Modern Democrats and Republicans agree in many ways. Both support our constitutional form of government. Both want a good life for all people in the United States. Both support a strong law-enforcement system. Both want people to have medical care and education. Both want the country to have a good transportation system, adequate energy supplies, and a pollution-free environment. Because of all the things they agree on, some people feel there is really no real difference between the two parties. The two parties stand for the same things. They do differ, however, on how to achieve these things.

Republicans believe that the state governments, more than the federal government, should take care of people's needs. They want to keep down federal government spending and to cut taxes.

Democrats, on the other hand, believe that the federal government can do more for the people than the state governments. They believe the federal government has more of a responsibility to help the people than the state governments.

Third Parties

There are other political parties whose views differ from those of the two major parties. The number of people who belong to these so-called third, or minor, parties is quite small. Usually **third parties** support special causes. Rarely do their candidates win elections. Occasionally, a third party candidate will win a seat in Congress or in a state legislature. The Republican party of today, in fact, was once a third party. It is the only third party in history that eventually became a major party. It was formed in 1854 to oppose the extension of slavery. It nominated a presidential candidate, but he lost. In the next presidential election in 1860, its candidate, Abraham Lincoln, won.

Third parties can influence the major parties. Several times in our history the views of a third party have been adopted by one of the major parties.

In the presidential election of 1892, for example, several farm organizations joined to form the Populist Party. They formed the party to protest low incomes, high prices, long working hours, and unhealthy working conditions. They asked Congress to pass a law to limit the work day to eight hours. They wanted to help farm and factory workers who often had to work 12 to 14 hours a day.

The Populists campaigned for the direct election of United States Senators. (Up to that time, Senators were chosen by state legislatures.) They felt that farmers and city workers were not fairly represented in the Senate. The Populists pointed out that, in many states, groups with selfish interests, such as railroads, oil companies, sugar companies, and manufacturers, controlled the legislatures. The legislatures often chose United States Senators who supported the interests of these groups.

Mary Lease, a Kansas orator and author, was one of the most important spokespersons for the Populist Party.

The Populists were against tariffs on imported goods, because they caused rising prices that hurt the poor more than the wealthy. The Populists felt that only the wealthy should be taxed.

The Democratic Party adopted the Populist ideas about an eight-hour day for workers, a national income tax, and the direct election of Senators. Eventually, both of the major parties supported Constitutional amendments for the direct election of Senators and a national income tax in 1913. In 1916, Congress passed a law to give government workers an eight-hour day. In 1935, Congress passed a similar law for nongovernment workers.

Some current third parties in the United States are the Socialist Labor Party, the American Independent Party, the Communist Party, and the Libertarian Party.

SECTION *1* *Review*

Defining Key Terms
1. Define: political party, two-party system, third party.

Recalling the Facts
2. What is the purpose of a political party?
3. What are some of the current third parties?

Reviewing the Main Idea
4. Answer "As you read . . ." question 1 on page 329: What are the two major political parties in the United States today?

Critical Thinking
5. Testing Conclusions. Mr. Lee has concluded that he will always vote for a Republican candidate for President. Explain any flaws you find in his conclusion.

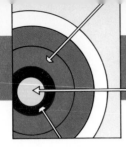

Sharpening Your Skills

Critical Thinking Skills

Recognizing Bias

Presidential Candidate A: "During my administration, government helped create many jobs. There are more jobs now than when my opponent's party was in power. Reelect me to keep our economy strong."

Presidential Candidate B: "During my opponent's Presidency, unemployment rose alarmingly. We cannot afford another four years like that. Elect me for a stronger economy and more jobs."

Which candidate should you believe? How can you tell if the candidates are distorting information to favor their own positions? Recognizing bias is an important skill that keeps us from being misled and from making poor decisions.

A *bias* is a particular slant or attitude with which a person may view a given situation. Biases develop as a result of past experiences, beliefs, and self-interest (personal advantage). Everyone has biases, and most of us occasionally act in a biased way. When you root for the home team, for example, you are showing a bias or preference for one group of players.

Biased information can take several forms. It can be inaccurate or incomplete. A biased speech, for example, may discuss only one side of an issue. It may use facts that support the speaker's opinion and it may ignore other, contradictory facts. Biased information can also be distorted by propaganda. Propaganda, as you read in Chapter 16, is information designed to sway people's opinions by appealing to their emotions.

Whatever form bias takes, you can learn to recognize it. The following hints will help you avoid being misled.

- Identify and focus on the facts.
- Look for points on which different sources of information agree.
- Ask yourself how complete any presentation seems to be.
- Be on the watch for distortion. Look for "loaded" words that come with strong ideas already attached to them. For example, to describe someone as a miracle-worker or as a lunatic is to use loaded language.

Practicing Skills

1. Excerpt *a* below is from the 1988 Democratic Party platform. Excerpt *b* is from the 1988 Republican Party platform. What examples of bias do you see in each statement?
   a. "The time has come for America to once again take charge of its economic future, to reverse seven years of 'voodoo economics'."
   b. "This election will bring change. The question is: Will it be change and progress with the Republicans or change and chaos with the Democrats?"

2. **Recognizing Ideologies.** Read the following statements. Then decide which ones might be made by someone biased in favor of the two-party system.
   a. Having more than one political party leads to confusion and disorder.
   b. The two-party system is one of the greatest features of American government.
   c. Most Americans would prefer a one-party system.
   d. Having two major parties gives voters a choice among candidates.

2 Party Structure

Political parties are made up of many people. There are the voters. There are the party leaders outside of government, such as members of state and county committees. Party leaders frequently are important people in their communities. There are the **party activists** who work for the party in many ways. They serve as delegates to county, state, and national conventions, and they do the day-to-day work on which parties depend. Finally, there are the party leaders in government, including the President, the leaders in Congress, and party leaders of state and local governments. All of these people work together to try to gain control of the government by winning elections.

Political parties in the United States are not very tightly organized. They are **decentralized**; that is, there are different levels—city or county, state, national—of organization in a party. At each level, there are specific tasks to perform.

Party Organization

AMERICAN ALMANAC

The Man Behind the Symbols

If you were to visit the Republican National Headquarters, you would see elephants on posters and banners. At the Democratic National Headquarters, you would find plenty of drawings of donkeys. These animals have represented our two major parties for more than 110 years.

The man who turned them into familiar political symbols was cartoonist Thomas Nast. In the 1870s, Nast began featuring these animals in the political cartoons he published in *Harper's Weekly* and other New York City newspapers. At the time, Republicans dominated the national government. The years after the Civil War were, in fact, a very lean period for the Democratic Party. Republicans charged Democrats with having caused the war, and

the charge stuck. It was not until 1884 that a Democrat—Grover Cleveland—entered the White House.

Because of the power the Republicans held, the mighty elephant made a fitting symbol for their party. The feisty donkey, meanwhile, seemed to capture the stubborn, challenging spirit of the Democrats.

The lasting popularity of Nast's animals is no surprise. Nast is the same artist who gave us the modern version of Santa Claus. In the 1860s, he sketched Santa with white beard, twinkling eyes, and generous belly. Nast can also take some credit for the reelection of President Ulysses S. Grant in 1872. Nast helped Grant win by drawing cartoons that were critical of his opponent.

ORGANIZATION OF A MAJOR POLITICAL PARTY

National
Chairman

National
Committee

State Central
Committee

City and County
Committees

Precinct Workers

The City, Town, and County Level.   At the local level, a central committee is elected by party members in a city, town, or county. The central committee directs the party's activities at this level. It provides money and workers to help the party's local candidates. It also chooses the delegates for the party's state convention.

The central committee directs the work of several precinct captains and their workers. A **precinct** is an election district in a town or city that usually has from 300 to 500 voters. Each precinct has a place where people can vote. At election time, a party captain and a committee in every precinct conduct campaign activities for the party's candidates. These workers also register voters for the party. Precinct captains and committees are either elected by the voters of the precinct, or they are selected by the central committee of the party. Several precincts make up a **ward**.

The State Level.   A state committee, elected by party members, directs the party's work at this level. It advises the national party organization. It supports the campaigns of the party's candidates for state offices with money, advisers, and workers. Leaders of the state committee are well-known party members. They usually know the governor and state legislators well.

The state party committee also organizes the state convention. The state convention is held in the years when there are elections for national and state offices. It is a meeting of party members from the entire state. The convention decides the position the party will take on state issues. It also decides which candidates it will support to run for state offices. In some states, the convention names delegates to the party's national convention.

The National Level.   The national committee is made up of one man and one woman from each state, the District of Columbia, and the territories. It directs the party's work throughout the country. The national committee has members chosen from the states and the Congress. The Republican National Committee includes all the chairpersons of the state parties. National committee members are usually people who have participated in the party's work for many years.

The national committee organizes the party's national convention. It helps decide the party's program. It makes plans to help the party's candidates for President and Vice President campaign for election. The national committee meets only rarely, however. Between elections, a small permanent staff in Washington, D.C. works mainly to raise money for the party. Most of the real work of a political party occurs at the state and local levels.

SKILL BUILDER   How does the national committee stay in touch with what is happening on the level of cities and towns?

A citizen who is 18 or older can become a member of a political party by registering to vote. A person writes the name of the party he or she wants to join on a registration form. Some people indicate that they wish to be **Independent**, that is, they do not wish to belong to a political party. After you **register**, your name is placed on a voter's list. Then, when you go to vote, your name is checked off the list. In some states you must register again when you change addresses or if you missed voting in the previous general election.

Some people identify with a particular party because they believe it represents their views and interests. Some people join a party because it is a family tradition.

One problem which all parties face is that many of their members do not vote. Party leaders try to make it clear that voting is very important. By voting, a person can help decide how our government will be run. Each party tries to get its members to go to the polls on election day. The party that gets the most people to the polls has the best chance of winning.

Most people help their political party by voting. Some contribute money. Others volunteer to help candidates campaign for an election. The most active party members usually work on committees that decide what issues the party supports or opposes.

Party Membership

The Meaning of Party Membership

SECTION 2 *Review*

Defining Key Terms
1. Define: party activist, decentralized, precinct, ward, Independent, register.

Recalling the Facts
2. How does one decide to join a particular political party?
3. What tasks are performed at each level of a political organization?

Reviewing the Main Idea
4. Answer "As you read . . ." question 2 on page 329: What are the levels of organization in a political party?

Critical Thinking
5. **Checking Consistency.** Why might a person not vote for a certain candidate of his or her political party?

3 What Do Political Parties Do?

Political parties propose programs that concern voters. Voters hold public officials accountable. Unless a party makes its program work, voters may vote for the other party in the next election. Thus, the parties provide a way for people to express their support for, or opposition to, the government.

Political Parties and Candidates

One of the most important goals of either the Democratic Party or the Republican Party is to win elections. Each party nominates candidates for public office. The party needs workers and money to get its candidates elected. Therefore, the party must constantly look for workers to help candidates, and raise money to support candidates.

Political parties buy advertising time on television, and advertising space in newspapers. They organize public meetings where candidates can speak. They send workers to homes, shopping centers, factories, and other places to get people to register and to vote. Parties pass out campaign pamphlets and urge people to vote for their candidates. On election day, party workers telephone people registered with their party to remind them to vote. They drive voters to the polls. They offer babysitting services. It would be very difficult, if not impossible, for a candidate to win an election without party support.

Political Parties in Congress

The Constitution states that each house of Congress may set up its own rules of operation and select its own leaders. In practice, it is the majority party in each house that selects the leaders and decides what the rules will be. Usually the same party has a majority in both houses. Sometimes, however, one party has a majority in the Senate and another has a majority in the House of Representatives.

At the beginning of a new Congress, the members of each party in each house hold a party caucus. At a caucus, each party elects its leaders and assigns its members to various committees. The majority and minority leaders are their party's floor leaders and key planners. They try to influence party members to vote on important bills as the party recommends. When 75 percent of the party's legislators vote the same way, it is considered a **party vote**.

The majority party in Congress usually has enough support from its members to pass bills. When it does not have this support, the leaders of the majority party may work with leaders of the minority party to get help to pass bills.

Ron Brown was selected as the Democratic Party National Chairperson at the 1988 national convention.

One of the advantages of a two-party system is that the two parties will debate issues and work out compromises. Most compromises are made when the majority party needs the minority party's help to pass a bill. At such times, the minority party can have influence over what the bill will contain.

Political Parties and State Legislatures

The Democratic and Republican Parties are represented in state legislatures too. The power and influence of the parties in the state legislatures are similar to their power and influence in Congress. Party caucuses elect leaders and assign members to various committees. The majority party elects the leaders in each house. The leaders of each party try to persuade their members to support the bills their party proposes.

The President as a Party Member

You learned in Chapter 7 that Presidents are legislators as well as leaders of their parties. The President, the President's advisers, and the leaders of the President's party in Congress often work together to develop bills.

There are times when the President's views on issues are different from the views of party members in Congress. When this happens they try to compromise, but at times they fail to reach agreement. Members of Congress, for example, may want a large tax cut. The President may feel that taxes should not be reduced. As a result, the President may veto a tax bill that some of his own party members helped to pass.

In 1989, Elizabeth Dole was appointed Secretary of Labor by President Bush.

The President uses the position as party leader and the power to make appointments to reward party members who support presidential programs in Congress. The President may ask these members to suggest people to be appointed as judges, Cabinet members, and ambassadors. The President also rewards loyal party members by campaigning for them—making personal appearances and issuing statements of support for them.

SECTION 3   *Review*

Defining Key Terms
1. Define: party vote.

Recalling the Facts
2. How do political parties try to help their candidates win public office?
3. What roles do political parties play in Congress?
4. What role does the President play as party leader?

Reviewing the Main Idea
5. Answer "As you read . . ." question 3 on page 329: What are some of the goals of political parties?

Critical Thinking
6. **Recognizing Ideologies.** When voting on bills, should a member of Congress who belongs to the President's party be guided more by his or her own view or by the views of the President? Explain your answer.

Citizenship

Politically Active Teens

Too young to vote? That doesn't stop hundreds of thousands of teenagers from taking part in politics. Teenagers can become Democrats or Republicans through youth groups that each party sponsors. Young people between the ages of 13 and 19 can join the Teen Age Republicans. Anyone age 16 through 35 can become a member of the Young Democrats of America. Not only do members of each group learn about the political party system but also they can influence local, state, and national elections.

A member of the Teen Age Republicans or the Young Democrats might assist in registering people to vote. He or she will typically help with a variety of other activities, too. Political club members may arrange for speakers to discuss local, state, and national issues and foreign policy before audiences in their neighborhoods.

Wherever politics is in the air, club members can fill a need. For example they might:

- welcome presidential candidates at airports
- attend political rallies
- serve as ushers at party dinners
- work at campaign headquarters, helping to stuff envelopes and answer telephones
- pass out campaign flyers in shopping malls or on street corners
- build and ride floats in community parades
- drive people to the polls on election day or babysit so parents can vote
- write letters for or against bills being discussed in Congress

Teenage campaign workers are valuable assets to their parties.

Young Democrats of America has about 300,000 members. Teen Age Republicans number more than 100,000. Each organization supports its parent political party. Both groups, however, give teenagers a taste of politics—before they ever enter a voting booth.

Questions to think about

1. What factors might influence which political party a teenager joins?
2. Why do you think the Democratic and Republican Parties created organizations that accept members who are too young to vote?

CHAPTER 17 REVIEW

CHAPTER SUMMARY

Section 1   When the United States was founded, there were no political parties. In time, however, people with different opinions about what a government should do formed two parties. The Federalists wanted a strong central government while the Anti-Federalists favored more state power. Today's major political parties—the Republicans and the Democrats—share many goals but often disagree on ways to achieve them. Although third-party candidates rarely win election to the highest offices, their ideas often influence major parties.

Section 2   Political parties are made up of party activists, voters, and leaders. All of these persons work together to win elections. Political parties are organized at the local, state, and national levels. Most voters register as Democrats or Republicans, but others register as Independents. People support their parties by voting for party candidates, contributing money, and volunteering to work during election campaigns.

Section 3   Political parties select candidates, collect money for the candidates, and provide workers to help win elections. Party organization is strong in Congress. Both parties hold caucuses to discuss plans or select floor leaders. The majority party holds leadership positions on all committees. Members of Congress often vote along party lines, but not always. Presidents usually seek support for their programs from their own party members in Congress.

Reviewing Key Terms

On a separate sheet of paper, use the following terms to complete the sentences below.

register
two-party system
Independent
ward

third party
precinct
party vote

1. The Populist Party is an example of a __?__ .

2. A person who votes but does not belong to a political party is an __?__ .

3. A __?__ means that at least 75 percent of a party's legislators voted the same way.

4. An election district in a city is a __?__ .

5. Several election districts in a city make up a __?__ .

6. Eligible voters must __?__ in order to be allowed to vote.

7. The __?__ in the United States allows voters a choice of candidates.

Understanding Main Ideas

1. What were the first two political parties in the United States? How did they differ?

2. What are the roots of today's Democratic Party? Today's Republican Party?

3. How are major parties and third parties different?

4. Which third party succeeded in becoming a major party? Who was the first President to come from this party?

5. What people often join the Democratic Party? The Republican Party?

6. How do Democrats and Republicans generally differ in their views?

7. What do precinct workers do?

8. What are three functions of a party's national committee?

9. How do people work for a political party?

10. Describe at least five ways that political parties help candidates win elections.

11. What happens at party caucuses?

12. How can Presidents use their political power to help their parties?

Critical Thinking

1. **Recognizing Cause and Effect.** What role do third parties play in our political system? Why is this role important? What might happen if there were no third parties?

2. **Formulating Questions.** Suppose you are trying to decide whether to join a political party. Write at least six questions that you would want answered about the party before you made your decision.

3. **Testing Conclusions.** In our system, the presidential candidate who wins the majority of a state's popular vote generally receives all of the state's electoral votes. This makes it very difficult for third-party candidates to get enough electoral votes to win an election. Some people believe the electoral process should be changed to make it easier for third-party candidates to gain support. Do you agree with this position? Why or why not?

Practicing Skills

1. **Recognizing Bias.** Look for biased statements in advertisements in magazines or your local newspaper and bring them to class. How are the statements biased?

2. **Recognizing Ideologies.** Compare the views of a Democratic and a Republican candidate for the same office in your community or state. On what points do the two candidates agree? On what points do they disagree? Are these differences of opinion based on party philosophies or on other issues?

Focusing on Citizenship

1. **Researching Political Parties.** Call or write to the headquarters of a political party in your community. Ask them to mail you information about how the party is organized and how many members it has. Report your findings to the class.

2. **Conducting an Opinion Poll.** Ask ten people why they do or do not belong to a political party. Make a list of the reasons they give. Compare your list with the lists of other students. What reasons are given for belonging to a party? What reasons are given for not belonging? How do these reasons differ?

CHAPTER 18

Choosing Our Leaders

This Texan exercises a Constitutional right by voting to elect government leaders.

Previewing the Chapter

Every four years, thousands of people gather at the national meetings of the Republican Party and the Democratic Party. The scene has been described as "the greatest political show on earth." Beneath all the fun and frivolity, however, there is a serious purpose: selecting candidates for President of the United States. This chapter discusses the democratic process by which we choose our President and other political leaders.

■ **Before you read,** look up these key terms in the Glossary at the back of this book: *national convention, Electoral College, political action committee, secret ballot, absentee ballot.*

■ **As you read,** look for answers to these questions:
1. What are the typical characteristics of those elected to public office?
2. How does a political candidate win his or her party's nomination in order to run for election?
3. What are some ways by which political candidates can raise campaign money?
4. What groups of people tend to vote, and why?

1 Who Runs for Office?

A homemaker and mother from a large suburban community runs for a position on the school board of her community. She has been angered by school district plans to bus children to schools in other neighborhoods. She wants to be on the school board in order to try to stop these plans.

A high school social studies teacher campaigns for the state legislature. He decides he wants to take part in government after teaching about it for so many years.

A police officer runs for mayor of a large city. She has spent years catching criminals on the street and helping to put them behind bars. Now she wants to develop new laws and programs to reduce crime in her city.

A Mexican American social worker runs for the city council. He feels that there are not enough minority people in city government. He also feels that city officials are neglecting issues that are important to the Hispanic community.

A black woman runs for the legislature of her state. She feels that more women are needed in government.

People run for office for a variety of reasons. Most of the people you just read about have not previously been active in politics, except as voters or as contributors to political campaigns. They now want to take a more direct role in bringing their ideas into government at the national, state, and local levels.

Characteristics of Candidates

Candidates for public office have certain characteristics. Most candidates are male, white, business people or professionals such as lawyers, doctors, and teachers. In the past, politics has been mostly a male occupation. Few women have been elected to public office. Members of minority groups rarely took part in politics, nor did low-income people. (See the graphs on pages 346 and 347. They show the characteristics of the Congress according to sex, race, religion, and occupation.)

Many business and professional people believe that citizens can affect government policies. They have learned how to organize people, how to raise money, and how to campaign. They have seen their own candidates win elections. Many have enough money to be able to take time off from their jobs to work in campaigns.

Most poor people, on the other hand, have had little or no experience in politics. They have not learned how to organize workers or to raise money. Since they have little or no savings and no other source of income, they cannot afford to leave their jobs to work in a campaign. As a result, poor people seldom run for political office.

Characteristics of Congress

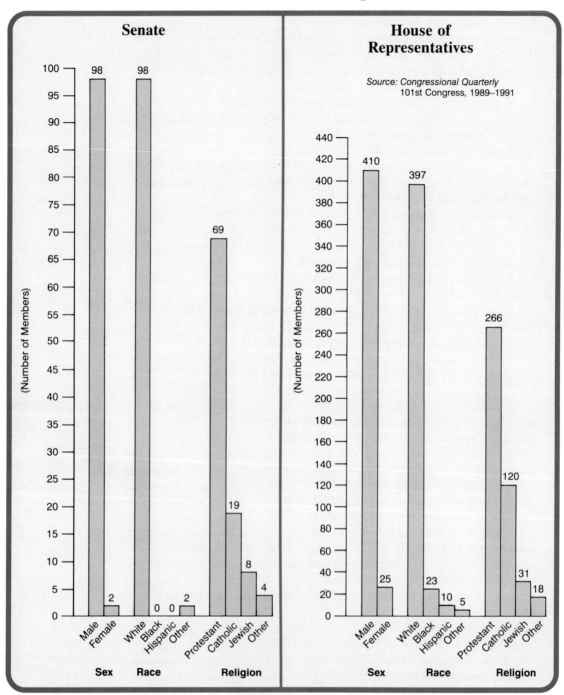

Senate

House of Representatives

Source: Congressional Quarterly
101st Congress, 1989–1991

(Senate)
- Male: 98
- Female: 2
- White: 98
- Black: 0
- Hispanic: 0
- Other: 2
- Protestant: 69
- Catholic: 19
- Jewish: 8
- Other: 4

Sex   Race   Religion

(House of Representatives)
- Male: 410
- Female: 25
- White: 397
- Black: 23
- Hispanic: 10
- Other: 5
- Protestant: 266
- Catholic: 120
- Jewish: 31
- Other: 18

Sex   Race   Religion

SKILL BUILDER   Do you think that the members of Congress represent the population of the United States accurately in terms of race and sex? Explain.

Occupations Reported by Members of Congress*

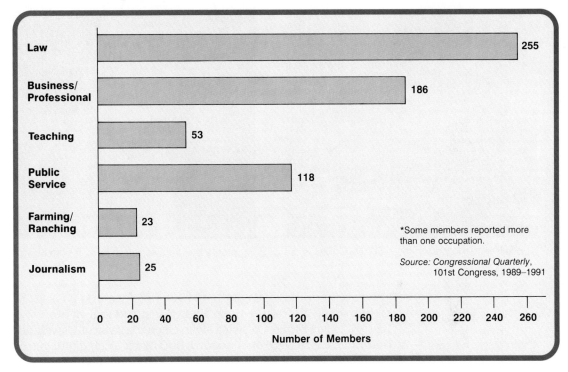

Occupation	Number of Members
Law	255
Business/Professional	186
Teaching	53
Public Service	118
Farming/Ranching	23
Journalism	25

*Some members reported more than one occupation.

Source: Congressional Quarterly, 101st Congress, 1989–1991

Number of Members

SKILL BUILDER

Which occupations are the most common among members of Congress? Why do you suppose this is?

A look at the background of recent members of the United States Congress shows what kinds of people are elected to that lawmaking body. Almost all members of the House and Senate are white men between 40 and 59 years of age. There are 25 women serving in the House and two serving in the Senate. Most members are lawyers, business people, or teachers. A few are farmers.

All Presidents have been white males. The two major parties have never nominated a black person or a Hispanic person for either President or Vice President. The first woman vice presidential candidate, Geraldine Ferraro, was nominated by the Democrats in 1984. Neither of the major parties has nominated a woman for President. Only two Democratic candidates for President—Alfred E. Smith in 1928 and John F. Kennedy in 1960—have been Catholics. Most Presidents have been lawyers or business leaders. A few have been military officers or farmers.

Women and Minorities

Many more blacks, Mexican Americans, and women have become active in politics in recent decades. The passage of federal laws to protect the rights of all people and the movement to pass the Equal Rights Amendment encouraged women and minorities to take a more active part in government. Many people in the civil

Above is Illinois Representative Cardiss Collins.

Senator Daniel Inouye, shown here, is from Hawaii.

rights movement met with national leaders to demand passage of laws that would guarantee them their Constitutional rights.

In 1967, Carl Stokes, a black, was elected mayor of Cleveland. At that time, there were only about 1,000 black elected officials at all levels of government; by 1987, there were more than 6,640. In recent years, blacks have served as mayors in several large cities. Hispanics elected to state legislatures numbered 120 in 1988. In 1987, more than 1,160 women served as state legislators. Clearly, the trend is toward more diversity in government.

SECTION *1* *Review*

Recalling the Facts

1. For what reasons do people run for public office?
2. How has the profile of a candidate for state office changed in the last 20 years?

Reviewing the Main Idea

3. Answer "As you read . . ." question 1 on page 344: What are the typical characteristics of those elected to public office?

Critical Thinking

4. **Recognizing Bias.** Why do you suppose American politics has been dominated by white males?

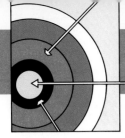

Sharpening Your Skills

Study Skills

Reading an Election Map

Suppose you wanted to quickly review how each state voted in a presidential election. You could look at a table, but that might take longer than you wanted. A better way would be to read an election map.

Election maps can show voting results in several ways. They can show the popular vote or the electoral vote. They can show election results state by state, region by region, or county by county.

The election map below shows electoral votes in the 1988 presidential election. The candidate who wins the majority of the popular vote in a state normally receives *all* that state's electoral votes. On the map below, the numbers tell how many electoral votes each state had. Blue shows the states whose electoral votes went to George Bush. Red shows the states whose electoral votes went to Michael Dukakis.

To get the most information from an election map, read the map title and key first. Then review the map itself. You can see at a glance that Bush won the most states. You can also quickly see the total number of electoral votes each state has. Note, too, the information about the popular vote that the map key provides.

Practicing Skills

Study the map and answer the following questions on a separate sheet of paper.

1. Which candidate won California's electoral votes? Who won New York's?
2. How many electoral votes does Utah have? Which candidate won them?
3. **Testing Conclusions.** Based on the map, which of the following conclusions is reasonable? Explain your answer.
   a. There are more registered Republicans than Democrats in Louisiana.
   b. Michael Dukakis won the majority of the popular vote in Oregon.

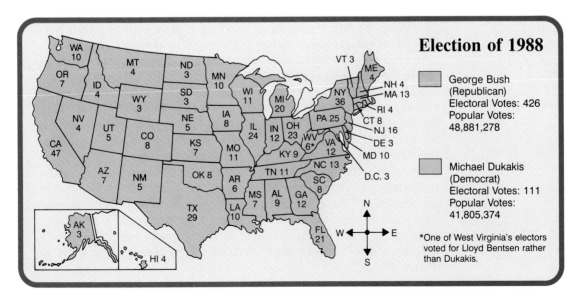

2 Selecting Our Leaders

Presidential candidates of the major parties must conduct two campaigns. In the first campaign, a candidate must win the party's nomination; that is, the candidate must be selected as the one who will run for the Presidency in the name of the party. The second campaign takes place after the parties nominate their candidates. The Republican and Democratic candidates campaign against each other before the presidential election. Presidential elections are held every four years on the first Tuesday after the first Monday in November.

A candidate's campaign for the Democratic or Republican nomination usually begins in the fall before a presidential election year. The candidate wants to get the support of delegates to the party's national convention. The **national convention**, as you know, is a meeting of the entire political party, held every four years. **Delegates** are party members from every state who nominate the party's candidates for President and Vice President.

Convention Delegates

In order to win a party's nomination, a candidate must have a majority of the delegates' votes. In 1988, there were 4,213 delegates at the Democratic National Convention and 2,277 at the Republican National Convention. Each party has its own formula to decide how many delegates each state may send to the convention.

Delegates are chosen in a number of different ways. Most delegates are chosen at presidential preference primaries in many of the states. At these primaries, voters elect delegates by voting (showing a preference) for a particular presidential candidate. The election procedure varies from state to state.

In some states, the candidate who wins the most votes wins all the delegates of that state. In other states, the candidate gets a certain number of delegates, based on the number of votes received in the primary election. In still other states, the people vote for delegates directly. Beside the delegate's name on the ballot is his or her choice of a presidential candidate. The voters vote for the delegate whose choice of a candidate they prefer.

In states that do not have primary elections, delegates to the national conventions are chosen by state committees or at state conventions. The chief difference between these groups is size. The state committee is usually a small group, while a state convention is a statewide meeting of many party members. Party members are the only ones involved in the selection process in either group.

The person who gets a majority of delegate votes at the national convention becomes the party's presidential candidate in the general election. The delegates vote according to a number of different rules. Some state laws require delegates to vote for the candidate who has won the most votes in the state primaries. However, this requirement is often dropped after the first ballot has been taken. Other states send uncommitted delegates. These delegates go to the convention without being pledged to vote for any of the candidates. At times, a state's delegates will go to the convention pledged to vote for a **favorite son**—a governor or other well-known state official—on the first ballot. This is a custom meant to honor the "favorite son."

After the delegates have nominated a presidential candidate, the next step is to choose a candidate for Vice President. By custom, the presidential candidate selects a running mate. The delegates are expected to approve the choice by unanimous vote. The vice-presidential candidate must have the same qualifications for office as the presidential candidate.

On the last evening of a national convention, bands play, delegates shout and applaud, balloons float over the convention hall, and the party's nominees for President and Vice President make their acceptance speeches. They describe what they hope to do for the nation when they are elected. (They show their confidence by speaking of *when* they win, not *if* they win.) They ask the delegates to work hard for them in the coming campaign.

SKILL BUILDER   What is the message of this political cartoon?

the small society

Presidential Campaigns

When the conventions are over, both Republican and Democratic presidential candidates meet with party heads to decide upon campaign plans. The plans include selecting a number of persons to direct campaign activities in different parts of the country. The goal of all candidates is to get enough votes to win the Presidency. To achieve this goal, they must campaign. The key to any campaign is forming an organization that will help the candidate get the votes needed to win the election.

Every presidential candidate needs a group of people who will give overall direction to the campaign. A candidate needs a campaign manager and a small group of top-level aids to plan the campaign. The candidate also needs someone to take charge of raising funds to pay for the campaign, which usually costs millions of dollars. Other people are needed to arrange for the candidate's personal appearances and to write the candidate's speeches. Finally, there must be thousands of volunteers throughout the country to do minor but important jobs.

A successful campaign is a well-planned campaign. Speaking schedules are arranged for the presidential candidate in various states. Plans are made for the candidate to meet people at rallies, parades, dinners, factories, office buildings, and even in homes. Plans for making the candidate's name, face, experience, and ideas familiar to the voters are also very important.

Campaign Wins and Losses

Not every horse trots into the winner's circle after a race. Likewise, not every candidate ends up triumphant. Nonetheless, the losers often leave a lasting mark.

William Jennings Bryan, for example, made three bids for the Presidency, in 1896, 1900, and 1908. Bryan's name has not gone down in history as a President, but rather as a brilliant speaker whose passion impressed millions.

More recently, Jesse Jackson, a minister and civil rights activist, tried to win the Democratic nomination for President in 1984 and again in 1988. His campaigns were unsuccessful, but he did succeed in drawing attention to the problems of blacks and other minorities. Jackson came out of the 1988 race with a reputation as an inspirational leader and a powerful voice in the Democratic Party.

Geraldine Ferraro, a Democrat from New York, was another contestant who lost at the ballot box but won a victory all the same. In 1984, Ferraro became the first woman chosen as a vice-presidential candidate by a major American political party. Though she and her running mate, Walter Mondale, lost the election, Ferraro's nomination was a step forward for women in politics.

A presidential campaign needs many workers, and uses many forms of communication. Campaign buttons play an important part. Campaign workers must speak personally to as many people. as possible.

All forms of communication are used in presidential campaigns—television, radio, and newspaper advertising; pamphlets, billboards, bumper stickers, lapel buttons, letters, and telephone calls. Campaign managers decide what kind of image the candidate should present, since success may depend on how the candidate comes across to the voters. Organization, planning, money, communication, and a candidate's image can affect the outcome of an election.

Campaigning is long and tiring. The candidates campaign back and forth across the country. They travel thousands of miles—sometimes for as long as 16 hours a day—on trains, buses, and airplanes. They meet thousands of citizens face to face, speak to many special interest groups, make television appearances, and sometimes participate in debates. On the night before the election, the candidate of each party appears on national television to give a final speech. The next day the voters make their choices.

The Electoral College

When the voters go to the polls on election day, they do not vote directly for the President and Vice President. Instead, they select a group of persons called **electors**. The electors vote for the President and Vice President at a later time. Their vote is called the **electoral vote**. The group of electors is known as the **Electoral College**. Each state has as many electors as it has Senators and Representatives in Congress.

The electoral votes are assigned to a candidate on a winner-take-all basis. All the electoral votes of a state go to the Democratic or Republican candidate who wins the popular vote in that state. Thus, it is possible that a candidate may win a majority of the popular vote and still lose the election if he or she doesn't win the popular vote in the states with many electoral votes.

The electors vote in their state capitals on the Monday following the second Wednesday in December. The votes are counted before both houses of Congress on January 6. In order to become

SKILL BUILDER

Who seems to have more power in electing the President—the voters or the political parties and electors?

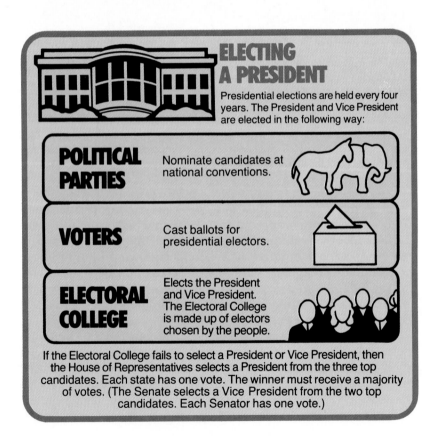

ELECTING A PRESIDENT

Presidential elections are held every four years. The President and Vice President are elected in the following way:

POLITICAL PARTIES
Nominate candidates at national conventions.

VOTERS
Cast ballots for presidential electors.

ELECTORAL COLLEGE
Elects the President and Vice President. The Electoral College is made up of electors chosen by the people.

If the Electoral College fails to select a President or Vice President, then the House of Representatives selects a President from the three top candidates. Each state has one vote. The winner must receive a majority of votes. (The Senate selects a Vice President from the two top candidates. Each Senator has one vote.)

President, one candidate must receive a majority of the electoral votes. If it should happen that none of the candidates receives a majority of the votes, the House of Representatives chooses the President, and the Senate chooses the Vice President.

Candidates for state offices and the United States Senate are nominated by their parties either in primary elections, state conventions, or caucuses. State conventions, although smaller, are similar to the national conventions. Candidates for the House of Representatives and the state legislatures are usually nominated by primary elections or by party caucuses in voting districts.

To become a candidate for a local office, a person must file papers with the registrar of voters. Within their states, candidates for governor and United States Senator conduct campaigns similar to a presidential campaign. Like a presidential candidate, they travel a great deal, give many speeches, meet many people, and raise much money.

Candidates for local offices travel very little and have less costly campaigns. How much they have to campaign depends on the size of their communities. A candidate for the city council of Dallas, Texas, for example, will have a bigger campaign than a candidate for the city council in a smaller city. Local candidates often go from door to door to meet people at their homes.

SECTION 2 *Review*

Defining Key Terms
1. Define: national convention, favorite son, elector, electoral vote, Electoral College.

Recalling the Facts
2. What does a campaign organization do for a candidate?
3. How does the Electoral College work?
4. How does a person become a candidate for Congress? For state office?

Reviewing the Main Idea
5. Answer "As you read . . ." question 2 on page 344: How does a presidential candidate win his or her party's nomination in order to run for election?

Critical Thinking
6. **Determining Relevance.** How important is "image"—the way voters see a candidate—in winning an election?

3 Campaign Financing

Successful candidates usually are those who have—or can get—money to spend. Running for elected office is expensive. Many campaign workers are volunteers, but some workers must be paid. There are countless other expenses, too. On many occasions, candidates have to give up their hopes for being elected because they do not have enough money to pay for a campaign.

Campaigning Costs

The cost of campaigning depends on the office a candidate wants to win. For 1988, the total campaign spending by all political parties in this country was about $2.5 billion. The presidential campaign cost much of this amount. Total spending in all of the United States House and Senate races in 1988 reached nearly $500 million. Some Senators spent nearly $1 million on their individual campaigns.

The cost of campaigning for governor, state legislator, mayor, or city council member depends on the size of the state, election district, or city. In the larger states, a candidate for governor may

SKILL BUILDER

What aspect of political campaigning does this cartoon criticize?

The 1988 Democratic Presidential candidate Michael Dukakis, shown playing the trumpet at a fundraiser, raised more campaign money than any Democrat in history.

spend from three to four million dollars to win the primary and general elections. In the larger cities of the nation, candidates for mayor can spend $500,000 or even one million dollars. Candidates for other offices (school-board trustee, local judge, sheriff, city clerk, county superintendent of schools, city treasurer, commissioner of parks and recreation) may spend only a few thousand dollars.

There are several ways by which candidates and parties raise money for political campaigns. For example they sponsor fund-raising dinners or luncheons. The major parties charge $500 to $1,000 per person to attend dinners at which the President or presidential candidates have been invited to speak. It is not uncommon for one of these dinners to raise as much as a million dollars. Dinners at which the speaker is a Senator, a governor, or a mayor may cost anywhere from $25 to $500 per person.

A second way to raise campaign money is to sponsor a big event such as a television spectacular where well-known entertainers appear. Such events attract many people. They can raise thousands of dollars for a candidate.

A third way to raise campaign money is to ask for donations. Corporations, labor unions, farmers' associations, business people, teachers, doctors, and many other groups often give large sums of money to the candidate they prefer. The National Association of Manufacturers, for example, usually gives a large amount to the Republican party. The AFL-CIO, the nation's largest labor union, usually gives money to the Democratic party. Large contributions are important to parties and candidates. The greatest

Raising Money for Campaigns

source of campaign money, however, comes from many donations of $100 or less from individual voters and small organizations.

Corporations and labor unions may not contribute directly to election campaigns. Instead they donate money through political action committees. A **political action committee** (PAC) is the political branch of an interest group that seeks to influence elections and government decisions. During 1987 and 1988, PAC contributions totaled almost $350 million.

Federal Election Campaign Act

In 1971, Congress passed the Federal Election Campaign Act, allowing presidential candidates to accept federal money to pay for their campaigns. The purpose of this law is to free presidential candidates from having to seek contributions from private organizations. In the past, private organizations such as large corporations and labor unions often wanted political favors in exchange for their contributions. To qualify for money from the campaign fund, a candidate must raise $5,000 in each of at least 20 states. If presidential candidates accept federal money, they cannot spend more than they receive, nor can they seek private contributions. Private organizations, however, may spend money to support candidates.

Where Does the Money Go?

Radio and television costs are by far the biggest single expense in a political campaign. Advertising, lapel buttons, mail, and telephone calls all cost a lot. Payments for polls, printing of posters and literature, and workers' salaries also add to expenses.

SECTION 3 *Review*

Defining Key Terms
1. Define: political action committee.

Recalling the Facts
2. Why is money important in a political campaign?
3. What are the biggest expenses of an election campaign?

Reviewing the Main Idea
4. Answer "As you read . . ." question 3 on page 344: What are some ways by which political candidates can raise campaign money?

Critical Thinking
5. **Predicting Consequences.** How would limiting campaign spending help provide a wider choice of candidates?

4 The Voters

To be able to vote in the United States, a person must be at least 18 years of age, a citizen, and a registered voter. Although the Constitution guarantees that all citizens 18 or older may vote, many do not. In recent presidential elections, only a little more than half of the people eligible to vote did so. An even smaller percentage of people vote in congressional elections. Elections for state and local officials have the lowest turnout of all.

Voting in Presidential Elections

Year	Winning Candidate	Percentage of Actual Voters Who Elected Winner	Percentage of Eligible Voters Who Elected Winner
1900	William McKinley	51.7%	17.6%
1904	Theodore Roosevelt	56.4%	16.8%
1908	William Taft	51.6%	15.4%
1912	Woodrow Wilson	41.9%	11.7%
1916	Woodrow Wilson	49.3%	15.8%
1920	Warren Harding	60.4%	25.6%
1924	Calvin Coolidge	54.0%	23.7%
1928	Herbert Hoover	58.1%	30.1%
1932	Franklin Roosevelt	57.4%	30.1%
1936	Franklin Roosevelt	60.8%	34.6%
1940	Franklin Roosevelt	54.7%	32.2%
1944	Franklin Roosevelt	53.4%	29.9%
1948	Harry Truman	49.6%	25.3%
1952	Dwight Eisenhower	55.1%	34.0%
1956	Dwight Eisenhower	57.4%	34.1%
1960	John Kennedy	49.7%	31.2%
1964	Lyndon Johnson	61.1%	37.8%
1968	Richard Nixon	43.4%	26.4%
1972	Richard Nixon	60.7%	33.7%
1976	Jimmy Carter	50.1%	27.2%
1980	Ronald Reagan	50.7%	28.1%
1984	Ronald Reagan	59.1%	31.3%
1988	George Bush	53.4%	26.8%

SKILL BUILDER

Which President was elected by the highest percentage of eligible voters?

What Kinds of People Vote?

Older citizens vote at a much higher rate than younger citizens. Sixty-eight percent of people between the ages of 45 to 64, and 69 percent of those 65 and over voted in the 1988 presidential election. Only 33 percent of the people who were 18 to 20 years old voted.

More whites than nonwhites vote. Slightly more women than men voted in the 1988 presidential election. College graduates tend to vote more often than people with high school or grade school educations. Employed people vote in larger numbers than unemployed people.

Candidates need to know what kinds of people vote. Members of minority groups, young people, and people with lesser amounts of education, for example, usually vote Democratic. But many of these same people do not vote at all. This means that Democratic candidates often have a difficult time getting the people who will vote for them to go to the polls. Republican candidates, on the other hand, have a somewhat easier task. Their supporters tend to be white, older, better educated, and to have higher incomes. These people who vote Republican tend to vote more often than the people who vote Democratic.

Why Do People Vote?

People vote because they want to influence what government leaders do. They want to protect their interests. Many government workers vote because they are worried about salaries and pension programs which local, state, and national legislatures determine. They want to elect lawmakers who will support their interests. People with high incomes vote because they are concerned about taxes. They are likely to vote for candidates who promise to try to keep government spending and taxes low. Many people feel that by voting for certain candidates at the local level they can get more and better government services such as parks, schools, and police and fire protection.

Many voters have decided how they will vote before a campaign begins. A campaign is not very likely to change the minds of these people. About 35 percent of the voters, however, make up their minds *during* the campaign. These are the *undecideds*. They hold the key to victory in close elections.

Some people vote only at certain times. They vote when they feel the issues may affect them. They vote when they find one candidate especially appealing. They vote when they have met a candidate personally. They vote when they think their votes will make a difference in the outcome of an election.

Of course, many people do not vote at all. They give several reasons for not voting. Most nonvoters say they don't vote because they are not registered. Others say that candidates do not live up to their promises after they are elected. Some nonvoters believe it doesn't make any difference who is elected. Some say they do not like any of the candidates. Some feel that their votes will not make any difference. Some are ill, disabled, or traveling at election time.

"I would have voted, but I didn't want to wait in line."

SKILL BUILDER

What attitude does the man speaking in this cartoon have toward the importance of voting?

Often, even a few votes can make a difference in the outcome of a close election. In such elections, especially at the local level, candidates have won by as little as two or three votes. If only a few more people had voted in these elections, the results could have been different.

Ballots

Citizens vote for their candidates on a piece of paper or card called a **ballot**. The ballot lists the names of candidates, their political parties, and the offices for which they are running. A voter places a checkmark ($\checkmark$) or an X on the ballot after the names of the candidate(s) of his or her choice.

Ballots also list and summarize various propositions the voters are being asked to approve or disapprove. A proposition may propose a pay raise for police officers, an increase in property taxes, or the raising of money to build new schools in a community. Propositions deal only with local and state issues. There are no propositions in federal elections.

The **secret ballot** allows people to vote in private. This method was not adopted by every state in the United States until 1950. Before the Civil War, citizens often announced their vote aloud at the polling place. Later, ballots were printed by each political party. The ballots of one party were often a different color from those of the other party. This practice allowed others to see how a person voted. The secret ballot made elections more fair.

The first voting machine was used in 1892 in Lockport, New York. A **voting machine** is a machine voters use in order to cast their votes. Instead of making X's or checkmarks, a voter pulls levers to vote for his or her choices. The machine automatically counts all the votes cast on it. A curtain in front of the machine provides privacy. The machine will not operate until the voter closes the curtain. Almost all states now use voting machines in at least some elections.

Ballots in the United States were once printed in English only. However, many of our citizens do not know English very well. So ballots have begun to be printed in English, Spanish, and Chinese. In some cities with large Filipino populations, the printing of ballots in the Filipino language is being considered.

All ballots cast in an election are counted after the polls have closed. Voting machines are locked at closing time so that no more votes can be registered on them. Two or more individuals usually count paper ballots to make sure that the total count is correct. Election results are not announced until officials are certain that all votes, including absentee ballots, have been counted. An **absentee ballot** is a ballot cast before election day by a voter who knew he or she would be away from home on that day.

Candidates and party officials may observe the counting of votes. They may ask for an investigation and a recount if they suspect mistakes have been made in the vote counting. They may also ask for a recount of votes if the outcome of an election is close.

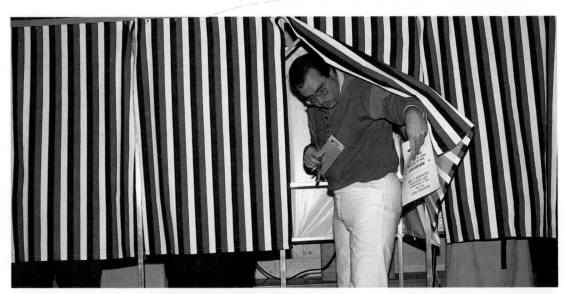

Citizens of the United States have the privilege of voting in privacy when they exercise their right to vote.

This voter has a voting information packet that gives personal statements of candidates, a list of the candidates' supporters, and information about propositions.

Before an election, each voter may receive a sample ballot and an election information packet from the county registrar of voters or from a state office. Such packets tell a voter the location of his or her voting place. They tell the day and time the polls will open. In every packet there is a card for voters to mark and take to the polls to help them remember how they wish to vote.

A voting information packet includes personal statements of candidates, along with a list of each candidate's supporters. The packet also contains a brief summary of each proposition, along with arguments in favor of it and against it.

Voter
Information
Packets

SECTION 4 *Review*

Defining Key Terms

1. Define: ballot, secret ballot, voting machine, absentee ballot.

Recalling the Facts

2. Why do people vote? Why do some not vote?

3. When does a voter use an absentee ballot?

Reviewing the Main Idea

4. Answer "As you read . . ." question 4 on page 344: What groups of people tend to vote, and why?

Critical Thinking

5. Demonstrating Reasoned Judgment. How would you convince someone that voting is important?

Government and Law

The Iowa Caucus

In January of each election year, the nation's political spotlight turns to Iowa. The normal routine is broken as presidential hopefuls, their staffs, reporters, journalists, and television crews descend upon cities and towns around the state.

In 1988, no fewer than 2,400 campaign workers and volunteers settled in and began working for the candidate of their choice. Within the space of a few weeks, Iowans from Sioux City to Grand Rapids were flooded with more than 2 million pieces of mail and as many as 3 million phone calls. The airwaves were jammed, as well, with both radio and television ads. Representatives of the media—2,500 strong—conducted hundreds of interviews, wrote thousands of articles, and polled just about every Iowan of voting age.

Michael Dukakis (in blue suit) stepped ahead of Democratic rivals for President after the 1988 Iowa caucus.

All this attention was due to the Iowa caucus. A caucus is a closed meeting of the members of a political party. In many ways a party caucus is like a primary. The purpose of both is to select the candidate that the party will support in an upcoming election. The way the candidate is selected, however, is different.

In a primary, there is basically one simple step. Registered voters go to the polls to cast their ballots, much as they do in an election. A caucus, however, is only the first of three steps. In the caucus itself, the voters go to a meeting held by either the Democratic or the Republican Party. After a discussion that often becomes quite heated, a vote is taken by a show of hands.

The caucus results are used to choose delegates to 99 county conventions. The county delegates in turn then choose the national convention delegates.

In the 1988 Iowa caucus, about 200,000 Democrats and Republicans turned out for the caucus. They met on the evening of February 8th in schools, public buildings, the back rooms of restaurants, or in private homes. In all, 2,943 caucuses were held across the state.

Many political science experts consider the results of the Iowa caucus to be extremely important. One reason is its timing. The Iowa caucus is held a week before the first primary in New Hampshire. This means that the Iowa caucuses provide the first real opportunity for voters to show what they think of the presidential candidates.

Another reason Iowa is watched so closely is that some political experts think that election results in Iowa indicate election results across the nation. Experts say that the percentages of Iowa voters who call themselves conservative, liberal, or moderate is about the same as the percentages for the nation as a whole. These experts hope that examining the results in Iowa will help them decide how to run a successful national campaign.

It was not until 1976 that the importance of the Iowa caucus was generally acknowledged. That was the year that a little-known Southern politician named Jimmy Carter won the Iowa caucus. Later that fall Carter went on to win the Presidency. As a result, Iowa became known as the place an unknown candidate could show strength. Thus at the beginning of the presidential race the efforts of lesser-known candidates focus on Iowa rather than on New Hampshire.

Not all the experts agree, however, on the importance of the Iowa caucus. Some point out that there is no guarantee that the winners of the Iowa caucus will be nominated by their party. In 1988, for example, Robert Dole won the Republican Iowa caucus, but it was George Bush who won the Republican nomination and the Presidency.

These experts also point out that in many ways Iowa does not reflect the conditions of a national election. For example, the style of campaigning that works in Iowa will not work nationally. Caucuses take place among small groups of highly motivated voters, which means that one-on-one campaigning is best. To be successful in Iowa, candidates need to spend more time than money on voters. Personal campaigning is very important.

In contrast, to be successful in a national campaign, personal campaigning runs a poor second to media management. The national candidate also needs an almost endless supply of money to fund media advertising.

Despite all this, most political experts believe that the candidates need to make a good showing in both Iowa and New Hampshire if they are to make it to the White House. Candidates who fare poorly in these two states are likely to lose financial contributions and press coverage. Money and media attention are two crucial factors in a successful, modern presidential campaign.

Has the Iowa caucus become more of a media event than a true political event? People on both sides of the issue hold strong opinions. But one thing seems certain: as long as the candidates and the media think the results are important, they will be.

Questions to think about

1. Do you think that the Iowa caucuses deserve all the attention that they receive from the candidates and the media? Explain your answer.
2. Do you think a caucus is more democratic than a primary? Explain.

CHAPTER SUMMARY

Section 1   People run for political office for many reasons. Most political candidates (and all Presidents) have been white males with a professional or business background. Today, however, more and more women and members of minority groups are seeking public office. To be a candidate, a person must have the time and money to take part in a campaign.

Section 2   Presidential candidates must win their party's nomination and then campaign against the other party's candidate. A successful campaign requires good planning, plenty of money, dedicated workers, and widespread publicity. Campaigning is a long and tiring job. Presidents are actually elected by a majority vote in the Electoral College. Generally, all the electoral votes of a state go to the candidate who wins the popular vote in that state.

Section 3   Money is an important part of a campaign. Expenses are high for presidential and congressional candidates. Candidates raise money by sponsoring fundraising events, asking for donations, and using the federal campaign fund. Most campaign money is spent for television or radio advertisements.

Section 4   Voter turnout in the United States is often quite low. Whites, older citizens, and college graduates vote in larger numbers than do minorities, younger adults, or people with high school or grade school educations. People vote in order to influence what government does, to protect their interests, and to support issues. Voting takes place in private using paper ballots, voting machines, or absentee ballots.

Reviewing Key Terms

On a separate sheet of paper, use the following terms to complete the sentences below.

national convention   Electoral College
secret ballot   political action committee
absentee ballot

1. A __?__ seeks to influence elections and public policy decisions.

2. Voters who are away from home on election day may use an __?__.

3. The __?__ is the group of people who officially elect the President and Vice President.

4. A party's candidates for President and Vice President are nominated at a __?__.

5. A __?__ allows people to cast their votes in private.

Understanding Main Ideas

1. What are the characteristics of most candidates for political office?

2. Why are poor people unlikely to run for office?

3. How often are presidential elections held?

4. Describe three ways that national convention delegates are chosen.

5. How is the vice presidential candidate selected?

6. What is the purpose of a campaign organization?

7. How are each state's electoral votes assigned?

8. Describe three ways that candidates raise money.

9. What is the federal campaign fund?

10. What are "undecided" voters? Why are they important?

11. What is the purpose of the secret ballot?

12. What is a sample ballot? A voter information packet?

Critical Thinking

1. **Predicting Consequences.** Would the election process be more democratic if the government required all candidates to limit their spending to sums of money the government provides? How might this affect the chances of less wealthy candidates?

2. **Determining Relevance.** Should people be required to read English before they can register to vote? Why or why not?

Practicing Skills

1. **Making an Election Map.** At your school or local library, find out the electoral vote of each state in the election of 1984. Consult *Facts on File* for 1984 (under "Presidential election results" in the index) or check the *Readers' Guide to Periodical Literature.* Then use the information to draw an election map for the 1984 election. Use different colors to show the states won by each candidate.

2. **Making a Bar Graph.** Contact your state legislature to find out the occupations of its members. Then make a bar graph showing the number of members in each occupation.

3. **Distinguishing False from Accurate Images.** Obtain a pamphlet for a candidate in a current or recent election campaign. What image does the candidate present? What facts support that image? Can you find any evidence (for example, a newspaper analysis or a rival candidate's campaign literature) that suggests the image is false?

Focusing on Citizenship

1. **Interviewing Candidates.** Interview three people who ran for office in your community to find out their reasons for running. Share your findings with the class. What seem to be the major reasons for which people run for public office?

2. **Researching Campaign Fund Raising.** Find out how much money candidates in your community spent on their latest campaigns. Make a list of the candidates' names, the office each sought, and the amount of money each spent. This information can be obtained from your local city hall.

CHAPTER 19

Interest Groups

These farmers, members of an agricultural interest group, are making their voices heard in the nation's capital.

Previewing the Chapter

For every issue there are at least two points of view. On matters as complex as balancing the budget or as seemingly simple as declaring a new holiday, you are bound to find people with different opinions. When like-minded people unite behind a cause, though, they can be a powerful force in government. This chapter explores how various interest groups try to influence the decisions made by government leaders.

■   **Before you read,** look up these key terms in the Glossary at the back of this book: *union, right-to-work law, coalition.*

■   **As you read,** look for answers to these questions:
    1. What are some types of interest groups?
    2. How do interest groups help political candidates?
    3. How does the First Amendment protect the right to lobby?

1 What Are Interest Groups?

There are more than 100,000 clubs and organizations in the United States. Not all of these groups, however, are interested in influencing government. People who like to collect stamps or grow roses, for example, may get together once a month just to exchange ideas and to enjoy each other's company. However, when a group of individuals unites and spends money in an effort to influence Congress or a state legislature, it becomes an interest group.

Interest Groups

As you know, an interest group is an organized group of people who try to influence the decisions of local, state, or federal government officials. People might organize an interest group to support the passage of a new bill or to oppose a bill. In some cases, an interest group may work to change an existing law. A group of concerned parents, for example, may organize to put pressure on the members of the city council to have a stoplight installed at a dangerous street corner. State government workers may organize to try to get the state legislature to pass a bill to raise their salaries. Elderly people may organize to try to get the Congress to pass laws to provide special tax benefits to people over 65.

There are thousands of interest groups in the United States. They are known by many names—pressure groups, special interests, lobbies, and vested interests. Some interest groups are small, with only a dozen members or so. Others are very large, with thousands of members. Whatever the size, there is an interest group for just about any purpose you can think of. New interest groups form as new political issues arise.

Types of Interest Groups

Business Groups.   One of the most active groups working in the interests of business in the United States is the Chamber of Commerce. This interest group has a national organization with headquarters in Washington, D.C. There are hundreds of local Chamber of Commerce chapters throughout the nation. For the most part, the local chapters try to promote the interests of the small business firms in their areas of the country. Another business interest group, the National Association of Manufacturers, works in behalf of large industrial firms.

The business interest groups do not always work together. Those who represent the trucking industry, for example, have tried to encourage the use of federal money for building highways. Airline and railroad interest groups, on the other hand, have been opposed to this idea.

Labor Groups. The most powerful of the labor interest groups is the American Federation of Labor-Congress of Industrial Organizations (AFL-CIO). This single organization represents about 14 million workers who belong to more than 100 separate unions. (A **union** is an organization that seeks to improve working conditions, salaries, and so forth for working people.) The AFL-CIO has worked for such goals as tax reform and housing assistance. It has also supported increased defense spending. This would mean more jobs for its members.

Unions tend to agree on certain issues. Almost all unions are in favor of a high minimum wage and increased unemployment benefits. Almost all are opposed to right-to-work laws. A **right-to-work law** is one which allows a company to hire a non-union worker. To get the job, the worker does not have to belong to the union or agree to join the union later. On other issues, different labor unions may disagree. An auto workers union, for example, may favor higher import taxes on foreign cars. They believe that higher taxes will help the sale of automobiles made in the United States and provide more jobs for the union's members. On the other hand, dock workers who unload imported foreign cars at the docks may see higher import taxes as a threat to their jobs.

There are thousands of interest groups in the United States. This group is asking for health care for all.

On many issues, business and labor groups are directly opposed to one another. For example, many business firms such as restaurants are against a minimum wage for young people. Their argument is that teenagers are more likely to get jobs if business firms do not have to pay them the same salary as adults. Unions, on the other hand, want young people to be paid the minimum wage. They argue that the business firms simply want young people as cheap labor.

Farm Groups. A number of interest groups work in the interests of farmers. Among such groups are the National Grange, the American Farm Bureau Federation, and the National Farmer's Union. There are also groups which represent certain types of farmers, such as cotton growers or livestock breeders. All of these interest groups favor laws to keep the prices of farm products high. Sometimes farmers have different interests. At one time, for example, dairy farmers were able to get a federal tax placed on margarine, a substitute for butter.

Other Interest Groups. The American Association of Retired Persons wants to promote the interests of senior citizens (individuals over the age of 65). The American Legion and the Veterans of Foreign Wars try to promote the welfare of the nation's veterans. Some organizations try to improve the position of black people in our society. Among them are the National Association for the Advancement of Colored People (NAACP), the National Urban League, and the Congress of Racial Equality (CORE). The American Indian Movement (AIM) wants to improve living and working conditions of Native Americans.

In recent years, some interest groups have tried to help the many disabled people in our society. One such group is the Center for Independent Living. Branches are found in several states. This interest group has put pressure on local governments to construct sloping curbs on street corners to make getting on and off sidewalks easier for people in wheelchairs. Another of its achievements has been to get special parking places for handicapped drivers.

Public Interest Groups

A public interest group is a group which tries to influence government to protect the interests of the public as a whole—all the people in the United States. The League of Women Voters, for example, is a national organization that tries to encourage citizens to take an active part in politics and government affairs. At the local level, chapters of the league publish pamphlets that explain how state and local governments work. In past years, the league has sponsored debates between leading presidential candidates. The league is a nonpartisan group. That is, it does not favor or endorse the candidates or issues of any particular party.

Members of the Gray Panthers, an organization whose motto is "age and youth in action," demonstrate against recent cuts in government funding for social service programs.

The American Civil Liberties Union (ACLU) seeks to protect the constitutional rights of all people who live in the United States. It is often called the "Defender of the Bill of Rights." People who feel their constitutional rights have been taken away can seek help from the ACLU. This includes assistance in a court of law. The ACLU will often provide lawyers for people who cannot afford them. Lawyers from the ACLU have even argued cases before the United States Supreme Court.

Common Cause is an organization that works for the improvement of the lawmaking process in Congress. The chief goal of this group is to make legislators think about the needs of the people. Common Cause has received credit for helping to bring about the Federal Election Campaign Act of 1974. This act limits the amount of contributions that can be given to candidates for political office. It also provides for public financing of presidential campaigns. Common Cause has also campaigned against secret committee meetings in Congress as well as for many other congressional reforms.

The National Organization for Women (NOW) is an organization that seeks to promote the welfare of all women of the United States. NOW has worked for equal employment opportunities and for the passage of the Equal Rights Amendment to the United States Constitution.

SECTION 1 *Review*

Defining Key Terms
1. Define: union, right-to-work law.

Recalling the Facts
2. What is an interest group?
3. How has an interest group helped change conditions for the handicapped?

Reviewing the Main Idea
4. Answer "As you read . . ." question 1 on page 368: What are some types of interest groups?

Critical Thinking
5. **Testing Conclusions.** Some critics have described interest groups as selfish because they promote their own causes. Do some causes need special representation? Explain.

2 Interest Groups and Government

All interest groups have points of view that they want the government to support. For this reason, interest groups usually support political candidates who share their views. The AFL-CIO, for example, usually helps Democratic candidates in their political campaigns. Business groups such as the National Association of Manufacturers usually assist Republican candidates. However, some interest groups support any candidate who agrees with their points of view. A group may even give financial aid to two opposing candidates—just to be on the safe side.

Interest groups help political candidates in a number of ways. During a political campaign, they provide workers to ring doorbells and pass out pamphlets. They provide people to speak in favor of candidates at club meetings, social gatherings, and college assemblies. Most important, perhaps, they provide money to help pay for campaign expenses. The American Medical Association contributes millions of dollars to candidates around the country. Unions and business firms have contributed even larger amounts to support the campaigns of candidates they favor.

Interest Groups and Candidates

Tenants' rights organizations form special interest groups. They look for candidates who are willing to support their point of view.

SKILL BUILDER

Why do you think these groups contributed such large sums of money to election campaigns?

Presidential and Congressional Campaign Contributions (1987–1988):

Top Five Contributors

1. National Association of Realtors	$3,040,969
2. International Brotherhood of Teamsters	2,856,724
3. American Medical Association	2,136,496
4. National Education Association	2,104,689
5. National Association of Retired Federal Employees	1,979,850

Source: Federal Election Commission

Interest groups do not give contributions directly to candidates, however. This is against the law. Thus, the AFL-CIO as an organization cannot give money to individuals running for office. Instead, as you learned in Chapter 16, the money is given through political action committees (PACs). A union member may, however, give up to $1,000 out of his or her own pocket to any number of different candidates.

Money that is given to a candidate by an interest group can be used only to pay for campaign expenses. It is a crime for a political candidate to use this money for personal expenses. It is also against the law to give a candidate money in return for a political favor or in return for the candidate's promise to vote in a certain way. Likewise, money that comes from a PAC representing corporation officials cannot be taken in return for a promise to sponsor a bill favorable to business interests.

Interest groups not only try to help candidates win elections, they also try to affect how the candidates will vote once they are elected. The American Tobacco Institute, for example, has been a major force in helping to defeat proposed anti-smoking laws in various states. These state laws would have forbidden smoking in elevators, restaurants, theatres, and other public places throughout the United States. The institute saw these proposals as threats to the sale of tobacco products and spent millions of dollars to defeat their passage into law.

The power of money to influence people cannot be denied. However, big spenders do not always get their way. All the money of the American Tobacco Institute, for example, has not stopped many city councils from passing laws to forbid smoking in public places. In a few cases, interest groups with little money have formed coalitions and won victories over wealthy organizations. A **coalition** is made up of several interest groups that band together for a common purpose.

As mentioned in Chapter 5, a lobbyist is a paid representative of an interest group. A lobbyist's job is to further the interests of the group that pays her or him. In most cases, these interests are economic. Labor union lobbyists, for example, work for the passage of minimum wage laws and laws that protect the right of workers to strike for higher wages. Lobbyists for farm groups work for laws that will help increase the sale of United States farm products in other countries. Lobbyists for real estate groups support laws to protect people who wish to buy and sell property.

Interest Groups and Voting

Interest Groups Band Together

Lobbyists

Interest groups seeking to bring about environmental protection laws are very active. This ecology group is an example.

The National Organization of Women, NOW, is a very active interest group working for social justice.

Lobbyists for steel companies promote laws that limit the amount of steel that can be brought into the United States from other countries.

Lately, even cities have hired lobbyists to represent their interests in Washington, D.C., the nation's Capital. Again, the reason for their doing this is an economic one. Every year, the federal government gives millions of dollars to cities and other units of local government. (See Chapter 14.) Having the services of a lobbyist in Washington is one way a city can improve its chances of getting some of this federal money.

The word *lobbyist* comes from the English term *lobby-agent* which has a similar meaning. In earlier years, there was a waiting room outside the House of Commons, one part of the lawmaking body of the English government. Individuals who wished to meet members of the House of Commons had to wait in this waiting room, or lobby. After a lawmaking session was over, these lobby-agents, as they were called, rushed to meet the legislators.

At any given time, there are several thousand lobbyists registered in Washington, D.C. There are even more in the various state capitals. Most lobbyists have expert knowledge of the workings of government. Some of them are ex-legislators, former government workers, or past employees of the interest groups they represent. In many cases, their salaries may be higher than those of the legislators they try to influence. Besides their salaries, lobbyists are given generous expense accounts by their employers. They use their expense accounts to entertain members of Congress or to provide services to lawmakers.

Lobbyists also work within the executive branch. They try to influence government officials who make decisions about public policy or those who carry out laws passed by Congress or state legislatures. The members of the Federal Aviation Administration (FAA), for example, set safety standards for commercial aircraft companies. Before an important decision is made, lobbyists for the airlines will probably contact these officials.

Lobbyists are often very helpful to legislators. They prepare summaries of proposed laws. This saves legislators and their staffs a considerable amount of time. They sometimes write speeches or letters for members of Congress. They are always willing to prepare drafts of bills that are important to the interest groups they represent.

Lobbyists Help Legislators

The tools of a lobbyist are said to be friendliness, persuasion, and helpfulness. Taking a legislator to lunch, to the theater, or to a ballgame is a good way to make a possibly helpful friend.

Many observers feel there is no harm in a legislator accepting free lunches or tickets to the theater. On the other hand, critics say it is often difficult to distinguish between a friendly gift and a bribe (an attempt to "buy" a legislator's vote). At what point, for example, is a free lunch, a weekend at an expensive resort, or a gold watch more than just a gift?

SECTION 2 *Review*

Defining Key Terms
1. Define: coalition.

Recalling the Facts
2. What regulations are placed on contributions made by interest groups to political candidates?
3. What do lobbyists do?
4. How do lobbyists help legislators?

Reviewing the Main Idea
5. Answer "As you read . . ." question 2 on page 368: How do interest groups help political candidates?

Critical Thinking
6. Recognizing Bias. Under what conditions should a member of Congress accept a gift from a lobbyist? How do legislators decide what is a gift and what is a bribe?

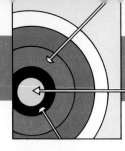

Sharpening Your Skills

Citizenship Skills

Working Together in Groups

Throughout your life, you will often find yourself working in groups. Perhaps you will participate in political interest groups like those mentioned in Sections 1 and 2. You may also belong to cultural or athletic groups, school groups, or work groups.

To work successfully in any group, a few basic skills are essential. These include compromising, organizing and holding meetings, listening to others, and communicating clearly.

Compromising. In most groups you will discover a mix of people with a variety of opinions. In spite of these differences, the members of a group must work together. One way to do this is through compromise. In a compromise, each side gives in a little to opposing viewpoints. This will often happen through negotiation (a discussion between the different sides to reach an agreement). Members of each side decide what demands they are willing to give up and what demands they must stand firm on. Eventually the group reaches a solution that all members can accept.

Organizing Meetings. Groups work best when they are well organized. Thus, an important task is choosing a leader, one who understands the group's purpose and can effectively set an agenda (an outlined plan) for each meeting.

Any group meeting must have a specific purpose. The leader begins the meeting by clarifying that purpose. A union group might meet, for example, to share information about a proposed factory closing.

Once the meeting's purpose becomes clear, the group discusses the topic. The leader keeps the discussion moving and makes sure that everyone has a chance to contribute as a secretary takes notes to record the discussion.

Listening and Communicating. During the meeting, each member has two responsibilities. One is to listen closely. The other is to communicate effectively.

To be a good listener, focus carefully on what each speaker says. Try to grasp the speaker's main point and purpose. Examine whether the speaker supports his or her main point. If possible, take notes as you listen. Ask questions if you need further clarification, but do not interrupt.

When your turn to speak comes, present your views clearly and concisely. Do not stray from the main point. Support your views with details. Speak loudly and slowly enough to be understood.

Practicing Skills

1. After a major oil spill on the Atlantic Ocean, an ecology group meets. Which would be the best opening statement by their leader? Why?
   a. "I've written a letter stating our view on the recent oil spill. I'd like all of you to sign it."
   b. "We're meeting today to formulate a group response to the oil spill."
2. **Determining Relevance.** Which of the following statements would be most relevant at a neighborhood meeting to improve relations between landlords and tenants? Why?
   a. "Perhaps we should start a monthly meeting for landlords and tenants."
   b. "My landlord doesn't make any repairs but keeps raising the rent."
   c. "One of my tenants plays loud rock music every night until 1:00 a.m."

3 The Regulation of Interest Groups

The First Amendment to the United States Constitution is the basic law that allows the activities of interest groups. The First Amendment guarantees that all citizens have the right to petition the government. In our society, individuals and groups have a right to try to influence the decisions of lawmakers.

From time to time, however, some state and federal lawmakers have been convicted of granting favors to lobbyists and of spending campaign donations for personal use. In 1977, many members of Congress were charged with taking favors from a lobbyist of the South Korean government. In return for money and trips to Asia, the members of Congress were expected to encourage the flow of United States military aid to South Korea.

In 1979, undercover FBI agents approached some members of Congress. The agents pretended to represent wealthy Arabs. They offered certain legislators $50,000 in cash in return for introducing bills that would allow these Arabs to come into the United States to set up a business. Some of the legislators accepted the bribes and were later tried in court. Illegal activities like these have led to demands for stricter laws regulating lobbyists.

PEOPLE HELPING PEOPLE

Blood Donors on a Leash

Thirty cats and dogs arrived at the Angell Memorial Animal Hospital in the spring of 1989, prepared to help their fellow creatures live a little longer. The pets were part of a first-in-the-nation campaign to build up the Boston hospital's blood bank for sick and injured animals.

In the human community, blood drives are a regular feature of life. People in the hospital often need large amounts of blood in order to survive accidents or operations,

and hospitals must have the right type on hand. Animals are no different. In 1988 alone, Angell Memorial gave more than 300 blood transfusions to cats and dogs in its care.

The pets who donated blood were treated like heroes. Each one was wheeled into a recovery room containing dog and cat treats and vitamins. "We think he should be on call when they need blood," Gail Novick told reporters as she smiled at her golden retriever Timmy. "It's kind of like he is doing his canine civic duty."

Lobbyists often meet one-on-one with members of Congress to try to influence their votes.

Regulation of Lobbying Act

The first attempt to regulate lobbyists through legislation came with the passage of the Regulation of Lobbying Act of 1946. This law requires lobbyists to register with the Clerk of the House of Representatives and the Secretary of the Senate. Lobbyists are also required to file reports showing their salaries and the amount of money they spend on lobbying activities each year. The year after the law was passed, 250 persons registered as lobbyists in Washington, D.C. Today, about 5,500 people are registered as lobbyists. There are about 20,000 people, however, who earn at least part of their living by lobbying Congress.

The 1946 act, and others that followed, have not always worked as Congress intended. The 1946 act requires the registration of a person or organization that collects and spends money for the principal purpose of influencing legislation. Many large organizations do not register, however. They claim that "influencing legislation" is not the principal purpose for which they collect and spend money.

The courts have ruled that only persons who contact members of Congress *directly* must register. Hence a person who spends large sums of money on newspaper advertisements, letters, and similar activities does not have to register. Even though these activities are intended to influence legislation, they do not involve direct contact. Individuals or groups who spend their own (not an organization's) money on lobbying activities do not have to register either.

Most people would defend the right of a lobbyist to try to influence the government. There are many other people, however, who feel that lobbying is now out of control. They argue that lobbyists too often speak only for their own special interests. If the welfare of the people of the United States is the same as those interests, all is well. But if those interests are opposed to the welfare of the people, the special interests come first.

During the 1970s, John Gardner, the former president of Common Cause, appeared before a committee of Congress. He offered the following suggestions about lobbying and what needs to be done to keep it more in line with the public interest:

Regulating Lobbyists

- Define lobbying as all forms of communication with government officials for the purpose of influencing public policy. Such forms of communication would include not only direct personal contact, but letters, telegrams, phone calls, and newspaper advertisements as well.
- Require lobbyists to include more detail in the reports which they file with Congress than is required by present law. Lobbyists should report the source of their income as well as the amount. They should give a detailed explanation of how they spend their money. They should be required to name the government officials they have contacted. They should also be required to name all congressional and other government activities which they have tried to influence.

SECTION 3 *Review*

Recalling the Facts

1. How does the Regulation of Lobbying Act of 1946 try to regulate the activities of lobbyists?
2. What suggestions have been proposed to improve the system of lobbying?

Reviewing the Main Idea

3. Answer "As you read . . " question 3 on page 368: How does the First Amendment protect the right to lobby?

Critical Thinking

4. **Identifying Assumptions.** In November, 1980, a member of Congress was reelected even though he had admitted taking a gift of $50,000. How would you explain his reelection?

Lobbying on Gun Control

IN 1985, HANDGUNS KILLED
46 PEOPLE IN JAPAN
8 IN GREAT BRITAIN
31 IN SWITZERLAND
5 IN CANADA
18 IN ISRAEL
5 IN AUSTRALIA
AND 8,092 IN THE UNITED STATES.

GOD BLESS AMERICA.

A Child A Day Is Killed With A Handgun

CONSTITUTIONAL RIGHTS IN JEOPARDY: JEOPARDY: JEOPARDY: JEOPARDY: JEOPARDY: JEOPARDY:

Interest groups promote their views on gun control with posters, pamphlets, and bumper stickers.

Think of the television shows and movies you have seen in the past month. Did you watch westerns, science fiction, crime thrillers? How many programs showed scenes with guns? How many scenes involving guns do you suppose you have watched in your entire lifetime?

Guns are so familiar on television and in the movies that we take them for granted. But in real life guns are the focus of much debate. Do all American citizens have the right to bear arms? Or should the right to bear arms be regulated? Powerful interest groups have spoken out on both sides of this question. The National Rifle Association (N.R.A.) is the best-known group lobbying in favor of the right of every citizen to bear arms. Groups such as Handgun Control, Inc., and the Center to Prevent Handgun Violence lead the fight to limit the sale and possession of firearms.

No one denies that guns play a significant role in violent crimes. But interest groups disagree whether or not gun control is an effective way to stop crime. Opponents of gun control argue that private citizens often need guns to protect themselves. A homeowner, for example, might own a gun to stop an intruder from breaking in and stealing property. Some foes of gun control further contend that crime would increase if citizens could not own guns, because criminals then would be able to get away with more crimes.

Gun control advocates see things differently. They believe that owning a gun does not significantly improve one's chances of defending oneself against a criminal. They also point out the great number of accidents that were caused by guns. In 1987, gun accidents were the fourth leading cause of accidental death for children under the age of 15 in the United States.

Supporters of gun control believe that violent crime would be reduced if criminals found it harder to get guns. The 1968 Gun Control Act forbids the purchase of guns by convicted felons, minors, drug addicts, and mentally ill persons. Some states have laws against carrying concealed weapons. Others require pistol owners to register their guns. Supporters of gun control want more; they would like to see a two-week waiting period in all states before anyone can purchase a gun. This would allow time to check the buyer's background.

Groups like the N.R.A. oppose such regulations. They argue that gun control laws affect only law-abiding people who want to own guns. Criminals, they say, will get guns no matter what the laws are. The N.R.A. puts its faith in better law enforcement and stiffer penalties for criminals.

Much of the debate on gun control focuses on the Second Amendment to the Constitution. The Amendment reads:

> A well-regulated militia being necessary to the security of a free state, the right of the people to keep and bear arms shall not be infringed.

Interest groups that support gun control point out that when the Amendment was written, the War for Independence was fresh in the minds of Americans. People remembered that British soldiers had taken charge of the colonial militia, and they wanted an amendment that would prevent the new federal government from ever disarming a state's militia. Gun control supporters insist that the Second Amendment gives the military, not individual citizens, the right to carry guns.

Interest groups opposing gun control could not disagree more. The Second Amendment, they argue, says in black and white that all American citizens have the "right to bear arms." This includes owning guns for self-defense, target shooting, and hunting.

The Supreme Court has not ruled directly on whether individuals can own guns. But citizens of Morton Grove, Illinois, presented the question to lower courts in 1973. Morton Grove was the first town in the United States to ban the possession of handguns. The two federal courts that heard the case both ruled that the town's ban did not violate the Second Amendment.

Crackling gunfire continues to keep the gun control issue alive. In 1981, John Hinkley, Jr., wounded President Reagan and Press Secretary William Brady with a handgun. More recently, the use of semiautomatic, or "assault," rifles has stirred public controversy. These military-type guns are often linked to drug-related violence. In February, 1989, five schoolchildren in Stockton, California, were killed in their school playground by a man with a semiautomatic rifle. Gun control groups have called for a ban on these weapons. Opponents of gun control reply that semiautomatic weapons should be allowed for lawful purposes such as hunting.

The debate over guns is not likely to be resolved soon. Interest groups for both sides will continue to lobby for their positions. The final verdict, when it arrives, will determine whether citizens have the right to buy any weapon they choose—or whether they can own a gun only under strict regulation.

Questions to think about

1. Do you think that your community should make it more difficult to purchase guns? Explain your answer.
2. Do you believe that the Second Amendment guarantees the rights of individual citizens to own guns? Why or why not?

CHAPTER SUMMARY

Section 1   Interest groups are organized groups of people who try to influence government policy. There are special interest groups that represent businesses, labor unions, farmers, retired persons, veterans, women, minorities, and many other segments of the population. These interest groups concentrate on issues that are important to their members. Public interest groups, on the other hand, try to promote the welfare of the public as a whole. The League of Women Voters, Common Cause, and the American Civil Liberties Union are three of the largest public interest groups.

Section 2   Interest groups support political candidates by giving money to cover campaign costs (through PACs), by promoting candidates to their members, and by providing campaign workers. Interest groups also try to affect how elected officials vote on particular issues. Lobbyists are paid employees of interest groups. Most of them work in Washington, D.C., or the state capitals. They try to influence legislation or government policy on behalf of their employers. Lobbyists are usually skilled in the workings of government and can offer valuable services to lawmakers.

Section 3   The First Amendment to the United States Constitution protects the right of interest groups to try to influence our government. Interest groups, however, are not allowed to give money directly to candidates, and lawmakers must not accept gifts in return for granting favors to particular groups. Abuses of these rules have led to a call for stricter laws regulating lobbyists.

Reviewing Key Terms

Match the following terms with the definitions below. Write your answers on a separate sheet of paper.

right-to-work law   union
coalition

1. an organization that tries to improve employment conditions for working people

2. a band of several interest groups

3. a law that allows companies to hire non-union workers

Understanding Main Ideas

1. What is the purpose of interest groups?

2. What are three different types of interest groups?

3. Name four kinds of laws supported by many unions.

4. How do public interest groups differ from other interest groups?

5. Identify two public interest groups and describe their activities.

6. What are three ways that interest groups can help a political candidate?

7. What are two restrictions placed on campaign contributions made by interest groups?

8. Name three services that lobbyists perform for lawmakers.

9. What are some criticisms of lobbyists?

10. What does the Regulation of Lobbying Act do?

11. How have lobbyists avoided registering?

12. What are John Gardner's suggestions for the regulation of lobbying activities?

Critical Thinking

1. **Identifying Central Issues.** What are the main effects of interest groups in the lawmaking process? If there were no organized interest groups, how could the public influence government?

2. **Drawing Conclusions.** Should government officials be forbidden from taking any kind of gift from a lobbyist, however small its value? Why or why not?

Practicing Skills

1. **Working Together in Groups.** Hold a meeting with five to ten other students to decide on a problem or issue in your school or community that you want to resolve. Decide what kind of action to take on this issue. Will you lobby the school principal, write letters to the local paper, or solve the problem directly? Have all group members participate in choosing an issue and taking steps to settle it.

2. **Organizing Information.** Collect newspaper and magazine clippings, pamphlets, bumper stickers, and buttons to make a bulletin board display showing the activities and slogans of various interest groups.

3. **Analyzing the News.** Look in your local newspaper or in a weekly news magazine for an article about the activities of an interest group. Summarize the article for a report to the class.

Focusing on Citizenship

1. **Presenting a Report.** Prepare and present an oral or written report on the activities of a public interest group such as Common Cause, the League of Women Voters, or the American Civil Liberties Union.

2. **Writing Your Lawmakers.** Imagine that you wish to encourage the federal government to make more money available to local school districts. State your reasons in a letter that could be sent to your Representative or to one of your Senators.

3. **Holding a Class Discussion.** Hold a class discussion on whether or not there are any interest groups (or "cliques") in your school. What efforts (if any) does your school make to control the actions of these interest groups? Are there any groups that try to look out for the interests of all students?

Focus on Decision Making

Should Nuclear Power Plants Be Shut Down?

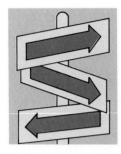

"There are more than enough power plants out there to meet our present needs if only we use their electricity more efficiently."

The Issue in Question

A Massachusetts resident made the statement above in November, 1988. That month, the citizens of Massachusetts were voting on a referendum concerning the future of nuclear power in their state.

Since 1946, nuclear power has gained ground as an energy source around the world. The first American nuclear reactor came on line in 1957. Currently there are some 85 nuclear plants in the United States generating about 13 percent of the nation's electricity.

But the debate about of nuclear power is hotter than ever. Nuclear power advocates say their technology uses less fuel and creates less air pollution than coal- or oil-burning systems. Opponents worry about the high costs of building nuclear plants and the risk of accidents.

Two nuclear accidents in particular have brought a sense of urgency to the debate. The Three Mile Island plant near Harrisburg, Pennsylvania, suffered a partial meltdown of its radioactive fuel in 1979. Seven years later, at Chernobyl in the Soviet Union, 31 people died and hundreds more suffered from radiation exposure when the full meltdown of a nuclear plant occurred. Experts estimated that

6,000 to 24,000 more would become sick or die from radiation exposure over the next 70 years as a result of this accident.

Background on the Referendum

The Massachusetts referendum on nuclear energy grew out of citizens' concerns about nuclear power plants. Volunteers for dozens of interest groups began collecting signatures in the spring of 1987. They gathered 120,000 signatures—enough to put a referendum on the November, 1988, ballot calling for the shutdown of Massachusetts's two nuclear power plants, Yankee Rowe and Pilgrim.

After a summer of heat waves and power shortages, many people worried about giving up an energy source they had come to count on. Nuclear industry officials estimated that replacing the lost power could cost as much as $4 billion. This would mean higher electric bills for consumers. Nuclear power advocates also noted that shutting the nuclear plants would mean opening more coal- and oil-burning plants, thus causing more air pollution.

The anti-nuclear forces argued that steps should be taken to make better use of existing power. More efficient lightbulbs, motors, and heating and cooling systems were the answer, they said. They also called for the development of new energy sources.

In addition, the opponents of nuclear power claimed that the risk of a serious accident at the two nuclear plants was high. Yankee Rowe was 30 years old and the plant's design was old-fashioned. The Nuclear Regulatory Commission ranked Pilgrim as one of the country's worst-run reactors.

Arguments for the Shutdown.

1. Nuclear power is a dangerous technology, as the accidents at Three Mile Island and Chernobyl have proved.
2. The wise use of other energy sources can easily replace the power lost through the shutdown of the Yankee Rowe and Pilgrim plants.

Arguments Against the Shutdown.

1. Massachusetts needs the power provided by these two nuclear plants. Other sources of power will cost more.
2. Shutting down Yankee Rowe and Pilgrim will damage the environment because coal- and oil-burning plants create more pollution than nuclear reactors.

Making Decisions

1. **Understanding Points of View.** Assume that you are asked to speak at a televised debate between pro- and anti-nuclear forces on the Massachusetts referendum. Flip a coin to determine which position you will argue: heads for "Yes" (in favor of the shutdown) and tails for "No" (opposed to the shutdown). Then switch sides and argue the opposite point of view. Explain which argument you find most convincing.
2. **Predicting Consequences.** If the referendum were approved, what effects on energy usage might result? What public health issues might stem from defeat of the referendum?
3. **Demonstrating Reasoned Judgment.** If you were a Massachusetts voter, what position would you take on the referendum? Why? Use the "Arguments For," the "Arguments Against," and "The Decision-Making Checklist" on this page to help you make your decision and develop your answer.

The Decision-Making Checklist

✔	**Clarify the problem.** (What is the issue or conflict?)
✔	**Create a list of possible solutions.** (How might you resolve the problem?)
✔	**Compare the pros and cons of each solution.** (What are the strengths and weaknesses of each solution?)
✔	**Consider your values and goals.** (What is important to you in choosing a course of action, and why?)
✔	**Choose a course of action and evaluate the results.** (What would you decide, and how could you judge the outcome?)

Previewing the Unit

It is 3:59 P.M. on a typical business day. New York City's Wall Street, the center of America's financial activity, is alive with sound and motion. Cars honk impatiently. Men and women with briefcases move briskly from one appointment to another. And inside the New York Stock Exchange building, heat and wildness rule. Hundreds of harried stockbrokers are racing to make their final sales or purchases of the day. They elbow their way frantically through the crowd and shout instructions to their partners, who will quickly negotiate the deals. The action resembles a football scrimmage, or a full-scale riot. At precisely 4:00 P.M., a bell clangs loudly and all trading comes to a sudden halt.

The stock market is only one part of the complex system that is the American economy. This unit explores the many aspects of this system and describes how it interacts with government.

Chapters in This Unit

◄ On the floor of the New York Stock Exchange, shares of stock change hands at a blinding pace.

CHAPTER 20

Economics and Economic Systems

A robotic arm welds together a car body in this modern automobile factory.

Previewing the Chapter

If you walk into a typical American department store, you can choose from a vast array of goods. If you decide to open your own business, no one will tell you what to sell or how much to charge. Free choice is a hallmark of the American economic system. Not all economies work like ours, however. This chapter describes different economic systems and how they work.

- **Before you read,** look up these key terms in the Glossary at the back of this book: *market economy, consumer, inflation, production, gross national product (GNP), standard of living, recession.*

- **As you read,** look for answers to these questions:
  1. What are three major types of economic systems that societies have used to make economic decisions?
  2. What are the roles of consumers and producers in an economic system?
  3. How do economists use economic indicators?

1 What Is Economics?

A farmer borrows money from a bank to buy seed for spring planting. A husband and wife make a down payment on a new home. You decide to purchase a new radio. All of these activities have something to do with money. Money is part of a wider topic called economics.

The word *economics* comes from the ancient Greek word, *oeconomia*, which referred to household management. In the early years of our country, *economics* was used with that meaning. Think about a family living in the wilderness of Ohio in the 1700s. What did economics mean to them? It meant obtaining food and shelter for the long winter months. It meant making decisions about how to use whatever resources there were, resources such as livestock, land, seeds, and tools. These resources had to be used wisely if the family was to survive. If the resources were used unwisely, it might mean hardship and hunger.

The Study of Economics

The word *economics* still refers to the wise management of resources, but the word has come to mean organizing the resources of a country, rather than of just a family. In this chapter, **economics** will mean "the study of the ways in which the people of a society make a living." **Economists** are the scientists who study how people produce the things they need and want. They also study a whole series of related activities, such as buying, selling, taxing, and investing.

Economics is a very complex subject. The growth of world population and the development of science and industry have produced many changes in the ways countries manage their resources. Economists study everything about such management. They collect information on the output of factories and farms. They gather information about workers and the buying and selling of goods. They compare the information they gather in one year with information from earlier years. Sometimes they use this information to advise business firms or the government. The President of the United States has several economists as advisers. With the information they gather, they try to make predictions; that is, they try to answer questions about the future, such as:

- Will there be more jobs for workers next year?
- What might happen if the government reduced taxes?
- If prices are too high, what can be done to lower them?
- Can different business firms afford to build new plants?
- If farmers plant more crops next year, will they be able to sell them?

Answering questions like these (predicting) is not easy. Why? Because the answers to the questions depend upon people and things that economists cannot control. People do not always act as we expect. One year, they may spend heavily on cars and on travel. The next year, they may put most of their money into buying clothing and paying for entertainment. Another year, they may decide to put their extra money into savings accounts. Also, unexpected things affect the economists' predictions. Natural disasters such as storms and droughts (lack of rain) can affect farming and other industries in unexpected ways.

Economics is a *social science.* Economists use the methods of science to study social problems such as unemployment and inflation; then they make predictions about them. They do not rely on guesswork. They cannot predict what will happen with as much certainty as the physical scientists can. Physical scientists can be certain what will happen when two chemicals are mixed in a test tube. However, economists cannot say for sure whether the rate of unemployment and inflation will be higher or lower from year to year.

An Economic System

An **economic system** is an organized way of satisfying people's needs and wants. **Goods** are things that satisfy our needs and wants. Goods include such needs as food, clothing, and homes. They include such wants as automobiles, bicycles, and record albums. Some goods are called **services**. People such as doctors, mechanics, teachers, taxi drivers, and hairdressers provide us with services. Services are used as they are provided.

All countries have some form of economic system to help them deal with the problem of scarcity. **Scarcity** means that there are not enough goods and services for everybody. No society has ever been able to give its people everything they want or need.

In some countries, growing food is limited by poor soil, low rainfall, or a cold climate. Making goods with machinery is difficult or impossible in countries which lack coal, oil, or other sources of energy. Many countries do not have enough schools to educate their people, or enough money to send them to other countries for educations. A lack of money is often a basic cause of other shortages.

Three Important Economic Questions.   Every society must answer three economic questions: (1) What goods and services shall we produce? (2) How shall we produce these goods and services? (3) Who will get the goods and services we produce?

What goods and services should a society produce? Should it build bombs and tanks or houses and hospitals? Should the factories turn out cars, bikes, trains, or airplanes? Should they be large, small, or medium in size? Should soil be used to grow corn and wheat, or grapes and tobacco? Should schools train young people to become farmers and cooks, or engineers and mechanics?

A society must also decide *how* to produce its goods. Should factories use human labor, or should machines do most of the work? Should autos be produced one at a time, or should an assembly line be used to speed up production? Should the harvesting of crops be done by machine, or should farm workers perform this task by hand?

Society plans, produces, and uses goods such as these bicycles.

Decisions must also be made about *who* is to get the goods and services that are produced. Will they go to the few who are wealthy, or will they be divided equally among all the people? How are the important needs of those without work, skills, money, or jobs to be provided for? Will the schools train only those who can pay, or will all persons be given an education?

A Traditional Economic System

Different countries have different ways of making these decisions. In a **traditional economy**, things are done the way they have always been done. Farmers grow the same crops, using the same methods. Hunters and fishers use the same skills they have always used. Homes are built in a certain way, and no other.

Traditional economic systems are found among people who have little industry. The Bushmen of the Kalahari Desert in southern Africa are an example. For ages, these people have been hunters. They have survived from one generation to the next by passing on their hunting skills.

A war, a natural disaster, or a change in climate may bring a traditional economy to a halt, however. Changing the economic system is difficult or even impossible, because people in a traditional economy have come to believe that there is only one way of doing things. For a long time, Native American tribes in the Great Plains lived off the herds of buffalo that roamed their land. Then in the 1800s, railroads were built across their hunting grounds. The railroads brought hunters who killed the buffalo in great numbers and sold the skins for profit. Soon, most of the buffalo were gone. The tribes of the Plains knew no way of surviving other than as hunters. Their economic system was destroyed.

A Command Economic System

Some countries make economic decisions through a command economy. In a **command economy**, the government makes all the major decisions. The word *command* is used to describe this economic system because the economy operates somewhat like an army. Orders about what to produce and how much to produce are made by top government officials. Their orders are passed on to supervisors or managers at a lower level. They, in turn, give orders to the workers. As orders go from the highest to the lowest levels, no one questions them. The Soviet Union is an example of a command economy in operation today.

In some command systems there is very little or no private property. All land, factories, stores, and railroads are owned by the government. Farmers turn their crops over to the government, which gives them a share in return.

During World War II, the United States was in part a command economy. The government controlled the making and distribution of all goods. Automakers were ordered to make tanks or trucks rather than cars. Farmers were told what and how much to grow. Prices, wages, and rents were set by the government. When the war was over, the government released its controls.

A third way of making decisions is through a **market economy**. The word *market* is used in different ways. In one use, a market is a place such as the corner grocery store. In another use, *market* describes the desire of consumers to buy certain products. In times of high gasoline prices, for example, there is a good market for small cars.

In a market economy, the choices are not made by command or tradition. They are made by individuals. A market economy system is also known as a **free enterprise system.** In such a system, people (or groups of people) are free to enter into business as producers of goods or services. The people who start up new businesses are called **entrepreneurs**. They take the risk of the success or failure of the operation. The United States has a free enterprise economic system.

A free enterprise economy operates in a free market. The producers of goods or services are free to sell where they choose.

A Market
Economic
System

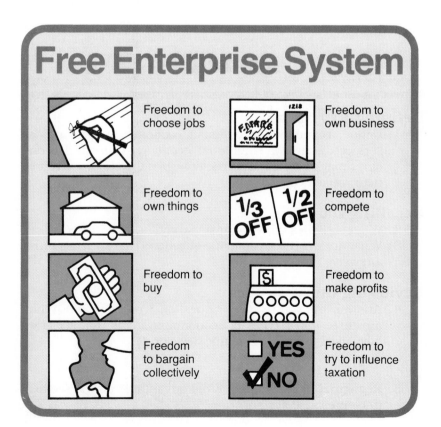

SKILL BUILDER

Which of the freedoms shown in this chart have you exercised?

Buyers are free to buy or not to buy. The producer wants to make a profit. The buyer wants to buy goods and services at a low price.

For example, people starting a small shoe business decide how to make the shoes and how much to charge for them. If the shoes are well made and not priced too high, the company should make a profit. If the shoes are poorly made or cost too much, the company may lose money or even fail.

The United States is an example of a market economy. It is not a pure market system, however. In a *pure* market system, the government does not make *any* decisions about what to produce or about wages, prices, and the like. In our country, the federal government and the states do make some economic decisions. The United States has what is called a **mixed economy,** in which economic decisions are made by both government and individuals. The federal government, for example, decides whether or not farmers may sell surplus grain to foreign countries. Many large industries are privately owned, yet the states and the federal government set minimum wages for workers. The United States government owns and operates businesses of its own. The postal service and veterans' hospitals are examples. Nevertheless, the United States economy is basically a free-enterprise system.

SECTION 1 *Review*

Defining Key Terms
1. Define: economics, economist, economic system, goods, services, scarcity, traditional economy, command economy, market economy, free-enterprise system, entrepreneur, mixed economy.

Recalling the Facts
2. What activities do economists study?
3. What are the three economic questions that societies must answer?

Reviewing the Main Idea
4. Answer "As you read . . ." question 1 on page 390: What are three major types of economic systems that societies have used to make economic decisions?

Critical Thinking
5. **Recognizing Ideologies.** What advantages do you see to a free-enterprise system?

2 What Makes an Economy Work?

The United States produces more goods and services than any other country in the world. This is not an accident. Consumers, producers, workers, managers, natural resources, and our government all contribute to this high rate of production.

Consumers. A person who buys and consumes (or uses) things is a **consumer**. The United States is a consumer economy. This means that most of the output of our factories is geared to the needs and wants of our people. About two-thirds of all the goods and services produced in a year are purchased for personal use. The remaining one-third is purchased by the government or by business organizations.

People in the United States spend more than a trillion dollars a year on goods and services. We spend most money for food, housing, medical care, and transportation. We also spend a lot for alcoholic beverages, tobacco, and luxury items.

Economists are very interested in the spending habits of consumers. The purchases we all make decide the success or failure of many businesses, from a corner grocery store to a large corporation. What goods and services you and other consumers are willing to buy and what amount you are willing to spend on them is called **demand**.

Consumption

Blue jeans are a popular consumer good among Americans of all ages.

Demand is influenced in part by price. If the price of a product becomes too high, most of us buy less of it. If the price of butter is too high, we may buy margarine. If coffee is too high, we may buy tea. If the price goes down, we may decide to buy the product again.

Sometimes price does not have much effect on demand, however. The demand for some products—gasoline, heating oil, and certain medicines—continues, even when they are high in price. These products are *necessities* for many of us. We must have them, no matter how much they cost.

The law of supply and demand has an effect on prices. **Supply** is the amount of a product a producer makes available to a market. If the supply of goods is greater than the demand, prices tend to go down. If supply is less than the demand, prices tend to go up. When supply and demand are equal, the prices tend to stay unchanged.

Inflation results when there is an increase in the money supply and a stable supply of goods. During periods of inflation, prices rise higher than wages and salaries.

Production

Goods and services cannot be used until they have been produced. Making goods and services is called **production**. There are four factors of production: management, labor, land, and capital goods.

Management. Managers are the people who plan and supervise the production of goods and services. The demands of consumers have a strong effect on what is produced. When shopping for goods or services, most of us look for good value. We look for the best products or services we can get for the price. Producers generally try to keep quality high and prices low. Their reward comes in a high number of sales. Management has to make a profit so that it can produce more goods and services.

SKILL BUILDER

According to the graph, about how many dollars did it take in 1989 to equal the buying power of one dollar in 1967?

The Decrease in Buying Power of a Dollar

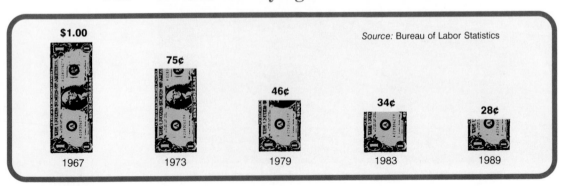

Source: Bureau of Labor Statistics

$1.00 — 1967
75¢ — 1973
46¢ — 1979
34¢ — 1983
28¢ — 1989

Labor.   Workers are important in the production of goods and services. **Labor** is the term used to refer to all the workers in an economic system. The kinds of work usually change from one generation to the next. In 1776, at the time of the American Revolution, most of the workers in the United States were farmers. One hundred years later, only half the labor force worked on farms. By 1980, only 2.2 percent of all workers were farmers. Mechanized farming and improved methods of planting and growing crops brought about this change.

In the last 30 or 40 years, more workers have been needed to provide services than to make goods. A great many people in service jobs work for the government. More than half of all workers today work in service jobs.

There are about 124 million workers in the labor force in the United States. Several million work for themselves. A few million work on farms. The greatest number by far—about 80 percent— work in business or government.

Land or Natural Resources.   Land includes the soil and other natural resources. **Natural resources** are the materials provided by nature—bodies of water, forests, and minerals, for example. Natural resources are limited. They are very important to the

Men and Women in the Labor Force, 1900–2000*

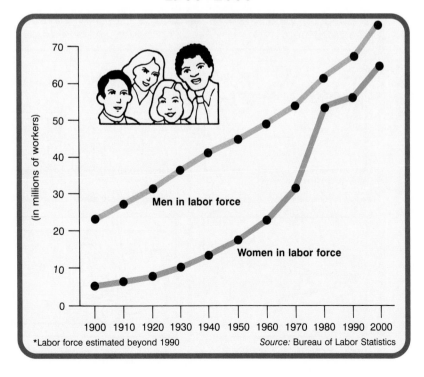

*Labor force estimated beyond 1990

Source: Bureau of Labor Statistics

SKILL BUILDER

In what decade did the number of women in the work force rise most dramatically?

economy of a country. In the United States, there is enough fertile soil to grow a wide variety of fruits, grains, and other crops. In some years, farmers harvest more corn, wheat, and other crops than consumers need.

Rivers provide a good source of electric power used in the homes and factories of the United States. Fairly large amounts of minerals such as iron ore are available. Our coal supply is one of the world's largest. At the present time, however, we use far more oil and natural gas than coal. We have only limited supplies of these two fuels. Therefore, the United States has to import about half of the petroleum (oil) it uses.

Obtaining oil may cause some serious problems for the United States in the future. Foreign exporters of oil have changed their prices again and again in the last few years. Since we depend heavily on imported petroleum, these price changes have created serious inflation. At present, other sources of energy are being explored.

Capital and Capital Goods. The money needed to produce goods and services is **capital**. **Capital goods** are the tools, machines, and buildings used to make goods and provide services. The tools used by a plumber, the machines used to make things, and the factories where the things are made are all capital goods.

SKILL BUILDER

Why is management an important factor of production?

The Factors of Production

MANAGEMENT

LABOR

LAND OR NATURAL RESOURCES

CAPITAL OR CAPITAL GOODS

Defining Key Terms

1. Define: consumer, demand, inflation, supply, production, labor, natural resources, capital, capital goods.

Recalling the Facts

2. Explain why the economy of the United States is called a consumer economy.

3. What is the law of supply and demand?

4. What are the four factors of production?

Reviewing the Main Idea

5. Answer "As you read . . ." question 2 on page 390: What are the roles of consumers and producers in an economic system?

Critical Thinking

6. Identifying Alternatives. Some state governments have placed price controls on certain products such as butter or milk. That is, the governments have said prices may not rise above a certain point. Do you think any products or services should be price controlled? If so, which ones?

3 Measuring the Economy

Buyers of new cars are usually concerned about how cars perform. How many miles to the gallon will this car get? How well does that car perform on turns or at high speeds? Answers to these and similar questions often help buyers decide to buy one car rather than another. In a similar way, economists often raise questions about the performance of the economy. Is production increasing or slowing down? Are consumers spending more money this year than last? Are farmers' profits high or low? In order to answer such questions, economists make studies of wages, production, spending, and other things that affect the economy. The answers to the economists' questions are called **economic indicators**. They indicate how the economy is performing. The most important economic indicator is the gross national product.

The Gross National Product

Economists do a lot of counting. They count the number of goods—cars, fishing rods, shoes, or fountain pens—made in a single year. They also count the money paid for services—in theater tickets, doctor bills, restaurant checks, and lawyer's fees, for example. When they have finished counting, the economists come up with a figure that is called the gross national product (GNP). The **gross national product** is the value in dollars of all the goods and services produced in a year.

The actual figuring of the GNP is done by specialists in the United States Department of Commerce. To get the total amount, the specialists count only final products. For example, in the manufacture of a truck, a great deal of steel is used. This steel was once iron ore. A mining company sells the ore to a steel company. The steel company uses the ore to make steel and sells the steel to a truck maker. Only when the steel has become a finished product—a truck—is its value counted. The Department of Commerce specialists count services in a similar way.

Another way of looking at the GNP is to consider the worth of goods and services. In 1900, for example, the worth of all goods and services produced in the United States was $118.9 billion. By the middle of the 1900s, the figure was $500 billion. In the last few years, the GNP has been over $4.2 *trillion!* A fast growth in the GNP means that more goods and services are being produced. Demand is high. When there is a fast growth, shortages are likely to develop. Prices for goods increase. Your dollar buys fewer goods and services. On the other hand, when the GNP decreases, fewer goods and services are being produced. This can mean a loss of jobs.

Personal Income

Personal income is the money people receive from wages, rent from property, interest on savings, and profits from investments. Social Security and unemployment payments are also personal income.

After taxes have been paid on personal income, what remains is called disposable income. **Disposable income** is the money that all of us may dispose of, or spend, as we choose. The amount of disposable income has increased by a small percent each year for the past 25 years.

What does a rise in disposable income tell us about the economy? Economists say that it indicates a rise in the standard of living. A person's **standard of living** refers to the kinds of goods and services that he or she needs and wants and can afford. A rise in the standard of living in the United States means that most families can afford to spend more money on such things as education, housing, recreation, and medical care. A great many families, however, continue to have a low standard of living because their incomes are far below the national average.

Pay Among Workers in the United States, 1988

Occupation	Average Weekly Pay Before Taxes
Lawyers	$914.00
Airplane pilots and navigators	811.00
Engineers	723.00
Physicians	716.00
Secondary school teachers	521.00
Registered nurses	516.00
Mail carriers	495.00
Mechanics	439.00
Construction workers (not supervisors)	407.00
Bus drivers	358.00
Computer operators	342.00
Butchers and meat cutters	313.00
Secretaries	312.00
Hairdressers	237.00
Sales clerks	213.00
Farm workers	202.00
Food counter service workers	161.00

Source: United States Department of Labor

SKILL BUILDER

Which occupation shown has the highest average weekly pay before taxes? The lowest?

Consumer Spending

How do the consumers in this country spend their disposable income? About 70 percent of it goes into housing, food, health care, and clothing. Spending on other items varies from year to year. This depends on the amount of money that families have left over after paying for necessities. It is estimated that consumers in the United States spend about $4 billion a day.

Economists have made many studies of consumer spending. The results are not surprising. They show that families in the lowest income bracket spend most of their money for food, shelter, or clothing. When shopping, they tend to buy less expensive foods such as beans, rice, or potatoes. They have little money left for medical care, recreation, or education.

The Business Cycle

One problem with a market economy like ours is that it does not always move at a steady pace. For the past 100 years, our economy has gone through a series of ups and downs that seem to be unavoidable. Economists often refer to these up-down series as cycles. A **business cycle** might begin with a period of prosperity with high production and full employment (up). Prosperity may be followed by a period of recession (down). A **recession** is caused by a slowdown in business activity and a rise in unemployment. A recession is sometimes followed by a depression (down). A **depression** is a serious decline in production and a sharp increase in unemployment. After the worst is over, the economy goes into a recovery period. A **recovery** is a period when economic conditions start to improve (on the way up). This is followed by a return to prosperity (up). The change from prosperity to recession (to depression) to recovery back to prosperity is known as a business cycle.

The Great Depression

The worst depression took place during the 1930s. Economic conditions were so bad that it was called the Great Depression. During the Great Depression, the number of people without jobs rose from 1.6 million (1929) to almost 13 million (1933). Factories closed down because people did not have money to buy their products. The GNP fell from $129 billion in 1929 to $56 billion in 1933. Prices for farm goods dropped so low that farmers didn't think it was worth bringing their crops to market. People who

How Far Does a Dollar Go?

The average dollar bill, once printed and placed in circulation by the United States Treasury Department, has a life span of a year and a half. During that time it will change hands about 400 times. Intrigued by the idea of following a dollar bill on its path, *Life* magazine assigned a reporter to select a bill at random and track it from pocket to pocket over a week's time.

Kevin Horan, the reporter in question, began his quest at the Exchange National Bank in Chicago. Horan changed $5 and taped a red *Life* logo to the back of one bill for easy identification. He then used the dollar to buy a bowl of chicken noodle soup at Mike's Rainbow Restaurant.

Five minutes later, taxi driver Bob Clarke visited Mike's, picked up the bill in change, drove around for a while, and left it in payment for a cup of coffee at a downtown coffeeshop. Five hours passed before Mary Ellen Flynn stopped by, received the

marked bill in change, and took it home to south Chicago in her pocketbook.

In the next three days, the greenback changed hands 21 times. It skipped through a sandwich shop, a fish market, several taverns, a beauty parlor, a Chicago Bears playoff game, a hospital emergency room (where it paid off a loan), and a cafeteria (where it bought a cup of tea). Bob Clark III, a businessman who was about to take a plane to Los Angeles, pocketed the bill in a lounge atop Chicago's Hancock Building.

The *Life* dollar flew coach to California. In a suburban deli, it helped pay for breakfast. Lurena Black, a cheerleader at Pacific Palisades High School, popped in to the deli on her way to class and took away the bill in change. When last seen, the dollar was speeding north in a white ice cream truck. It had chalked up 39 transactions in seven days and traveled a total of more than 1,700 miles.

had invested money lost millions of dollars. Both the federal and the state governments started relief programs to help those who were left homeless or hungry by this great economic disaster.

What happened to cause the Great Depression? Some economists blame it on questionable practices used in buying and selling stocks (shares of a company). Many historians agree that the collapse of the stock market triggered the final economic breakdown of the Great Depression. Of course, there were other conditions that played a part. During the 1920s, the rate of factory production increased greatly, but people's wages did not increase at the same rate. As a result, people did not have enough money to buy all the goods the factories produced. The goods remained on the shelves of stores. This surplus of goods led to a decrease in production and, therefore, a loss of jobs . By 1929, about one-third of all personal income was going to the five percent of the people who had the highest incomes.

Also, during most of the 1920s one important group of workers in the economy—the farmers—was going through hard times. After World War I ended in 1918, there was less need for large amounts of food, yet farmers kept on producing huge crops. This created a surplus, and farmers found it more and more difficult to sell their harvests. As a result, they lowered their prices until often they made barely enough money to support their families.

SECTION 3 *Review*

Defining Key Terms

1. Define: economic indicator, gross national product, disposable income, standard of living, business cycle, recession, depression, recovery.

Recalling the Facts

2. What are four major economic indicators?

3. On what goods and services do people spend most of their disposable income?

Reviewing the Main Idea

4. Answer "As you read . . ." question 3 on page 390: How do economists use economic indicators?

Critical Thinking

5. Making Connections. How is a country's standard of living related to its gross national product?

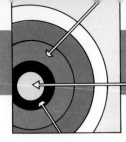

Sharpening Your Skills

Study Skills

Summarizing Information

What was the movie about? What happened in school? How did the game go? When someone asks you questions like these, the person wants the highlights or major points about an event. In other words, the person is expecting a summary.

A **summary** is a brief review of information. An effective summary is careful to focus on just the central issues (the main ideas) and perhaps a few interesting examples that help to explain or illustrate the central issues.

A written summary can take the form of an outline or of several paragraphs. The key to writing a good summary is learning how to select only the most necessary information. Here are some guidelines for the selection process:

- Identify the central issues.
- For each central issue, include one or two examples to support it. Do not simply give long lists of examples.
- Eliminate less important details and information. These details may be interesting, but if they don't serve to make the main ideas clearer they should be left out.
- Since summaries are short, do not repeat information. You will have to rely on your examples to make your main idea clear just once.

Review Section 2 of this chapter. Then read the two possible summaries of the section below:

Summary 1: Natural resources are important to the economy of a country. A nation needs raw materials such as land, soil, water, forests, minerals (such as iron ore),

and petroleum to produce goods. The United States is lucky to have plenty of fertile soil, rivers, iron ore, and coal.

Summary 2: The two basic parts of an economy are production and consumption. Production—the creation of goods and services—involves management, labor, natural resources, capital, and capital goods. Consumption is the buying and using of goods and services. The people who purchase goods and services are called consumers. They create the demand for goods and services.

Which do you think is the better summary? Summary 1 includes many details about natural resources but does not give the reader an overview of the entire section. Summary 2, however, tells what the main ideas of the section are without going into excessive detail. Therefore, Summary 2 is the more effective summary.

Practicing Skills

1. Review Section 3 of this chapter. Then read the list of facts from the section below. Explain why you would or would not include each fact in a brief summary of the section.
   a. An economic indicator tells how an economy is performing.
   b. By the mid-1900s, the United States GNP was $500 billion.
   c. An example of economic depression was the Great Depression of the 1930s.
2. **Identifying Central Issues.** Write a summary for a magazine article that you have read or a television show that you have seen recently.

Government and Law

Insuring the Nation's Banks

In the 1930s, the United States economy was in ruins. One-quarter of the country's work force was unemployed. Thousands of men, women, and children were homeless. Some Americans even feared a revolution. People with money in banks began to worry about its safety. Late in 1932, depositors panicked and rushed to banks across the country to withdraw their money. Many people were too late. The banks had already run out of money and closed. People lost the money they had spent their whole lives saving. Today, depositors are luckier. Savings deposits are insured by the federal government.

The banking industry. Banks are in business to make money. The money you deposit into a savings account is not simply stored in a vault somewhere inside the bank building. Banks use your savings to make more money. One way banks use depositors' money is by making loans. For example, a person who wants to borrow money may mortgage his or her house to a bank in exchange for a loan. The fact that the person owns a house serves as a guarantee that the bank will be able to collect on the loan. Banks also make loans to students who need money to pay for college. In both cases, banks charge interest, or a fee paid over time, for the use of their money.

Banks compete with other institutions that offer some of the same services. For example, savings and loan associations (S&Ls) and credit unions accept deposits and make loans to customers. Together,

The government protects the money in people's savings accounts through the Federal Deposit Insurance Corporation.

banks, S&Ls, and credit unions are known as thrift institutions.

Savings and loan associations began to spring up in the 1800s. They were started to encourage home ownership. Many people who did not have the cash to buy houses were able to buy homes with the help of a loan from the local S&L. Today, savings and loan institutions still invest most of their funds in mortgages.

Protection for troubled times. During the late 1970s and early 1980s, S&Ls were hurt by rising interest rates. Most of their money had been loaned to consumers before the interest rates had increased. They had little money left to loan at the higher rates. As a result, they were not making enough of a profit to increase their interest rates on deposits. Depositors began to panic and take their money to banks where the interest rates were higher. More than 800 savings and loan institutions went out of business. The last time so many financial institutions closed was during the Great Depression in the 1930s.

This time, however, depositors did not lose their money. Their accounts were protected by a government agency, the Federal Savings and Loan Insurance Corporation (FSLIC). The FSLIC insures accounts in savings and loan associations up to $100,000.

Likewise, the National Credit Union Share Insurance Fund (NCUSIF) insures credit unions. And the Federal Deposit Insurance Corporation (FDIC) protects deposits in banks. Today, deposits in almost all American thrift institutions are insured by the national government.

Federal insurance funds act as a safety net. If a bank runs out of money, federal insurance can be used to pay back the depositors. It is unusual, however, for the FDIC to pay off depositors. Usually, the government steps in and helps a failing bank to merge with a healthy one.

In 1987 alone, 265 banks, savings and loans, and credit unions went out of business. Many others survived only with the help of federal insurance. The rescue cost about $1 billion or more for each financial institution.

The worst trouble in the banking industry today is with the savings and loans. In 1988, the FSLIC was $13.7 billion in debt because of failed thrift institutions. Some banking experts think that the figure could climb as high as $157 billion by 1999.

Why is the S&L industry in so much trouble? In the early 1980s, Congress allowed S&Ls to invest in business real estate deals. These are riskier than residential mortgages but earn higher interest rates. These investments allowed S&Ls to attract depositors by offering higher interest rates. When many of the real estate deals failed, the S&Ls had to absorb the losses. Another ruling by Congress permitted many of the hurting S&Ls to stay open. As a result, the cost of the federal bailout grew.

No matter how big the federal insurance debt grows, though, depositors' money is protected. The federal government guarantees it. Americans can have the security of knowing that money they have spent years saving will be in the bank tomorrow.

Questions to think about

1. Do you think that the benefits of insured money are worth the risks of higher taxes and inflation? Explain your answer.
2. One way to fund the FSLIC, the FDIC, and the NCUSIF would be to tax savings deposits. Do you think this is a good idea? Why or why not?

CHAPTER SUMMARY

Section 1   Economics is the study of the ways in which people make a living. Economists are social scientists who try to answer questions about the performance of an economic system. An economic system, or economy, is made up of all the ways in which a group of people makes decisions about the production and distribution of goods and services. In a traditional economy, the decisions are based on the way people have always done things. In a command economy, government leaders make the major economic decisions. In a market economy (a free enterprise system), only private individuals make the decisions. In the mixed economy of the United States, both government officials and private individuals make economic decisions.

Section 2   There are several elements that make an economy work. Consumers, the people who purchase and use products, create the demand for goods and services. If there is a great demand for a certain product but only a small supply, the price will tend to go up. This is called the law of supply and demand. Inflation, or an increase in the money supply, often affects prices, too. There are four factors of production: (1) managers who plan and supervise production; (2) workers who produce goods and provide services; (3) land and natural resources that provide the raw materials of production; and (4) capital, or the money needed to start and maintain production.

Section 3   Economists measure the performance of the economy by studying economic indicators such as the gross national product (GNP), personal income, and consumer spending. From these figures, they try to judge how healthy the economy is and where it is headed.

Reviewing Key Terms

1. Use each term below appropriately in a sentence. Write your sentences on a separate sheet of paper.

   a. consumer
   b. production
   c. recession

2. On a separate sheet of paper, use the following terms to complete the sentences below.

inflation	gross national product
standard of living	market economy

   a. When people's income rises, their _?_ usually rises as well.

b. The value of the goods and services produced by a country in one year is called ___?___.

c. A sharp increase in prices is often caused by ___?___.

d. A system in which economic decisions are made freely by individuals is called a ___?___.

Understanding Main Ideas

1. What do economists do?

2. What is the difference between goods and services?

3. What are three economic questions facing every society?

4. How do sudden changes affect people in a traditional economy?

5. What is the difference between a command economy and a market economy?

6. What is a mixed economy?

7. How does the law of supply and demand affect prices?

8. In what kinds of jobs do most Americans work today?

9. Why is the gross national product an important economic indicator?

10. What is an economic depression?

Critical Thinking

1. **Testing Conclusions.** Socialists believe that all natural resources—air, water, minerals, timber—should belong to all of the people and not to private individuals or corporations. What would be the advantages and disadvantages of this system?

2. **Recognizing Cause and Effect.** Many people buy a great many unhealthful things, such as tobacco, candy, and alcoholic beverages. What might explain this?

3. **Supporting an Opinion.** Some economists favor making consumers pay cash for all purchases as one way to stop inflation. Would you support such an idea? Why or why not?

Practicing Skills

1. **Summarizing.** Look at a weekly news magazine to find an article about economics or the economy. Write a one-paragraph summary of the article. Ask a classmate to check your summary to see if it includes the main ideas and the most important details.

2. **Distinguishing False from Accurate Images.** Consider the following statement: "People in the United States spend more money per year on tobacco and alcohol than on public education." Do research to find out if this statement is true or false.

Focusing on Citizenship

1. **Making a Bulletin Board Display.** Look through copies of several magazines. Find pictures that show items that make up part of the GNP of the United States. Bring these pictures to class and prepare a bulletin board display on the GNP.

2. **Doing Field Research.** Your own school district operates as a separate economic unit in the community. Interview the financial director (or another staff member) of the district. Find out how much the school district spends on each student every school year. On what else does the district spend its money?

CHAPTER 21

Business, Labor, and Government

Projects such as the construction of buildings require the cooperation of business, labor, and government.

Previewing the Chapter

At a meat processing plant, a government inspector talks with workers and company executives about plant operations. At the headquarters of a major airline, government negotiators help settle a dispute between company managers and mechanics. What do these two scenes have in common? They both illustrate the subject of this chapter—the relationships among business, labor, and government.

■ **Before you read,** look up these key terms in the Glossary at the back of this book: *partnership, corporation, dividend, subsidy, collective bargaining, monopoly.*

■ **As you read,** look for answers to these questions:
  1. What are the four types of private business organizations in the United States?
  2. How does the federal government check on business practices?
  3. How has the relationship between employers and workers changed since the early 1800s?
  4. What does the federal government hope to prevent by enforcing anti-trust laws?

411

1 Types of Business Organizations

How would you like to work for a busines firm thousands of kilometers from home? That is fairly common these days. Some firms make and sell products all over the world. United States citizens work in places like Hong Kong, Tel Aviv, and London, and people from other countries work in the cities of the United States. The business world is growing to include new products and locations every year.

Single Ownership

There are more than 10 million business firms in our country today. Most are small businesses owned by individuals—restaurants, stores, beauty shops, gas stations. A look through the pages of a telephone book will show you many more.

Some people want to be their own boss. They like being able to make all the decisions about their hours of work, the price of their products or services, and the locations of their businesses. They also like knowing that whatever profits are made from their work do not have to be shared with someone else.

Most firms in our country are small businesses owned by individuals.

There are some disadvantages to owning your own business. Setting up a business requires money for supplies, rent, and advertising. The single owner may have trouble raising enough money. Failure can be very costly. There is no one to share the losses. Paying off debts to banks may take years.

Partnerships

In a **partnership**, two or more persons agree to set up a business. Often their agreement is in the form of a written contract. Oral (unwritten) agreements also are legal, however. The partners usually share equally in providing money to start the business and in the daily work. Partnerships have generally been more successful than single ownership. One reason for this may be that the partners have different skills. Thus, one partner may have special talent in taking care of money, while the other works better at turning out products.

One problem in this type of business is that one or more of the partners may not live up to the terms of the partnership agreement. Court action is often necessary to settle such problems.

Corporations

The word **corporation** comes from the Latin word *corpus*, meaning body or person. In many ways, a corporation is like a person. It can buy or sell a product. It can enter into a contract. It can sue or be sued in court. Corporations must pay taxes and must obey state and federal laws. Unlike a single ownership or partnership, a corporation lives on even if the original members die.

Among firms with a large number of employees, the corporation is the most common form of business. A charter (permit) must be obtained from a state government to start a corporation. Each state has its own regulations for corporation charters. All of them, however, require detailed information about the proposed business. Charters are usually drawn up by lawyers who are specialists in this type of work. After state approval of a charter, the corporation is free to start business. Corporations are the most successful form of business in the United States.

There are advantages to a corporation. Corporations can raise money by selling shares of stock. A **share of stock** is a certificate saying a person is a part owner of the company. The people who buy stock are known as **stockholders**. They vote for a board of directors. The board appoints managers to run the company. Some of the profits of the corporation may be paid to stockholders. These payments are called **dividends**.

Another advantage of a corporation is the *limited liability* of the owners. This means that a stockholder is not responsible for the debts of a corporation. If a corporation were to fail, and go into debt, the owner of 200 shares of stock would lose the amount of money he or she paid for those shares, but nothing more.

Owning stock makes a person part owner of a company. Stockholders are those who own stock. This photo shows a meeting of stockholders of a company.

There are more than a million corporations in the United States today. Many mining companies, trucking firms, airlines, banks, and natural gas companies are corporations. Corporations account for more than half of the national income and almost two-thirds of all business activity.

Cooperatives

Just as some workers join unions to protect their interests, producers and consumers may form cooperatives. A **cooperative** is an organization in which people join together to buy and sell goods. In some cases, cooperatives provide important services to producers. Farmers use this kind of organization to help store, process, and deliver their products. Prices are set by the cooperative, so each farmer gets the same price for crops.

Another form of cooperative is the retail store started by consumers. People become members of such cooperatives by buying one or more shares of stock. Goods are sold to members at reduced prices. The members are the real owners of the store. They share in any profits.

Defining Key Terms

1. Define: partnership, corporation, share of stock, dividend, cooperative.

Recalling the Facts

2. What usually makes a partnership more successful than single ownership of a business?

3. What are some of the advantages of corporations?

Reviewing the Main Idea

4. Answer "As you read . . ." question 1 on page 411: What are the four types of private business organizations in the United States?

Critical Thinking

5. Checking Consistency. Each year thousands of businesses fail. Yet thousands more are started every year. How would you explain this?

2 The Government and Business

For almost 100 years the federal government did not check on the activities of businesses. In the 1880s, however, a dispute between farmers and railroads over rates led to the creation of the Interstate Commerce Commission (ICC). The ICC was set up to establish fair rates. In later years, other commissions and agencies were created to check on businesses.

The Federal Trade Commission (FTC) is the chief agency which checks on businesses. The FTC was created in 1914. It consists of five commissioners who are nominated by the President and approved by the Senate. A majority of the businesses that take part in interstate commerce come under the supervision of the FTC.

The FTC promotes free and fair competition among companies that take part in interstate commerce. For example, the commission tries to prevent **price fixing**. This is an illegal agreement among large companies to charge the same price for similar products. Price fixing prevents smaller companies from competing

The Government Checks on Business

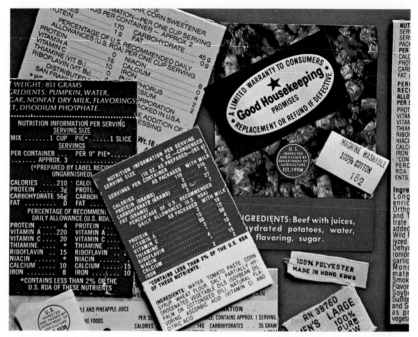

The FTC is responsible for protecting consumers from false and misleading advertising. One way of doing this is by checking all the packaging and labeling of consumer products. Note these labels from various products.

with the large companies. The FTC also tries to prevent companies from illegally agreeing not to compete with one another in certain parts of the country. Illegal agreements of this kind usually make free and fair competition impossible and result in higher prices for the consumer.

Another responsibility of the FTC is to protect consumers from false and misleading advertising. FTC investigators check television commercials as well as advertisements in magazines and newspapers. The claims manufacturers make about their products are examined carefully. Manufacturers of over-the-counter medicines who promise that their products will cure the common cold must be able to prove their claim. The same proof is required of those who advertise weight-reduction schemes, facial creams to remove wrinkles, hair restorers, or cures for cancer.

The FTC checks the packaging and labeling of consumer products. All packages must tell what they contain. The ingredients of a can of chopped meat, for example, must be listed on the label. Packaged food in cardboard boxes must state the weight of the contents. Investigators from the FTC also check the labels on fur and textile products for accuracy. A sweater with "all wool" printed on the label must live up to that description.

Another government agency which tries to protect the public is the Consumer Product Safety Commission (CPSC). This commission was set up in 1972 as a result of a study of consumer safety ordered by President Lyndon Johnson. According to this study, 20 million people in the United States were injured by consumer products every year. The study claimed that 110,000 people were permanently disabled and 30,000 were killed. To prevent death and injury, the CPSC has done several things.

- It has set packaging requirements for poisonous substances. Poisonous items must be placed in safe containers with "Poison" clearly marked on their labels.
- It has required that refrigerators have doors that can be opened from the inside. Many children have suffocated by locking themselves in abandoned refrigerators.
- It has required manufacturers to take back consumer products that do not meet safety standards.

The Government Helps Business

Complaints about too much government regulation of business are heard often. However, many government departments also provide valuable services to businesses.

The Census Bureau takes a formal count of the nation's population every ten years. Bureau staff members also keep track of the output of manufacturing, wholesale, and retail industries. Studies conducted by the bureau show the number of men, women, and children living in different areas of the country. All of this information provided by the Census Bureau can be valuable to those who may be thinking of opening a store, a bank, or another type of business.

The Office of Minority Enterprise gives advice to people of minority groups who want to begin or improve a business. To do this, the office draws on information from other federal agencies such as the Department of Commerce.

The Small Business Administration (SBA) makes loans to small businesses. These loans usually are meant to help build a plant, expand a business, or buy needed supplies. Sometimes a loan may be given for other reasons, for example, to help a business move to a new location. As of 1988, the maximum SBA loan was $750,000 per borrower.

The Maritime Administration, for many years, has granted **subsidies** (money given to private enterprise) to shipbuilders, operators, and owners. The subsidies were to help United States companies compete with companies in other countries. Staff workers in the Maritime Administration also study problems related to designing, building, and safely operating ships.

The subsidies discussed above are direct. There are also indirect subsidies to help businesses. Tariffs are an example. A tariff placed on imported watches serves to protect United States watchmakers. It forces foreign watchmakers to raise their prices. The higher prices of foreign watches encourage consumers to buy

The Office of Minority Enterprise gives advice to people of minority groups who want to begin or improve a business. This man, a Native American, works for a Navajo-owned lumber company.

the lower-priced watches made in this country. Another indirect subsidy is given by the United States Postal Service. Reduced rates are given to firms that mail catalogues, books, and other printed materials.

Through the Department of Agriculture, farmers are able to obtain loans to buy homes, farmland, livestock, and equipment. The Agriculture Department also helps farmers sell their crops. It searches for new markets (at home and in other countries) where United States farm products can be sold. It collects information on weather conditions and crop prices. It broadcasts this information to farmers on radio or television. Workers in this department also carry out studies in soil conservation, disease control, fertilizing methods, and other farming matters.

Other government agencies offer services of various kinds to businesses. The federal government as a whole, however, provides the greatest help of all. As the nation's biggest consumer, it spends more than $1 trillion a year. Most of that money is spent on goods and services produced within the United States. Every month, federal checks go to millions of civilian workers, military personnel, retired persons, and people on welfare. The people who receive these checks spend them in supermarkets, beauty shops, auto dealerships, department stores, and other businesses throughout the country.

The Government Helps Housing and Transportation

The federal government helps the housing industry by providing credit programs. These credit programs supplement private financing of business and housing. For example, the Federal Housing Administration (FHA) insures loans for people with low or moderate incomes who are buying homes for the first time. The Government National Mortgage Association (GNMA) estimated guaranteed loan commitments of $66 billion for 1990.

In the area of transportation, the federal government estimated expenditures of $28.3 billion in 1990. This money is spent on highways, mass transit systems, railroads, air transportation, and water transportation.

SECTION 2 *Review*

Defining Key Terms

1. Define: price fixing, subsidy.

Recalling the Facts

2. Which federal agency checks on the way business is conducted in the United States?

3. What is the purpose of the Consumer Product Safety Commission?

4. What are some of the ways in which federal government agencies help businesses?

Reviewing the Main Idea

5. Answer "As you read . . ." question 2 on page 411: How does the federal government check on business practices?

Critical Thinking

6. Identifying Central Issues. In 1979 the Chrysler Corporation announced it would go bankrupt without government help. Critics felt that the company's managers were responsible and that the government should not help. The United States government decided to provide a federal loan guarantee for several million dollars. Why do you think the government did this for an automobile company and not for other companies in trouble.

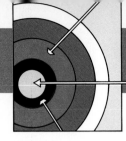

Citizenship Skills

Making Career Choices

"What do you want to be when you grow up?" You have probably heard that question since you were very young. A useful strategy for career planning begins with learning more about your interests and the career opportunities that exist.

Focusing on your interests and goals. People are usually happiest doing work that matches their interests, skills, and values. Answering the questions in the following list can help you to identify career fields that might be good choices for you.

1. *What are your interests?* Perhaps you enjoy playing music or writing stories. How about performing scientific experiments or cooking gourmet meals? Perhaps you enjoy a combination of things.
2. *What are your skills?* You probably have some skills you have worked hard to develop, and other "gifts" that come easily to you. Are you good at making people laugh? At fixing cars? At explaining things to other people? Do you speak a second language? Can you type or use a computer?
3. *What are your values?* In other words, what things matter most to you? Your values may be global (concerned with the world at large), personal (concerned with your individual place in the world), or some combination of the two.

Exploring career opportunities. After you have narrowed down your interests, your school guidance or career counselor can help you explore career possibilities. One resource your counselor may show you is *The Dictionary of Occupational Titles,* which lists approximately 20,000 kinds of jobs. *The Guide to Occupational Explora-* tion categorizes jobs by interests and abilities required. To predict future trends or directions in the job market, *The Occupational Outlook Handbook* is useful.

Investigating jobs. Reading books and magazine articles about your field of interest will help you learn more about it. So will talking to people who already work in that field. Informational interviews, as these are called, let you see the workplace and get a general feel for what a job is like. Set up an informational interview as follows:

- Call for an appointment with someone holding a job that interests you.
- Bring a list of questions to ask the person you will be interviewing. Your list might include, "What would I do on this job?" "What preparation do I need?" "What is the salary range for a job like this?"
- Dress neatly for the interview and arrive for your appointment on time.

Once you have collected information about the careers that interest you, you can begin whatever training or further education you might need. With planning and preparation, the choices you make can lead you to a fulfilling career.

Practicing Skills

1. What book would you use to find a list of jobs for people interested in music? What book would tell you about the need for engineers in the next few years?
2. **Drawing Conclusions.** Carlos is an excellent writer. He values excitement and is interested in current events. What career field would you recommend for him? What specific jobs?

3 Business and Labor

Before 1800, most businesses were quite small. The owner usually worked side by side with the employees. Working conditions were the same for workers and owners alike.

As the use of large machines increased during the 1830s, businesses began to change. Large factories were built. Hundreds of workers operated machines under the watchful eyes of a supervisor. Owners were no longer workers. Some of the owners lived far away from the plant. Workers and owners no longer had a close relationship.

By the 1840s, working in factories was a way of life for many wage earners. The work was very tiresome and often dangerous. The working day ranged from 12 to 16 hours. The 6½-day week

The drawing above shows Frank Farrell (left) and Terence Powderly (right) at a Knights of Labor meeting.

was common. Factory machinery caused frequent accidents, but injured workers received no help from owners for medical bills. There were no insurance plans for workers injured or killed on the job.

Workers' salaries were extremely low. In order to increase family income, many women and children went to work in textile (cloth) mills. Women received lower salaries than men, and children were paid the lowest salaries of all.

There was little that the individual worker could do about poor working conditions. Those who complained about wages or working conditions often were fired. A common attitude during those years was that the owner of a business had rights, but that workers had none.

SKILL BUILDER

How have the lives of union workers improved since 1880, according to this table?

GAINS MADE BY LABOR UNIONS

	1880	Today
Workday	10 hours	8 hours or less
Workweek	6–7 days	4–5 days
Overtime pay	Almost none	1½ times regular pay
Paid vacation	Almost none	2–4 weeks a year
Paid holidays	Almost none	10–12 days a year
Hospital insurance	Paid by union or individual	Paid by most employers

Labor Organizations

Many workers began to think about joining together to protect their interests. They began to form labor unions. As mentioned in Chapter 19, a labor union is an organization formed by workers to try to improve working conditions and to bring about increased pay and benefits.

Early attempts to form unions were strongly opposed by owners. Business firms did not want any kind of union activity. Workers who were suspected of organizing or joining a union were fired. Unions in turn organized strikes or work stoppages to get what the workers wanted. When strikes were called, owners obtained injunctions (court orders) forbidding workers to go on strike. During a strike, police were called to protect the safety of nonunion members going to work. Many strikers were killed by police or by agents hired by owners. Throughout the 1800s, Massachusetts was the only state to recognize the rights of workers to organize to protect their interests. In 1842, the Massachusetts Supreme Court ruled that unions had a legal right to exist. However, it was many years before the labor movement would receive the full approval of the federal government.

Before the end of the 1800s, several large unions were formed. One of the first—the Knights of Labor—was begun in 1869 and

TWO ROADS FOR THE WORKINGMAN ONE LEADS TO PROSPERITY AND THE OTHER TO VIOLENCE AND RUIN.

Labor organizations had great opposition in the late nineteenth century. This 1886 cartoon depicts the Knights of Labor and trade unions as lawless, the Brotherhood of Locomotive Engineers as orderly.

had about 700,000 members by 1886. In that same year, the American Federation of Labor (AFL) was formed. The AFL was a group of *craft* unions. Its membership was limited to workers, such as plumbers or carpenters, who had a craft, or skill. By 1900, the AFL had almost 500,000 members.

The federal government's approval of unions came in the 1930s, at a time when millions of workers were unemployed. In 1935, during the Great Depression, Congress passed the National Labor Relations Act. This act protected the right of workers to form a union. The most important part of that law was the guarantee of collective bargaining. **Collective bargaining** requires the representatives of the owners to meet and discuss working conditions, salary, and benefits with the elected representatives of a union. If both sides can agree about such matters during the bargaining process, a *labor contract* is signed. Should there be disagreement, a vote of the union members decides whether a strike is to be called.

In 1938, the Congress of Industrial Organizations (CIO) was formed. This was an *industrial* union. It invited all workers in a major industry, skilled or unskilled, to join. It was started because the AFL had excluded unskilled workers from membership. In 1955, the AFL and the CIO combined into one labor union—the AFL-CIO.

Many people felt that the unions were gaining too much power. They argued that the National Labor Relations Act had

The Taft-Hartley Act

given too many privileges to labor and not enough to management (business owners) or the general public. Pressure was put on Congress to "restore the balance between unions and management." In 1947, Congress responded by passing the Taft-Hartley Act.

The Taft-Hartley Act forbids unions to engage in certain practices. One such practice is **featherbedding**, that is, requiring an employer to hire more workers than are actually needed. The act also forbids the **closed shop**. This is a place of employment where only union members may be hired.

The act allows the **union shop**. This is a place of employment in which nonunion workers may be hired but must join the union a short time after being hired. The union shop is legal when more than half of the workers in a company agree to it, in those states where the law does not forbid it. Because of the Taft-Hartley Act, some states have passed right-to-work laws. These laws outlaw both the closed and the union shops. They permit only the **open shop**. In an open shop, workers may join or not join a union as they choose.

Labor unions are against right-to-work laws, but most businesses are for them. Union members see these laws as an attempt to destroy unions. Others see the laws as protectors of individual rights. At the present time, most of the states do not have right-to-work laws.

SKILL BUILDER

How many people belonged to the United Auto Workers in 1987? How would their union protect them?

The Ten Largest Unions in the AFL-CIO, 1987

Union	Estimated Membership
1. Teamsters	1,600,000
2. American Federation of State, County, and Municipal Employees	1,032,000
3. United Food and Commercial Workers International Union	1,000,000
4. United Auto Workers	900,000
5. International Brotherhood of Electrical Workers	765,000
6. Service Employees International Union	762,000
7. United Brotherhood of Carpenters and Joiners	609,000
8. Communications Workers of America	515,000
9. Association of Machinists and Aerospace Workers International	509,000
10. American Federation of Teachers	499,000

Sources: Bureau of National Affairs; AFL-CIO

SECTION 3 *Review*

Defining Key Terms

1. Define: collective bargaining, featherbedding, closed shop, union shop, open shop.

Recalling the Facts

2. Why did unions begin?

3. What is the Taft-Hartley Act?

Reviewing the Main Idea

4. Answer "As you read . . ." question 3 on page 411: How has the relationship between employers and workers changed since the early 1800s?

Critical Thinking

5. Drawing Conclusions. Should a worker be required to join a union in order to be hired? Why or why not?

4 Regulation of Business

Competition is another word for rivalry. Competition exists when two or more firms offer the same product or service. Each firm tries to make its product or service the best and to charge the lowest price. When a firm is the only one that makes a certain product or provides a certain service, the firm is said to have a monopoly on the product or the service. When there is a monopoly, consumers have no choice of goods or services. There is nothing to stop the producer from raising prices. Competition encourages producers to provide high-quality goods and services at fair prices.

Monopolies became a problem during the 1880s. Giant corporations began to gain control over the steel, meat, sugar, oil, and tobacco industries. Consumers had to pay high prices for products. They had no protection against poor quality because there were no competing companies.

A large oil and gas company, for example, would open a branch in a small town. The company would lower prices drastically. The low prices would attract customers away from the small firms in the town. In time, the small firms had to close, because they could not compete. The large companies would then raise prices, often making them higher than they had been before.

Monopolies

Monopolies, such as the Standard Oil Trust organized by John D. Rockefeller, were a problem in the United States during the 1880s.

The Sherman Anti-Trust Act

The first attempt to deal with the monopolies came in 1890. Congress passed the Sherman Anti-Trust Act. This act gave the federal government the power to break up companies that had a monopoly on a product or service. A **trust** was a giant corporation that owned and controlled many smaller business firms.

The Standard Oil Trust, organized by John D. Rockefeller in 1882, was typical. Over a period of several years, Rockefeller persuaded the officers of several smaller companies to give him their stock in return for a share of the profits. As a major stockholder, Rockefeller had the power to run all the companies. He and his associates made all the decisions on prices, wages, and production for all these firms.

At first, Standard Oil was made up mostly of refineries. However, as Rockefeller acquired the stock of more and more companies, Standard Oil began to control oil fields, pipelines, shipping companies, and retail stores. Rockefeller ran an efficient operation. His methods, however, were often open to question. Many companies that tried to compete with Standard Oil were driven out of business.

The Sherman Act did not stop the trusts. The trusts in the steel, railroad, and meat packing industries continued to grow. This was, in part, because the wording of the law was very general. The word *monopoly* was never clearly defined. Furthermore, the courts were unwilling to make decisions against large companies accused of breaking the law.

The failure of the Sherman Anti-Trust Act led Congress to make two new attempts to deal with monopolies. In 1914, the Federal Trade Commission Act was passed. The Federal Trade Commission was formed to serve as a watchdog over unfair business practices. The Clayton Anti-Trust Act, passed later in the same year, defined these practices. One part of the law forbade a company to buy the stock of a competing company in order to form a monopoly. Another part forbade the practice of price cutting, which some businesses had done in order to drive other firms out of business.

Some people feel that our government's enforcement of the monopoly laws is not as strict as it should be. In recent years, a new type of enforcement has appeared. Business firms are suing other business firms in court for unfair practices. In one such suit, one company charged another with false and misleading advertising about its products. A court ruled that the advertising had to be stopped. In other court cases, business firms have been required to pay fines for unfair activities.

Many state governments and the national government allow some monopolies to exist. These are called **legal monopolies**.

Public utilities, such as electric companies, are legal monopolies.

PEOPLE HELPING PEOPLE

Banking with a Conscience

A brave bank in Brattleboro, Vermont, has created a special fund that loans money to people in the local community who need it most. The program, began in 1989, has been dubbed "social banking." The idea behind it is simple—to back visions of a better world with cold, hard cash.

Under the program, a customer at Vermont National Bank can invest his or her money at regular rates of return. The depositor is guaranteed that the money will support loans for pressing local needs. In its first year, the bank's Socially Responsible Banking Fund helped low-income Vermonters buy mobile homes and enabled debt-ridden farmers to save their farms.

The chief reason these monopolies are allowed is that competition would cause waste and loss of efficiency. For example, if three electric companies were allowed to provide services in a city, an enormous number of electric wires would be needed. Public utilities monopolies are watched closely by government agencies. In most states, for example, a public utilities commission sets the rates that such companies may charge.

SECTION 4 *Review*

Defining Key Terms
1. Define: trust, legal monopoly, public utility.

Recalling the Facts
2. What was the Sherman Anti-Trust Act?
3. Why are some monopolies legal?

Reviewing the Main Idea
4. Answer "As you read . . ." question 4 on page 411: What does the federal government hope to prevent by enforcing anti-trust laws?

Critical Thinking
5. **Expressing Problems Clearly.** What are some reasons for breaking up a monopoly?

Citizenship

Special Groups in the Work Force

If you flip through the Help Wanted section of the Sunday paper, you will come across advertisements for all kinds of jobs—computer programmers, truck drivers, nurses, short order cooks, and many more. To some people, these ads offer openings into a pleasant future. To others, they resemble a stone wall.

Many people belong to groups that face unusual obstacles in finding employment. These groups include minorities, young people without proper training, the elderly, and the disabled. But there is hope for those at a disadvantage. Working side by side with government support programs, private organizations and employers all over the country are striving to ease more people into the work force.

- **Eden Express,** in Hayward, California, looks like just another small storefront restaurant. In fact, the restaurant's purpose is unique—it functions as a training ground for the mentally retarded. At Eden Express, people with disabilities gain skills that can make them valuable employees in any restaurant.

    Trainees usually begin working in the laundry or the kitchen. As they progress, they learn to interact with customers as waiters and waitresses. After-hours classes and counseling sessions give the retarded men and women practical tips on social behavior, personal budgeting, math, reading, and coping with stress.

    The training program lasts for five months. Eden Express trainees are

Minority students in this job training program are learning to make furniture.

closely watched by a staff member who charts their progress. Many of the program's trainees have spent a large part of their lives wandering the streets or shut away in hospitals. Yet a stunning 90 percent of these "graduates" are able to move on to paid jobs in the work force.

- **Operation ABLE** began in the city of Chicago and then branched out with additional offices in New York City, in Boston, and in Little Rock, Arkansas. ABLE stands for "Ability Based on Long Experience." The "long experience" in the organization's name refers to the knowledge and maturity of people 45 and older who find themselves competing in the job market.

Older workers face special hurdles here. Many are not familiar with the latest job-hunting strategies. They may also be up against hidden age-discrimination by employers. One of Operation ABLE's main challenges, in fact, involves educating employers about the advantages of hiring and keeping older, seasoned workers.

To aid older workers in their job hunt, Operation ABLE sponsors career counseling and support groups. It helps its members polish their interviewing skills and spruce up their resumes. And although the organization does not place people in jobs directly, it runs a toll-free hotline to put job seekers in touch with potential employers.

- Young people who have dropped out of high school are another group requiring special assistance. These young people lack the skills needed to compete in today's job market. **Jobs For Youth** (JFY), located in Chicago, New York, and Boston, helps groom them for better jobs and long-term careers.

As a first step, JFY makes GED (high school equivalency) classes available to the young people enrolled in its program. Students also learn how to track down a job possibility, apply for it, and communicate in an interview. After students have completed the program, they have gained the self-confidence and knowledge needed to apply for entry-level positions in any number of companies nationwide.

Many other programs around the country help people in special groups find gainful employment. Team Work, for example, in northern Virginia, matches disabled young people with volunteers aged 55 and older. These seniors serve as "job coaches" who guide the young job-seekers on their path. Lift, Inc., trains physically disabled people to work as home-based computer programmers for firms in New Jersey, Illinois, and California.

All of these programs help men and women to sharpen their skills and enter the American work force in a meaningful way. The nation gains by harnessing the intelligence of its young, old, and disabled citizens. These special people, in turn, are able to feel the satisfaction of a job well done.

Questions to think about

1. Why might employers sometimes discriminate against minorities, young people, elderly people, and the disabled?
2. What advantages might people who belong to special groups bring to their jobs?

CHAPTER SUMMARY

Section 1   In addition to working for someone else, there are four other ways a person can enter the world of business: through a single ownership, a partnership, a corporation, or a cooperative. Corporations have some special advantages. They can sell shares of stock to raise money, and the stockholders have limited liability.

Section 2   The Interstate Commerce Commission, created in 1887, was the first attempt by government to control business activities. Today, other federal agencies encourage fair trade and business practices and test consumer products for safety. The federal government also helps businesses by collecting useful information, giving business advice and loans, and providing subsidies for certain businesses.

Section 3   Labor unions were formed to improve poor working conditions in 19th-century industries. When workers first took steps to gain rights, they met with strong opposition. In the mid-1800s, labor unions were legal in only one state. By the 1930s, however, several large labor unions had formed, and Congress recognized the right of collective bargaining. In 1947, reaction against the power of unions led to the Taft-Hartley Act, which limited certain union practices.

Section 4   A single firm that has control over most or all of the output of a certain product or service is called a monopoly. Monopolies may lead to high prices for poor-quality goods. In the past 100 years, Congress has passed a number of laws to control monopolies. Still, some people feel that stricter enforcement of monopoly laws is needed. Public utilities are examples of legal monopolies.

Reviewing Key Terms

Use each term below appropriately in a sentence. Write your sentences on a separate sheet of paper.

1. partnership
2. corporation
3. dividend
4. collective bargaining
5. monopoly
6. subsidy

Understanding Main Ideas

1. What are some of the advantages and disadvantages of single ownership?
2. How does a business partnership differ from a corporation?
3. How does a corporation raise money?
4. What is limited liability?

5. What are cooperatives? Describe one type of cooperative.

6. What are three things the Federal Trade Commission does to check on business activity?

7. What kinds of subsidies does the government give to certain businesses?

8. What is an injunction?

9. What is collective bargaining? Why is it important for workers?

10. What did the Taft-Hartley Act do?

11. What is a closed shop? A union shop? An open shop?

12. Why do unions usually oppose right-to-work laws? Why do businesses support them?

13. What are some of the drawbacks of monopolies for consumers?

14. What was the Sherman Anti-Trust Act and why did it fail?

15. Give an example of a legal monopoly. Why does the national government allow such monopolies to operate?

Critical Thinking

1. **Demonstrating Reasoned Judgment.** Many people say it is not the government's job to control business practices. They argue that it is the responsibility of every adult to look out for his or her own interests. Do you agree? Explain your answer.

2. **Recognizing Ideologies.** Is the union shop undemocratic? Would it be fair for workers who receive all the benefits of a union contract to refuse to join the union? Explain your reasoning.

Practicing Skills

1. **Making Career Choices.** Choose a field that interests you and do research to learn about a specific career within that field. Find out the training or education required, working conditions, salaries, room for growth, and so on.

2. **Making a Graph.** In the most recent almanac, look up statistics on the number of work stoppages (strikes) involving 1,000 or more workers. Put this information in graph form. Did the number of strikes increase or decrease in the 1980s? What might explain this trend?

Focusing on Citizenship

1. **Making Comparisons.** How much evidence of competition can you find at the local supermarket? Make a study of the prices of different brands of products such as soap, breakfast food, or canned goods. Be sure to notice the size and weight of the contents of each package when comparing prices. Report your findings to the class.

2. **Watching the Stock Market.** Form several groups. Each group will decide to buy stock in one of the corporations listed in the financial pages of the daily newspaper. Keep a record of the weekly gains or losses of your group's stock. Draw a graph showing the stock's price changes over a period of several weeks.

3. **Learning About Unions.** Interview someone who belongs to a union and someone who does not belong. What are the goals of the union? What advantages does the member find in belonging to the union? Why did the non-member decide not to join?

American shoppers can choose from a wide variety of foods at the supermarket.

CHAPTER 22

Making Consumer Decisions

Previewing the Chapter

Shopping has been called "the all-American pastime." By some estimates, the average 16-year-old in the United States today has about $60 a week in spending money from jobs and allowances. This chapter explains how to budget your money, decide which items are worth buying, and select the best methods for saving and spending your money. You will also learn what to do if a product you have purchased does not perform as it is supposed to.

■ **Before you read,** look up these key terms in the Glossary at the back of this book: *budget, expenditures, unit price, interest, down payment, credit rating.*

■ **As you read,** look for answers to these questions:
1. What is a budget and why is having one important?
2. How can you get the most for your shopping dollars?
3. What are some reasons for saving money?
4. What steps should a consumer take when he or she has a complaint against a business?

1 Planning and Using a Budget

"Biggest bargains of the year! Prices slashed! Stock up now, and save! Sweaters, jackets, and pants—30% to 60% off!" You may have seen advertisements like these in your newspaper or on television. Many stores have special sales in which they offer merchandise at reduced prices. They usually advertise these sales as bargains. Learning how to evaluate sales is just one part of managing money.

The ability to manage money is an important skill. To manage money means to spend and save it carefully. It means to use it wisely in order to have enough to pay for necessities. The failure of many people to manage their money wisely has become a serious problem in the United States.

The Need for a Budget

Each year, thousands of individuals spend far more money than they have. Many cannot pay their debts (money they owe to people). They declare themselves bankrupt. A statement of bankruptcy is a public declaration that a person cannot pay his or her debts.

Thousands of personal bankruptcies occur in the United States each year. All of a bankrupt person's money and property is turned over to a court. The court divides the money, including any received from selling the property, among the person's creditors. As mentioned in Chapter 2, creditors are people to whom money is owed. In most cases, a bankrupt person does not have enough money to pay off all of her or his creditors. In recent times, creditors have lost millions of dollars a year because of the occurrence of bankruptcies.

Planning a Budget

A **budget** is a plan for using money. It consists of two parts. One part lists a person's income. The other part lists a person's **expenditures**—money spent on various goods and services.

Different types of expenditures include needs, wants, debts, taxes, and savings. Needs include food, rent, electricity, water, garbage collection, and transportation. Wants are goods and services that help to make life pleasant—a new refrigerator, a color television set, a vacation trip, or a meal at a restaurant.

Expenditures may be fixed or flexible. *Fixed* expenditures remain the same. They do not change over time. House payments, loan payments, and life insurance payments are examples of fixed expenditures. *Flexible* expenditures change with time, depending on changes in prices or amount of use. Payments for food, clothing, or entertainment are examples of flexible expenditures. Since we can't know the exact amount of our flexible expenditures, we must estimate (guess intelligently) what they will be. Flexible expenditures are often hard to budget accurately.

It is a good idea to set priorities when budgeting. A priority is one of the important items in a budget. The more important an item, the higher priority it has. Needs have a high priority for most of us. We find it very difficult to do without them. Debts and taxes also rank high, since they must be paid on a regular basis. Once a budget has been planned, it is important to follow it.

Budgets show us our spending patterns. A **spending pattern** is a regular way we spend money. A budget can show us if we are spending money on things we really need or want.

In many communities, the Consumer Credit Counseling Service provides help for people who wish to make budgets, but do not know how. This is a nonprofit agency. Its advice is free. The Government Printing Office in Washington, D.C., also has publications that give information about making budgets.

Using a Budget

SKILL BUILDER

What specific kinds of expenses do you think would come under "Transportation"? Under "Recreation"?

How People Spend Their Money
Percent of Money Spent in 1988

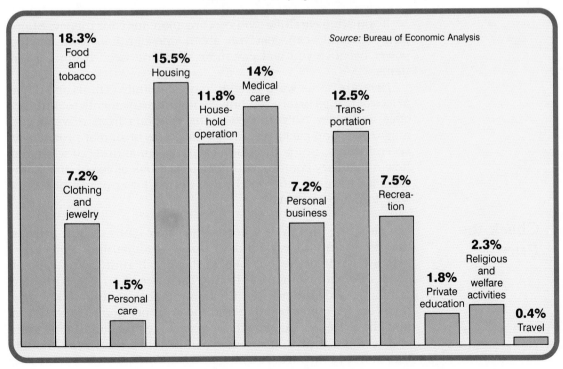

Source: Bureau of Economic Analysis

18.3% Food and tobacco
15.5% Housing
14% Medical care
11.8% Household operation
12.5% Transportation
7.2% Clothing and jewelry
7.2% Personal business
7.5% Recreation
1.5% Personal care
1.8% Private education
2.3% Religious and welfare activities
0.4% Travel

Defining Key Terms

1. Define: budget, expenditures, spending pattern.

Recalling the Facts

2. What happens when a person files a statement of bankruptcy?

3. What is the difference between fixed expenditures and flexible expenditures?

Reviewing the Main Idea

4. Answer "As you read . . ." question 1 on page 433: What is a budget and why is having one important?

Critical Thinking

5. Formulating Questions. Create a list of questions that you would need to answer to make a budget.

2 Be a Careful Shopper

If you shop carefully, you can buy more for your money. Shopping carelessly can cost you about one-eighth of your buying power because you will pay more than you need to for certain items.

Here are some ways to shop more carefully. Think about the prices of things before you buy. Study advertisements to find specials and sales. Clip money-saving coupons from newspapers, magazines, and packages. Check the prices of similar products at several stores. Study the labels on packages to find out what and how much they contain. A higher-priced box of cereal, for example, may have no more food value than a lower-priced box. It is wise to make comparisons.

Check the Price

Check the unit price of foods and other items. A **unit price** is the cost of an ounce, pound, or quart of something. Many markets give unit prices on their shelf tags. If unit prices are not given, they can be figured. To find the price of an ounce of some product, divide the price by the total number of ounces. Multiply the price per ounce by 16 to find the price per pound, or by 32 to find the price per quart. Products in large-size containers often cost less per unit than products in small containers, although this is not always true.

A **discount** is a price reduction. Discount stores buy merchandise in very large quantities. As a result, they are able to sell many items for 10 to 30 percent less than other stores. Be sure to check for quality items, however. Just because a product is cheaper at a discount store does not mean it is a bargain. The product can still be of poor quality.

An impulse shopper is one who buys suddenly without really thinking. Don't be tempted by the shape, size, or color of packages, displays, or sales signs. Make a list of what you want to buy before you go shopping. Then buy only what is on your list.

Try to buy things out of season. Next year's holiday cards and wrappings, for example, can be bought at lower prices for several days after the holidays each year. Summer clothes are often marked down near the end of July or August.

Buy in large quantities with friends or relatives in order to take advantage of reduced prices. Subscribe to magazines for two or three years instead of one. You will pay less per copy.

A **bargain** is an item of high value that is sold at a low price. Do not be deceived by misleading or vague claims. Here are some examples that could deceive you because they are misleading or unclear.

"Special purchase"   "Now only $7.99"
"An unbelievably low price"   "Made to sell for $8.95"

Look for the original price tags on articles of clothing that are offered at "special" prices. Check for quality by looking at seams, zippers, buttons, pockets, and labels. Look for damage, such as rips and holes.

Ask for a rain check when an advertised bargain has been sold out. A **rain check** is a slip of paper given in a store that says you can buy the item later at the sale price.

Look for stores that have high-quality merchandise and that offer true bargains. Shop at stores where the salespeople give honest answers to your questions.

Read signs in stores. See if the store will accept returned merchandise. Ask if cash refunds are given. Sometimes no returns or exchanges are allowed when a store holds a special sale. Some stores allow exchanges but will not give cash refunds. You should find out such things *before* you buy anything.

Look for warranties on the products, and carefully read what they say. A **warranty** is a promise by the maker of a product to repair or replace the product if it does not work. Check to see for how long the warranty is good.

Read all sales contracts before you sign them. A **sales contract**

Check Out
Discount Stores

Do Not Buy
on Impulse

Take Advantage
of Sales

Look for
Bargains

Buy at Reliable
Stores

Comparison shopping, especially on expensive items such as televisions, can save consumers money.

explains when and how payments are to be made when you buy on credit. A contract also tells the amount of interest you must pay on a credit purchase. Ask an adviser at a consumer agency to explain a contract that you do not understand.

Read Before You Buy

Consumer Reports and *Consumers' Research* are two monthly magazines that report on the quality and safety of products such as cars, cosmetics, and foods. Each magazine has staff people who test products in laboratories. Many libraries carry back issues of these magazines.

SECTION 2 *Review*

Defining Key Terms

1. Define: unit price, discount, rain check, warranty, sales contract.

Recalling the Facts

2. How can you tell when a "bargain" really *is* a bargain?

3. What purpose do consumer magazines serve?

Reviewing the Main Idea

4. Answer "As you read . . ." question 2 on page 433: How can you get the most for your shopping dollars?

Critical Thinking

5. Identifying Central Issues. Why is it important to read the "fine print" in a sales contract?

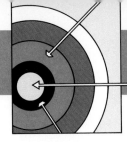

Critical Thinking Skills

Evaluating Evidence

Evaluating evidence is a skill you'll use often as a consumer and a citizen. Evidence is something that furnishes proof. As a consumer, you'll want proof that the stereo speakers you're thinking of buying perform as well as the salesperson says they do. As a citizen, you'll want facts that prove a political candidate is qualified.

How do you get proof? You evaluate pieces of evidence. First you must find information that is relevant, or useful, for your purpose. Next you determine how credible, or believable, the information is. Finally, you synthesize pieces of evidence. This means putting the pieces of evidence together to form a whole.

Finding evidence and determining relevance. In the case of buying stereo speakers, evidence can come from several sources. You could check the library for *Consumer Reports* articles on the best brands and models. You could visit stereo stores and talk to salespeople. You could talk to friends who already own speakers.

Once you've collected a piece of evidence, you need to be sure it is relevant to your decision. For example, a *Consumer Reports* article may tell you which speakers give the best sound for the lowest price. That kind of information would be relevant. On the other hand, a magazine ad may say that a famous rock musician uses a certain kind of speaker. This information has little to do with your consumer decision.

Determining credibility. Once you have found relevant evidence, you next try to find out how credible, or believable, it is. Suppose a stereo salesperson says his or her store has the largest selection of speakers. You could check this statement by visiting other stores to compare.

In addition to checking the accuracy of the information you've collected, ask yourself if the information is consistent, or without contradictions. For example, suppose a salesperson tells you that Brand X speaker has the best sound quality. He or she also says that the Brand X speaker makes a buzzing noise past a certain sound level. The second statement contradicts, or goes against, the first.

Synthesizing the evidence. The last step in evaluating evidence is synthesizing. To do this, consider all the evidence you have and use it to draw a conclusion. You might want to write down the information you collect. You can also list the evidence in order of most importance to you.

Practicing Skills

1. Suppose you want to purchase a new pair of tennis shoes. Which information would be relevant in getting the best buy? Which would not be relevant? Explain your answers.
   a. Your favorite athlete wears Brand X shoes.
   b. A discount store sells the same brands as the downtown stores, but for 30 percent less.
   c. Brand Y is the leading seller of tennis shoes.
2. **Checking Consistency.** Are the following two sentences consistent? Explain.
   a. "We assure you that all of our rental cars run perfectly."
   b. "Any mechanical defects you find will be repaired by our experts."

3 Saving, Borrowing, and Buying on Credit

Saving

When people budget, they often try to keep or *save*, some of their money. They do this:

- to have money in case of illness or another emergency
- to earn **interest** (money a bank pays to people who place their savings in the bank for a certain length of time)
- to be able to go to college
- to prepare for retirement
- to go on a vacation trip
- to buy things which they cannot pay for all at once

There are several ways you can save money. One way is to deposit (place) money in a savings account in a bank, a savings and loan association, or a credit union. A **credit union** is a savings and loan company operated by the employees of a company. Money deposited in a savings account earns interest.

A second way is to buy savings certificates. They are sold by banks and savings and loan associations. A **savings certificate** is a written document which says a person has a certain amount of money in the bank. These certificates usually earn a higher amount of interest than savings accounts. The money must be kept for a certain length of time to collect the full amount of interest offered. If you cash your certificate before that time, you may lose all or part of the interest that has been earned. Money in a

Putting money in a savings bank is an excellent way to save.

savings account, on the other hand, may be withdrawn (taken from the bank) at any time. The interest earned up to the time of withdrawal is not lost.

A third way to save is to buy government savings bonds. A **bond** is a promise to pay someone a certain amount of money plus interest. Bonds also must be kept for a certain length of time before the full amount of interest can be collected. The end of this period of time is called the *maturity date* of the bond. In addition to government bonds, there are corporate bonds that you can buy.

A fourth way to save is to buy property or stocks. Property can be rented or sold at a later date for a profit. As you know, a share of stock is a certificate of ownership in a company. Buying stocks can be risky. If the company has a loss, you as a stockholder will share the loss. The amount you lose depends on the number of shares you own.

Money can be saved regularly through payroll deductions. A **payroll deduction** is money taken from an employee's paycheck by his or her employer. The money is deposited in a bank or used to buy stocks or government bonds. Having money deducted from the paycheck is a way to make sure a certain amount will be saved each month.

All of these ways to save have both advantages and disadvantages. Savings accounts, savings certificates, and government bonds are safe, but the interest they pay amounts to less money than can be earned through buying and selling stocks or property. Also, savings certificates and government bonds must be kept a certain length of time before all the interest paid on them can be collected. Stocks and property may bring a profit if they rise in price, but they can also fall in price. If it becomes necessary to sell stocks or property when prices are low, much of the original price paid for them could be lost.

When you are ready to save some money, ask these questions. How safe will my money be? How much interest will be paid on it? How much profit can I make? How long must I wait before collecting any interest? How quickly can I get my money back if I should need it?

Borrowing

People borrow money for many reasons. They may wish to buy homes or cars. They may wish to start businesses or make improvements on their homes. They may want to pay off their debts. Suppose a family wishes to add a room to their home. They find out it will cost $20,000. If the family only has $5,000, they may decide to borrow the additional $15,000 from a bank. They agree to repay the loan with interest over ten years. In this case, the interest is the money the family pays the bank for lending the money.

You must go through certain steps to get a loan from a bank or a savings and loan company. First, you have to fill out a loan application, listing your assets (money and property you own), and your debts. The bank then checks to be sure that what you say in the application is true. It wants to make sure you will be able to repay any money loaned to you. People who already owe a large amount of money may not be able to get another loan until they pay what they already owe.

Buying on Credit

"Buy now, pay later!" Many people do this. Buying now and paying later is called **buying on credit.** In the United States, consumers owe more than $600 billion for goods and services bought on credit.

There are two kinds of credit—charge accounts and credit cards. A **charge account** allows a customer of a store to buy goods and/or services and have the price put on his or her account. The customer is charged interest on the unpaid amount in the account every month. The interest rate in many stores may be 18 percent or higher per year.

Charge accounts also permit what is known as buying on the **installment plan**. A customer buys an item and then pays a certain amount of money (an installment) every month until the item is paid for. To buy a $1,000 dining room set, for example, a customer might agree to pay $100 down and $50 for 18 months, plus interest. The $100 is a down payment on the dining room set. A **down payment** is the amount of money a buyer agrees to pay before the credit payments begin. In order to attract customers, some stores do not require a down payment.

Credit cards are very convenient, but users must be prompt in paying bills.

Millions of people buy with credit cards such as Visa, Master Card, and American Express. A person with a **credit card** can buy things and be billed for them every month. The card contains a person's name, an identification number, and a date when the card expires. Credit cards are usually good for one or two years, and they can be renewed. To buy something, a cardholder presents the credit card to a salesperson who stamps the information from the card onto a special sales slip with three copies. One copy goes to the customer, one to the store, and one to the bank or company providing the card.

A cardholder receives a statement once every month. The statement lists places where the credit card was used, the dates of use, the amount of each purchase, and the total amount the cardholder owes that month. The cardholder may pay all or part of the balance shown on the monthly statement. As with charge accounts, interest is charged each month on any unpaid balance.

Stores, banks, and companies that give credit cards may take back goods that have been bought if the cardholder fails to make the monthly payments. Taking back the goods is called **repossession**. If this happens, the cardholder loses not only what was bought on credit, but also all of the money already paid on the balance. The cardholder may also lose his or her good credit rating. A **credit rating** is a buyer's reputation as a safe or unsafe credit risk. Businesses often refuse to give credit to people who are rated as unsafe credit risks.

SECTION 3 *Review*

Defining Key Terms
1. Define: interest, credit union, savings certificate, bond, payroll deduction, buying on credit, charge account, installment plan, down payment, credit card, repossession, credit rating.

Recalling the Facts
2. What are some ways to save money?
3. What are two methods of buying on credit?

Reviewing the Main Idea
4. Answer "As you read . . ." question 3 on page 433: What are some reasons for saving money?

Critical Thinking
5. **Recognizing Cause and Effect.** Why do you think many people go into debt using their credit cards?

4 Protecting the Consumer's Interests

There are many laws and government and nongovernment agencies which protect consumers. How many of the following do you already know about?

Federal Laws

The Fair Packaging and Labeling Act requires that package labels list the weight and contents. Directions must tell how the contents can be used. A warning must be given if the contents are dangerous. The Textile Fiber Products Identification Act and the Wool Products Labeling Act require labels on clothing to tell what kinds of fibers (nylon, wool) the clothing is made of. The label must tell how to care for the clothing, too. The Federal Hazardous Substance Act requires that consumers be warned if there is anything harmful in such products as cleansers and insect sprays.

The Truth in Lending Act requires that all installment and credit card contracts tell what finance charges have to be paid. The yearly rate of interest must also be stated. The Pure Food and Drug Act requires that foods, cosmetics, drugs, medicines, and other products that people eat, drink, or put on their bodies be tested for harmful effects.

AMERICAN ALMANAC

Finding a Recipe for Success

Coca-Cola™, the world's most popular soft drink, began in a three-legged iron pot in a backyard in Georgia in 1886. John S. Pemberton, the man stirring that first experimental batch, was a Civil War veteran who ran a small drugstore in Atlanta. His sweet, dark, syrupy drink soon lured many new customers to his soda fountain.

Business boomed. By 1985 Coca-Cola™ claimed 21.8 percent of the $23 billion soft-drink market in the United States.

Then, out of the blue, the company announced it was changing its formula for Coke™. The new version was promoted as being even better than the original, but consumers were not convinced.

They said they liked the original taste just fine. Many protested the change in formula. Bowing to consumer pressure, Coca-Cola™ announced that it had made a mistake. Two kinds of Coke™, both old and new, would be sold from then on.

Ralph Nader has made a career as an advocate for consumers.

Federal Agencies

You read about many federal agencies and departments that check on business practices and standards in Chapter 9. Besides those mentioned, the Office of Consumer Affairs advises consumers about how to deal with unfair treatment. This federal office investigates business practices and suggests how businesses can better serve consumers.

State and Local Agencies

State and local governments, too, have agencies to check on business practices and standards. A state public utilities commission decides what rates gas, electric, and telephone companies may charge. A state department of agriculture enforces laws that limit the use of sprays and chemicals in growing food. State inspectors make regular checks on scales and gasoline pumps to be sure that they measure accurately. City health inspectors see to it that food stores and restaurants are clean and free of germs.

State and local agencies investigate complaints about businesses. If a law has been broken, they issue warnings. You can get information about county agencies from your county consumer affairs department. The county district attorney's office and the state attorney general's office prosecute companies that cheat or trick people. Consumers may also file a suit for from $300 to $5,000 in small claims court. As you remember, the amount varies among the states. Local legal aid societies give free advice.

Nongovernment Organizations

The Better Business Bureau is a nongovernment organization that assists dissatisfied consumers. It is run by the business people of a community. You can write or visit the local office of the bureau to find out which businesses in your area have excellent reputations. The Better Business Bureau checks out complaints and speaks to business people who treat consumers unfairly.

Public Citizen, Inc., is an organization that checks business practices, studies consumer protection laws, and keeps watch over government agencies. Ralph Nader is the head of this organization. He became well-known in the 1960s after writing *Unsafe at Any Speed.* This book described the dangerous features of some automobiles. Nader and his assistants collect information on products, services, and business practices. They write articles and books about their findings. They make suggestions to Congress and to government agencies about how to protect consumers.

Processing Complaints

Consumer affairs agencies give the following advice to consumers who have complaints. First, contact the company from which you bought a product or service. Sometimes the company's customer service department can settle your complaint. If not, you should ask to see a supervisor or manager. If you are still dissatisfied, you should get in touch with a consumer protection agency or the Better Business Bureau. You should bring sales slips, receipts, contracts, and warranties. You should also bring any letters you sent and received about the complaint.

SECTION 4 *Review*

Recalling the Facts
1. What are some of the federal laws that protect consumers?
2. How do local governments help to protect the interests of consumers?
3. What is the Better Business Bureau?

Reviewing the Main Idea
4. Answer "As you read . . ." question 4 on page 433: What steps should a consumer take when he or she has a complaint against a business?

Critical Thinking
5. **Demonstrating Reasoned Judgment.** What would you guess are the most common complaints customers have against businesses? Why?

Government and Law

Regulating Children's Advertising

Promoting everything from super-hero dolls to sugar-coated cereals, American companies spend over $500 million a year on advertisements aimed at children. To look at it another way, out of the four hours a day the average child in the United States spends watching television, almost an hour of this time is spent viewing ads.

Studies have shown that children can become easy victims to advertising. They are far more trusting and easily influenced than are adults, and often they cannot tell the difference between reality and fantasy. Most children lack the reasoning skills and the knowledge necessary to make good consumer decisions. Clever ads can make them want to buy almost any product.

The Federal Trade Commission (FTC) and the Federal Communications Commission (FCC) are two government agencies that regulate advertising. The FTC has the power to put a stop to any advertising campaigns it thinks are unfair or misleading. Citizen groups with a special interest in children's welfare, such as Action for Children's Television (ACT), have helped to persuade the FTC and FCC that children need special protection from television advertising.

Children are especially easy targets for advertisers when a familiar personality is used to advertise a product. For example, ACT showed that when Captain Kangaroo recommended a product, children wanted to buy it. They saw no difference between a paid ad and a personal recommendation. As a result, the FCC no longer permits hosts of children's shows to recommend products.

Television often seems very real to children. Therefore the government closely monitors TV ads aimed at children.

Questions to think about

1. Do you think that children need more protection from advertising than teenagers or adults? Explain.
2. Many children's television shows are now based on actual toys. How does this trend help toy manufacturers? What effect might this have on children?

CHAPTER SUMMARY

Section 1   Many people spend more money than they make. Bankruptcy is often the result. Living on a budget is one way to prevent bankruptcy. In many communities, the Consumer Credit Counseling Service will help people prepare budgets.

Section 2   Consumers can get more for their money by reading labels and checking unit prices of products before buying. They can take advantage of bargains and sales. They can shop at stores with good reputations. They can learn the exchange and return policies of stores. They can read warranties and contracts before buying. Shoppers who aren't sure of the best buys can read magazines such as *Consumer Reports.*

Section 3   Saving for future needs is a good policy for everyone. There are many ways to save—by depositing money in savings banks and by buying savings certificates, bonds, property, or stocks. Savings accounts and other safe investments pay small returns, but there is no risk of loss. There are better returns but more risks to investing money in stocks. Banks will lend money, but they will check credit ratings before approving loans. Credit cards or charge accounts can be used to buy on credit. There is a risk, however, in buying on credit. Failure to make payments can result in heavy losses.

Section 4   Federal laws protect the interests of consumers in many ways. There are laws related to packaging, labeling, finance charges, and the content of certain foods. A number of federal agencies have been set up to inspect the drug and food industries to make sure their products are safe. At the state level, there are agencies that enforce health and consumer protection laws. There are also nongovernment organizations to protect consumers.

Reviewing Key Terms

Match the following terms with the definitions below. Write your answers on a separate sheet of paper.

down payment   unit price
interest   budget
credit rating   expenditures

1. a buyer's reputation as a safe or unsafe credit risk

2. a plan for the wise use of money

3. money spent on goods and services

4. money a bank pays to people with savings deposited in the bank

5. the cost of an ounce, pound, or quart of something

6. the amount of money a buyer pays before credit payments begin

Understanding Main Ideas

1. What happens to a person who declares bankruptcy?

2. What are the main parts of a budget?

3. How do fixed expenditures differ from flexible expenditures?

4. What are some practices that wise shoppers follow?

5. What is a warranty?

6. Why do many people try to set aside some of their income as savings? What are some of the ways that people save?

7. What is a charge account? A credit card?

8. What is a payroll deduction plan?

9. How does the government try to protect consumers?

10. Who is Ralph Nader?

Critical Thinking

1. Supporting an Opinion. Should the government make supermarkets and other stores mark unit prices on their shelves? Why or why not?

2. Demonstrating Reasoned Judgment. Would you favor a law that did not allow people to buy on credit unless they earned over $20,000 per year? Why or why not?

3. Formulating Questions. Imagine that you are an investment counselor. People come to you for advice on how to invest their savings profitably. They want your recommendations about whether to put their money into savings accounts, stocks, bonds, property, and so forth. What questions would you ask a prospective client before giving advice?

Practicing Skills

1. Evaluating Evidence. Identify a product you would like to buy, such as a typewriter or tape recorder. Gather information about different brands, models, and prices from advertisements and consumer magazines. Then evaluate the evidence and decide which item is the best buy.

2. Budgeting. Prepare a one-week budget for a family of four. Show all expenditures for the week. Then discuss the budget with your parents or another adult and ask them if they think it is reasonable. What do they say? Compare your budget with the budgets made by your classmates.

3. Making Comparisons. Imagine you have $100 to spend. Make up a list of items you would like to buy. Compare prices for these items at several stores. What differences, if any, do you find?

Focusing on Citizenship

1. Doing Field Research. Visit the local office of the Better Business Bureau. Find out how this organization helps consumers, and report your findings to the class.

2. Identifying Government Resources. Use the telephone directory to prepare a list of names, addresses, and telephone numbers of local government agencies that help consumers.

Should the Minimum Wage Be Increased?

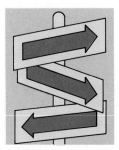

"When Franklin Roosevelt signed the original minimum wage into law in 1938, he stated: 'Except for the Social Security Act, it is the most far-reaching, far-sighted program ever adopted here or in any other country.' Nothing has happened in the past 49 years to change that assessment."

The Issue in Question

Senator Edward Kennedy, Democrat from Massachusetts, delivered the above words on the floor of the United States Senate on March 25, 1987. At the time, Kennedy was introducing the Minimum Wage Restoration Act of 1987.

Should American workers be guaranteed a basic minimum wage, as Kennedy believes? The answer to that question will vary depending on the economist, business leader, or politician you ask. Some people believe that the minimum wage hurts the economy. They claim that business failures, rising unemployment, and rising inflation can all be traced to increases in the minimum wage. Other people claim that the economy has shown no ill effects from raising the minimum wage in the past. These people think that the minimum wage safeguards the well-being of workers at the bottom of the economic ladder.

In other words, more than half a century after it first became law, the minimum wage continues to stir heated debate.

Background on the Bill

The first federal minimum wage law was a product of President Franklin Roosevelt's New Deal. Passed in 1937, when the nation was still in the grip of the Great Depression, this law set a minimum wage of 25 cents an hour. Between 1937 and 1977, Congress passed six laws increasing the minimum wage. At the time of Senator Kennedy's speech, the last increase had taken effect in 1981, raising the hourly rate from $2.55 to $3.35.

Although Senator Kennedy introduced the Minimum Wage Restoration Act in March, 1987, Congress did not take action on the bill for more than two years. Then, in the spring of 1989, Congress considered a bill that proposed increasing the minimum wage from $3.35 to $4.55 over a three-year period. This bill also included a lower 60-day training wage for people who had never worked before.

Those who opposed a minimum wage increase argued that employers would respond by laying off workers. Opponents also said a higher minimum wage was unneccessary because most minimum-wage earners did not depend on their income for survival. They cited figures showing that most of these workers were young people, between the ages of 16 and 24, who did not come from poor families and were not heads of households.

Those who supported the increase in the minimum wage claimed that it would be unfair to do otherwise. They noted that the cost of living had gone up by 36 percent since the last increase and that the minimum wage had never remained unchanged for so long. They also argued that workers earning $3.35 an hour were earning less than $7,000 a year—$3,000 below the official 1989 poverty level.

Arguments for Raising the Minimum Wage.

1. The minimum wage had not been raised between 1981 and 1989, while inflation had decreased the value of the dollar by more than a third during that period.
2. Raising the minimum wage had never caused dramatic increases in unemployment or inflation in the past.

Arguments Against Raising the Minimum Wage.

1. Raising the minimum wage would lead to business failures, as well as increases in inflation and unemployment.
2. The typical minimum wage worker does not come from a poor family and does not need the income to support a family.

Making Decisions

1. **Identifying Alternatives.** What might Congress do, other than raise the minimum wage, to protect low-paid workers from poverty? Do you think this action would be better or worse than raising the minimum wage? Explain.
2. **Formulating Questions.** Develop a list of five questions that would help you gather additional information regarding the decision to raise the minimum wage. Where would you go to find the answers to these questions?
3. **Demonstrating Reasoned Judgment.** If you had been a member of Congress in 1989 and had to vote on the proposed increase in the minimum wage, what position would you have taken? Why would you have taken that position? Use the "Arguments For," the "Arguments Against," and "The Decision-Making Checklist" on this page to help you make your decision and develop your answer.

The Decision-Making Checklist

✔	**Clarify the problem.** (What is the issue or conflict?)
✔	**Create a list of possible solutions.** (How might you resolve the problem?)
✔	**Compare the pros and cons of each solution.** (What are the strengths and weaknesses of each solution?)
✔	**Consider your values and goals.** (What is important to you in choosing a course of action, and why?)
✔	**Choose a course of action and evaluate the results.** (What would you decide, and how could you judge the outcome?)

6 Government and World Affairs

Previewing the Unit

The first snow of the season was drifting through the streets of Reykjavik, Iceland, in late 1986. Even inside the white-shingled house where President Ronald Reagan and Soviet leader Mikhail Gorbachev sat talking, a chill seemed to hang in the air. The two men had agreed to discuss cutting back the number of nuclear weapons each of their countries had. Yet years of mistrust between the United States and the Soviet Union kept the men wary of each other. When they ended their meeting neither one felt it had been a success.

Nonetheless, the Iceland trip was a step toward warmer relations between the two superpowers—and a step toward peace. One year later, Reagan and Gorbachev signed the Intermediate Nuclear Forces (INF) Treaty in Washington, D.C. In this unit, you will learn about America's often complicated relations with other countries of the world.

Chapters in This Unit

◀ This brilliant display of international flags underscores the close ties that exist today among the countries of the world.

CHAPTER 23

Making Foreign Policy

Sections in This Chapter

This Marine Corps drill team symbolizes the nation's readiness to defend itself, a key part of foreign policy.

Previewing the Chapter

When George Washington left the Presidency in 1796, he hoped that the United States would "steer clear of permanent alliances with any portion of the foreign world." For many years, government leaders tried to follow Washington's advice. Today, however, the United States takes an active role in foreign affairs. This chapter explains how our government decides on its foreign policies, and how those policies have changed over time.

■   **Before you read,** look up these key terms in the Glossary at the back of this book: *satellite, containment, mutual defense pact, terrorism, isolationism.*

■   **As you read,** look for answers to these questions:
   1. What have been the major foreign policy goals of the United States in recent years?
   2. What is the President's role in American foreign policy?
   3. What are two factors that help shape American foreign policy?
   4. What are the three main periods of American foreign policy, and how do they differ from each other?

1 What Is Foreign Policy?

The **foreign policy** of the United States is a plan that determines how our country acts toward the rest of the world. The ideas in this plan change from time to time depending on what is happening in the world. The President, along with many advisers, decides what the country's foreign policy is to be. Plans are then made to decide how to carry out this policy.

In recent times, the foreign policy of the United States has had three main goals. One goal is to protect and to promote our interests around the world. A second is to help other countries further their interests if they don't conflict with ours. A third is to promote peace and friendship among all countries.

We have tried to achieve these foreign policy goals in a number of ways—opposing communism, working for peace and friendship, raising the standard of living for all people, and encouraging understanding between the United States and other countries.

Leaders in the United States have been concerned about the efforts of the Soviet Union to set up communist dictatorships in other countries. During World War II, the Soviet army moved into many Eastern European countries. It remained there when the war ended in 1945. These Soviet-controlled countries are often called satellites. A **satellite** is a weak country controlled by a more powerful country. The Soviets did not give the people in the satellite countries the right to choose the kinds of government they wanted.

Opposition to Communism

At the same time that Eastern Europe was struggling with the Soviet Union, communist troops and government troops fought a war in China. In 1949, the communists won. The non-communist leaders of China set up a government on the island of Taiwan. Taiwan is in the China Sea about 160 kilometers (100 miles) southeast of mainland China.

The success of communist forces in Eastern Europe and China alarmed leaders of the United States government. They feared that communist-supported armies would try to take over other countries in the world. As a result, the United States developed a policy of **containment**. To contain something is to keep it from spreading. As part of its foreign policy, the United States gave military equipment, money, and military advisers to countries in danger of communist takeover. Our leaders also developed military alliances around the world.

The United States decided to send weapons and other military aid to non-communist countries to help them resist communist

Military Assistance

The United States gave aid to non-communist countries after World War II to help them resist communism. In 1948, Greece was one of the first countries to receive this aid.

forces. In 1948, Greece and Turkey were the first to receive this aid. Both countries shared borders with the Soviet Union or its satellites. In later years, the United States sent billions of dollars worth of military equipment and supplies to dozens of other countries in Asia, Latin America, and Africa. It continues to do so today.

In 1948, the United States and several countries in Europe formed the North Atlantic Treaty Organization (NATO). The NATO countries signed a mutual defense pact. A **mutual defense pact** is an agreement among countries to come to each other's aid if one of them is attacked.

Since 1948, the United States has signed several other mutual defense pacts. These agreements have expanded to involve 40 or more countries in Europe, Asia, and Latin America. Under the terms of some of these defense pacts, the United States has stationed thousands of military persons in other countries. It has spent billions of dollars building bases and providing equipment and weapons to other nations. Today, the United States continues to maintain bases in many countries. Also, the United States Navy patrols the seas around the world.

Reuniting a War-Torn Family

Back in 1980, Quoc Tan Pham left Vietnam in a small boat he had helped to build. Four days later, he was picked up by a U.S Navy ship and taken to Singapore. Eventually he made it to the United States and began a new life.

Pham, a former officer in the South Vietnamese navy, had fled his homeland after the North Vietnamese took over. He was forced to leave behind his wife and three young children. But his missing family members were never far from his thoughts during the nine years it took him to win their freedom. He wrote them every month, but he was just one man with little influence thousands of miles away.

The struggle was not his alone. Friends and neighbors in Methuen, Massachusetts, where Pham had settled, were touched by his dream of a family reunion. Students and teachers at Methuen High School wrote 1,400 letters asking the Vietnamese government to let the Phams leave Vietnam and come to the United States.

All this hard work and community involvement paid off on the evening of March 15, 1989. A plane landed at Logan Airport in Boston. Three Vietnamese children and a young woman rushed joyfully from the plane into Pham's waiting arms. "If I had known it would take nine years to get them out of Saigon, I never would have left," Pham said.

Peace and Friendship

Since the United Nations (UN) was created in 1945, all Presidents of the United States have supported its efforts to preserve world peace. On many occasions, the United States has supported UN resolutions calling for peaceful settlement of disputes between countries. It was at a meeting of the UN in 1955 that the United States announced to the world its policy of utilizing nuclear power only for peaceful uses. Our leaders have asked other countries to follow a similar policy. The United States has joined with other members of the UN in trying to bring peace to the Middle East, an area of great tension for more than 40 years. Our Secretary of State has worked with leaders of Israel and the Arab nations to establish a permanent peace in the Middle East.

The United States has tried to develop friendly relations with the Soviet Union and the People's Republic of China. All three countries have expressed their interest in peaceful coexistence. The leaders of these countries want to live peacefully and not threaten each other's interests. Treaties have been signed with the Soviet Union to reduce armaments. Friendly relations with the People's Republic of China were restored in 1972. Tensions returned, however, in 1989 when the Chinese government used violence against Chinese students demanding democratic reform.

Musicians from the United States sometimes go to foreign countries to perform. This man is a member of an American orchestra that has given concerts in the People's Republic of China.

Increasing the Standard of Living

In 1949, President Harry Truman stated: "Our aim should be to help the free peoples of the world, through their own efforts, to produce more food, more clothing, more materials for housing, and more mechanical power to lighten their burdens. The American people desire, and are determined to work for, a world in which all nations and all people are free to achieve a decent and satisfying life."

Since World War II, the United States has made President Truman's statement an important part of its foreign policy. We have given more than $400 billion in aid to more than 100 countries. Thousands of our technicians, farmers, teachers, engineers, and other experts have gone to other countries to help people build homes, factories, hospitals, and schools.

Promoting Knowledge and Understanding

The United States has sent scientists, educators, writers, artists, athletes, and musicians to visit, study, and perform in other countries. Similar people from other countries are invited to visit, study, and perform in our country. Thousands of foreign students have been given special permission to study in the United States. Scholars and artists from many countries have been brought together to exchange knowledge in science, medicine, technology, and the arts.

For the most part, the foreign policy of the United States tries to make the world a better place. Some people say, however, that sometimes the United States government has given aid to dictatorships. They say that, at times, it has failed to help ethnic groups in other countries who were seeking fair treatment from their governments.

Defining Key Terms

1. Define: foreign policy, satellite, containment, mutual defense pact.

Recalling the Facts

2. What is the purpose of NATO?

3. What has the United States done to improve the standard of living in developing countries?

Reviewing the Main Idea

4. Answer "As you read . . ." question 1 on page 454: What have been the major foreign policy goals of the United States in recent years?

Critical Thinking

5. Demonstrating Reasoned Judgment. Should the United States ever help a country that is unfriendly toward it? If so, under what circumstances?

2 Who Makes Foreign Policy?

The Constitution gives both the President and the Congress power to make foreign policy. The President can:

- negotiate treaties
- receive ambassadors (official representatives) from other countries
- appoint United States ambassadors to other countries
- command the military forces of the United States

In Chapter 7, you learned that the President is not only Commander in Chief of the armed forces, but also chief legislator and chief diplomat. The President fills all these roles in conducting foreign policy. As chief legislator, the President suggests laws that involve relationships with other countries. In the yearly State of the Union Message to Congress, the President says what should be done in foreign relations. The President meets with leaders of Congress on foreign matters. Presidential assistants attend the meetings of congressional committees and present in-

The President and Foreign Policy

formation about foreign policy. Information is given to explain why Congress should support presidential policies.

In 1978, President Jimmy Carter sent the Panama Canal Treaty to the Senate for approval. In the treaty, the United States agreed to turn over the Canal Zone to Panama before the year 2000. President Carter's advisers gave the Senators information about the treaty and answered their questions. Some Senators asked for changes in the treaty. The President accepted some of these changes to please these Senators. He knew that their support was needed to approve the treaty.

Sometimes Congress does not agree with the President. At such times, it may not appropriate the money the President needs to carry out foreign policy. Sometimes Congress may pass laws which limit presidential power in dealing with foreign matters.

The President Meets Foreign Leaders

As chief diplomat of the United States, the President meets with the leaders and representatives of other countries. Much of the diplomatic work of the government is done by the Secretary of State. The Secretary of State is the President's chief assistant in foreign affairs. There are also special and regular ambassadors who help the President in shaping foreign policy. The President not only meets leaders of other countries when they come to the United States but also travels to other countries to discuss world affairs.

President Richard Nixon went to the People's Republic of China in 1972. This was the first time a United States President

President George Bush is shown walking with South Korean leaders during a visit to their country in February, 1989.

had ever visted that country. President Jimmy Carter went to Egypt and Israel in 1978 to help these two nations develop a peace agreement. In the spring of 1988, President Ronald Reagan made a historic visit to Moscow for talks with Soviet leader Mikhail Gorbachev.

Several Presidents have used the Army and the Navy to carry out the foreign policy of the United States. President Harry Truman sent United States troops into combat in 1950 when North Korea attacked South Korea. Presidents John Kennedy, Lyndon Johnson, and Richard Nixon sent several thousand troops to help the South Vietnamese in the 1960s and early 1970s. President Jimmy Carter ordered naval ships to the Persian Gulf area in 1980 after the Soviet Union invaded Afghanistan. In 1987, President Reagan again sent naval forces to the Persian Gulf.

Congress and Foreign Policy

Since the Constitution does not clearly state limits on how much power the President or the Congress may use in foreign policy, the two often conflict. At various times in history, one has been more powerful than the other. Since World War II, the President has been the more powerful.

The President's powers as Commander in Chief are limited, however. Only Congress—not the President—may declare war. Furthermore, Congress authorizes how much money the President may spend on the military. In 1973, because of the growing unpopularity of the war in Vietnam, Congress passed the War Powers Act. This act forbids the President to commit troops to combat for longer than 60 days without Congress's approval.

The President must have the support of Congress to develop and carry out our country's foreign policy. Suppose the President makes an agreement with another country to lower tariffs on certain products. The agreement would go into effect only if approved by Congress. Congress examines the President's foreign policy proposals that need its support. It questions the President's advisers in committee meetings.

The President talks about foreign policy matters with congressional leaders of both parties and with members of the Foreign Relations, Armed Services, and other key committees. These congressional leaders can influence the way other members of Congress vote. In statements to the press, they can also persuade the public to support or oppose the President's foreign policy.

Presidential Advisers

Each President chooses many advisers on foreign policy. Some of these advisers hold government positions. Others are private citizens whose opinions the President values, such as former Cabinet members, professors, and retired military leaders.

The Secretary of State, the Secretary of Defense, the Joint Chiefs of Staff, the Director of the CIA, and the National Security

Adviser, however, are the President's main advisers on foreign policy. They report to the President on the foreign policies of other countries. These advisers keep the President informed about the military strength of the United States and other countries. They give their opinions about what policies the United States should follow and how the country should act when a crisis develops. The President seriously considers their advice when making decisions.

In carrying out foreign policy, the President is also assisted by the United States Foreign Service. The Foreign Service consists of all the ambassadors who represent the United States abroad, and other professional diplomats who hold key positions in the State Department. The ambassadors are the President's personal representatives to the governments of other countries. Ambassadors and other diplomats carry out the day-to-day relations between the United States and other governments.

Other agencies help the President in foreign policy making: the Agency for International Development (AID), the United

This Peace Corps volunteer shares his building skills with some Kenyans.

States Information Agency (USIA), the Peace Corps, and the Arms Control and Disarmament Agency. The job of AID is to grant loans and provide technical help to countries that need either or both. The task of USIA is to encourage the people of other countries to have a positive attitude toward the United States. It does this by setting up libraries and information centers for the people to use. USIA also broadcasts a radio program called The Voice of America.

The Peace Corps was created by President John F. Kennedy in 1961. The corps is made up of men and women who volunteer to help people in developing countries. Thousands of volunteers have served as teachers, doctors, farmers, and in many other jobs in over 60 countries. Men and women af all ages and walks of life have joined the Peace Corps. They are trained for a 9- to 14-week period in the language and culture of the people they will serve. They are also taught technical skills. Volunteers serve for a two-year period. During their service, they live among the people of their host countries. Peace Corps volunteers usually work in projects related to agricultural and rural development, health, ecucation, and small businesses.

The Peace Corps

SECTION 2 *Review*

Recalling the Facts
1. How must the President acquire the funds he or she needs to carry out foreign policy?
2. How does the War Powers Act of 1973 limit the President's power to carry out foreign policy?
3. Who are the President's chief advisers with regard to making and carrying out foreign policy?

Reviewing the Main Idea
4. Answer "As you read . . ." question 2 on page 454: What is the President's role in American foreign policy?

Critical Thinking
5. **Identifying Assumptions.** Why do you think the Framers of the Constitution gave Congress, rather than the President, the power to declare war? Do you think this was a wise decision?

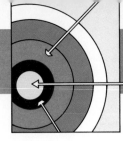
Interpreting Political Cartoons

Political cartoons are clever drawings that focus on people, events, and issues related to government. The underlying purpose of many political cartoons is to criticize someone or something related to government, often by using humor. Beyond the cartoon's humor, there is usually a serious message that expresses the cartoonist's view on a current political issue.

Interpreting political cartoons involves some of the same skills you use to interpret pictures: describing what you see in the cartoon; telling how the objects, people, and actions are related; identifying the main idea or purpose of the cartoon; and describing the feelings or mood the cartoon suggests.

There are several important points to remember about political cartoons:

- Political cartoons are not meant to be realistic drawings. Sometimes details are left out. Sometimes figures are drawn much larger or smaller than they really are to emphasize the cartoonist's message. For example, to show that one person is more powerful than another, a cartoonist might make the first figure much larger than the second.
- Caricatures, or exaggerated likenesses of people, are common in political cartoons. For example, cartoonists often drew President Ronald Reagan with a thick crop of jet-black hair. Cartoons of Michael Dukakis, the Democratic candidate for President in 1988, often showed him with very bushy eyebrows.
- Cartoonists may use symbols to give information. One familiar symbol for the

United States is Uncle Sam (whose name bears the same initials as those of the United States—U.S.). The cartoon on page 469 shows Uncle Sam as an older man with white chin whiskers and a red, white, and blue costume of stripes and stars.

How do you interpret a political cartoon? Begin by checking for a title, caption, or any labels written within the cartoon itself. Next, ask yourself these questions:

- What topic or issue does the cartoon address?
- What is the cartoonist's message or point of view?

Be sure that you also look for symbols and caricatures and think about what the cartoonist is using them to express.

Study the political cartoon below and then answer the questions that follow.

Practicing Skills

1. What symbols has the cartoonist used?
2. **Drawing Conclusions.** What is the message of this cartoon? How does the cartoonist convey this meaning?

3 What Influences American Foreign Policy?

Several factors and forces influence those who shape the foreign policy of the United States. A desire to protect our business investments abroad or to obtain needed raw materials, for example, may cause the United States to sign treaties with one country or another. A wish to help a friendly nation keep a democratic government in power and resist the spread of communism may cause us to form a military alliance.

Various factors can affect foreign policy. Let us use the foreign policy of the United States toward the nations of the Middle East as an example. The Middle East is the area at the eastern end of the Mediterranean Sea. It includes the countries of Southwest Asia and North Africa.

The United States and the Middle East

Several developments influenced United States foreign policy toward the Middle East in the 1970's. One was the conflict between the Arab nations—Egypt, Syria, Jordan, Iraq, and Saudi Arabia—and Israel. The Arab nations and Israel have long been unfriendly toward each other. The Arabs claim that the area occupied by the state of Israel belongs to the Palestinian people. The Palestinians are Arabs who lived in areas that are either now part of Israel or controlled by it. Many Palestinians left their homes when Israel became independent in 1948. Others left during the war in 1967 when Israel seized their land. Since leaving, many have had to live in refugee camps.

Since 1948, four wars have been fought between Israel and the Arab nations. In each war, the Arab nations could not achieve their goal: the destruction of Israel as a sovereign (self-governing) state. As a result of these wars, the number of Palestinians in refugee camps has climbed.

The plight of the Palestinians in refugee camps has been a major cause of ongoing tension in the Middle East. Sympathy for those living in the refugee camps has also increased public support for a Palestinian homeland.

In 1964, the Palestine Liberation Organization (PLO) was formed to represent Palestinian Arabs. The PLO's goal was, at first, to free their homeland from Israel's control. By 1967, the PLO had become an extremist group committed to the destruction of the state of Israel. The methods the PLO has employed have included many acts of terrorism around the world. **Terrorism** is the use of violence to achieve a political goal. The PLO and other Arab terrorist groups that oppose American support for Israel have hijacked airplanes, carried out bombings, and taken Americans hostage. Such activities continue to hurt peace efforts in the Middle East.

The Soviet Union and the Middle East

Another influence on the Middle Eastern policy of the United States is the effort of the Soviet Union to set up military bases in the Middle East. The Suez Canal in Egypt is part of an important ship route between Europe and Asia. Neither Egypt nor the United States wants the Soviet Union to be in a position to control the canal. The Middle East has large oil supplies that are needed by many countries, including the United States. The United States does not want the Soviet Union to influence or to control the countries that own this oil.

By the early 1970s, the Soviet Union had supplied weapons and advisers to Egypt, Syria, and Iraq in their wars against Israel. It had armed Palestinian fighters who attacked Israel from bases in Syria, Lebanon, and Iraq. The Soviets had also obtained a naval base at Alexandria, Egypt, on the Mediterranean Sea.

The United States and Israel

The United States has supported Israel since it became a nation. A chief reason for this support is that Israel is the only democracy in the Middle East. The leaders of the United States believe that Israel can help block Soviet activity in the area. Some United States citizens have economic interests in Israel. Others have cultural or family ties. These citizens use their influence to persuade Congress to send aid to Israel.

The United States and the Arab States

The United States is friendly with some of the Arab states of the Middle East. Many Arabs living in the United States want our government to help the Arab countries. They want the United States to recognize the Palestinians' claims to land held by Israel. United States companies, especially those involved in oil, want their interests in the Arab states protected. The Arab-Israeli wars and the threat of Soviet influence have threatened these interests.

Egypt and Israel

In the late 1970s, President Jimmy Carter met with the leaders of Egypt and Israel to bring about a peace agreement. He invited them to the United States and he also went to their countries. In March of 1979, the leaders of Egypt and Israel signed the treaty in Washington, D.C. President Carter was considered for the Nobel Peace Prize because of his efforts. Egypt's leaders ordered the Soviets to leave their country before the peace talks started. Egypt then turned to the United States for military and economic assistance. The United States agreed to provide this aid to Egypt and other Arab states as well as to Israel.

Many United States companies do business with Saudi Arabia.

President Reagan issued a peace plan for the Middle East in 1982. The plan attempted to satisfy both Israel and the Arab states. Israel rejected the plan because it forbade Israelis to live on the West Bank, land gained by Israel in a 1967 war. The Arab states rejected the plan because it did not provide for an independent Palestinian state.

Also, the war in Lebanon demanded attention. Israel invaded southern Lebanon in 1982 vowing to drive out the PLO and the Soviet-backed Syrians. Civil war broke out as Christian forces supported by the U.S. and Israel fought Islamic forces backed by Syria. The U.S. attempted to aid the Christian Lebanese government and negotiate a troop withdrawal for Israel and Syria. President Reagan ordered U.S. Marines to serve as a peacekeeping force during the negotiations. In 1984, when a terrorist attack on Marine headquarters killed over 200 Marines, American troops were withdrawn. Israel withdrew its troops in 1985, but Lebanon has remained a trouble spot.

Lebanon and Israel

In recent years, especially since 1979, another major problem area in the Middle East has involved a non-Arab nation—Iran. From 1979 to 1989 Iran was under the rule of the Ayatollah Khomeini, who pursued fiercely anti-Western policies.

In 1980, a series of border disputes led to open warfare between Iran and Iraq. Attacks by fighter-bombers and heavy ground fighting resulted in heavy casualties on both sides. In 1984, the Iran-Iraq war expanded to the Persian Gulf. Planes from both nations attacked oil tankers. These attacks threatened the access of many nations, including the United States, to the oil of the Middle East. In 1988, President Reagan ordered the U.S. Navy to escort oil tankers through the Persian Gulf. Finally, the bloody nine-year Iran-Iraq war was halted by a 1988 ceasefire.

Iran and Iraq

Defining Key Terms

1. Define: terrorism.

Recalling the Facts

2. What interests does the United States want to protect by promoting peace in the Middle East?
3. What is the main issue behind the Middle East conflict?

Reviewing the Main Idea

4. Answer "As you read . . ." question 3 on page 454: What are two factors that help shape American foreign policy?

Critical Thinking

5. **Demonstrating Reasoned Judgment.** Do you think the United States should become involved in disputes between other countries? If so, under what circumstances?

4 A Brief History of American Foreign Policy

The history of the foreign policy of the United States can be divided into three parts. First, there was a period of noninvolvement in the affairs of other countries. The second period saw an increased interest in the outside world. In the third period, the United States became involved throughout the world.

An Era of Isolationism

When he retired as President in 1797, George Washington stated that it was the policy of the United States not to become involved in the problems of other countries. President Thomas Jefferson stated that the United States wanted to be friendly with all countries, but enter into special alliances with none.

To a great extent, Presidents in the 1800s conducted foreign policy according to Washington's advice. Our foreign policy was one of **isolationism**. The United States did not get involved in the problems of other countries. Through purchases, agreements, and war, it acquired most of its territory.

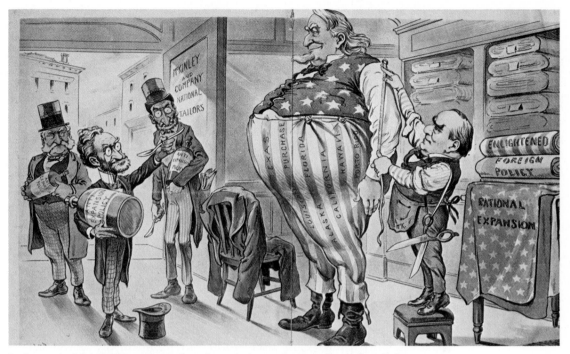

By the end of the 1800s public sentiment was in favor of expanding United States influence in other countries. Here President McKinley fits Uncle Sam with new clothes. Foes of expansionism offer Uncle Sam diet medicine.

In 1823, President James Monroe issued a statement, now called the Monroe Doctrine. The Monroe Doctrine was intended to protect the United States and Latin America from European powers. The United States promised not to interfere in the affairs of the countries of Europe. It also warned Europe not to interfere in the affairs of Latin America or the United States. The Monroe Doctrine became the policy of many Presidents after Monroes's term in office.

Interest in the Outside World

By the end of the 1800s, our foreign policy began to change. The United States began to take a greater interest in the affairs of other countries. We fought a war with Spain in 1898 and acquired Puerto Rico, Guam, and the Philippines. We sent troops to Mexico and other Latin American countries when we felt our interests were threatened. The United States sent troops into Latin America to put down uprisings. In 1903, territory was obtained in Panama to build a canal connecting the Atlantic and Pacific oceans. The United States built military bases in the Panama Canal Zone and in Cuba. The United States bought the Virgin Islands from Denmark to protect the Canal and Latin America as well as its own interests.

The United States took part in World War I from April 1917 to November 1918. But after the war ended, we returned to a policy of noninvolvement. From 1918 to 1941, the United States did sign several agreements with Japan and other countries of Europe to reduce armaments. However, the United States did not join the League of Nations, a world organization like the UN, that was formed at that time. Our government did not want to become involved in disputes between other nations. Several wars did break out during this period, but the United States stayed out of them.

Global Involvement

In 1939, World War II broke out in Europe and in the Far East. The United States took part from 1941 to 1945. The United States wanted to stop Germany, Japan, and Italy from conquering the world. After World War II, the United States stopped following President Washington's advice about noninvolvement, for several reasons. The United States felt it could no longer ignore what happened elsewhere. It became more involved with other countries. A war-torn world had to be rebuilt, and the United States had the resources to help rebuild it.

Only a few years after World War II ended, the Soviet Union succeeded in imposing communist-style dictatorships upon many governments in Eastern Europe. Opposition to these Soviet "takeovers" from the United States and Western Europe nearly touched off fighting several times. A condition of tension and hostility continued that came to be called a **cold war.** The cold war was a war of opposing policies and ideas, not a war of armed conflict. It was waged by the United States to achieve two major goals. One of these goals was to stop the spread of communism. The other goal was to support the right of free people to choose their own government and political leaders without interference.

Starting in 1947, our government formed several military alliances to prevent communist expansion and to protect itself. It set up military bases around the world and has given or sold billions of dollars worth of military equipment to other countries. Between 1950 and 1953, as part of a United Nations military action, United States forces fought to stop North Korea's attempt to conquer South Korea. From 1956 to 1973, our government supported and then sent troops to fight on the side of the government of South Vietnam against anti-government forces. The United States believed these forces (some coming from North Vietnam and others from within South Vietnam) were communist, and were being supplied by the Soviet Union. In 1973, United States forces withdrew and the anti-government forces took control of all of Vietnam.

In the 1980s, the United States stepped up its efforts to keep communism from spreading in various parts of the world. In 1979, the Soviet Union invaded Afghanistan to force support for a communist government. The United States sent equipment and supplies to help the people there resist the Soviets. In 1989, under the leadership of Mikhail Gorbachev, the Soviets finally withdrew from Afghanistan. Another example involves Central America. Under the Reagan Administration, secret aid was sent to forces in Nicaragua to fight a communist government in that country. Many people, including members of Congress, opposed this action, and public policy toward Central America remains controversial.

The foreign policy of the United States has often been criticized, especially when our nation has engaged in wars or interfered in the affairs of other nations. Many people were against our participation in World Wars I and II. In recent times a great many Americans spoke out against our participation in the Vietnam War and our involvement in Central America.

Public opinion surveys show that our people went the United States to follow a foreign policy that not only promotes peace but also protects our country's interests. People differ, however, on how the United States should accomplish both of these goals.

SECTION 4 *Review*

Defining Key Terms
1. Define: isolationism, cold war.

Recalling the Facts
2. What was the purpose of the Monroe Doctrine?
3. Why did the United States stop its policy of noninvolvement in world affairs after World War II?

Reviewing the Main Idea
4. Answer "As you read . . ." question 4 on page 454: What are the three main periods of American foreign policy, and how do they differ from each other?

Critical Thinking
5. **Drawing Conclusions.** Many Americans want the United States government to follow a foreign policy that promotes peace and protects our interests. In today's world, do you think these goals can be achieved with a policy of non-involvement?

Citizenship

Student Exchanges with the Soviet Union

To some, the term RAFT means an inflatable rubber boat used to ride the fierce currents of white-water rapids. To others, RAFT stands for "Russians and Americans for Teamwork."

It was no accident that the name RAFT was chosen for a unique exchange program between American and Russian youths. Since 1987, hundreds of Americans and Soviets, ages 17 to 22, have worked together while white-water rafting on challenging rivers. "When you're going through a rapid together, it doesn't matter if you speak the same language, think the same, or even like one another. If you don't paddle together, you'll both end up in the water," says the director of Project RAFT.

Each Project RAFT exchange consists of two rafting trips, one in the Soviet Union, and one the following year in the United States. Ten Americans and ten Soviets together learn to solve problems under pressure—and to trust one another.

Project RAFT is just one of many exchange programs for American and Soviet students. Limited exchange programs have existed for years. But, as never before, an ease now exists between our two countries, due in part to the new era of *glasnost,* or openness, under Soviet President Mikhail Gorbachev.

In May 1988, former President Reagan met with Gorbachev in Moscow. The two leaders signed agreements that created a United States–Soviet Union High School Academic Partnership Program. The exchange program, begun in 1989, aims to

These American students in Moscow have a valuable opportunity to learn about Soviet life.

develop education, improve relations, and deepen mutual understanding between Soviets and Americans. Thousands of students now cross the Atlantic to visit the superpower on the other side.

Questions to think about:

1. Project RAFT aims to be a model of cooperation. How do you think this model could help political relations between the Soviet Union and the United States?
2. What value do you think student exchange programs have?

CHAPTER SUMMARY

Section 1   The term *foreign policy* describes the way in which our government deals with other countries. For the most part, the President is in charge of shaping foreign policy. Our foreign policy is designed to protect our interests and the interests of friendly nations. This is accomplished by opposing the spread of communism, promoting peace and friendship, raising the standard of living for all people, and encouraging understanding between the United States and other countries.

Section 2   The Constitution gives the President the power to negotiate treaties, appoint and receive ambassadors, command the army and navy, and propose laws that relate to foreign affairs. There are limits to a President's power over foreign policy. Only Congress may declare war, for example. Most Presidents work closely with Congress to shape foreign policy.

Section 3   Foreign policy decisions are influenced by many factors. Among these are business interests and a concern for democracy abroad. In the Middle East, for example, the United States tries to stay on friendly terms with the Arab countries, where many American firms have oil wells. At the same time, our foreign policy is designed to support Israel, the only democratic country in the region.

Section 4   For a long period, the United States stayed out of foreign affairs. In the late 19th century, the United States began a policy of intervention, particularly in Latin America. Since World War II, the United States has been involved in foreign affairs all over the globe.

Reviewing Key Terms

On a separate sheet of paper, use the following terms to complete the sentences below.

   terrorism
   satellite
   isolationism
   mutual defense pact
   containment

1. A weak country controlled by a more powerful country is called a __?__ .

2. The term __?__ refers to a policy of trying to control the growth of communism.

3. An agreement among countries to come to each other's aid is called a __?__ .

4. Staying out of the disputes of foreign nations is a policy of __?__ .

5. Using violence to achieve a political end is called __?__ .

Understanding Main Ideas

1. What three main goals have guided American foreign policy in recent years?

2. Why does the United States send weapons to other countries?

3. How has the United States pursued peaceful coexistence with the Soviet Union and the People's Republic of China?

4. What roles does the President play in conducting foreign policy?

5. Describe three ways that Congress limits the President's power over foreign policy.

6. Who are the President's most important foreign policy advisers?

7. What was the Monroe Doctrine?

8. How did United States foreign policy change after World War II?

9. Since 1947, how has the United States tried to prevent communist expansion?

Critical Thinking

1. **Checking Consistency.** Some people claim that the United States cannot promote peace when it engages in wars, sells weapons, and interferes in the affairs of other countries. Do you agree that these activities are inconsistent with the goal of promoting peace? Explain your reasoning.

2. **Expressing Problems Clearly.** Reread Section 3 of this chapter. Then write a paragraph or two that clearly describes the problem the United States has in trying to keep friendly ties with both Israel and the Arab countries.

3. **Predicting Consequences.** Some people say that the President's powers to conduct foreign policy should be reduced and the powers of Congress increased. Do you agree or disagree? Why?

Practicing Skills

1. **Interpreting Political Cartoons.** Look in a newspaper to find a political cartoon about a foreign policy issue. Write a paragraph telling what the cartoon is about, what the symbols represent, and what the cartoonist's message is.

2. **Making Comparisons.** Use *Facts on File* or *Congressional Quarterly's Almanac* for 1988 to look up the Democratic and Republican parties' platform statements on foreign policy. (Ask your librarian to help you, if necessary.) In what ways do the parties agree? In what ways do they disagree?

Focusing on Citizenship

1. **Making a Chart.** Look through the international news sections of the last four editions of either *Time, Newsweek,* or *U.S. News & World Report.* Read the articles that describe American participation in foreign affairs. Make a chart with three sections to show the three goals of our foreign policy. Place each event in the section of the chart where it belongs.

2. **Writing to Government Decision Makers.** Identify a current foreign policy issue that interests you, such as U.S. aid to Central America. Write a letter to the President or to your Senator or Representative describing the policy you think the United States should follow.

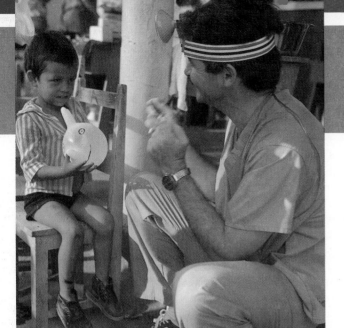

This American health care worker volunteers medical aid to Central Americans.

Participating in the World Community

Previewing the Chapter

Since the 1600s, people from around the globe have come to America in search of a better life. Today, many Americans believe that the things enjoyed by citizens of the United States—freedom, prosperity, the chance to achieve happiness—should be shared with people in all countries. This chapter focuses on the global community and the role played by the United States in this community.

■ **Before you read,** look up these key terms in the Glossary at the back of this book: *interdependent,* glasnost, *unfavorable balance of trade, proliferate, human rights, genocide, covenant.*

■ **As you read,** look for answers to these questions:
1. What are some ways in which the countries of the world depend on each other?
2. What is the main purpose of the United Nations?
3. How has the UN tried to protect human rights?

1 Global Problems and Relationships

The United States is often said to be a nation of immigrants. That means that the ancestors of most of us came from other countries to live in the United States. Allowing people from many lands to settle and work in the United States is one way in which our government takes part in the world community of nations.

In many ways, the United States and the countries in the rest of the world are interdependent. Countries that are **interdependent** need each other. Interdependence also means that events in one country can affect people in another country. A frost in Brazil may kill the coffee-bean crop and mean Brazil has fewer coffee beans to export. This in turn, may cause the price of coffee in the United States to go up. A strike by airline workers in Europe may force people in many countries to change their vacation plans. Low wages paid to Japanese steel and automobile workers may make it possible for Japanese companies to sell cars in our country at prices lower than the prices of United States manufacturers. A decision by the government of China to become friendly with the United States may allow citizens of the two countries to visit each other's lands.

Likewise, events in the United States can affect other countries. A large crop of wheat or corn may cause United States farmers to lower their prices. This may make it easier for other countries to buy our grain. A strike by dock workers in the United States may prevent the exporting of products by the factory workers of our country. The sale of a new computer may help another country increase its industrial production. A government decision not to sell fuel or equipment for atomic-power plants may cause other countries to look elsewhere for what they need.

Dependence on Oil

Oil is very important to the United States. It is used in our automobiles, homes, and factories. Our country produces about half the oil it needs, however. It depends on other countries for the other half. It buys much oil from countries that are members of the Organization of Petroleum Exporting Countries (OPEC). Thirteen countries, including Nigeria and Saudi Arabia (two of the world's largest oil producers) belong to this organization. Since 1973, OPEC members have competed somewhat with each other in selling oil. As a result, the price of oil has varied. This has caused gasoline prices in the United States to increase. Compare today's price of a gallon of regular gasoline, for example, with the 1973 price of 34 cents a gallon!

The lives of all of us are affected when the OPEC countries cut down on the amount of oil they send to the United States. Saudi Arabia stopped shipments in 1973, and Iran did the same in 1979. In 1973–1974, people waited in line for hours to fill their gas tanks. Many gas stations were open for only a few hours each day. In 1974, Congress set a national speed limit of 55 miles per hour because experts pointed out that driving at lower speeds cuts down on the amount of gasoline a car uses. Leaders in government urged people to use less fuel. Many people bought small cars because they use less gas. People saved energy by lowering thermostats on heaters and by insulating their homes.

U.S.–Soviet Relations

When Soviet leader Mikhail Gorbachev took steps to ease cold-war tensions in the 1980s, he also made reforms in the Soviet Union itself. One such reform was that of **glasnost**, a new "openness" that permitted greater freedom of the press and more tolerance for those who criticized the government. Gorbachev also urged a major restructuring of the Soviet Union's economic and political systems.

Gorbachev's policies have led to improved relations between the Soviet Union and Western nations such as the United States and Great Britain. Many Americans, however, continue to distrust Gorbachev's intentions. Nevertheless, President Reagan began a policy of opening discussions with the Soviets on issues such as arms reductions. When President Bush took office in 1989, he pledged to continue efforts to promote world peace.

Secretary of State James Baker (front, left) and Soviet diplomat Eduard Shevard-nadze (front, right) discuss relations between the two superpowers.

The policies of the Soviet Union and the United States influence events elsewhere. Both nations send experts and advisers to other countries. Both sell them military equipment, food, and industrial products. Both have military bases elsewhere. The Soviet Union, for example, has helped Cuba build up its economic and military strength. The Soviet Union has invaded countries to put leaders it can control into power. It has sent advisers to many African countries.

The United States has made efforts to win the friendship of countries by sending them food, supplies, and military equipment. It has set up military bases in the Persian Gulf, in South Korea, Japan, and the Philippines. It has continued to supply Taiwan with weapons and equipment.

The leaders of the Soviet Union and the United States understand that world peace can come only if their countries work together. So, from time to time, they have made agreements to cut back on the production of military arms, to increase trade, and to have more exchanges of scientists, artists, and tourists. Both countries, however, continue to compete for influence and power in various parts of the world.

Global Pollution

International cooperation is important in fighting pollution. The people of all countries share the earth's air and water. The way people in one country use these resources often affects how people in other countries live. Garbage dumped into oceans, for example, has washed up on foreign shores and ruined beaches. American cars produce exhaust that may be carried by wind currents to places as far away as Paris and London. Factories release chemicals into the air that may return to the earth as acid rain—that is, rain, snow, or sleet carrying harmful acids. In Canada, acid rain caused by pollution from American factories has killed fish, damaged crops, and withered forests. President Bush met with Canadian Prime Minister Brian Mulroney in February, 1989, to discuss ways to reduce acid rain.

All countries have problems with pollution. Many Presidents of the United States have worried about these problems and about how best to protect the environment. Through the United Nations, our government works with other countries to find ways to decrease pollution worldwide. In 1987, 31 nations including the United States signed the Montreal Protocol, an agreement to curb the use of certain chemicals that pollute the air. In March, 1989, 20 more nations pledged their support for the pact.

Other international meetings have been held to talk about ocean pollution, the destruction of tropical rain forests, and global warming of the earth. There is growing recognition that we must take action now if we want our children and grandchildren to inherit a healthy planet.

Pollution is a world-wide problem. An oil spill such as this one in Virginia has far-reaching effects.

The United States depends upon the rest of the world for many natural resources, raw materials, and products. It also depends upon many countries to buy United States products. In the United States, coffee, bananas, chocolate, pineapples, and sugar are imported. We also import television sets, automobiles, furniture, glassware, clothing, toys, games, and many other products. United States manufacturers import tungsten for light bulbs, manganese for airplanes, copper for electric wires and pipes, and tin for many products. As mentioned before, we produce only about half the oil we use. The rest must be imported.

Some United States companies have built factories in other countries because the costs of labor and materials there are lower than they are at home. These factories ship finished products and parts to the United States. Some American automobiles, for example, are made in Japan, as are many parts for sewing machines.

Some foreign companies in Germany and Japan now have assembly lines in the United States. They employ many of our citizens. The United States also sells or exports many products to other countries. We export farm machinery, chemicals, computers, and airplanes, to name just a few products.

Trade and Business Development

Selected Imports from Four Areas of the World, 1987*

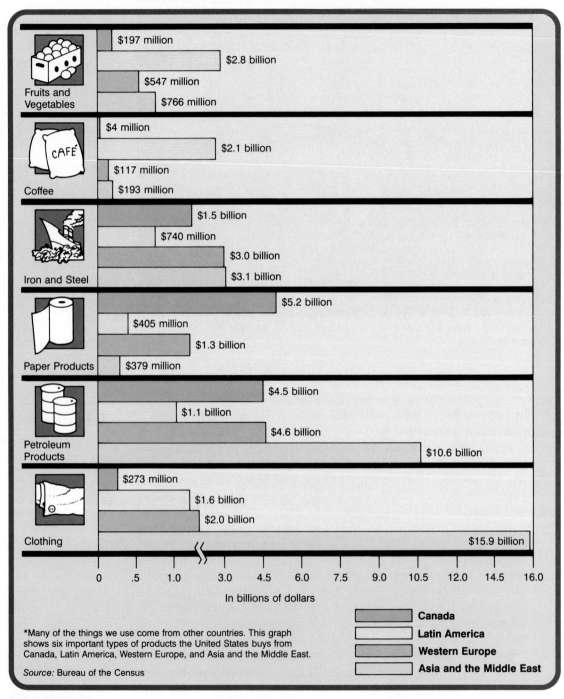

Fruits and Vegetables
- $197 million
- $2.8 billion
- $547 million
- $766 million

Coffee
- $4 million
- $2.1 billion
- $117 million
- $193 million

Iron and Steel
- $1.5 billion
- $740 million
- $3.0 billion
- $3.1 billion

Paper Products
- $5.2 billion
- $405 million
- $1.3 billion
- $379 million

Petroleum Products
- $4.5 billion
- $1.1 billion
- $4.6 billion
- $10.6 billion

Clothing
- $273 million
- $1.6 billion
- $2.0 billion
- $15.9 billion

0   .5   1.0   3.0   4.5   6.0   7.5   9.0   10.5   12.0   14.5   16.0

In billions of dollars

Canada
Latin America
Western Europe
Asia and the Middle East

*Many of the things we use come from other countries. This graph shows six important types of products the United States buys from Canada, Latin America, Western Europe, and Asia and the Middle East.

Source: Bureau of the Census

SKILL BUILDER   How much does the United States spend on imports of petroleum products?

United States companies are located in other countries. A major oil-producing company in Saudi Arabia is partly owned by a United States company. United States companies own hotels, fast-food restaurants, and car-rental agencies all over the world. Soft drinks from the United States are also sold in many countries.

Foreign trade has both good and bad effects. On the one hand, we can buy more goods. Foreign products can sometimes cost much less than products made in this country. Sometimes, however, the United States has an unfavorable balance of trade. An **unfavorable balance of trade** means that the United States imports more than it exports. This is one of several reasons for unemployment in the United States. When consumers here buy products made in other countries, they usually buy less from companies in our country. Manufacturers in the United States, for example, have purchased a great deal of steel from Japan, so our steel companies have had to fire some of their workers. As a result, many people have urged that the United States manufacturers buy only steel made at home. They have suggested that United States steel companies try to sell more of their products to other countries.

SKILL BUILDER

How is the American economy affected when the United States imports more than it exports?

Dollar Value of Imports and Exports

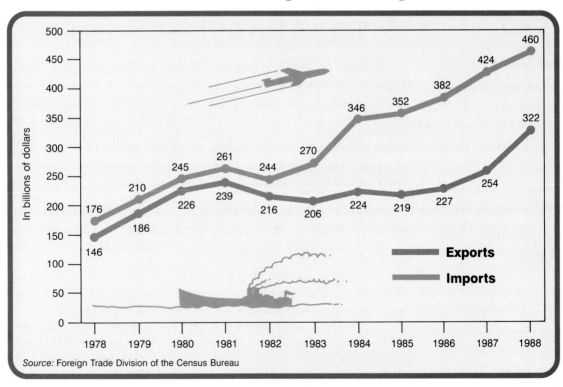

Source: Foreign Trade Division of the Census Bureau

SECTION *1* *Review*

Defining Key Terms

1. Define: interdependent, *glasnost,* unfavorable balance of trade.

Recalling the Facts

2. How did OPEC's 1973 decision to stop oil shipments affect American consumers?

3. Why is international cooperation needed to solve the problem of global pollution?

Reviewing the Main Idea

4. Answer "As you read . . ." question 1 on page 475: What are some ways in which the countries of the world depend on each other?

Critical Thinking

5. Identifying Central Issues. Is it possible for any country to be totally independent in today's world? Explain.

2 The United Nations

One way in which the United States takes part in the world community is by supporting the United Nations (UN). You have probably heard of the United Nations. It is a world organization that was set up in 1945 at the end of World War II. Its main purposes are to prevent wars, to promote human rights, and to bring about a better standard of living for people everywhere. Fifty-one countries belonged to the United Nations when it began. Now 159 countries are members.

Main Parts of the United Nations

There are six main parts of the United Nations: the General Assembly, the Security Council, the Economic and Social Council, the Secretariat, the International Court of Justice, and the Trusteeship Council.

The General Assembly. All member countries are represented in the **General Assembly**. Each country has one vote. In the General Assembly, members discuss and pass resolutions about world problems, new members, and the budget. The estimated 1990–1991 budget for the UN was about $1.9 billion. The United States pays about one-fourth of the budget. Other UN members must provide at least 0.01% of the total UN expenses.

The Security Council. This second part of the UN proposes ways to solve disputes. It may ask members to stop trading with countries that make war, or it may call upon UN forces to prevent war. In 1950, the Security Council called upon the member countries to stop North Korea's invasion of South Korea. Sixteen countries sent troops. Other UN peace-keeping forces have been sent to Cyprus, Africa, and the Middle East.

The Security Council has 15 members. China, France, Great Britain, the Soviet Union, and the United States are permanent members. Ten other members are selected by the General Assembly—five each year. Nine votes are required in order to put a proposal into effect. Five of those votes must be those of the permanent members. Each of the permanent members has a veto vote. If even one permanent member votes no, a proposal is defeated.

The Economic and Social Council. This third part of the UN conducts studies, sponsors programs, and holds meetings on problems having to do with money or with human relations. The Economic and Social Council tries to promote a higher standard of living for all people. The council is made up of 27 members. Nine new members are chosen by the General Assembly each year. Each member serves a term of three years.

The Economic and Social Council works with the UN specialized agencies. You may have heard of some of the agencies. One, the *United Nations Educational, Scientific, and Cultural Organization* (UNESCO), supports programs that bring education and scientific information to many countries. UNESCO sends text-

PEOPLE HELPING PEOPLE

The Homesick Press

"Being homesick is one of the things I think we all have to go through," a student wrote recently in her high school newspaper. Sharing such feelings—and solutions—is common in the *Silver International*, a collection of articles, essays, and poems written entirely by foreign students at Montgomery Blair High School in Silver Spring, Maryland. The newspaper is helping students develop their English skills and their self-confidence.

The first issue of the paper rolled off the presses in 1987. Within two years, the *Silver International* had a staff of 19 students —teenage immigrants from Thailand, Bulgaria, El Salvador, and several other nations.

A typical 16-page issue includes tips for foreign students on how to function in their new land, but most articles are highly personal in nature. "I want the kids to learn about each other," says their teacher Joseph Bellino, "to help the students know other people feel the way they do."

Javier Perez de Cuellar, a diplomat from Peru, is the Secretary General of the United Nations.

books and other learning materials to schools in many places in the world. A second UN agency, the *Food and Agriculture Organization* (FAO), helps farmers improve food production. The *International Labor Organization* (ILO) works to improve working and living conditions. The *World Health Organization* (WHO) deals with health problems. This UN agency sends doctors, nurses, and medicine to needy countries. It tries to teach people good health habits. Thanks to the efforts of WHO, the disease of smallpox has been wiped out around the world.

The Secretariat. This fourth main part of the UN manages the daily business of the United Nations. The Secretariat is headed by a secretary general. The Security Council nominates a secretary general and the General Assembly appoints the person.

The International Court of Justice. The fifth main part of the UN deals with legal problems. Two countries that have a dispute with each other may have their case heard in this court. However, both countries must agree to accept the decision of the court. If one country will not agree, the International Court of Justice cannot hear the case.

The Trusteeship Council. The sixth main part of the UN, the Trusteeship Council, was formed to help territories that were not self-governing. The Caroline and Mariana Islands in the Pacific Ocean, for example, were trust territories of the United States. The Trusteeship Council worked to help such trust territories become independent.

The United Nations System

SKILL BUILDER

Why does this chart show the General Assembly as the center of activity at the United Nations?

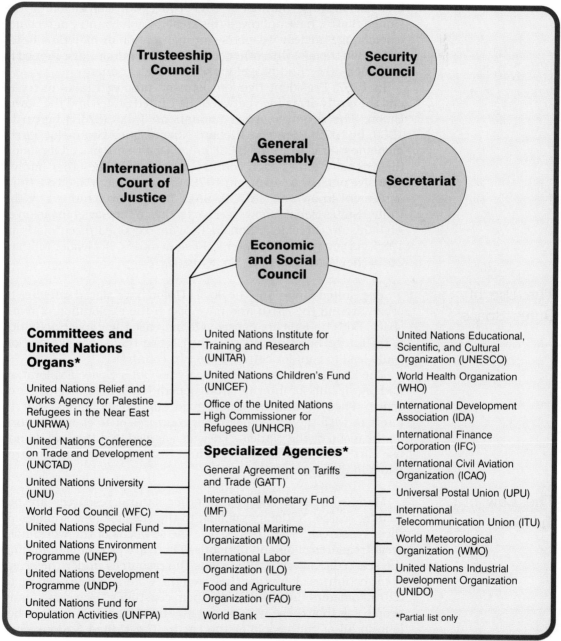

Trusteeship Council

Security Council

International Court of Justice

General Assembly

Secretariat

Economic and Social Council

Committees and United Nations Organs*

United Nations Relief and Works Agency for Palestine Refugees in the Near East (UNRWA)

United Nations Conference on Trade and Development (UNCTAD)

United Nations University (UNU)

World Food Council (WFC)

United Nations Special Fund

United Nations Environment Programme (UNEP)

United Nations Development Programme (UNDP)

United Nations Fund for Population Activities (UNFPA)

United Nations Institute for Training and Research (UNITAR)

United Nations Children's Fund (UNICEF)

Office of the United Nations High Commissioner for Refugees (UNHCR)

Specialized Agencies*

General Agreement on Tariffs and Trade (GATT)

International Monetary Fund (IMF)

International Maritime Organization (IMO)

International Labor Organization (ILO)

Food and Agriculture Organization (FAO)

World Bank

United Nations Educational, Scientific, and Cultural Organization (UNESCO)

World Health Organization (WHO)

International Development Association (IDA)

International Finance Corporation (IFC)

International Civil Aviation Organization (ICAO)

Universal Postal Union (UPU)

International Telecommunication Union (ITU)

World Meteorological Organization (WMO)

United Nations Industrial Development Organization (UNIDO)

*Partial list only

Participating in the World Community   485

Nuclear Weapons Control

Several countries now have the scientific knowledge needed to produce and use nuclear energy. The UN has tried to get its members to use this scientific knowledge for peaceful purposes rather than for nuclear bombs. The world organization fears that countries that already have nuclear weapons may give or sell them to other countries. As a result, the UN sponsored the Treaty on the Non-Proliferation of Nuclear Weapons. (To **proliferate** means to increase in large numbers.) Over 100 countries, including the United States, have approved this treaty. Each country agreed not to exchange nuclear weapons—or information or materials needed to build them—with other countries. The nations also agreed to help each other find peaceful uses for nuclear energy.

In 1967, President Lyndon Johnson proposed talks to try to end the costly arms race between the United States and the Soviet Union. The Strategic Arms Limitations Talks (SALT) began in 1969. In 1972, President Richard Nixon signed two major agreements resulting from the SALT talks. One treaty placed limits on the defensive forces each country could build. The other limited offensive nuclear weapons. In 1979, the two nations signed a third agreement known as SALT II. SALT II was never ratified by the United States Senate, however, partly due to the Soviet invasion of Afghanistan. President Ronald Reagan reopened discussions in 1985. As you read in Chapter 7, Reagan and Soviet leader Mikhail Gorbachev signed the INF Treaty in 1987.

The Use of Outer Space

The United States and the Soviet Union have placed satellites in orbits around the earth and have begun the exploration of outer space. Both nations are expected to increase their space activities in the future. Some members of the UN fear that space exploration could lead to conflict between the two countries.

The UN has sponsored the Treaty on Outer Space Exploration and Use. It calls for international cooperation in the peaceful use of space. Those countries that signed this treaty agreed not to interfere with the projects of other countries or to claim territory on the moon or the planets. They also agreed that they would not use earth satellites as weapons and that they would help astronauts in distress.

The Law of the Sea

Many sources of energy and other natural resources are becoming scarce. Nations now look to the seas for new supplies of these resources. Scientists believe the sea beds of the world hold great treasures of oil and minerals. There are problems in mining the sea beds, however. Who owns the resources under the seas? Some countries claim that they own the waters and sea bed up to 320 kilometers (200 miles) off their coastlines. However, many people say that these waters and any treasures they contain belong to all of the people of the earth. The United Nations conducted a series of conferences to work out agreements. In 1982, the Law of the Sea Treaty was completed. The United States, however, did not sign it. President Reagan argued that the treaty would not be fair to U.S. companies that wanted to mine the sea.

In one of his yearly reports, a former secretary general of the United Nations said: "It is necessary to convince people that the struggle for peace, justice, equity, and human dignity which is waged at the United Nations is very much their struggle." The United States agrees. The goals of the United Nations and the goals of the people of the United States are similar.

The UN and You

Who owns the resources under the sea?

Defining Key terms
 1. Define: proliferate.

Recalling the Facts
 2. Which part of the United Nations has representatives from all member nations and controls the UN budget?
 3. What is the Treaty on the Non-Proliferation of Nuclear Weapons?

Reviewing the Main Idea
 4. Answer "As you read . . ." question 2 on page 475: What is the main purpose of the United Nations?

Critical Thinking
 5. **Drawing Conclusions.** Do you think the United States should continue to support the United Nations with more money than any other nation? Explain your answer.

3 Human Rights

Political, economic, and social rights are human rights. **Human rights** are rights that people are entitled to simply because they are human beings.

As mentioned earlier in this book, the United States Constitution guarantees us certain rights. These rights include the freedom to say and write what we believe and the right to fair treatment in a court of law. In addition, laws passed by Congress and the states try to provide equal rights in jobs and housing by forbidding discrimination because of race or sex.

Not all citizens of the United States have full social and economic rights, however. Many of our citizens do not enjoy the benefits of decent housing, adequate income, and proper medical care, because of discrimination. Much still needs to be done to guarantee the rights of every person, even in the United States.

Human rights are often discussed in the United Nations. In some parts of the world, governments show little or no concern for the rights of their people.

Political Rights

In some countries, people who criticize the government are put in prison, tortured, or killed. Over the years, the Soviet Union has put thousands of people in prison for speaking against

Andrei Sakharov (pictured second from right with his family in Russia) gained worldwide attention for his human rights efforts.

the government. Alexander Solzhenitsyn, a famous Soviet writer, wrote about the horrible conditions for political prisoners held in Soviet prison camps. The only "crime" of these prisoners is that they dared to criticize the Soviet government. Solzhenitsyn has left the Soviet Union. He now lives in the United States.

Andrei Sakharov was also jailed for criticizing the Soviet government. Sakharov is a well-known scientist and winner of the 1975 Nobel Peace Prize. In 1987, Soviet leader Mikhail Gorbachev allowed Sakharov to return home.

The Soviet Union is not the only country with a poor record on human rights. In South Africa, for example, blacks are denied full political rights under a system of racial separation known as apartheid. In some countries, newspapers have been shut down because they printed stories against government policies. People who have spoken out against the government have disappeared. Members of religious groups have not been allowed to worship. Women have not been allowed to vote or to hold government office. Entire racial, cultural, or religious groups of people have been murdered. Such an act of mass murder is called **genocide**.

Social and Economic Rights

One out of every ten children born in some **developing countries** (countries that have a low standard of living) will die before the age of five. Adults in these countries suffer as well. Many cannot read or write. Many do not have regular jobs. Many have diseases that shorten their lives. Half of the world's people go to bed hungry every night. The average lifespan of people in Asia and Africa is 20 years shorter than that of Americans.

American singers, including Tracy Chapman (second from left) and Bruce Springsteen (far right), performed in 1988 to benefit Amnesty International—an independent, worldwide human rights organization.

Helping these people is very difficult. For many years, the United States and other countries have given their surplus (extra) food to countries in need. However, there are limits to the amount of food any country can spare. In any year, lack of rain or damage by insects destroys crops and may cause a shortage of food.

Protecting Human Rights

The United Nations has tried to protect human rights. In 1975, UN member countries ratified two **covenants,** or agreements. These covenants set down rights that all persons should have, regardless of where they live. The members who signed these covenants agreed to try to protect these rights.

The first covenant dealt with economic, social, and cultural rights. Some of the rights set down in this covenant include freedom from hunger, an adequate standard living, an education, and freedom to take part in the cultural life of one's society.

The second covenant dealt with civil and political rights. Many of these rights are in the Bill of Rights and other amendments to our Constitution. They include the rights to life and liberty, humane treatment in prison, movement from one country to another, privacy, free worship, voting and running for office, and free practice of customs and traditions.

Representatives from many countries are on the Human Rights Committee of the United Nations. People who feel their rights have been taken away by their governments may send a written complaint to this committee. The committee investigates these complaints. If they find that the complaints are true, they ask the governments to stop violating the people's rights. The member countries also encourage citizens around the world to write letters of protest to governments. The letters often help.

The UN covenants on human rights have two weaknesses. One is that over one-third of the member countries have not yet voted to accept them. The second is that some countries are unwilling to obey the agreements even after they sign them.

Women's Rights. The UN proclaimed an International Women's Year in 1976. The next 10 years were labeled the Decade for Women. The UN sponsored an international conference in Nairobi, Kenya, in 1985 to assess the progress that had been made for women's rights over the past ten years, to provide a forum to discuss women's issues, and to plan for the future. At the end of the conference, the "Nairobi Forward-Looking Strategies for the Advancement of Women" called for such things as "equal pay for work of equal value" and government funding of women's organizations and child care.

Children's Rights. The UN is also dedicated to securing special rights for children. The United Nations Declaration of the Rights of the Child establishes ten principles that outline the rights of every child, regardless of his or her "race, color, sex, language, religion, political or other opinion, property, birth, or other status." Principle Seven, for example, states, "The child shall be given an education which will promote his general culture and enable him . . . to develop his abilities." In 1989, ratification of the Declaration of the Rights of the Child was being discussed in the Economic and Social Council of the UN.

SECTION 3 *Review*

Defining Key Terms
1. Define: human rights, genocide, developing country, covenant.

Recalling the Facts
2. How are human rights denied in some countries?
3. What are the weaknesses of the United Nations covenants on human rights?

Reviewing the Main Idea
4. Answer "As you read . . ." question 3 on page 475: How has the UN tried to protect human rights?

Critical Thinking
5. **Identifying Central Issues.** Explain what you think is meant by the right to an adequate standard of living.

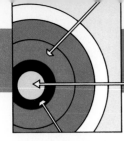

Critical Thinking Skills

Predicting Consequences

As our nation participates in the world community, our government's leaders face complex decisions. Should we send aid to El Salvador? Will the Soviet Union honor treaties with us? How much oil will we need to import over the next 20 years?

How can leaders make such decisions? They almost need to look into the future to determine the best choices. And, in fact, that is just what they do. Policy makers constantly forecast the future to try to predict the consequences of their decisions and actions.

Of course, these leaders do not have a crystal ball or magical powers. Instead, they use a reasoned approach to predict consequences. They begin by studying history, current events, and trends. Then they make reasonable guesses about how these factors might affect the future. Finally, they decide which possible development is most likely to occur.

One example of how history and current events can help policy makers predict consequences is in U.S.-Soviet relations. The historical record shows that since Mikhail Gorbachev came to power, the Soviet government has been more willing to discuss arms reductions. In addition, the Soviets seem to be loosening the rigid control over their people. Past events and current events have led some American leaders to predict that our nation can trust our rival superpower a bit more and have more confidence in treaties with the Soviets.

The table on this page shows an example of how trends can help in predicting consequences. The table shows the number of nuclear weapons tests held by the United States and the Soviet Union from

Nuclear Weapons Tests

	United States	Soviet Union
1945–1949	8	1
1950–1959	188	89
1960–1969	344	168
1970–1979	162	198
1980–1987	125	157

Source: *The World Almanac and Book of Facts*

1945 to 1987. The figures show a downward trend in the number of American tests. One consequence of such a trend might be a continued reduction of nuclear weapons tests in the United States.

Each example discussed above presents a view of the future. Remember, though, that each view represents only a reasonable guess. Differing interpretations, new facts, or unexpected developments can always affect our predictions. Even the events we think are most likely to occur may not, in fact, come to pass.

Practicing Skills

1. The table shows that Soviet testing declined only after the United States reduced the number of its tests. If the number of nuclear weapons tests in the United States continues to decline, how might Soviet testing be affected?
2. **Drawing Conclusions.** Based on the figures in the table, what conclusion can you make about the importance of nuclear weapons tests in both the United States and the Soviet Union?

Citizenship

Protecting Human Rights

"For years I was held in a tiny cell. . . . My only company were the cockroaches and mice. . . . On Christmas Eve, the door to my cell opened and the guard tossed in a crumpled piece of paper. It said: 'Take heart. The world knows you're alive. We're with you. Regards, Monica, Amnesty International.' That letter saved my life."

These are the words of a released prisoner of conscience from Paraguay in South America. Prisoners of conscience are people jailed for their political beliefs, ethnic background, or religion who have neither used nor urged the use of violence. This prisoner's release came about because of a unique human rights organization called Amnesty International.

Founded in 1961, Amnesty International is a nonpolitical group with more than 700,000 members and supporters in over 150 countries. Amnesty members believe that governments must not deny people their fundamental human rights. The organization is dedicated to freeing prisoners of conscience all over the world. The group also works for fair and prompt trials for all political prisoners and for an end to torture, execution, and religious persecution.

One of the group's most effective tactics is to organize letter-writing campaigns. Amnesty's research staff first learns the facts about prisoners of conscience. Members then receive the names of foreign government officials to whom they can write on behalf of individual prisoners. Letters may ask for a prisoner's release. Or they may ask that a prisoner be given medical attention or better treatment. Sometimes Amnesty members also write

Amnesty Internation helped to free these Cuban political prisoners, who are shown being greeted by friends and family in Miami, Florida.

directly to the prisoners themselves, boosting their spirits with moral support.

The efforts of Amnesty International have freed thousands of prisoners of conscience around the world. Recently, junior and senior high school students in the United States have joined the group. They and other Amnesty members take pride in knowing that, for the price of a stamp, they are helping to protect human rights.

Questions to think about

1. Why do you think governments are influenced by letters from citizens of other countries?
2. Could people in this country ever be jailed simply because of their political views, ethnic background, or religion? Explain.

CHAPTER SUMMARY

Section 1   Nations depend upon one another, just as people do. For example, the United States depends on other countries for one-half of its oil needs. The United States and the Soviet Union are affected by each other's foreign policy actions. Because all nations share the earth's air and water, fighting global pollution and its effects on the environment requires international cooperation. The United States depends on other countries for raw materials and finished products. In fact, this country now buys more products than it sells.

Section 2   The United States participates in global affairs by supporting the United Nations. The UN is a world organization that tries to prevent wars, promote human rights, and improve the world's standard of living. The UN consists of six main divisions and many agencies that focus on special problems. In recent years, the UN has worked on programs to stop the spread of nuclear weapons, to encourage space exploration, and to manage ocean resources.

Section 3   Human rights are important to people in every nation. Human rights are the political, economic, and social rights to which people are entitled just because they are human. In some countries, not everyone has these rights. In 1975, the United Nations ratified two human rights covenants, but many countries, including the United States, have not signed them. The UN also promotes the rights of women and children.

Reviewing Key Terms

On a separate sheet of paper, use the following terms to complete the sentences below.

genocide
covenant
proliferate
unfavorable balance of trade

human rights
glasnost
interdependent

1. Nations that need one another are said to be ___?___.

2. To increase in large numbers is to ___?___.

3. Having more imports than exports creates an ___?___.

4. The killing of an entire group of people is called ___?___.

5. An agreement among countries is sometimes called a ___?___.

6. Freedom of speech and freedom from hunger are examples of ___?___.

7. The recent policy of more openness in the Soviet Union is called ___?___.

Understanding Main Ideas

1. How do decisions made by OPEC affect the United States?

2. Give one example of how pollution from the United States affects other countries.

3. How does an unfavorable balance of trade affect consumers and workers in the United States?

4. What are the six main parts of the United Nations?

5. What is the purpose of the Security Council? Who are its members?

6. How does the work of United Nations agencies such as WHO and UNESCO agree with the foreign policy of the United States?

7. What has the United Nations done to stop the spread of nuclear weapons? Has the United States supported these efforts?

8. Identify three important political rights and three important economic and social rights.

9. What has the United Nations done to protect human rights?

Critical Thinking

1. **Testing Conclusions.** To reduce the dependence of the United States on foreign oil, the rationing of oil and oil products has been suggested. Would you favor or oppose such an idea? Why?

2. **Checking Consistency.** Reread the rights listed in the two human rights covenants. Are there any rights that are not provided to all citizens in the United States? If so, what are they? What could be done to guarantee these rights for everyone?

Practicing Skills

1. **Predicting Consequences.** Choose one of the following questions: (a) What is likely to happen if the world runs out of oil in the next 30 to 50 years? (b) What will happen to the United States as a global power if we continue to import more goods than we export? Do some research to answer the question. Then discuss your predictions with the class.

2. **Using Maps.** Look at the United States map. (a) What major cities might be putting pollutants into the Pacific Ocean? The Gulf of Mexico? The Atlantic Ocean? (b) What rivers might be dumping pollutants into these coastal waters? (c) What cities might be polluting these rivers?

Focusing on Citizenship

1. **Doing a Field Study.** Check the products in your home and make two lists: one of products made in the United States and the other of products made in foreign countries. Which list is longer? Mark the items that are most important to you. Which list includes more of these items?

2. **Inviting a Guest Speaker.** Contact the local offices of the Peace Corps or the Returned Volunteers of the Peace Corps. Arrange to have someone come to talk to the class about Peace Corps experiences.

3. **Preparing a Directory.** Find out about nonprofit organizations that are involved in international efforts to protect the environment or promote human welfare. You might start with the Red Cross, Oxfam-America, Amnesty International, and Greenpeace. Put together a listing of the organizations with addresses, telephone numbers, and brief descriptions of their work.

Focus on Decision Making

Should the United States Continue To Develop SDI?

"Let me share with you a vision of the future which offers hope. It is that we embark on a program to counter the awesome Soviet threat with measures that are defensive . . . What if . . . we could intercept and destroy strategic ballistic missiles before they reached our own soil or that of our allies?"

The Issue in Question

On the evening of March 23, 1983, President Ronald Reagan introduced his Strategic Defense Initiative (SDI) to the nation in a television speech. He called for the development of a space-based defense system that could "shield" the United States from attack by long-range intercontinental ballistic missiles (ICBMs).

Americans have debated the wisdom of the nuclear arms race for decades. Some people believe that the continued buildup of nuclear weapons will lead inevitably to nuclear war. Other people think that nuclear weapons have actually prevented a major war from breaking out since World War II.

Until President Reagan's SDI proposal, the debate focused on *offensive* nuclear weapons—those used to attack an enemy. Reagan, however, saw SDI as a *defensive* system that could detect, target, and destroy enemy missiles before they reached the United States. The SDI proposal thus signaled a major shift in the debate over nuclear weapons.

Background on the Issue

Since 1983, research into the Strategic Defense Initiative (or "Star Wars," as it is often called) has become a major issue in American foreign policy.

Supporters of "Star Wars" claim that SDI research could lead to an effective national defense that would reduce the chances of war. They believe that SDI would give the United States more flexibility to respond in the event of an enemy attack. They admit that an effective defense system would require the development of complex new technologies, but they believe that a "limited shield" could soon be ready.

Supporters of "Star Wars" also believe that the system need not be perfect to be an effective deterrent to war. They claim that the Soviet Union felt threatened enough just by SDI *research* to take arms control talks more seriously. They say this is partly why the Soviets signed the INF Treaty in 1987 (see page 126).

Opponents of "Star Wars" believe the system will not offer any real protection for the United States. They point out that SDI would provide no defense against low-flying enemy bombers, cruise missiles, or submarine-launched attacks. Critics also say that the system could never be accurately tested except during an actual attack. By that time, it would be too late to correct any flaws.

SDI opponents believe that "Star Wars" might trigger a new arms race to develop offensive weapons that could slip through

SDI defenses. Finally, SDI critics claim that the $16 billion spent on "Star Wars" research between 1983 and 1989 could have been better used to deal with pressing national problems such as the war against drugs.

Arguments for the Strategic Defense Initiative.

1. An effective SDI system is technologically possible and will ensure greater protection for the United States.
2. Even if the system is never fully operational, the United States can continue to use SDI as a bargaining chip in the future. SDI has already forced the Soviet Union to negotiate on arms reductions.

Arguments Against the Strategic Defense Initiative.

1. SDI will not protect the United States because it relies on complex technologies that are not yet developed and cannot be accurately tested in advance.
2. "Star Wars" stands in the way of negotiations with the Soviet Union and could trigger a new arms race.

Making Decisions

1. **Making Comparisons.** Supporters and critics of SDI disagree on many aspects of the system. Compare their views on each of the following: (a) the expense of SDI; (b) the technological reliability of SDI; (c) the impact of SDI on Soviet-American relations.
2. **Predicting Consequences.** In recent years, relations between the Soviet Union and the United States have improved. How do you think this improvement will affect the debate over SDI research?
3. **Demonstrating Reasoned Judgment.** If you were President of the United States or a member of Congress, and you had to decide whether or not to devote more money to SDI research, what position would you take? Why would you take that position? Use the "Arguments For," the "Arguments Against," and "The Decision-Making Checklist" on this page to help you make your decision and develop your answer.

The Decision-Making Checklist

✔	**Clarify the problem.** (What is the issue or conflict?)
✔	**Create a list of possible solutions.** (How might you resolve the problem?)
✔	**Compare the pros and cons of each solution.** (What are the strengths and weaknesses of each solution?)
✔	**Consider your values and goals.** (What is important to you in choosing a course of action, and why?)
✔	**Choose a course of action and evaluate the results.** (What would you decide, and how could you judge the outcome?)

Reference Section

◀ The Library of Congress in Washington, D.C., contains one of the largest collections of reference resources in the world.

499

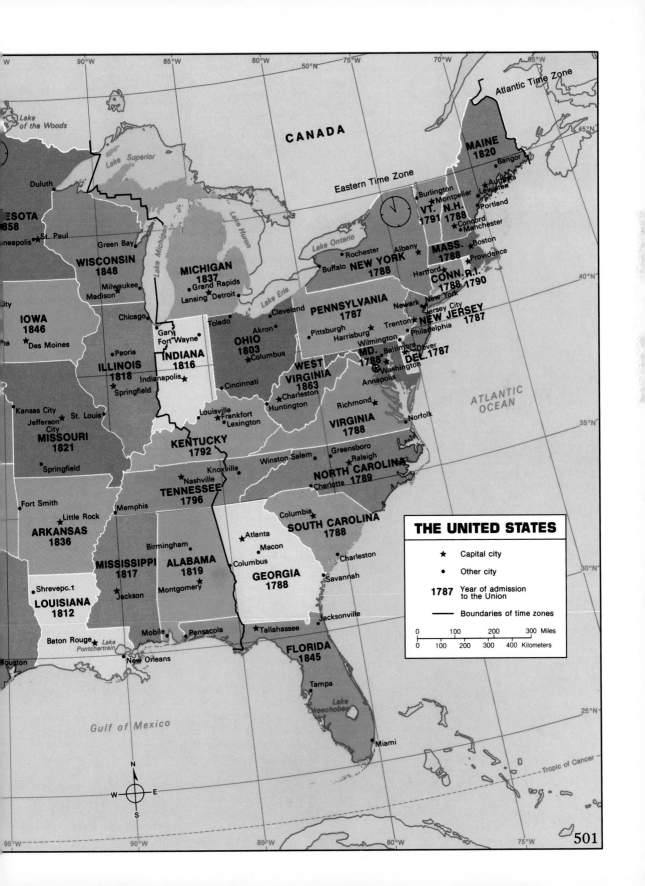

THE UNITED STATES

★	Capital city
•	Other city
1787	Year of admission to the Union
——	Boundaries of time zones

0   100   200   300 Miles
0 100 200 300 400 Kilometers

501

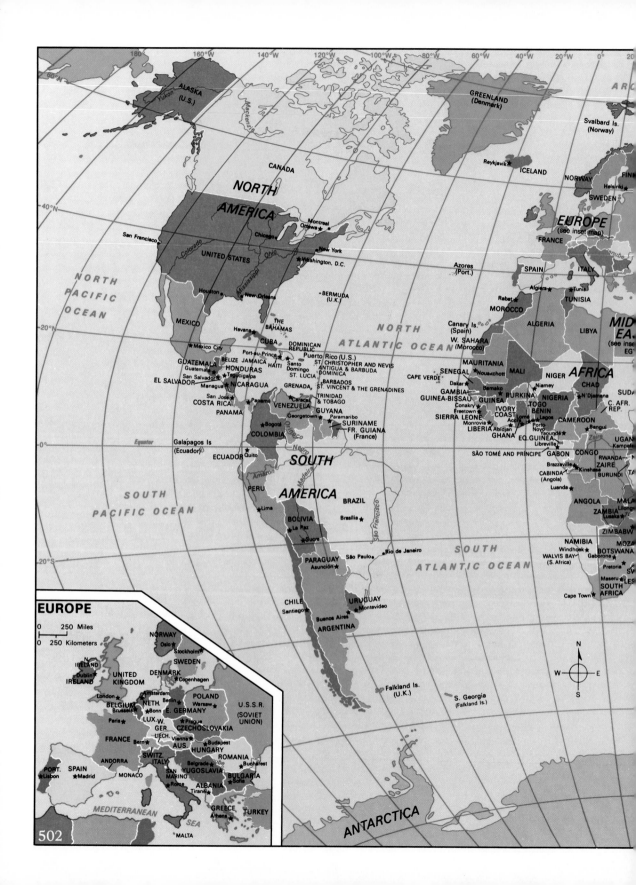

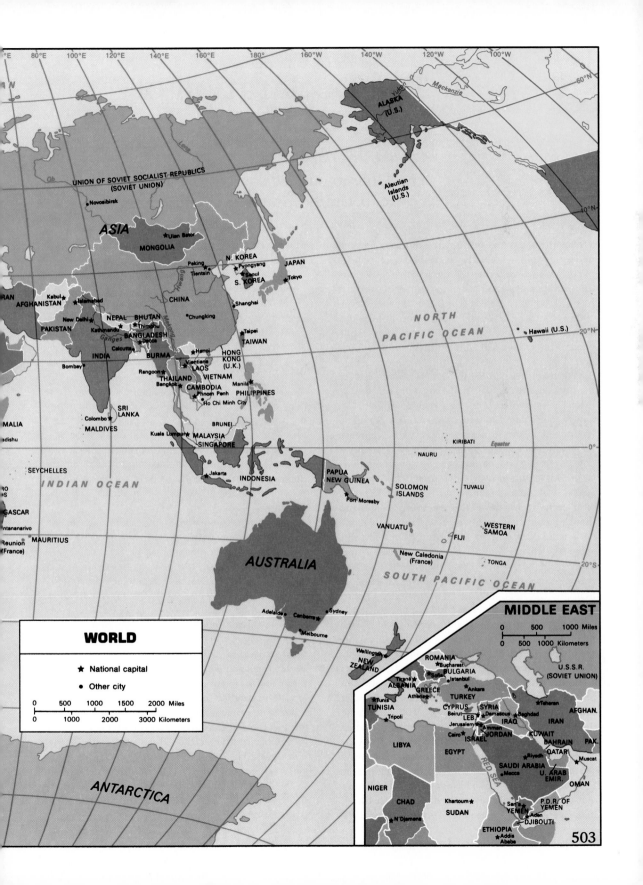

WORLD

★ National capital

● Other city

0	500	1000	1500	2000 Miles

0	1000	2000	3000 Kilometers

MIDDLE EAST

0	500	1000 Miles

0	500	1000 Kilometers

503

The Declaration of Independence

In Congress, July 4, 1776

The Unanimous Declaration of the Thirteen United States of America

When in the Course of human events, it becomes necessary for one people to dissolve the political bands which have connected them with another, and to assume among the powers of the earth, the separate and equal station to which the Laws of Nature and of Nature's God entitle them, a decent respect to the opinions of mankind requires that they should declare the causes which impel them to the separation.

We hold these truths to be self-evident, that all men are created equal, that they are endowed by their Creator with certain unalienable Rights, that among these are Life, Liberty and the pursuit of Happiness. That to secure these rights, Governments are instituted among Men, deriving their just powers from the consent of the governed; That whenever any Form of Government becomes destructive of these ends it is the Right of the People to alter or to abolish it, and to institute new Government, laying its foundation on such principles and organizing its powers in such form, as to them shall seem most likely to effect their Safety and Happiness. Prudence, indeed, will dictate that Governments long established should not be changed for light and transient causes; and accordingly all experience hath shown, that mankind are more disposed to suffer, while evils are sufferable, than to right themselves by abolishing the forms to which they are accustomed. But when a long train of abuses and usurpations, pursuing invariably the same Objects evinces a design to reduce them under absolute Despotism, it is their right, it is their duty, to throw off such Government, and to provide new Guards for their future security—Such has been the patient sufferance of these Colonies; and such is now the necessity which constrains them to alter their former Systems of Government. The history of the present King of Great Britain is a history of repeated injuries and usurpations, all having in direct object the establishment of an absolute Tyranny over these States. To prove this, let Facts be submitted to a candid world.

He has refused his Assent to Laws, the most wholesome and necessary for the public good.

He has forbidden his Governors to pass Laws of immediate and pressing importance, unless suspended in their operation till his Assent should be obtained; and when so suspended, he has utterly neglected to attend to them.

He has refused to pass other Laws for the accommodation of large districts of people, unless those people would relinquish the right of Representation in the Legislature, a right inestimable to them and formidable to tyrants only.

He has called together legislative bodies at places unusual, uncomfortable, and distant from the depository of their public records, for the sole purpose of fatiguing them into compliance with his measures.

He has dissolved Representative Houses repeatedly, for opposing with manly firmness his invasions on the rights of the people.

He has refused for a long time, after such dissolutions, to cause others to be elected; whereby the Legislative powers, incapable of Annihilation, have returned to the People at large for their exercise; the State remaining in the mean time exposed to all the dangers of invasions from without, and convulsions within.

He has endeavored to prevent the population of these States; for that purpose obstructing the Laws for Naturalization of Foreigners; refusing to pass others to encourage their migration hither, and raising the conditions of new Appropriations of Lands.

He has obstructed the Administration of Justice, by refusing his Assent to Laws for establishing Judiciary powers.

He has made Judges dependent on his Will alone for the tenure of their offices, and the amount and payment of their salaries.

He has erected a multitude of New Offices, and sent hither swarms of Officers to harass our people and eat out their substance.

He has kept among us in times of peace, Standing Armies, without the Consent of our legislatures.

He has affected to render the Military independent of, and superior to, the Civil power.

He has combined with others to subject us to a jurisdiction foreign to our constitutions, and unacknowledged by our laws; giving his Assent to their Acts of pretended Legislation:

For quartering large bodies of armed troops among us;

For protecting them, by a mock Trial, from punishment for any Murders which they should commit on the Inhabitants of these States;

For cutting off our Trade with all parts of the world;

For imposing Taxes on us without our Consent;

For depriving us, in many cases, of the benefits of Trial by Jury;

For transporting us beyond Seas, to be tried for pretended offenses;

For abolishing the free System of English Laws in a neighboring Province, establishing therein an Arbitrary government, and enlarging its Boundaries, so as to render it at once an example and fit instrument for introducing the same absolute rule into these Colonies;

For taking away our Charters, abolishing our most valuable Laws, and altering, fundamentally, the Forms of our Governments;

For suspending our own Legislatures, and declaring themselves invested with Power to legislate for us in all cases whatsoever.

He has abdicated Government here, by declaring us out of his Protection, and waging War against us.

He has plundered our seas, ravaged our Coasts, burned our towns, and destroyed the lives of our people.

He is at this time transporting large Armies of foreign Mercenaries to complete the works of death, desolation and tyranny, already begun with circumstances of Cruelty and perfidy scarcely paralleled in the most barbarous ages, and totally unworthy the Head of a civilized nation.

He has constrained our fellow Citizens taken Captive on the high Seas to bear Arms against their Country, to become the executioners of their friends and Brethren, or to fall themselves by their Hands.

He has excited domestic insurrections amongst us, and has endeavored to bring on the inhabitants of our frontiers the merciless Indian Savages whose known rule of warfare is an undistinguished destruction of all ages, sexes, and conditions.

In every stage of these Oppressions We have Petitioned for Redress in the most humble terms. Our repeated Petitions have been answered only by repeated injury. A Prince whose character is thus marked by every act which may define a Tyrant, is unfit to be the ruler of a free people.

Nor have We been wanting in attentions to our British brethren. We have warned them from time to time of attempts by their legislature to extend an unwarrantable jurisdiction over us. We have reminded them of the circumstances of our emigration and settlement here. We have appealed to their native justice and magnanimity, and we have conjured them by the ties of our common kindred to disavow these usurpations, which, would inevitably interrupt our connections and correspondence. They too have been deaf to the voice of justice and of consanguinity. We must, therefore, acquiesce in the necessity, which denounces our Separation, and hold them, as we hold the rest of mankind, Enemies in War, in Peace Friends.—

We, therefore, the Representatives of the United States of America, in General Congress, Assembled, appealing to the Supreme Judge of the world for the rectitude of our intentions, do, in the Name, and by the Authority of the good People of these Colonies, solemnly publish and declare, That these United Colonies are, and of right ought to be Free and Independent States; that they are Absolved from all Allegiance to the British Crown, and that all political connection between them and the State of Great Britain, is and ought to be totally dissolved, and that as Free and Independent States, they have full Power to levy War, conclude Peace, contract Alliances, establish Commerce, and to do all other Acts and Things which Independent States may of right do. And for the support of this Declaration, with a firm reliance on the protection of Divine Providence, we mutually pledge to each other our Lives, our Fortunes and our sacred Honor.

The Constitution of the United States of America

We, the people of the United States, have written and adopted this Constitution for the following reasons:

- so that all the states may work together as part of a strong, united nation;
- so that everyone will be treated fairly;
- so that there will be peace within the nation;
- so that the nation will be safe from attack;
- to promote the happiness and well-being of all the people;
- to make sure that our children and grandchildren will enjoy the same freedoms that we do.

Preamble

We the people of the United States, in Order to form a more perfect Union, establish Justice, insure domestic Tranquility, provide for the common defence, promote the general Welfare, and secure the Blessings of Liberty to ourselves and our Posterity, do ordain and establish this Constitution for the United States of America.

Article One.

Congress has the power to make laws. There are to be two separate houses in Congress, a Senate and a House of Representatives.

Section 1.

Members of the House of Representatives are to be elected every two years by the people of the district they represent.

Members of the House must be at least 25 years old. They must also have been a citizen of the United States for

LEGISLATIVE DEPARTMENT

THE CONGRESS

All legislative powers herein granted shall be vested in a Congress of the United States, which shall consist of a Senate and House of Representatives.

THE HOUSE OF REPRESENTATIVES

a. Election and term of members. The House of Representatives shall be composed of members chosen every second year by the people of the several states, and the electors in each state shall have the qualifications requisite for electors of the most numerous branch of the state legislature.

b. Qualification of members. No person shall be a representative who shall not have attained to the age of twenty-five years, and been seven years a citizen of the United States, and who shall not, when elected, be an inhabitant of the state in which he shall be chosen.

c. *Apportionment of representatives and of direct taxes.* Representatives and direct taxes shall be apportioned among the several states which may be included within this Union, according to their respective numbers, which shall be determined by the whole number of free persons, including those bound to service for a term of years, and excluding Indians not taxed, three fifths of all other persons. The actual enumeration shall be made within three years after the first meeting of the Congress of the United States, and within every subsequent term of ten years, in such manner as they shall by law direct. The number of representatives shall not exceed one for every thirty thousand, but each state shall have at least one representative, and until such enumeration shall be made, the State of New Hampshire shall be entitled to choose three; Massachusetts, eight; Rhode Island and Providence Plantations, one; Connecticut, five; New York, six; New Jersey, four; Pennsylvania, eight; Delaware, one; Maryland, six; Virginia, ten; North Carolina, five; South Carolina, five; and Georgia, three.

d. *Filling vacancies.* When vacancies happen in the representation from any state, the executive authority thereof shall issue writs of election to fill such vacancies.

e. *Officers; impeachment.* The House of Representatives shall choose their Speaker and other officers; and shall have the sole power of impeachment.

The number of representatives for each state is based on the state's population. States with large populations will have more representatives than states with small populations. Every state must have at least one representative, no matter how small its population. A federal census is to be taken every ten years to determine how many persons live in each state.

If a representative dies or resigns, the governor of the state must call a special election to fill the vacancy.

Members of the House choose their own officers. One of these, the Speaker, is the presiding officer (chair) of the House. Only the House can impeach (bring charges of wrongdoing against) a government official. This is the first step in removing a government official. (At a later time, the charges may be acted on by the Senate.)

THE SENATE

a. *Number and election of members.* The Senate of the United States shall be composed of two senators from each state, chosen by the legislature thereof, for six years; and each senator shall have one vote.

b. *Classification.* Immediately after they shall be assembled in consequence of the first election, they shall be divided as equally as may be into three classes. The seats of the senators of the first class shall be vacated at the expiration of the second year, of the second class at the expiration of the fourth year, and of the third class at the expiration of the sixth year, so that one third may be chosen every second year, and if vacancies happen by resignation, or otherwise, during the recess of the legislature of any state, the executive thereof may make temporary appointments until the next meeting of the legislature, which shall then fill such vacancies.

c. *Qualifications of members.* No person shall be a senator who shall not have attained to the age of thirty years, and been nine years a citizen of

Section 3.

Each state is allowed to elect two senators. Their term of office is to be six years. At one time, senators were chosen by their state legislatures, but are now elected by the people (See Amendment 17).

Unlike members of the House, all senators do not run for office at the same time. One-third of the Senate is elected every two years.

Senators must be at least 30 years old, United States citizens for 9 years, and residents of the state in which they are

at least seven years and a resident of the state in which they are elected.

elected.

The Vice President is the President of the Senate. He or she may vote only to break a tie.

The Senate chooses its own officers. One of these, the President pro tempore (temporary President) presides when the President of the Senate is absent.

The Senate tries all impeachment cases. A two-thirds vote is necessary for a verdict of guilty.

A person found guilty of impeachment charges is to be removed from office. He or she can never again hold a position in the federal government. Any person found guilty of such charges can also be tried in a court of law if accused of breaking any laws.

the United States, and who shall not, when elected, be an inhabitant of that state for which he shall be chosen.

d. President of Senate. The Vice President of the United States shall be President of the Senate, but shall have no vote, unless they be equally divided.

e. Other officers. The Senate shall choose their own officers, and also a President pro tempore, in the absence of the Vice President, or when he shall exercise the office of President of the United States.

f. Trial by impeachment. The Senate shall have the sole power to try all impeachments. When sitting for that purpose, they shall be on oath or affirmation. When the President of the United States is tried, the Chief Justice shall preside; and no person shall be convicted without the concurrence of two thirds of the members present.

g. Judgment in case of conviction. Judgment in cases of impeachment shall not exceed further than to removal from office, and disqualification to hold and enjoy any office of honor, trust, or profit under the United States; but the party convicted shall nevertheless be liable and subject to indictment, trial, judgment, and punishment, according to law.

Section 4.

Rules that govern Congressional elections are set by the legislatures of each state. However, Congress has the power to pass election laws that all states must follow.

Congress must meet at least once a year. (Amendment 20 sets January 3 as the opening day of each session.)

ELECTION AND MEETINGS OF CONGRESS

a. Method of holding elections. The times, places, and manner of holding elections for senators and representatives shall be prescribed in each state by the legislature thereof; but the Congress may at any time by law make or alter such regulations, except as to the places of choosing senators.

b. Meeting of Congress. The Congress shall assemble at least once in every year, and such meeting shall be on the first Monday in December, unless they shall by law appoint a different day.

Section 5.

Each house of Congress may decide whether or not new members are qualified and have been elected fairly. In order to carry out its official work, each house must have a majority of its members present. (Such a majority is called a quorum.) Either house may require its members to be

RULES OF PROCEDURE

a. Organization. Each house shall be the judge of the elections, returns, and qualifications of its own members, and a majority of each shall constitute a quorum to do business; but a smaller number may adjourn from day to day, and may be authorized to compel the attendance of absent members, in such manner, and under such penalties as each house may provide.

b. Rules of proceedings. Each house may determine the rules of its proceedings, punish its members for disorderly behavior, and with the concurrence of two thirds, expel a member.

c. Journal. Each house shall keep a journal of its proceedings, and from time to time publish the same, excepting such parts as may in their judgment require secrecy; and the yeas and nays of the members of either house on any question shall, at the desire of one fifth of those present, be entered on the journal.

d. Adjournment. Neither house, during the session of Congress, shall without the consent of the other adjourn for more than three days, nor to any other place than that in which the two houses shall be sitting.

present, and may punish them if they are absent.

Each house sets its own rules of conduct. Members who are disorderly or who disobey house rules can be expelled by a two-thirds vote of the membership.

Each house must keep and publish a record of its activities (*The Congressional Record*). Neither house may stop meeting for more than three days without the consent of the other house.

COMPENSATION, PRIVILEGES, AND RESTRICTIONS

Section 6.

a. Pay and privileges of members. The senators and representatives shall receive a compensation for their services, to be ascertained by law, and paid out of the Treasury of the United States. They shall in all cases, except treason, felony, and breach of the peace, be privileged from arrest during their attendance at the session of their respective houses and in going to and returning from the same; and for any speech or debate in either house, they shall not be questioned in any other place.

b. Holding other offices prohibited. No senator or representative shall, during the time for which he was elected, be appointed to any civil office under the authority of the United States which shall have been created, or the emoluments whereof shall have been increased during such time; and no person holding any office under the United States shall be a member of either house during his continuance in office.

Members of Congress are to be paid by the federal government. They set their own salaries. They cannot be sued or arrested for anything they say in Congress. Like anyone else, they are responsible for any untrue statements they make outside of Congress.

Members of Congress cannot hold any other federal office while serving in Congress.

MODE OF PASSING LAWS

Section 7.

a. Revenue bills. All bills for raising revenue shall originate in the House of Representatives; but the Senate may propose or concur with amendments as on other bills.

b. How bills become laws. Every bill which shall have passed the House of Representatives and the Senate shall, before it become a law, be presented to the President of the United States; if he approve he shall sign it, but if not he shall return it, with his objections, to that house in which it shall have originated, who shall enter the objections at large on their journal and proceed to reconsider it. If after such reconsideration two thirds of that house shall agree to pass the bill, it shall be sent, together with the objections, to the other house, by which it shall likewise be reconsidered, and if approved by two thirds of that house, it shall become a law. But in all such cases the votes of both houses shall be determined by yeas and

Revenue (money) bills must start in the House, but the Senate may add amendments to such bills.

A bill passed by both houses of Congress must be signed by the President in order to become law. If the President vetoes a bill, it is sent back to Congress. The Congress may still pass it into law by a two-thirds vote of the members of both houses, however.

If a bill is not signed within a period of ten days (not including Sunday), the bill becomes law without the President's signature. But if Congress goes home before the ten days are up, the bill is dead. This is called a pocket veto.

Every order or resolution passed by Congress must be signed or vetoed by the President.

nays, and the names of the persons voting for and against the bill shall be entered on the journal of each house respectively. If any bill shall not be returned by the President within ten days (Sundays excepted) after it shall have been presented to him, the same shall be a law, in like manner as if he had signed it, unless the Congress by their adjournment prevent its return, in which case it shall not be a law.

c. *Approval or disapproval by the President.*   Every order, resolution, or vote to which the concurrence of the Senate and House of Representatives may be necessary (except on a question of adjournment) shall be presented to the President of the United States; and before the same shall take effect, shall be approved by him, or being disapproved by him, shall be repassed by two thirds of the Senate and House of Representatives, according to the rules and limitations prescribed in the case of a bill.

Section 8.   POWERS GRANTED TO CONGRESS

Congress may collect taxes. They can be used only to pay debts, to provide for the common defense, or the welfare of the people. Taxes must be the same for all states.

Congress may borrow money. One way is by selling Treasury Bonds.

Congress controls all commerce between the states or with foreign countries. Today, commerce can include almost everything that goes from one state to another.

Congress can pass laws that tell how foreign-born persons may become citizens, and laws about business failures.

Congress can coin money and set its value.

Congress decides the punishment for persons who print or coin money illegally.

Congress provides post offices and post roads. This power helps develop roads, waterways, and air routes.

Congress protects authors and inventors by giving them copyrights or patents.

Congress has the power to set up a system of federal courts: district, appellate, and

The Congress shall have power

a. To lay and collect taxes, duties, imposts, and excises, to pay the debts and provide for the common defense and general welfare of the United States; but all duties, imposts, and excises shall be uniform throughout the United States;

b. To borrow money on the credit of the United States;

c. To regulate commerce with foreign nations, and among the several states, and with the Indian tribes;

d. To establish a uniform rule of naturalization, and uniform laws on the subject of bankruptcies throughout the United States;

e. To coin money, regulate the value thereof and of foreign coin, and fix the standard of weights and measures;

f. To provide for the punishment of counterfeiting the securities and current coin of the United States;

g. To establish post offices and post roads;

h. To promote the progress of science and useful arts by securing for limited times to authors and inventors the exclusive right to their respective writings and discoveries;

i. To constitute tribunals inferior to the Supreme Court;

j. To define and punish piracies and felonies committed on the high seas and offenses against the laws of nations;

k. To declare war, grant letters of marque and reprisal, and make rules concerning captures on land and water;

l. To raise and support armies, but no appropriation of money to that use shall be for a longer term than two years;

m. To provide and maintain a navy;

n. To make rules for the government and regulation of land and naval forces;

o. To provide for calling forth the militia to execute the laws of the Union, suppress insurrections, and repel invasions;

p. To provide for organizing, arming, and disciplining the militia, and for governing such part of them as may be employed in the service of the United States, reserving to the states respectively the appointment of the officers and the authority of training the militia, according to the discipline prescribed by Congress;

q. To exercise exclusive legislation in all cases whatsoever over such district (not exceeding ten miles square) as may, by cession of particular states and the acceptance of Congress, become the seat of the government of the United States, and to exercise like authority over all places purchased by the consent of the legislature of the state in which the same shall be for the erection of forts, magazines, arsenals, dock-yards, and other needful buildings; and

r. To make all laws which shall be necessary and proper for carrying into execution the foregoing powers, and all other powers vested by this Constitution in the government of the United States, or in any department or officer thereof.

POWERS DENIED TO THE FEDERAL GOVERNMENT

a. The migration or importation of such persons as any of the states now existing shall think proper to admit shall not be prohibited by the Congress prior to the year one thousand eight hundred and eight, but a tax or duty may be imposed on such importation, not exceeding ten dollars for each person.

b. The privilege of the writ of habeas corpus shall not be suspended, unless when in cases of rebellion or invasion the public safety may require it.

c. No bill of attainder or ex post facto law shall be passed.

d. No capitation or other direct tax shall be laid, unless in proportion to the census or enumeration herein before directed to be taken.

e. No tax or duty shall be laid on articles exported from any state.

f. No preference shall be given by any regulation of commerce or revenue to the ports of one state over those of another; nor shall vessels bound to or from one state be obliged to enter, clear, or pay duties in another.

special courts.

Congress can punish those who commit crimes on the high seas.

Only Congress may declare war.

Congress can draft citizens and pay them.

Congress can establish a navy.

Congress can make rules for the armed forces.

Congress can allow the calling out of the National Guard in riots, floods, or other emergencies.

Congress sees to training and arming the National Guard.

Congress sets up a government for Washington, D.C., and makes laws for the control of federal land.

Congress may pass all laws necessary for carrying out its other powers. This "elastic clause" gives Congress the power to make laws not mentioned specifically.

Section 9.

The slave trade was not to be prohibited before 1808.

Habeas corpus is the right of a prisoner to be brought before a court of law. Unless there is reason for holding that person, he or she must be set free. This right can be set aside only in an emergency.

A bill of attainder law punishes a person without a trial in a court of law. An ex *post facto* law makes an act a crime before the law was passed.

A capitation tax collects money from every person. It must be the same for all.

No tax can be placed on goods sent out of state.

The Constitution of the United States of America   511

Federal laws cannot favor one port over another. All taxes on incoming goods must be the same. Ships that cross state lines cannot be taxed.

Congress must approve all money spent by the federal government. A record of spending must be published.

No government official can be given a title of nobility or receive gifts from a foreign nation without the permission of Congress.

Section 10.

The states cannot make treaties or alliances with one another, carry on a war, or coin money. They cannot pass a bill of attainder or an *ex post facto* law. They cannot pass a law that voids a contract, or create a nobility.

States cannot tax goods coming into or going out of their ports, other than a small fee to pay the cost of inspection.

States cannot tax tonnage (incoming ships) without the consent of Congress. States cannot have navies or armies (although they may have a state militia) and they cannot make war unless they are invaded or are in serious danger.

Article Two.

Section 1.

The President of the United States serves for four years. As Chief Executive, it is the President's duty to see that the laws of the land are carried out.

The President is actually

g. No money shall be drawn from the treasury, but in consequence of appropriations made by law; and regular statement and account of the receipts and expenditures of all public money shall be published from time to time.

h. No title of nobility shall be granted by the United States; and no person holding any office of profit or trust under them shall, without the consent of Congress, accept of any present emolument, office, or title, of any kind whatever, from any king, prince, or foreign state.

POWERS DENIED TO THE STATES

a. No state shall enter into any treaty, alliance, or confederation; grant letters of marque and reprisal; coin money; emit bills of credit; make any thing but gold and silver coin a tender in payment of debts; pass any bill of attainder, ex post facto law, or law impairing the obligation of contracts; or grant any title of nobility.

b. No state shall, without the consent of the Congress, lay any imposts or duties on imports or exports, except what may be absolutely necessary for executing its inspection laws; and the net produce of all duties and imposts laid by any state on imports or exports shall be for the use of the treasury of the United States; and all such laws shall be subject to the revision and control of the Congress.

c. No state shall, without the consent of Congress, lay any duty of tonnage; keep troops or ships of war in time of peace; enter into any agreement or compact with another state or with a foreign power; or engage in war, unless actually invaded or in such imminent danger as will not admit of delay.

EXECUTIVE DEPARTMENT

PRESIDENT AND VICE PRESIDENT

a. Term of office. The executive power shall be vested in a President of the United States of America. He shall hold his office during the term of four years, and, together with the Vice President, chosen for the same term, be elected as follows:

b. Electors. Each state shall appoint, in such manner as the legislature thereof may direct, a number of electors, equal to the whole number of senators and representatives to which the state may be entitled in the Congress; but no senator or representative, or person holding an office of trust or profit under the United States, shall be appointed an elector.

Former method of electing President and Vice President.   The electors shall meet in their respective states and vote by ballot for two persons, of whom one at least shall not be an inhabitant of the same state with themselves. And they shall make a list of all the persons voted for and of the number of votes for each; which list they shall sign and certify, and transmit sealed to the seat of government of the United States, directed to the President of the Senate. The President of the Senate shall, in the presence of the Senate and House of Representatives, open all the certificates, and the votes shall then be counted. The person having the greatest number of votes shall be the President, if such number be a majority of the whole number of electors appointed; and if there be more than one who have such majority, and have an equal number of votes, then the House of Representatives shall immediately choose by ballot one of them for President; and if no person have a majority, then from the five highest on the list the said house shall in like manner choose the President. But in choosing the President the votes shall be taken by states, the representation from each state having one vote; a quorum for this purpose shall consist of a member or members from two thirds of the states, and a majority of all the states shall be necessary to a choice. In every case, after the choice of the President, the person having the greatest number of votes of the electors shall be the Vice President. But if there should remain two or more who have equal votes, the Senate shall choose from them by ballot the Vice President.

c. *Time of elections.*   The Congress may determine the time of choosing the electors, and the day on which they shall give their votes; which day shall be the same throughout the United States.

d. *Qualifications of the President.*   No person except a natural-born citizen, or a citizen of the United States, at the time of the adoption of this Constitution, shall be eligible to the office of President; neither shall any person be eligible to that office who shall not have attained the age of thirty-five years, and been fourteen years a resident within the United States.

e. *Vacancy.*   In case of the removal of the President from office or of his death, resignation, or inability to discharge the powers and duties of the said office, the same shall devolve on the Vice President; and the Congress may by law provide for the case of removal, death, resignation, or inability, both of the President and Vice President, declaring what officer shall then act as President; and such officer shall act accordingly, until the disability be removed or a President shall be elected.

f. *The President's salary.*   The President shall, at stated times, receive for his services a compensation, which shall neither be increased nor diminished during the period for which he shall have been elected, and he

chosen by persons called electors. Each state has as many electors as it has Senators and Representatives.

Amendment 12 changes the above section as follows: the electors are to meet in their state capitals in December of a presidential election year. At that time, they cast their ballots for President and Vice President.

The ballots are sent to Congress and are counted on or about January 6. The counting takes place before both houses of Congress, with the Vice President in charge. A majority vote (270) is required to win the election.

If no candidate receives a majority of the electoral votes, the House of Representatives chooses the President. The choice must be made from the top three candidates. The Senate chooses the Vice President from the top two candidates.

Every four years, the people vote for the electors on a date set by Congress; the Tuesday after the first Monday in November.

The President must be a natural-born citizen of the United States, not less than 35 years of age, and must have lived in the United States for 14 years. The above requirements also apply to the Vice President.

If the President resigns, dies or is not able to carry out presidential duties, the Vice President takes over (see also the 25th Amendment).

Congress has set the line of succession after the Vice President as follows: the Speaker of the House, the President pro tempore of the Senate, and then the Cabinet officers in the order in which their departments were created (State, Treasury, Defense, and so on).

Congress sets the President's salary. This salary cannot be raised or lowered during a President's term of office.

At the inauguration, on January 20, the new President promises to support the Constitution.

shall not receive within the period any other emolument from the United States, or any of them.

g. Oath of office. Before he enter on the execution of his office, he shall take the following oath or affirmation: "I do solemnly swear (or affirm) that I will faithfully execute the office of President of the United States, and will to the best of my ability, preserve, protect, and defend the Constitution of the United States."

Section 2. POWERS OF THE PRESIDENT

The President is the head of all the military forces, including the National Guard. The President may grant pardons for federal crimes or postpone the carrying out of a sentence. No pardon may be granted in a case of impeachment.

The President can make treaties with foreign nations. All treaties must be approved by a two-thirds vote of the Senate. The President appoints many high officials, but the Senate must approve by a majority vote.

When the Senate is not in session, the President may make temporary appointments.

a. Military powers; reprieves and pardons. The President shall be Commander-in-Chief of the Army and Navy of the United States, and of the militia of the several states, when called into the actual service of the United States. He may require the opinion, in writing, of the principal officer in each of the executive departments, upon any subject relating to the duties of their respective offices, and he shall have power to grant reprieves and pardons for offenses against the United States, except in cases of impeachment.

b. Treaties; appointments. He shall have power, by and with the advice and consent of the Senate, to make treaties, provided two thirds of the senators present concur; and he shall nominate and, by and with the advice and consent of the Senate, shall appoint ambassadors, other public ministers and consuls, judges of the Supreme Court, and all other officers of the United States, whose appointments are not herein otherwise provided for, and which shall be established by law; but the Congress may by law vest the appointment of such inferior officers as they think proper in the President alone, in the courts of law, or in the heads of departments.

c. Filling vacancies. The President shall have power to fill up all vacancies that may happen during the recess of the Senate, by granting commissions which shall expire at the end of their next session.

Section 3. DUTIES OF THE PRESIDENT

The President must give reports to the Congress, such as the State of the Union message and the budget message.
The President must meet foreign visitors, appoint military officers, and see that the laws are carried out.

He shall from time to time give to the Congress information of the state of the Union and recommend to their consideration such measures as he shall judge necessary and expedient; he may, on extraordinary occasions, convene both houses, or either of them, and in case of disagreement between them with respect to the time of adjournment he may adjourn them to such time as he shall think proper; he shall receive ambassadors and other public ministers; he shall take care that the laws be faithfully executed, and shall commission all the officers of the United States.

IMPEACHMENT

The President, Vice President and all civil officers of the United States shall be removed from office on impeachment for, and conviction of, treason, bribery, or other high crimes and misdemeanors.

Section 4.

The President or the Vice President, like any other government official, can be impeached for breaking the law or misusing the power of the office.

JUDICIAL DEPARTMENT

Article Three.

THE FEDERAL COURTS

Section 1.

The judicial power of the United States shall be vested in one Supreme Court and in such inferior courts as the Congress may from time to time ordain and establish. The judges, both of the Supreme and inferior courts, shall hold their offices during good behavior and shall, at stated times, receive for their services a compensation which shall not be diminished during their continuance in office.

The Supreme Court is the only court mentioned in the Constitution. Congress is given the power to set up other federal courts. Judges have a lifetime job. They can only be removed by impeachment. Congress cannot reduce the salary of judges during their term of office.

JURISDICTION OF THE FEDERAL COURTS

Section 2.

a. Federal courts. The judicial power shall extend to all cases, in law and equity, arising under this Constitution, the laws of the United States, and treaties made, or which shall be made, under their authority; to all cases affecting ambassadors, other public ministers, and consuls; to all cases of admiralty and maritime jurisdiction; to controversies to which the United States shall be a party; to controversies between two or more states; between a state and citizens of another state; between citizens of different states; between citizens of the same state claiming lands under grants of different states, and between a state, or the citizens thereof, and foreign states, citizens, or subjects.

b. Supreme Court. In all cases affecting ambassadors, other public ministers, and consuls, and those in which a state shall be a party, the Supreme Court shall have original jurisdiction. In all the other cases before mentioned, the Supreme Court shall have appellate jurisdiction, both as to law and fact, with such exceptions and under such regulations as the Congress shall make.

c. Rules respecting trials. The trial of all crimes, except in cases of impeachment, shall be by jury; and such trial shall be held in the state where the said crimes shall have been committed; but when not committed within any state, the trial shall be at such place or places as the Congress may by law have directed.

Federal courts try cases involving the Constitution, federal laws, treaties, ships, ambassadors, public ministers, consuls, the U.S. Government, two or more state governments, citizens of different states, a state or its citizens against foreign countries or citizens of foreign countries.

Certain cases that deal with ambassadors, states, or foreign nations, may be tried only in the Supreme Court.

A person accused of a crime has the right to a trial by jury, except in impeachment. The accused must be tried in the state where the crime took place. When a crime is not committed within a state (at sea, perhaps), Congress sets the place of trial.

The Constitution of the United States of America   515

Section 3.

Treason means carrying on war against the United States or helping the enemies of our nation.

A person cannot be found guilty of treason unless there are two witnesses to the crime, or unless the accused confesses in court.

Congress sets the punishment for treason, but no punishment can be given to the families of those found guilty.

TREASON

a. Definition of treason.   Treason against the United States shall consist only in levying war against them or in adhering to their enemies, giving them aid and comfort. No person shall be convicted of treason unless on the testimony of two witnesses to the same overt act, or on confession in open court.

b. Punishment of treason.   The Congress shall have power to declare the punishment of treason, but no attainder of treason shall work corruption of blood, or forfeiture except during the life of the person attainted.

Article Four.

THE STATES AND THE FEDERAL GOVERNMENT

Section 1.

The official acts of one state must be accepted as legal in all other states. Official acts would include wills, birth certificates, and the like.

STATE RECORDS

Full faith and credit shall be given in each state to the public acts, records, and judicial proceedings of every other state. And the Congress may by general laws prescribe the manner in which such acts, records, and proceedings shall be proved, and the effect thereof.

Section 2.

Each state must treat citizens of other states as fairly as it treats its own citizens.

An accused person who escapes to another state must be returned to the state from which he or she fled.

The same rule once applied to runaway slaves. It is no longer in effect.

PRIVILEGES AND IMMUNITIES OF CITIZENS

a. Privileges.   The citizens of each state shall be entitled to all privileges and immunities of citizens in the several states.

b. Extradition.   A person charged in any state with treason, felony, or other crime who shall flee from justice and be found in another state shall, on demand of the executive authority of the state from which he fled, be delivered up, to be removed to the state having jurisdiction of the crime.

c. Fugitive slaves.   No person held to service or labor in one state, under the laws thereof, escaping into another shall, in consequence of any law or regulation therein, be discharged from such service or labor, but shall be delivered upon claim of the party to whom such service or labor may be due.

Section 3.

New states can be admitted into the Union by Congress.

NEW STATES AND TERRITORIES

a. Admission of new states.   New states may be admitted by the Congress into this Union; but no new state shall be formed or erected within the jurisdiction of any other state; nor any state be formed by the junction of two or more states, or parts of states, without the consent of the legislatures of the states concerned, as well as of the Congress.

b. Power of Congress over territory and property. The Congress shall have power to dispose of and make all needful rules and regulations respecting the territory or other property belonging to the United States; and nothing in this Constitution shall be so construed as to prejudice any claims of the United States, or of any particular state.

Congress makes the laws for governing the territories and for the control of all federal property.

GUARANTEES TO THE STATES

Section 4.

The United States shall guarantee to every state in this Union a republican form of government, and shall protect each of them against invasion; and on application of the legislature, or of the executive (when the legislature cannot be convened), against domestic violence.

Each state is guaranteed a republican form of government—a government by elected representatives of the people.

The federal government must protect the states against invasion, riot, or other threats to the peace.

METHOD OF AMENDMENT

Article Five.

The Congress, whenever two thirds of both houses shall deem it necessary, shall propose amendments to this Constitution, or, on the application of the legislatures of two thirds of the several states, shall call a convention for proposing amendments, which, in either case, shall be valid to all intents and purposes, as part of this Constitution, when ratified by the legislatures of three fourths of the several states or by conventions in three fourths thereof, as the one or the other mode of ratification may be proposed by the Congress; provided that no amendments which may be made prior to the year one thousand eight hundred and eight shall in any manner affect the first and fourth clauses in the ninth section of the first article; and that no state, without its consent, shall be deprived of its equal suffrage in the Senate.

Amendments to the Constitution may be proposed by a two-thirds vote of both houses of Congress or by a vote of two-thirds of the states. Amendments may be approved by either the legislatures of three-fourths of the states or by conventions in three-fourths of the states.

GENERAL PROVISIONS

Article Six.

a. Public debt. All debts contracted and engagements entered into, before the adoption of this Constitution, shall be as valid against the United States under this Constitution as under the Confederation.

The United States will pay back any money borrowed by the earlier government under the Articles of Confederation.

b. Supremacy of the Constitution. This Constitution, and the laws of the United States which shall be made in pursuance thereof; and all treaties made, or which shall be made, under the authority of the United States, shall be the supreme law of the land; and the judges in every state shall be bound thereby, anything in the Constitution or laws of any state to the contrary notwithstanding.

The Constitution, treaties, and laws of the United States are the supreme law of the land. State laws cannot conflict with federal laws.

c. Oath of office; no religious test. The senators and representatives before mentioned, and the members of the several state legislatures, and all executive and judicial officers, both of the United States and of the several states, shall be bound by oath or affirmation to support this Constitution;

All federal and state officials must take an oath of office in which they promise to uphold the Constitution.

There can be no religious re-

The Constitution of the United States of America   517

quirement for holding office at any level of government.

but no religious test shall ever be required as a qualification to any office or public trust under the United States.

Article Seven.

RATIFICATION OF THE CONSTITUTION

The Constitution becomes the law of the nation when nine states approve it.

The ratification of the conventions of nine states shall be sufficient for the establishment of this Constitution between the states so ratifying the same.

AMENDMENTS TO THE CONSTITUTION

Amendment 1

FREEDOM OF RELIGION, SPEECH, AND PRESS·1791

Congress cannot declare an official religion for this nation. People must be allowed to follow the religion of their choice. Congress cannot stop people from writing, printing, or speaking freely. The people must be given the right to hold peaceful public meetings, and the right to bring their complaints to their elected representatives.

Congress shall make no law respecting an establishment of religion, or prohibiting the free exercise thereof; or abridging the freedom of speech, or of the press; or the right of the people peaceably to assemble, and to petition the government for a redress of grievances.

Amendment 2

THE RIGHT TO KEEP AND BEAR ARMS·1791

The federal government cannot deny the states the right to keep an armed militia.

A well-regulated militia being necessary to the security of a free state, the right of the people to keep and bear arms shall not be infringed.

Amendment 3

THE QUARTERING OF TROOPS·1791

In peacetime, soldiers cannot be placed in private homes by the government. In wartime, this can be done, but only in accordance with rules set down by Congress.

No soldier shall, in time of peace, be quartered in any house without the consent of the owner, nor in time of war, but in a manner to be prescribed by law.

LIMITING THE RIGHT OF SEARCH • 1791

Amendment 4

The right of the people to be secure in their persons, houses, papers, and effects against unreasonable searches and seizures shall not be violated, and no warrants shall issue but upon probable cause, supported by oath or affirmation and particularly describing the place to be searched and the persons or things to be seized.

Police or other officials cannot search persons, homes, or other personal property without a search warrant. A warrant is a legal paper, signed by a judge, giving permission to carry on a search. A judge should not sign a warrant unless there is a good reason for the search. A warrant must list the place to be searched, and the persons or things to be taken.

RIGHTS OF THE ACCUSED AND OF PROPERTY • 1791

Amendment 5

No person shall be held to answer for a capital or otherwise infamous crime, unless on a presentment or indictment of a grand jury, except in cases arising in the land or naval forces, or in the militia, when in actual service in time of war or public danger; nor shall any person be subject for the same offense to be twice put in jeopardy of life or limb; nor shall be compelled in any criminal case to be a witness against himself, nor be deprived of life, liberty, or property, without due process of law; nor shall private property be taken for public use without just compensation.

The federal government cannot try a person for a crime unless a grand jury decides there is enough evidence.

A person tried and found not guilty cannot be tried again for the same crime.

During a trial, accused persons may remain silent, and cannot be forced to give evidence against themselves.

The government cannot take away a person's life, liberty, or property except by lawful means (due process of law).

The government must pay a fair price for seized property.

FURTHER RIGHTS OF THE ACCUSED • 1791

Amendment 6

In all criminal prosecutions, the accused shall enjoy the right to a speedy and public trial by an impartial jury of the state and district wherein the crime shall have been committed, which districts shall have been previously ascertained by law, and to be informed of the nature and cause of the accusation; to be confonted with the witnesses against him; to have

A person accused of a crime has the following rights:
- a public trial as soon as possible after arrest;
- a jury that will decide the

case fairly, and whose members live nearby;

- to be told the exact charges, so that a defense can be prepared;
- the chance to question unfriendly witnesses;
- the court's help getting friendly witnesses;
- a lawyer, paid by the government if the accused cannot afford to pay.

compulsory process for obtaining witnesses in his favor; and to have the assistance of counsel for his defense.

Amendment 7

THE RULES OF COMMON LAW · 1791

People have a right to a jury trial in all cases that involve more than $20.00.

In suits at common law, where the value in controversy shall exceed twenty dollars, the right of trial by jury shall be preserved, and no fact tried by a jury shall be otherwise re-examined in any court of the United States than according to the rules of common law.

Amendment 8

EXCESSIVE BAIL AND PUNISHMENT · 1791

Bail, fines, and punishments must be fair and reasonable.

Excessive bail shall not be required, nor excessive fines imposed, nor cruel and unusual punishments inflicted.

Amendment 9

RIGHTS KEPT BY PEOPLE · 1791

Although all of the peoples' rights are not named by the Constitution, the federal government cannot take away those rights simply because they are not named.

The enumeration in the Constitution of certain rights shall not be construed to deny or disparage others retained by the people.

Amendment 10

POWERS KEPT BY STATES AND PEOPLE · 1791

All powers that are not given to the federal government belong to the states or the people.

The powers not delegated to the United States by the Constitution, nor prohibited by it to the states are reserved to the states respectively, or to the people.

Amendment 11

LIMITING FEDERAL COURTS · 1798

Federal courts do not have the power to hear cases brought

The judicial power of the United States shall not be construed to extend to any suit in law or equity commenced or prosecuted against one of the

United States by citizens of another state or by citizens or subjects of any foreign state.

against a state by citizens of another state or by foreigners. Such cases must be heard in state courts.

ELECTION OF PRESIDENT AND VICE PRESIDENT · 1804

Amendment 12

This amendment is explained in Article 2, Section 1.

The electors shall meet in their respective states and vote by ballot for President and Vice President, one of whom, at least, shall not be an inhabitant of the same state with themselves; they shall name in their ballots the person voted for as President, and in distinct ballots the person voted for as Vice President, and they shall make distinct lists of all persons voted for as President, and of all persons voted for as Vice President, and of the number of votes for each, which lists they shall sign and certify, and transmit sealed to the seat of the government of the United States, directed to the President of the Senate; the President of the Senate shall, in the presence of the Senate and House of Representatives, open all the certificates and the votes shall then be counted; the person having the greatest number of votes for President shall be the President, if such number be a majority of the whole number of electors appointed; and if no person have such majority, then from the persons having the highest numbers not exceeding three on the list of those voted for as President, the House of Representatives shall choose immediately, by ballot, the President. But in choosing the President, the votes shall be taken by states, the representation from each state having one vote; a quorum for this purpose shall consist of a member or members from two thirds of the states, and a majority of all the states shall be necessary to a choice. And if the House of Representatives shall not choose a President whenever the right of choice shall devolve upon them, before the fourth day of March next following, then the Vice President shall act as President, as in the case of the death or other constitutional disability of the President. The person having the greatest number of votes as Vice President shall be the Vice President, if such number be a majority of the whole number of electors appointed, and if no person have a majority, then from the two highest numbers on the list, the Senate shall choose the Vice President; a quorum for the purpose shall consist of two thirds of the whole number of senators, and a majority of the whole number shall be necessary to a choice. But no person constitutionally ineligible to the office of President shall be eligible to that of Vice President of the United States.

THE ABOLITION OF SLAVERY · 1865

Amendment 13

Slavery is abolished.

Section 1. Abolition of slavery. Neither slavery nor involuntary servitude, except as a punishment for crime whereof the party shall have been duly convicted, shall exist within the United States or any place subject to their jurisdiction.

Section 2. Enforcement. Congress shall have the power to enforce this article by appropriate legislation.

Congress can pass laws to enforce this order.

Amendment 14

CIVIL RIGHTS GUARANTEED · 1868

Former slaves are made citizens. No state can take away the rights and privileges of its citizens. The Bill of Rights applies to state governments as well as to the federal government. All persons must have equal protection of the law.

If a state keeps certain citizens from voting, the state's representation in Congress should be reduced.

Former officials in the Confederate government who had previously taken an oath to support the Constitution before the Civil War cannot hold public office, except by approval of Congress through a two-thirds vote.

The U.S. government will not pay any debts of the Confederate government.

Section 1. Definition of citizenship. All persons born or naturalized in the United States, and subject to the jurisdiction thereof, are citizens of the United States and of the state wherein they reside. No state shall make or enforce any law which shall abridge the privileges or immunities of citizens of the United States; nor shall any state deprive any person of life, liberty, or property, without due process of law; nor deny to any person within its jurisdiction the equal protection of the laws.

Section 2. Apportionment of representatives. Representatives shall be apportioned among the several states according to their respective numbers, counting the whole number of persons in each state, excluding Indians not taxed. But when the right to vote at any election for the choice of electors for President and Vice President of the United States, representatives in Congress, the executive and judicial officers of a state, or the members of the legislature thereof, is denied to any of the male inhabitants of such state, being twenty-one years of age and citizens of the United States, or in any way abridged, except for participation in rebellion, or other crime, the basis of representation therein shall be reduced in the proportion which the number of such male citizens shall bear to the whole number of male citizens twenty-one years of age in such state.

Section 3. Disability resulting from insurrection. No person shall be a senator or representative in Congress, or elector of President and Vice President, or hold any office, civil or military, under the United States, or under any state, who, having previously taken an oath as a member of Congress, or as an officer of the United States, or as a member of any state legislature, or as an executive or judicial officer of any state, to support the Constitution of the United States, shall have engaged in insurrection or rebellion against the same, or given aid or comfort to the enemies thereof. But Congress may by vote of two thirds of each house remove such disability.

Section 4. United States debt valid; Confederate debt void. The validity of the public debt of the United States, authorized by law, including debts incurred for payment of pensions and bounties for services in suppressing insurrection or rebellion, shall not be questioned. But neither the United States nor any state shall assume or pay any debt or obligation incurred in aid of insurrection or rebellion against the United States, or any claim for the loss or emancipation of any slave; but all such debts, obligations, and claims shall be held illegal and void.

Section 5. Enforcement. The Congress shall have power to enforce by appropriate legislation the provisions of this article.

Amendment 15

VOTES FOR FREEDMEN · 1870

No citizen can be denied the right to vote because of race, color, or because that person

Section 1. The suffrage. The right of citizens of the United States to vote shall not be denied or abridged by the United States or by any state on account of race, color, or previous condition of servitude.

Section 2. Enforcement. The Congress shall have power to enforce this article by appropriate legislation.

was once a slave.

THE INCOME TAX • 1913

Amendment 16

The Congress shall have power to lay and collect taxes on incomes, from whatever source derived, without apportionment among the several states and without regard to any census or enumeration.

Congress is given the power to tax personal incomes (the money a person makes in salary or wages).

POPULAR ELECTION OF SENATORS • 1913

Amendment 17

a. Election by the people The Senate of the United States shall be composed of two senators from each state, elected by the people thereof, for six years; and each senator shall have one vote. The electors in each state shall have the qualifications requisite for electors of the most numerous branch of the state legislatures.

b. Vacancies. When vacancies happen in the representation of any state in the Senate, the executive authority of such state shall issue writs of election to fill such vacancies: provided that the legislature of any state may empower the executive thereof to make temporary appointments until the people fill the vacancies by election as the legislature may direct.

c. Not retroactive. This amendment shall not be so construed as to affect the election or term of any senator chosen before it becomes valid as part of the Constitution.

Senators are to be elected by the people of each state and not state legislatures.

A vacancy in the Senate is to be filled by a special election called by the governor of the state. The legislature may give the governor power to appoint someone until a special election is held.

PROHIBITION • 1919

Amendment 18

Section 1. Prohibition of intoxicating liquors. After one year from the ratification of this article the manufacture, sale, or transportation of intoxicating liquors within, the importation thereof into, or the exportation thereof from the United States and all territory subject to the jurisdiction thereof for beverage purposes is hereby prohibited.

Section 2. Enforcement. The Congress and the several states shall have concurrent power to enforce this article by appropriate legislation.

Section 3. Limited time for ratification. This article shall be inoperative unless it shall have been ratified as an amendment to the Constitution by the legislatures of the several states, as provided in the Constitution, within seven years from the date of the submission hereof to the states by the Congress.

The manufacture, sale, or transportation of any alcoholic beverages is forbidden. (This amendment was repealed [withdrawn] in 1933 by the passage of the 21st Amendment.)

VOTES FOR WOMEN • 1920

Amendment 19

Section 1. Woman suffrage. The right of citizens of the United States to vote shall not be denied or abridged by the United States or by any state on account of sex.

Women are given the right to vote.

The Constitution of the United States of America 523

Section 2. Enforcement. The Congress shall have power to enforce this article by appropriate legislation.

Amendment 20

The President's term of office begins on January 20.

The Congress must meet at least once every year. A session will start January 3, unless the members decide on a different date.

If the President-elect dies, or is not able to hold office, the Vice President becomes President.

TERMS OF THE PRESIDENT AND OF CONGRESS · 1933

Section 1. Terms of President, Vice President, and Congress. The terms of the President and Vice President shall end at noon on the 20th day of January, and the terms of senators and representatives at noon on the 3rd day of January, of the years in which such terms would have ended if this article had not been ratified; and the terms of their successors shall then begin.

Section 2. Sessions of Congress. The Congress shall assemble at least once in every year, and such meeting shall begin at noon on the 3rd day of January, unless they shall by law appoint a different day.

Section 3. Death of the President-elect. If, at the time fixed for the beginning of the term of the President, the President-elect shall have died, the Vice President-elect shall become President. If a President shall not have been chosen before the time fixed for the beginning of his term, or if the President-elect shall have failed to qualify, then the Vice President-elect shall act as President until a President shall have qualified; and the Congress may by law provide for the case wherein neither a President-elect nor a Vice President-elect shall have qualified, declaring who shall then act as President, or the manner in which one who is to act shall be selected, and such person shall act accordingly until a President or a Vice President shall have qualified.

Section 4. Choice of President by the House. The Congress may by law provide for the case of the death of any of the persons from whom the House of Representatives may choose a President whenever the right of choice shall have devolved upon them, and for the case of the death of any of the persons from whom the Senate may choose a Vice President whenever the right of choice shall have devolved upon them.

Section 5. Effective date. Sections 1 and 2 shall take effect on the fifteenth day of October following the ratification of this article.

Section 6. Limited time for ratification. This article shall be inoperative unless it shall have been ratified as an amendment to the Constitution by the legislatures of three fourths of the several states within seven years from the date of its submission.

Amendment 21

The 18th amendment is repealed.

REPEAL OF PROHIBITION · 1933

Section 1. Repeal of Amendment 18. The eighteenth article of amendment to the Constitution of the United States is hereby repealed.

Section 2. States protected.   The transportation or importation into any state, territory, or possession of the United States for delivery or use therein of intoxicating liquors, in violation of the laws thereof, is hereby prohibited.

Section 3. Limited time for ratification.   This article shall be inoperative unless it shall have been ratified as an amendment to the Constitution by conventions in the several states, as provided in the Constitution, within seven years from the date of the submission hereof to the states by the Congress.

PRESIDENTIAL TERMS · 1951

Amendment 22

A President is limited to two terms of office. A person who has held the office for more than two years can only be elected once.

Section 1. Definition of limitation.   No person shall be elected to the office of the President more than twice, and no person who has held the office of President, or acted as President, for more than two years of a term to which some other person was elected President shall be elected to the office of the President more than once. But this article shall not apply to any person holding the office of President when this article was proposed by the Congress, and shall not prevent any person who may be holding the office of President, or acting as President, during the term within which this article becomes operative from holding the office of President, or acting as President during the remainder of such term.

Section 2. Limited time for ratification.   This article shall be inoperative unless it shall have been ratified as an amendment to the Constitution by the legislatures of three fourths of the several states within seven years from the date of its submission to the states by the Congress.

VOTING IN THE DISTRICT OF COLUMBIA · 1961

Amendment 23

The people of Washington, D.C., have the right to vote for the President and Vice President.

Section 1. Appointment of Electors.   The District constituting the seal of government of the United States shall appoint, in such manner as the Congress may direct: A number of electors as President and Vice President equal to the whole number of senators and representatives in Congress to which the District would be entitled if it were a state, but in no event more than the least populous state; they shall be in addition to those appointed by the states, but they shall be considered, for the purposes of the election of President and Vice President, to be electors appointed by a state; and they shall meet in the District and perform such duties as provided by the twelfth article of amendment.

Section 2. Enforcement.   The Congress shall have power to enforce this article by appropriate legislation.

Amendment 24

No state may charge a tax on people as a condition for voting.

THE POLL TAX · 1964

Section 1. Prohibition in national elections. The right of citizens of the United States to vote in any primary or other election for President or Vice President, for electors for President or Vice President, or for senator or representative in Congress, shall not be denied or abridged by the United States or any state by reason of failure to pay any poll tax or other tax.

Section 2. Enforcement The Congress shall have power to enforce this article by appropriate legislation.

Amendment 25

If the President dies, resigns or is removed from office, the Vice President becomes President.

If the office of the Vice President becomes vacant, the President chooses a new Vice President, subject to the approval of Congress.

If the President is ill and unable to perform the duties of office, the Vice President becomes acting President.

If the Vice President and a majority of Cabinet officers decide that a President cannot perform the duties of the office, the Vice President shall become acting president.

When the President feels ready to go back to work, he or she will notify the Congress. But if the Vice President and the Cabinet officers believe that the President is not able to so perform, Congress will decide, by a two-thirds vote, whether or not the President can take over the office.

DISABILITY OF THE PRESIDENT · 1967

Section 1. Succession of the Vice President. In case of the removal of the President from office or of his death or resignation, the Vice President shall become President.

Section 2. Replacing the Vice President. Whenever there is a vacancy in the office of the Vice President, the President shall nominate a Vice President who shall take office upon confirmation by a majority vote of both Houses of Congress.

Section 3. The Vice President as Acting President. Whenever the President transmits to the President pro tempore of the Senate and the Speaker of the House of Representatives his written declaration that he is unable to discharge the powers and duties of his office, and until he transmits to them a written declaration to the contrary, such powers and duties shall be discharged by the Vice President as Acting President.

Section 4. Determining presidential disability. Whenever the Vice President and a majority of either the principal officers of the executive departments or of such other body as Congress may by law provide, transmit to the President pro tempore of the Senate and the Speaker of the House of Representatives their written declaration that the President is unable to discharge the powers and duties of his office, the Vice President shall immediately assume the powers and duties of the office as Acting President.

Thereafter, when the President transmits to the President pro tempore of the Senate and the Speaker of the House of Representatives his written declaration that no inability exists, he shall resume the powers and duties of his office unless the Vice President and a majority of either the principal officers of the executive department or of such other body as Congress may by law provide, transmit within four days to the President pro tempore of the Senate and the Speaker of the House of Representatives their written declaration that the President is unable to discharge the powers and duties of his office. Thereupon, Congress shall decide the issue, assembling within forty-eight hours for that purpose, if not in session. If the Congress, within twenty-one days after receipt of the latter written declaration, or, if Congress is not in session, within twenty-one days after Congress is required to assemble, determines by two-thirds vote of both Houses that the President is unable to discharge the powers and duties of his office, the Vice President shall continue to discharge the same as Acting President; otherwise, the President shall resume the powers and duties of his office.

LOWERING THE VOTING AGE • 1971

Amendment 26

Section 1. Eighteen-year-olds may vote. The right of citizens of the United States who are eighteen years of age or older to vote shall not be denied or abridged by the United States or by any state on account of age.

Citizens who are 18 years of age cannot be kept from voting because of age.

Section 2. Enforcement. The Congress shall have power to enforce this article by appropriate legislation.

Presidents of the United States

	President	Birth-Death	Occupation	State*
1	George Washington	1732–1799	Planter, Soldier	Virginia
2	John Adams	1735–1826	Lawyer	Maryland
3	Thomas Jefferson	1743–1826	Planter, Lawyer	Virginia
4	James Madison	1751–1836	Politician	Virginia
5	James Monroe	1758–1831	Politician, Lawyer	Virginia
6	John Quincy Adams	1767–1848	Lawyer	Maryland
7	Andrew Jackson	1767–1845	Lawyer	Tennessee
8	Martin Van Buren	1782–1862	Lawyer	New York
9	William H. Harrison	1773–1841	Soldier	Ohio
10	John Tyler	1790–1862	Lawyer	Virginia
11	James K. Polk	1795–1849	Lawyer	Tennessee
12	Zachary Taylor	1784–1850	Soldier	Louisiana
13	Millard Fillmore	1800–1874	Lawyer	New York
14	Franklin Pierce	1804–1869	Lawyer	New Hampshire
15	James Buchanan	1791–1868	Lawyer	Pennsylvania
16	Abraham Lincoln	1809–1865	Lawyer	Illinois
17	Andrew Johnson	1808–1875	Tailor, Politician	Tennessee
18	Ulysses S. Grant	1822–1885	Farmer, Soldier	Illinois
19	Rutherford B. Hayes	1822–1893	Lawyer	Ohio
20	James A. Garfield	1831–1881	Lawyer, Politician	Ohio
21	Chester A. Arthur	1830–1886	Lawyer	New York
22	Grover Cleveland	1837–1908	Lawyer	New York
23	Benjamin Harrison	1833–1901	Lawyer	Indiana
24	Grover Cleveland	1837–1908	Lawyer	New York
25	William McKinley	1843–1901	Lawyer	Ohio
26	Theodore Roosevelt	1858–1919	Author, Politician	New York
27	William H. Taft	1857–1930	Lawyer	Ohio
28	Woodrow Wilson	1856–1924	Lawyer	New Jersey
29	Warren G. Harding	1865–1923	Newspaper Editor, Publisher	Ohio
30	Calvin Coolidge	1872–1933	Lawyer	Maryland
31	Herbert C. Hoover	1874–1964	Engineer	California
32	Franklin D. Roosevelt	1882–1945	Lawyer	New York
33	Harry S Truman	1884–1972	Businessman, Politician	Missouri
34	Dwight D. Eisenhower	1890–1969	Soldier	New York
35	John F. Kennedy	1917–1963	Author, Politician	Massachusetts
36	Lyndon B. Johnson	1908–1973	Teacher, Politician	Texas
37	Richard M. Nixon	1913–	Lawyer, Politician	New York
38	Gerald R. Ford	1913–	Lawyer, Politician	Michigan
39	Jimmy Carter	1924–	Businessman, Politician	Georgia
40	Ronald Reagan	1911–	Actor, Politician	California
41	George H.W. Bush	1924–	Businessman, Politician	Texas

* State of residence at time of election.

Years in Office	Age When Elected	Party	Vice President(s)
1789–1797	57	None	John Adams
1797–1801	61	Federalist	Thomas Jefferson
1801–1809	57	Republican**	Aaron Burr, George Clinton
1809–1817	57	Republican**	George Clinton, Elbridge Gerry
1817–1825	58	Republican**	Daniel D. Tompkins
1825–1829	57	Republican**	John C. Calhoun
1829–1837	61	Democratic	John C. Calhoun, Martin Van Buren
1837–1841	54	Democratic	Richard M. Johnson
1841	68	Whig	John Tyler
1841–1845	51	Whig	
1845–1849	49	Democratic	George M. Dallas
1849–1850	64	Whig	Millard Fillmore
1850–1853	50	Whig	
1853–1857	48	Democratic	William R. King
1857–1861	65	Democratic	John G. Breckinridge
1861–1865	52	Republican	Hannibal Hamlin, Andrew Johnson
1865–1869	56	Republican	
1869–1877	46	Republican	Schuyler Colfax, Henry Wilson
1877–1881	54	Republican	William A. Wheeler
1881	49	Republican	Chester A. Arthur
1881–1885	50	Republican	
1885–1889	47	Democratic	Thomas A. Hendricks
1889–1893	55	Republican	Levi P. Morton
1893–1897	55	Democratic	Adlai E. Stevenson
1897–1901	54	Republican	Garret A. Hobart, Theodore Roosevelt
1901–1909	42	Republican	Charles W. Fairbanks
1909–1913	51	Republican	James S. Sherman
1913–1921	56	Democratic	Thomas R. Marshall
1921–1923	55	Republican	Calvin Coolidge
1923–1929	51	Republican	Charles G. Dawes
1929–1933	54	Republican	Charles Curtis
1933–1945	51	Democratic	John N. Garner, Henry A. Wallace, Harry S Truman
1945–1953	60	Democratic	Alben W. Barkley
1953–1961	62	Republican	Richard M. Nixon
1961–1963	43	Democratic	Lyndon B. Johnson
1963–1969	55	Democratic	Hubert H. Humphrey
1969–1974	56	Republican	Spiro T. Agnew, Gerald R. Ford
1974–1977	61	Republican	Nelson R. Rockefeller
1977–1981	52	Democratic	Walter F. Mondale
1981–1989	69	Republican	George H.W. Bush
1989–	64	Republican	J. Danforth Quayle

** The Republican Party of the early 1800s developed into what is today the Democratic Party. The modern Republican Party was not formed until 1854.

The United States: Facts and Figures

State	Date (and Order) of Entry to Union	Area in Square Miles	Population (1990 estimate)	Capital
Alabama	1819 (22)	51,705	4,181,000	Montgomery
Alaska	1959 (49)	591,004	576,000	Juneau
Arizona	1912 (48)	114,000	3,752,000	Phoenix
Arkansas	1836 (25)	53,187	2,427,000	Little Rock
California	1850 (31)	158,706	29,126,000	Sacramento
Colorado	1876 (38)	104,091	3,434,000	Denver
Connecticut	1788 (5)	5,018	3,279,000	Hartford
Delaware	1787 (1)	2,044	666,000	Dover
Florida	1845 (27)	58,664	12,818,000	Tallahassee
Georgia	1788 (4)	58,910	6,663,000	Atlanta
Hawaii	1959 (50)	6,471	1,141,000	Honolulu
Idaho	1890 (43)	83,564	1,017,000	Boise
Illinois	1818 (21)	56,345	11,612,000	Springfield
Indiana	1816 (19)	36,185	5,550,000	Indianapolis
Iowa	1846 (29)	56,275	2,758,000	Des Moines
Kansas	1861 (34)	82,277	2,492,000	Topeka
Kentucky	1792 (15)	40,409	3,145,000	Frankfort
Louisiana	1812 (18)	47,751	4,513,000	Baton Rouge
Maine	1820 (23)	33,265	1,212,000	Augusta
Maryland	1788 (7)	10,460	4,729,000	Annapolis
Massachusetts	1788 (6)	8,284	5,880,000	Boston
Michigan	1837 (26)	58,527	9,293,000	Lansing
Minnesota	1858 (32)	84,402	4,324,000	St. Paul
Mississippi	1817 (20)	47,689	2,699,000	Jackson
Missouri	1821 (24)	69,697	5,192,000	Jefferson City
Montana	1889 (41)	147,046	805,000	Helena
Nebraska	1867 (37)	77,355	1,588,000	Lincoln
Nevada	1864 (36)	110,561	1,076,000	Carson City
New Hampshire	1788 (9)	9,279	1,142,000	Concord
New Jersey	1787 (3)	7,787	7,899,000	Trenton

State	Date (and Order) of Entry to Union	Area in Square Miles	Population (1990 estimate)	Capital
New Mexico	1912 (47)	121,593	1,632,000	Santa Fe
New York	1788 (11)	49,108	17,773,000	Albany
North Carolina	1789 (12)	52,669	6,690,000	Raleigh
North Dakota	1889 (39)	70,703	660,000	Bismarck
Ohio	1803 (17)	41,330	10,791,000	Columbus
Oklahoma	1907 (46)	69,956	3,285,000	Oklahoma City
Oregon	1859 (33)	97,073	2,766,000	Salem
Pennsylvania	1787 (2)	45,308	11,827,000	Harrisburg
Rhode Island	1790 (13)	1,212	1,002,000	Providence
South Carolina	1788 (8)	31,113	6,623,000	Columbia
South Dakota	1889 (40)	77,116	708,000	Pierre
Tennessee	1796 (16)	42,144	4,972,000	Nashville
Texas	1845 (28)	266,807	17,712,000	Austin
Utah	1896 (45)	84,899	1,776,000	Salt Lake City
Vermont	1791 (14)	9,614	562,000	Montpelier
Virginia	1788 (10)	40,767	6,157,000	Richmond
Washington	1889 (42)	68,138	4,657,000	Olympia
West Virginia	1863 (35)	24,231	1,856,000	Charleston
Wisconsin	1848 (30)	56,153	4,808,000	Madison
Wyoming	1890 (44)	97,809	502,000	Cheyenne
District of Columbia		69	614,000	

Self-Governing Areas, Possessions, and Dependencies	Area in Square Miles	Population (1987)	Capital
Puerto Rico	3,515	3,292,000	San Juan
Guam	209	130,400	Agana
U.S. Virgin Islands	132	106,100	Charlotte Amalie
American Samoa	77	38,400	Pago Pago

The United States Flag: History and Etiquette

"I pledge allegiance to the Flag of the United States of America and to the Republic for which it stands, one Nation under God, indivisible, with liberty and justice for all."

As Americans, we recite the Pledge of Allegiance with hand over heart. Expressing respect and loyalty to the flag is important because it is a powerful symbol for Americans. Not only does the flag stand for our country and its republican form of government, but it also represents the ideals of liberty and equality upon which the United States of America was founded.

History of the Flag

Although its history is as old as our nation —over 200 years—the flag we know today, as shown on the next page, is quite different from early American flags. In colonial times, a variety of local flags were used. The colonists at first borrowed colors and designs from European flags. As America began to develop its own culture, colonial flags began to show symbols typical of particular regions, such as a pine tree or a beaver.

During the Revolutionary War, each military unit chose its own flag. Eventually, this practice produced such an assortment of different flags that during sea battles, foreign powers could not tell who or what each flag represented!

In 1776, General George Washington and other Revolutionary leaders pressed for the adoption of a national flag. Thus,

the first flag to represent the colonies as a whole was the Grand Union Flag, or Continental Colors, shown at the bottom of this page. This flag featured a replica of the British flag, the Union Jack, in the upper left corner.

After the colonies declared their independence from Great Britain, it was no longer appropriate to feature the British flag as part of the American flag. After seemingly endless debate, the first United States flag, the Stars and Stripes, was adopted on June 14, 1777, by a resolution of the Continental Congress. The new flag had 13 stars and 13 stripes, symbolizing the 13 original states.

Many sentimental stories have arisen about who made the first flag. One popular legend claims that Betsy Ross, an expert seamstress from Philadelphia, sewed the first flag at the request of George Washing-

The Continental Colors was first raised over George Washington's army camp at Cambridge, near Boston.

ton. Although Ross did make some flags during the Revolutionary War, this story cannot be proved by any written sources from this period.

When Kentucky and Vermont joined the Union in the 1790s, the question of changing the flag's design again arose. This time Congress decided to create a flag of 15 stars and 15 stripes. The 15-star flag flew over Fort McHenry in Baltimore Harbor during the War of 1812, inspiring Francis Scott Key to write the poem that would become the national anthem of the United States—"The Star Spangled Banner."

The United States began to grow rapidly, and by 1817 five more states entered the Union. It was soon apparent that the flag would be too cluttered if a new stripe and a new star were added for each new state. So, in 1818, Congress passed a law stating that the number of stripes on the flag would be fixed at 13, representing the original states. Then, each time a state joined the Union, the flag would receive a new star on the following Fourth of July. The present American flag has had 50 stars since July 4, 1960, when Hawaii's star was added to the flag.

Americans across the country proudly display the flag throughout the year.

free"—that is, the right edge of the flag should not be held or attached to anything. This practice symbolizes the freedom that Americans enjoy as citizens of the United States.

The Flag Code

Many countries have developed rules of etiquette, or a flag code, to set forth guidelines on how to honor and display a national flag. The flag code of the United States was enacted into law by Congress in 1942. Some of the code's main points are listed at the right.

The United States flag code is very long and detailed. It lists precise ways to display, carry, and salute the flag. The Pledge of Allegiance is also an official part of the flag code. And the code specifically states that the flag should always be allowed to "fall

Highlights of the Flag Code

1. The flag is displayed on or near the main building of all public institutions.

2. The flag is only displayed outdoors from sunrise to sunset.

3. The flag is displayed in or near every polling place on election days.

4. The United States flag is flown above and in the center of any other flags.

5. During the singing of the national anthem, all people present face the flag and stand at attention with the right hand over the heart.

Glossary

A

absentee ballot: a ballot cast in advance by a voter who will not be in the state on election day (p. 362)

administrative law: the rules and regulations of government agencies (p. 168)

alien: a citizen of another country who is living in the United States (p. 40)

amend: to improve or change (p. 23)

amendment: a written change or addition to a constitution (p. 46)

Anti-Federalist: a person opposed to the adoption of the Constitution in 1787–1788 (p. 29)

appeal: a request to have a trial court decision reviewed by a higher court (p. 169)

appeals court: any court that hears cases from other courts (p. 170)

appellate jurisdiction: the power of a court to hear an appeal from a lower court (p. 170)

appropriation: money set aside for a specific use (p. 27)

appropriations bill: a bill that allows the government to use money it has received from taxes or other sources (p. 109)

arbitrator: a person trained to settle specific disputes rather than a judge (p. 252)

Articles of Confederation: the first plan of government for the United States, designed to unite the 13 colonies and divide power equally between the central government and the states (p. 20)

B

bail: a payment of money that allows an accused person to stay out of jail until the trial (p. 56)

balanced budget: a budget in which income equals expenditures (p. 195)

ballot: paper on which a voter registers votes for candidates and issues (p. 361)

bankruptcy: a situation in which a person or city has no money to pay debts (p. 242)

bicameral: a two-house legislature (p. 216)

bill of attainder: a law that allows a person to be punished without a trial (p. 113)

Bill of Rights: the first ten amendments to the United States Constitution (p. 56)

bond: a written promise to pay someone a particular amount of money plus interest after a certain period of time (p. 441)

borough: the Alaskan term for county (p. 272)

boycott: a refusal to deal with a person or organization in order to express disapproval (p. 12)

brief: a written statement presented by a lawyer to a court (p. 177)

budget: a plan for using money (p. 434)

bureaucracy: the entire body of government workers and its agencies (p. 142)

business cycle: a term referring to the various periods an economy may go through in a given period of time (p. 403)

buying on credit: buying something today and paying for it in the future (p. 442)

C

Cabinet: the group of persons who head the major departments within the executive branch of the United States government (p. 142)

campaign: a contest for political office (p. 318)

candidate: a person running for political office (p. 120)

capital: the money needed to produce goods and services (p. 400)

capital goods: any tools or property used in the production or manufacture of goods and services (p. 400)

census: a population count (p. 99)

challenge for cause: a term meaning that a juror is dismissed for a particular reason (p. 263)

charge account: method of payment allowing a person to purchase goods and services on credit (p. 442)

charter: a city's basic law (p. 275)

checks and balances: the system by which the power of the national government is separated into three branches that check, or limit, the power of the others (p. 41)

circuits: the 11 judicial districts of the United States government (p. 170)

city council: a city's lawmaking body (p. 280)

city manager: a person hired by the city council to administer the city's affairs (p. 279)

city planner: person trained to plan for future growth and development of a city (p. 292)

civil law: all laws dealing with disputes between persons, or between persons and government (p. 168)

civil servant: individual who works in the Civil Service for the federal government (p. 154)

closed shop: a place of employment where only union members may be hired (p. 424)

cloture: procedure used to end a floor debate in a legislative body (p. 110)

coalition: interest groups who join together to work for a common goal (p. 375)

cold war: a condition of tension and hostility without armed conflict (p. 470)

collective bargaining: the process whereby representatives of business owners meet and discuss working conditions, salary, and benefits with elected union representatives (p. 423)

colonist: an original settler in a place (p. 12)

colony: land where the people are ruled by the government of another country (p. 12)

command economy: an economy in which the government makes all major economic decisions (p. 394)

commerce: trade (p. 27)

committee: a group of Senators or Representatives that is organized to study and propose bills (p. 104)

committee on committees: a group from each political party that names its respective members to serve on the various standing committees in its house (p. 105)

common law: law made by judicial decisions (p. 167)

community property: property owned equally by a husband and wife (p. 243)

commute: to reduce the length of a sentence for a prisoner (p. 234)

compromise: an agreement in which people make concessions to reach a common goal (p. 27)

concurrent jurisdiction: the right of both federal and state courts to try a case (p. 164)

concurrent powers: powers held by both national and state governments (p. 44)

conference committee: a joint committee, formed of members of both houses, that tries to work out differences in two similar versions of the same bill (p. 105)

Congress of the United States: the lawmaking body of the United States government, composed of two houses, or parts (p. 98)

congressional district: an area of a state with clearly defined boundaries (p. 98)

constituents: people represented by members of Congress (p. 105)

Constitution: the fundamental and supreme law of the United States of America (p. 6)

Constitutional law: law based on the United States Constitution (p. 167)

consumer: a person who buys and consumes, or uses, things (p. 397)

containment: United States foreign policy designed to keep communism from spreading (p. 455)

cooperative: an organization of producers and consumers who join to buy and sell goods (p. 414)

corporation: business owned by shareholders and given the authority to act like a single person under the law (p. 413)

corporation income tax: a tax placed on corporations by the federal government (p. 189)

council members at-large: city councilors elected from the city, rather than from voting districts (p. 280)

county: a major unit of local government (p. 272)

county board: the governing body of a county, elected by the voters (p. 272)

county commission: another name given to the governing body of a county (p. 272)

court: place where disputes or arguments about the law are settled (p. 163)

covenant: agreement (p. 490)

credit card: a card that allows a person to make purchases and make payments later (p. 443)

credit rating: a person's reputation as a credit risk (p. 443)

credit union: a savings and loan association operated by an employee association (p. 440)

creditor: person who loans money (p. 23)

criminal law: law that defines crimes and decides appropriate punishments (p. 168)

cross-examination: the examination of a defense witness by the lawyer for the prosecution or vice-versa (p. 259)

customs duty: an amount of money paid to the government when certain goods purchased in another country are brought into this country (p. 190)

D

debtor: someone who owes money (p. 24)

decentralized: term that relates to authority at state and local levels instead of at the central level (p. 335)

declaration of rights: another name for the bill of rights in several states' constitutions (p. 213)

deduction: a specific amount of money subtracted from taxable income (p. 187)

default: failure to pay a debt (p. 22)

defendant: person accused in a court of law (p. 168)

defense attorney: the lawyer for a defendant in a criminal trial (p. 258)

deficit spending: spending more than the income (p. 194)

delegate: a representative to a local, state, or national political convention (p. 13)

demand: the amount of goods and services consumers are willing to buy at a certain price (p. 397)

democracy: a system of government in which the people have the final power (p. 5)

dependent: a person who relies on someone else for support (p. 83)

depreciate: to decline in value (p. 197)

depression: time when production drops sharply and unemployment rises (p. 404)

developing countries: countries with a low standard of living (p. 489)

dictatorship: form of government in which an individual or a group rules, and where people have no say in government (p. 4)

diplomat: an official representative of a country who conducts relations with another country's government (p. 156)

direct democracy: a form of democracy in which the people express their views directly through group meetings (p. 5)

discount: selling a product or service at a lower–than–actual price (p. 437)

discrimination: unfair attitude toward or treatment of a particular person or group (p. 66)

disposable income: money a person has over and above the amount needed for necessities (p. 402)

dispute: an argument (p. 9)

dissenting opinion: an opinion in court in which one or more judges disagree with the decision of the majority (p. 177)

district court: a federal trial court (p. 170)

dividend: a payment issued at certain intervals to the owners of stock in a corporation (p. 413)

double jeopardy: an illegal practice in which a person is tried twice for the same crime (p. 58)

down payment: the amount of money a buyer pays on a purchase before the credit payments begin (p. 442)

drafting a bill: putting an idea for a bill in writing (p. 107)

due process of law: a guarantee that all people will receive fair and equal treatment in a court of law (p. 168)

E

economic indicators: things that show how well an economy is performing, such as the total number of goods and services being produced over a period of time (p. 401)

economic system: an organized way of satisfying people's needs and wants (p. 392)

economics: the study of how goods and services are produced, distributed, and consumed (p. 391)

economist: a person who studies economics (p. 391)

editorial section: part of a newspaper that presents the editors' opinions about issues and events (p. 323)

elastic clause: Article 1, Section 8, of the United States Constitution. It allows Congress to make laws necessary and proper to carry out its enumerated powers. (p. 45)

Electoral College: all of the electors, taken together (p. 354)

electoral vote: the vote of the electors for the President and the Vice President of the United States (p. 354)

electors: representatives elected to choose the President of the United States (p. 29)

eminent domain: government power to purchase private property for public use (p. 58)

entrepreneur: a person who owns a business and takes on the risk of its success or failure (p. 395)

enumerated powers: powers specifically given to Congress by the United States Constitution (p. 44)

equal opportunity: a term meaning that every person has the same chance to develop and function (p. 6)

estate: all of the money and property belonging to a person (p. 189)

estate tax: a tax placed directly on the estate of a person who has died, and paid by the dead person's heirs (p. 189)

excise tax: a tax on the manufacture, sale, or consumption of various items within a country (p. 187)

exclusive jurisdiction: the sole right to hear a case only in the federal courts (p. 164)

executive agreement: a written agreement between the President and the head of another country, which does not require Senate approval (p. 127)

executive branch: the President of the United States, the President's advisers, and all executive departments (p. 40)

Executive Office of the President: the name given to advisers and agencies, including the Vice President, who assist the President with presidential duties (p. 129)

executive session: a private meeting of a Congressional committee not open to the public (p. 109)

expenditure: money spent on goods and services (p. 434)

exported: sent from one country to another (p. 46)

exports: goods made in one country and sent to another (p. 113)

***ex post facto* law:** a law applying to an act that occurred before the law was passed (p. 113)

extradition: returning a prisoner from one state to the state from which escape was made (p. 50)

F

favorite son: a candidate supported by politicians from a particular state (p. 351)

featherbedding: union practice requiring an employer to hire more workers than a job actually needs (p. 424)

federal: national (p. 36)

federalism: an idea of government requiring that power be shared by the national and state governments (p. 44)

Federalist: supporters of the Constitution who favored a strong national government (p. 29)

fee: payment to obtain a government permit or service (p. 10)

felony: a serious crime, such as arson or murder (p. 251)

filibuster: non-stop talking in the Senate to prevent a bill from coming to a vote (p. 110)

fiscal: having to do with money (p. 193)

fiscal year: a 12-month period for the purpose of accounting money (p. 193)

floor leaders: leaders of the Democratic and Republican parties who guide their parties' bills through Congress (p. 102)

foreclose: to take away the right to a mortgage (p. 24)

foreign policy: plan that determines a country's actions toward the rest of the world (p. 455)

Framers: the writers of the United States Constitution (p. 29)

free enterprise system: an economic system that allows private individuals to make important economic choices (p. 395)

full faith and credit clause: the Constitution's requirement (Article IV, Section 1) that each state accept the public acts, records, and judicial proceedings of every other state (p. 49)

G

general welfare: the well-being of all the members of a society (p. 37)

genocide: the killing of an entire race of people (p. 489)

glasnost: a Soviet policy of greater openness both toward the West and within the Soviet Union (p. 477)

goods: things that satisfy our needs and wants (p. 392)

government: people who decide how a community is to be run (p. 3)

government corporation: any business operated by a government (p. 151)

grand jury: a group of about 20 persons who examine the evidence against an accused person to determine whether a trial is necessary (p. 257)

grant-in-aid: federal government money given to the states to pay for programs (p. 198)

gross national product (GNP): the dollar value of all the goods and services produced by a society within a given year (p. 402)

H

heir: anyone to whom an estate is left when the owner dies (p. 189)

home rule: powers given to cities to write their own charters and manage their own affairs (p. 275)

House of Representatives: the larger of the two houses of the Congress, consisting of 435 members with the number of members from each state determined by its population (p. 98)

human rights: rights to which all people are entitled (p. 488)

I

immigrant: person who comes from one country to live in another country (p. 86)

impeach: to bring charges against a government official (p. 39)

implied powers: any powers given the national government to pass laws to fulfill the other powers expressly stated in the Constitution (p. 46)

imports: goods brought into the United States (p. 113)

income tax: a percentage of a person's income paid to the government (p. 186)

independence: freedom from the control of others (p. 14)

Independent: the term given to people who are active in politics, but who do not belong to an organized political party (p. 337)

independent agency: an agency, commission, department, or corporation within the executive branch that performs specialized tasks outlined by the laws of Congress (p. 148)

indeterminate sentence: a prison sentence that does not specify when it will be over (p. 264)

indictment: a formal notice of a charge against a person (p. 257)

indirect democracy: a form of government in which the people elect representatives to run government affairs for them (p. 6)

inflation: an increase in the money supply, and a rise in prices (p. 398)

information: a formal charge against an accused person made by a city's district attorney (p. 257)

initiative: a process that allows voters to take a direct part in passing or vetoing state or local laws (p. 219)

injunction: a court order forbidding or directing a certain course of action (p. 173)

installment plan: payment plan offered by businesses so customers may pay smaller amounts at regular intervals until the entire debt has been paid (p. 442)

interdependent: dependent on each other (p. 476)

interest: an increase or addition over the amount of money that is owed (p. 440)

interest group: any group of individuals who have organized themselves to promote the group's interests (p. 91)

interpret: to explain or give meaning to something (p. 88)

interstate: between or among states (p. 28)

investing: placing money in business, such as bonds, to obtain a profit (p. 197)

isolationism: a policy of a government whereby it has little or no relationships with other countries (p. 470)

item veto: a means of striking out one or more parts of a bill. The governors of most states have this power, but the President of the United States does not. The President must sign or veto an entire bill. (p. 235)

J

joint committee: a committee with members from both houses of Congress (p. 104)

judicial branch: one of three branches of the United States government, composed of the Supreme Court and other federal courts (p. 40)

judicial review: the power of the United States Supreme Court and the Courts of Appeals to determine whether or not certain laws are Constitutional (p. 176)

jurisdiction: the term referring to the types of cases a court can hear and decide (p. 163)

jury: a group of people selected to decide the guilt or innocence of an accused person in court, on the basis of the evidence presented to them (p. 170)

L

labor: the term used to refer to all the workers in an economic system (p. 399)

law: written rule stating how members of a society should behave (p. 8)

legal monopoly: any business that is permitted by law to control all of the production of a particular good or service (p. 426)

legislative branch: the United States Congress, one of the three main branches of our government, charged by the Constitution with making the laws of the land (p. 39)

legislator: member of a state legislature (p. 216)

libel: the publication of statements that wrongfully damage another person's reputation (p. 57)

liberty: freedom to do as one pleases as long as the law is obeyed and others' rights are not taken away (p. 38)

M

majority opinion: the decision of the majority of judges in a case heard before the Supreme Court (p. 177)

majority party: the party that has the most members in a house of Congress at a particular time (p. 100)

majority rule: a basic idea of democracy that helps to settle any disagreement between two different groups by establishing what the majority of the people want (p. 6)

majority vote: at least more than one-half (50 percent) of the total votes in an election (p. 6)

mandatory referendum: any bill that must be referred to the voters before it can become a law (p. 220)

mandatory sentence: a situation in which a judge is required to give a sentence instead of probation to a convicted criminal (p. 264)

market economy: an economic system in which all economic decisions are made by private individuals (p. 395)

master plan: detailed outline of a city's present and future needs (p. 291)

mayor: the chief executive of a city (p. 282)

merit system: a system of employment in which all promotions are based on ability (p. 155)

metropolitan area: an urban center and its surrounding suburbs (p. 275)

militia: an emergency army of civilians (p. 57)

minority group: persons set apart from the majority of people by their color, religion, or national background (p. 66)

minority party: the party with fewer members in either house of Congress (p. 100)

misdemeanor: a minor crime (p. 251)

mixed economy: an economic system in which economic decisions are made by both government and individuals (p. 396)

monopoly: exclusive control by a single business of all the production of a good or service (p. 240)

mutual defense pact: an agreement between two or more countries to come to each other's aid in the case of an attack by enemies (p. 456)

N

national convention: a meeting of representatives of each of the political parties in the United States every four years to nominate candidates for President and Vice President (p. 350)

national debt: total amount of money owed by a country (p. 193)

natural resources: any materials provided by nature such as land and water (p. 399)

natural-born: a term that refers to a person born in the United States, or born in another country but having one or both parents as United States citizens (p. 120)

naturalized citizen: a person who was not a citizen of the United States at birth but became one later (p. 61)

negotiate: to bargain or discuss a matter with the purpose of coming to some mutual agreement (p. 22)

news media: term referring to television, radio, newspapers, and news magazines (p. 321)

nonpartisan: not favoring any particular side or position in a dispute (p. 255)

null and void: having no legal force, binding power, or validity (p. 251)

nullify: to cancel (p. 7)

O

open shop: a place of employment where workers may choose whether or not to join a union (p. 424)

opinion: a written statement by a state attorney general that explains a part of a state's constitution or law (p. 238)

ordinance: a law (p. 273)

original jurisdiction: the power of a court of law to hear a case for the first time (p. 170)

P

pardon: an act by the governor of a state setting a convicted person free from prison (p. 234)

parish: the term used in Louisiana for a county (p. 272)

parole: release of a prisoner before the prison term is complete (p. 234)

partnership: an arrangement in which two or more persons agree to share equally in the risks and rewards of a business (p. 413)

party activist: individual who works for a political party (p. 335)

party caucus: a closed meeting of the members of a political party (p. 100)

party vote: term referring to a time when 75 percent of the party's legislators vote the same way (p. 388)

party whip: the assistant to the party leaders in each house of the United States Congress (p. 102)

payroll deduction: an amount of money deducted before a person's salary is paid (p. 441)

peremptory challenge: the opportunity for lawyers to reject a juror without giving a reason (p. 263)

petition: a document voters sign that asks the government to do or stop doing something (p. 68)

pigeonholing: the act of putting aside a bill that has been sent to a committee for study and recommendation (p. 108)

plaintiff: one who brings charges against another person in a court of law (p. 168)

plea: a statement of guilt or non-guilt in a court of law (p. 257)

plea bargaining: a court agreement in which an accused person pleads guilty in return for reduced charges (p. 261)

pluralistic: having many parts (p. 66)

plurality: the largest number of votes, which doesn't have to be a majority, in an election (p. 230)

pocket veto: a method of killing a bill. This term is used if Congress has adjourned within ten days of submitting a bill and the President has not signed it (p. 110)

policy: an official position on some matter (p. 79)

political action committee (PAC): the political arm of a group that seeks to influence elections and public policy decisions (p. 360)

political party: an organized group of people who have similar ideas about government, such as the Republican or Democratic Party in the United States (p. 330)

poll: a survey of the reactions of people to important issues (p. 314)

poll tax: a tax, now illegal in the United States, that people were required to pay before they could vote (p. 64)

pollster: a person who conducts a public opinion poll, or compiles information gathered in such a poll (p. 314)

pollute: to make something dirty or impure (p. 84)

popular referendum: an arrangement that allows the people to approve or disapprove a measure passed by the legislature (p. 220)

posterity: future generations (p. 38)

Preamble: introduction to the United States Constitution (p. 36)

precedent: past court rulings used to decide present cases (p. 167)

precinct: an election district in a town or city (p. 336)

prejudice: an unfair opinion or judgment not based on facts (p. 66)

President *pro tempore:* a leading member of the Senate, elected to preside when the President of the Senate is absent (p. 102)

price fixing: an illegal agreement between companies to charge the same price for a product (p. 415)

prime time: the time when television has its largest number of viewers (p. 322)

principle: a basic rule or code of conduct (p. 44)

probation: the freeing from prison of a convicted person with the condition that the person meet regularly with a probation officer (p. 257)

procedural rights: rights accused people have regarding procedures, or steps, in a court trial (p. 169)

production: the making of goods and services (p. 398)

progressive income tax: a tax that increases with income. The more a person earns, the greater percentage the person pays (p. 186)

proliferate: to grow rapidly (p. 486)

propaganda: the spreading of a message to persuade people to believe or act in a specific way (p. 310)

property tax: a tax paid by people on property they own (p. 243)

prosecuting attorney: the state's lawyer in a criminal trial (p. 258)

prosecution: the government in a criminal trial (p. 168)

protective tariff: a high tax on imported goods (p. 189)

public housing project: low-cost housing built by the government (p. 300)

public policy: a government's plan or course of action (p. 79)

public utility: a state or federal monopoly that provides essential products or services, such as light, water, and gas (p. 240)

R

rain check: a form issued by a store allowing a customer to buy a sold-out sale item at the same price at a later date (p. 439)

ratify: to approve or accept (p. 20)

reasonable doubt rule: a court rule requiring jurors to vote not guilty if the guilt of an accused person is in doubt (p. 258)

rebellion: an armed uprising against a government (p. 13)

recall: petition process by which voters can remove an elected state or local official from office in mid-term (p. 221)

recession: a period of time with low business activity and rising unemployment (p. 404)

recognize: to send an ambassador to a new country to admit formally that that country is now an independent nation (p. 128)

recovery: a period of time in which economic conditions improve, business output increases, and unemployment declines (p. 404)

referendum: process of referring a bill passed by a legislature to the voters for approval before the bill becomes law (p. 220)

register: to list one's name and political party with the registrar of voters in a city to become eligible to vote (p. 337)

regressive tax: any tax levied at a flat rate (such as sales tax), regardless of the income of those who must pay it (p. 242)

regulate: control (p. 21)

repeal: to do away with, usually by an act of authority (p. 12)

repossession: the act of taking back goods sold on credit if the purchaser does not pay on time (p. 443)

representative democracy: a form of government in which the people elect a few members, or representatives, to make decisions for them (p. 6)

representative sample: a smaller group selected from a larger group. All of the characteristics of the larger group are believed to be found in the smaller group. (p. 314)

reprieve: an order to delay punishment for a crime (p. 234)

republican form of government: a government where people elect representatives to govern them (p. 25)

reserved powers: powers that belong only to the states (p. 44)

resolution: a city council's statement of opinion (p. 281)

revenue: money raised from taxes (p. 108)

revenue bill: any bill designed to raise money (p. 108)

right-to-work law: a law that allows a company to hire a worker who does not have to join or belong to a union (p. 370)

S

sales contract: a document that explains when and how payments are to be made when something is bought on credit (p. 438)

sales tax: a tax on an item, collected for the government by the seller and paid by the purchaser (p. 242)

sample: a smaller group of people or things selected from a larger group (p. 314)

satellite: a smaller country controlled by a more powerful one (p. 455)

savings certificate: a written document that states that a person has a certain amount of money in a bank that will earn interest if left there for a given period of time (p. 440)

scarcity: a shortage of goods or other things (p. 392)

search warrant: a written statement, signed by a judge, permitting police to search a person's property or other possessions (p. 58)

secret ballot: a method by which people vote in private (p. 361)

selectman: elected official of a town's government (p. 272)

Senate: one of the two houses of Congress (p. 98)

seniority system: a system in which the chair of a congressional committee is automatically given to the oldest member of the majority party serving on the committee (p. 106)

separation of church and state: a basic principle in the United States stating that the government should not interfere in church affairs or vice-versa (p. 57)

separation of powers: a basic principle of United States government that divides governmental power among the executive, legislative, and judicial branches (p. 39)

services: work performed by one or more persons for others; specialized work performed for a fee (p. 10; p. 392)

share of stock: a written certificate stating that an individual owns a part of a business (p. 413)

slum: a city's run-down section (p. 295)

smog: unclean air that is a blend of smoke and fog (p. 298)

Social Security tax: payments made into a government retirement fund (p. 189)

social welfare: any government program providing assistance to people in need (p. 83)

special session: a session of Congress that is held in addition to the regular session (p. 234)

spending pattern: the way a person spends money (p. 435)

spoils system: a system of government appointments in which individuals are given government jobs as a reward or favor rather than because of their ability to perform the jobs (p. 155)

standard of living: a general measure of the material well-being of a person or group (p. 402)

standing committee: a permanent committee of Congress (p. 104)

State of the Union message: a message delivered every year by the President to the Congress describing conditions in the United States (p. 126)

statutory law: laws passed by a legislature and then written down (p. 167)

subcommittee: a small group formed from a committee of Congress to study parts of a bill or to conduct an investigation (p. 104)

subsidy: a government grant (p. 417)

suit: a court case (p. 163)

sunshine laws: laws that forbid committee hearings to be held in secret (p. 222)

supply: the amount of a product available to a market (p. 398)

syndicated: term referring to newspaper columnists (writers) whose work is printed in newspapers across the country (p. 323)

T

tariff: a tax on imports or exports (p. 88)

tax: a payment required by law to be made to the government (p. 10)

tax loophole: provision in the law allowing some businesses or individuals to escape paying taxes (p. 198)

territory: a political unit of the United States before it becomes a state (p. 212)

terrorism: the use of violence to achieve a political end (p. 466)

third party: in the United States, a term applied to any political party other than the Democratic or Republican parties (p. 332)

totalitarian: form of government that holds control over every part of a person's life (p. 5)

town: a political unit that is smaller than a city and larger than a village (p. 271)

town meeting: gathering where community members meet to discuss issues affecting their town (p. 5)

township: a subdivision of a county, in some states (p. 274)

traditional economy: an economic system in which all decisions are made as they always have been (p. 394)

treaty: a formal agreement between two or more countries (p. 127)

trial jury: a group of individuals chosen to make a court decision about the guilt or innocence of the accused in a criminal trial, or about who the injured party is in a civil case (p. 257)

trust: a very large corporation that owned or otherwise controlled many smaller firms (p. 426)

two-party system: a political system in which the candidates of only two (major) parties have a reasonable chance of winning an election (p. 331)

U

unanimous: having the agreement and consent of all (p. 257)

unfavorable balance of trade: condition when a country imports more goods than it exports (p. 481)

unicameral: a one-house legislature (p. 216)

union: an organization that seeks improved working conditions, salaries, and other benefits for working people (p. 370)

union shop: a business that can hire non-union members only if they join the union shortly after being hired (p. 424)

unit price: the cost of an ounce, pound, or quart of any product (p. 436)

urban: relating to cities (p. 275)

urban renewal: a government plan in which funds are provided to upgrade housing and surrounding areas (p. 300)

V

verdict: a jury's decision in court (p. 170)

veto: refusal to sign a bill into law by a state governor or the President of the United States (p. 41)

village: the smallest unit of local government in the United States (p. 272)

voting machine: an automatic vote counter (p. 362)

W

ward: a voting district (p. 280)

warranty: a product guarantee by the manufacturer to repair or replace it should it prove faulty during a given period of time (p. 439)

witness: a person who gives evidence in court (p. 259)

writ of *certiorari:* order issued by a higher court directing a lower court to send case records for a review (p. 175)

writ of *habeas corpus:* a court order that requires sufficient evidence for a prisoner to be held for trial (p. 113)

Z

zoning: the practice of dividing a city into districts or zones for building and other purposes (p. 292)

Index

C

Cabinet: 142–146

California Conservation Corps (CCC): 245–246

Campaign(s): 318; costs, 356–357, 358; other, 355; presidential, 352–353; raising money for, 357–358

Candidates: 120; characteristics of, 345–347; interest groups and political, 373–374; political parties and, 338; women and minority, 347–348

Capital, capital goods: 400

Carson, Rachel: 91

Carter, Jimmy: 81, 122, 131, 322, 461; his attempt to rescue hostages in Iran, 142; foreign policy of, 460, 461, 467; and Habitat for Humanity, 305; his Olympic boycott, 317; and Panama Canal Treaty, 460; influence on public opinion, 317

Castro, Fidel: 134

Caucus: party, 100; Iowa, 364–365

Census, Bureau of the: 144, 270, 275, 417

Center for Independent Living: 371

Central Intelligence Agency (CIA): 132

Certiorari, writ of: 175

Challenge: for cause, 263; peremptory, 263

Chamber of Commerce: 369

Charge account: 442

Charter: 275

Checks and balances: 41, 44

Children's rights: 491

Circuits: 170

City government: 275–276; city councils in, 280–281; city managers in, 279–280; mayors in, 282–283; three forms of, 276–278; *see also* Local governments

City planning: 290; in colonial times, 290; commissions, 291–293; and walking cities, 291

City problems: 295; city ordinances dealing with, 300; crime, 296–297; federal aid for, 302–303; housing, 295–296; income tax to deal with, 302; money for, 300–301; pollution, 298; poverty, 296; public housing projects, 300; urban renewal, 300

Civil law: 168, 250

Civil Service: 154–156; federal workers in, 156; formation of, 154–155

Civil Service Commission: 155

Claims court: 171

Clayton Anti-Trust Act (1914): 426

Clean Air Act Amendments (1970): 84

Closed shop: 424

Cloture: 110

Coalition: 306, 375

Cochran v. *Louisiana*: 71

Cold war: 471

Collective bargaining: 423

Collins, Cardiss: 348

Colonists: defined, 12; rebellion of, 13

Colony(ies): defined, 12; English, 12; taxing of, 12

Command economy: 394–395

Commerce: compromise on, 28; defined, 27; *see also* Trade

Commerce, Department of: 144

Commission on Civil Rights: 148–149

Committee(s), congressional: 104; committee on, 105; conference, 105; joint, 104–105; kinds of, 104–105; select, 104; selection, 105; and seniority system, 106; standing, 104

Common Cause: 372, 381

Common law: 167–168

Communism: 455, 470, 471

Community property: 243

Commuting a sentence: 234

Competition: 425

Compromise: commerce and slave trade, 28; Connecticut, 27–28; defined, 27; and Electoral College, 29; Three-fifths, 28

Concurrent jurisdiction: 164–165

Concurrent powers: 44–45

Congress: 97, 98; and foreign policy, 461; House of Representatives, 98–99; organization of, 100–102; political parties in, 338–339; and public policy, 88; Senate, 99–100; students go to, 115–116; *see also* Committee(s), congressional

Congressional districts: 98–99

Congress of Racial Equality (CORE): 371

Connecticut Compromise: 27–28

Constituents: 105, 112–113

Constitution, United States: 6–7, 9, 36–37; annotated, 506–507; Article 1 of, 39–40, 89, 506; Article 2 of, 40, 512; Article 3 of, 40, 515; Article 4 of, 48–50, 516; Articles 5, 6, and 7 of, 50, 517–518; compromises reached on, 27–29; preamble to, 36–38, 506; ratification of, 29–30; writing of, 25–27; *see also* Constitutional amendments

Constitutional amendments: 518–527; Bill of Rights, 29, 56–57, 61, 65, 113, 518–519; ERA (Equal Rights Amendment), 64, 347, 372, 527; First, 57, 74–75, 90, 379, 518; Second, 57, 518; Third, 58, 518; Fourth, 58, 518; Fifth, 58, 168, 519; Sixth, 58, 519; Seventh, 58, 520; Eighth, 58, 167, 520; Ninth, 58, 520; Tenth, 59, 520; Eleventh, 520; Twelfth, 521; Thirteenth, 28, 61, 521; Fourteenth, 61, 168, 522; Fifteenth, 62, 522; Sixteenth,

L

Labor: 399; business and, 421–422; Taft–Hartley Act, 423–424; unions, 422–423; groups, 370–371

Labor, Department of: 144

Land: 399–400

Law(s): administrative, 168; civil, 168, 250; common, 167–168; Constitutional, 167; criminal, 168, 250; due process of, 168–169; interpretation of, 167; making and enforcing, 8–9; statutory, 167; sunshine, 222

Law of the Sea Treaty: 486–487

League of Nations: 470

League of Women Voters: 371

Legal Aid Society: 66, 67, 265

Legal monopolies: 426–427

Legislative branch: 39–40

Legislators, state: 216; complaints of, 222; duties of, 218; high rate of turnover among, 222; in home district, 222–223; lawmaking process and, 217–218; lobbyists and, 377; number of, in legislatures, 216–217; qualifications for, 217; in state capitol, 223–224

L'Enfant, Pierre: 290

Libel: 57

License fees: 243

Limited government, principle of: 45

Lincoln, Abraham: 122

Loans: 441–442

Lobbyists: 112, 375–377; and legislators, 278; origin of term, 376

Local governments: 3, 270–271; counties and townships, 272–273; key decision makers in, 279–283; special districts, 274; towns and villages, 271–272; *see also* City government

Lotteries, state: 225–226

M

McGovern, George: 121–122

McKinley, William: 120

Majority: opinion, 177; party, 100; rule, 6–7; vote, 6

Management: 398

Mandatory referendum: 220

Mandatory sentence: 264

Marbury v. *Madison* (1803): 175–176

Maritime Administration: 417

Market economy: 395–396

Marshall, John: 175, 176

Marshall, Thurgood: 182

Martinez, Bob: 235

Mayors: 282–283

Mecham, Evan: 231

Media: effect of, on public opinion, 324; influence of, on public policy, 92; role of, in shaping beliefs, 321–324

Medicare: 84

Merit system: 155

Metropolitan area: 275

Middle East: 318, 457, 465–467, 483

Military assistance: 455–456

Militia: 57

Minority: groups, 66; party, 100; political candidates, 347–348; rights, 6–7

Miranda v. *Arizona* (1966): 178

Miranda Warning: 178–179

Misdemeanor: 250

Mondale, Walter: 128, 352

Money: federal, 186–187; sources of, 186–191; spending, 192–197; state, sources of, 242–244

Monopolies: 240, 425; legal, 426–428

Monroe Doctrine: 469

Montreal Protocol: 478

Mothers Against Drunk Driving (MADD): 325–326

Motley, Constance Baker: 173

Mutual defense pact: 456

N

Nader, Ralph: 445, 446

National Aeronautics and Space Administration (NASA): 148

National Association for the Advancement of Colored People (NAACP): 182, 374

National Association of Manufacturers: 357, 369, 373

National conventions: 350, 351

National debt: 193–194

National Drug Control Policy: 93

National Farmer's Union: 371

National Grange: 371

National Labor Relations Act (1935): 423–424

National Mediation Board: 149

National Organization for Women (NOW): 372, 376

National Rifle Association (N.R.A.): 382–383

National Science Foundation: 150

National Security Council (NSC): 130–131

National Transportation Safety Board (NTSB): 149

National Urban League: 371

Native Americans: 66, 91, 154, 371, 394

Naturalized citizen: 61

Natural resources: 399–400

Negotiation: 22, 406

Nixon, Richard M.: 81, 122, 123, 131, 179, 461; his visit to China, 460–461

Noninvolvement, policy of: 468, 470

North Atlantic Treaty Organization (NATO): 456

Nuclear power: 386–387

Nuclear Regulatory Commission: 151

Nuclear weapons control: 486, 496–497

V

Veterans Affairs, Department of: 148, 154
Veterans of Foreign Wars: 374
Veto: 41; item, 235; pocket, 110
Vice President of United States: 133
Vietnam War: 81, 461
Villages: 272
Vote: electoral, 354; kinds of people who, 359–360; methods used to, 361–362; party, 338; reasons why people, 360–361; right to, 61–62; amendments guaranteeing, 62–64
Voter information packets: 363
Voting Rights Act (1965): 62

W

Walters, Vernon: 157
Wards: 280, 336
War for Independence: 14, 19, 20, 21
War Powers Act (1973): 461
Warranty: 437
Warren, Earl: 178
Washington, George: 14, 25, 330, 468, 470
Welfare payments: 84, 296
White House Office: 129
Wilkie, Wendell: 121
Wilson, Woodrow: 136, 457
Women: Decade for Women, 491; in labor force, 399; Nairobi conference (1985), 491; National Organization for Women (NOW), 372, 376; political can-
didates, 347–348; voters, 360; and voting rights, 62, 88
Workers: federal, 156; in labor force, 399; public policy on, 85; special groups, 429–430; weekly pay of, 403
Writ: of *certiorari,* 175; of *habeas corpus,* 113

Y

Young Democrats of America: 341

Z

Zenger, John Peter: 57
Zoning: 292

Acknowledgments

PHOTOS

Front Cover: Statue of Liberty: Superstock; Flag: Al Fishek.

Back cover: Top: Dennis Brack, Blackstar; Middle: David Dempster; Bottom: Shepard Sherbell/Picture Group.

Front Matter: i, ii Statue of Liberty: Superstock; Flag: Al Fishek. **v** Bob Daemmrich. **vi** John Naubauer. **vii** Keller & Peet Assoc. **viii** Al Stephenson/Picture Group. **ix** James Pickerell. **x** Ben Barnhart/Offshoot. **xi** Chuck Nacke/Picture Group **xiii** Susan Steinkamp/Picture Group. **xiv L** David Hathcox/Woodfin Camp & Assoc; **R** Mike Grecco/Picture Group. **xv T** Shepard Sherball; **M** Chuck Nacke/Picture Group; **B** Susan Biddle. **xvi** Wesley Bocxe/Photo Researchers. **xvii T** W. Hubbell/Woodfin Camp & Assoc; **L** (Tanor) Russ Schleipman/Offshoot; **R** John Curtis/Offshoot; **B** Richard Howard/Offshoot. **xviii L** Kenneth Jarecke/Contact Press; **R** Jose Azel/Contact Press. **xix T** David Dempster/Offshoot; **BL** Doug Menuez/Picture Group; **BR** Russ Schleipman/Offshoot. **xx** Ben Barnhart/Offshoot. **xxi T** Ann States/Picture Group; **L** Michal Heron/Woodfin Camp & Assoc.; **B** Bob Daemmrich/Click Chicago/TSW.

UNIT ONE, xxii Everett C. Johnson/Folio Inc. **CHAPTER ONE, 2** Dennis Brack/Black Star. **5** Peter Arnold. **9** Daniel Brody/Stock Boston. **10L** Shostal Assoc. **10TR** Bohdan Hrynewych/Stock Boston. **10BR** Woodfin Camp & Assoc. **13** Bostonian Society. **15** (detail) Kennedy Galleries. **16** Robert Houser/Comstock. **CHAPTER TWO. 19** Henry Francis Du Pont Winterthur Museum. **21** Shostal Assoc. **23** The Granger Collection. **27** Wadsworth Atheneum. **28** Virginia Museum. **32** Dennis Dempster/Offshoot. Estate/Cinncinati Art Museum (VAGA). **CHAPTER THREE, 35** Keller & Peet Assoc. **41** A. Tannenbaum/Sygma. **49** Ted Wood. **51** Kevin Horan/Picture Group. **CHAPTER FOUR, 55** Bob Daemmrich. **59** Cooper/Coughlin. **62** UPI/Bettmann Newsphotos. **63** Talbot D. Lovering/Allyn & Bacon. **69** EGI-Medical Center of Princeton. **70** John Lei/Omni Photo Communications. **71** Elena Dorfman/Offshoot.

UNIT TWO, 76 John Neubauer. **CHAPTER FIVE, 78** Al Stephenson/Picture Group. **80** Suki Coughlin. **86** Edith Haun/Stock Boston. **87** Boroff/Texastock. **89** Brad Bower/Picture Group. **91** Shostal Assoc. **93** Mattew McKay/Picture Group. **CHAPTER SIX, 97** James Pickerell. **102** Consolidated News Pictures/Arnie Sachs. **106** Paul Conklin. **108** Keith Jewell. **109** Keith Jewell. **112** Dennis Brack/Black Star. **114** Story Litchfield/Stock Boston. **115** Courtesy of The Close-Up Foundation. **CHAPTER SEVEN, 119** John Naubauer. **124** Pam Price/Picture Group. **126** Sygma. **128** Diana Walker/Gamma-Liason. **132** White House/Black Star. **135** Judy Sloan/Gamma-Liason. **137** Michael Evans/Sygma. **CHAPTER EIGHT, 141** Brad Bower/Picture Group. **143** Dennis Brack/Black Star. **149** NASA. **152** Shostal Assoc. **156** Lib. of Congress. **157** Wide World Photos. **158** JP Laffont/Sygma. **CHAPTER NINE, 162** David Dempster. **164** Cary Wolinsky/Stock Boston. **165** UPI/Bettmann Newsphotos. **168** Jane Flavell Collins. **171** Cooper/Coughlin. **173** UPI/Bettmann Newsphotos. **178** AP/Wide World Photos. **179** Bill Polo. **181** Life Picture Service. **CHAPTER TEN, 185** James Pickerell. **188** Larry Lawfer. **190** Bob Smallman/DPI. **197** Dobbins/Boston Herald, from Rothco cartoon. **198** Dobbins/Boston Herald Traveler. **201** Brad Bower/Picture Group.

UNIT THREE, 206 Nathen Benn/Woodfin Camp & Assoc. **CHAPTER ELEVEN, 208** Paul Conklin. **209** Cooper/Coughlin. **210** Joel Gordon/DPI. **216** Nebraska State Legislature. **220** Mike Mazzaschi/Stock Boston. **223** Woodfin Camp & Assoc. **225** Richard Howard/Offshoot. **CHAPTER TWELVE, 229** K14 Group/The Image Bank. **231** Paul Conklin. **233** Larry Lawfer. **235L&R** Al Stephenson/Picture Group. **239** Centers for Disease Control, Atlanta, GA. **241** Jack Swedberg, Massachusetts Divisons of Fisheries and Wildlife. **244** Reprinted by permission of Tribune Company Syndicate, Inc. **245** California Conservation Corps. **CHAPTER THIRTEEN, 249** Keller & Peet Assoc. **251** Paul J. Vinci, Jr. **253** Sandra Johnson. **257** Bill Polo. **259** Roger Bradford. **260** Bill Polo. **263** Shostal Assoc. **266** David Dempster/Offshoot. **CHAPTER FOURTEEN, 270** John Neubauer. **271** Peter Arnold. **273** Michael Sullivan. **281** Woodfin Camp. **282** Acey Harper/Picture Group. **285** Mark Antman/The Image Works. **CHAPTER FIFTEEN, 289** Russ Schleipman/Offshoot. **290** Talbot F. Hamlin. **292L** Woodfin Camp. **292R** Peter Menzel/Stock Boston. **295** Shostal Assoc. **298** Shostal Assoc. **302L** Centers for Disease Control, Atlanta, GA. **302R** Texas Highway Department. **304** Reggie Parker.

UNIT FOUR, 310 Sullivan/Texastock. **CHAPTER SIXTEEN, 312** Bob Daemmrich. **314** Eric A. Roth/Picture Cube. **315** Bohdan Hrynewych/Stock Boston. **318** Larry Lawfer.

ART